Meta in Film and Television Series

Meta in Film and Television Series

David Roche

EDINBURGH
University Press

Edinburgh University Press is one of the leading university presses in the UK. We publish academic books and journals in our selected subject areas across the humanities and social sciences, combining cutting-edge scholarship with high editorial and production values to produce academic works of lasting importance. For more information visit our website: edinburghuniversitypress.com

© David Roche, 2022, 2024

Edinburgh University Press Ltd
The Tun—Holyrood Road
12 (2f) Jackson's Entry
Edinburgh EH8 8PJ

First published in hardback by Edinburgh University Press 2022

Typeset in Garamond MT Pro by
Cheshire Typesetting Ltd, Cuddington, Cheshire

A CIP record for this book is available from the British Library

ISBN 978 1 3995 0803 2 (hardback)
ISBN 978 1 3995 0804 9 (paperback)
ISBN 978 1 3995 0805 6 (webready PDF)
ISBN 978 1 3995 0806 3 (epub)

The right of David Roche to be identified as author of this work has been asserted in accordance with the Copyright, Designs and Patents Act 1988 and the Copyright and Related Rights Regulations 2003 (SI No. 2498).

Contents

List of Figures	viii
Acknowledgments	xii
Preface	xiii

Part I The Theory and History of Meta

Chapter 1	What Is Meta and Who Uses the Term?	3
	"That's so meta"	3
	Metafiction, Metanarrative, Metafilm, Metacinema, Metafilmic . . . and Reflexivity	6
	A Theoretical Proposition	15
Chapter 2	How Does Meta Work?	19
	Typologies of Metafiction, Metareference, Metacinema, etc.	19
	Problems when Doing Meta	25
Chapter 3	When, Where and Possibly Why Did Meta Appear?	35
	A Short History of Reflexivity and Meta in Film and Television	35
	Is Meta Specific to Western Culture?	38
	Did Meta Come from Literature?	41
	Did Meta Come from Modernism and/or the Avant-Gardes?	44
	Are the Origins of Meta the Same in Television as in Film?	48
	Can Silent Films Be Meta Anyway?	51
	A Series of Tentative Conclusions	56

Part II The Aboutness of Meta

Chapter 4	Industry and Creation	61
	Movies about Making Movies	61
	More than Just about the Industry (*Sunset Blvd.*, *Contempt*, *Mulholland Dr.*)	67

	Allegories of the Film and Media Industry (*Westworld*)	83
	Conclusion	90
Chapter 5	Apparatus and Spectatorship	92
	Movies about Movie-going	92
	Movie-going as Ritual (*Cinema Paradiso*)	95
	Adventures in Metalepsis (*The Purple Rose of Cairo*)	99
	Allegories of Spectatorship Revisited (*Rear Window, Blow-up, Blow Out*)	106
	Conclusion	120
Chapter 6	Medium and Materiality	122
	Synchretism, Intermediality, Remediation	122
	Cinema and the Fine Arts (*Fellini Roma*)	125
	Film, Television, Video (*Family Viewing*)	132
	Film and Comics (*American Splendor*)	139
	Digital and Interactive Media (*Black Mirror: Bandersnatch*)	145
	Conclusion	150
Chapter 7	Adaptation and Remake	152
	Engaging with the Original: Statements of Intent Part I (*The Portrait of a Lady*)	152
	Adapting the Metafictional Novel (*The French Lieutenant's Woman, A Cock & Bull Story, Inherent Vice*)	159
	Metadaptations (*Adaptation, Psycho, Bram Stoker's Dracula*)	169
	Conclusion	178
Chapter 8	Genre	180
	This Is a Genre Film/Series and You Know It: Statements of Intent Part II	180
	Is Parody Essentially Meta? (*Lemonade Joe, My Name Is Nobody, Blazing Saddles*)	185
	The Ethics of Genre Play (*Funny Games, Scream, Community*)	191
	Conclusion	203
Chapter 9	Seriality	205
	Metamoments in Series	205
	Allegories of Seriality (*This Is Us*)	208
	Metaseries (*LOST, The Prisoner, Twin Peaks*)	213
	Conclusion	230

Chapter 10	History and Historiography	232
	Historiographic Metafiction (*Culloden*)	232
	Are Allohistories Always Meta? (*Inglourious Basterds*, *The Man in the High Castle*)	239
	Self-conscious Historical Film (*Schindler's List*, *JFK*, *No*)	247
	Conclusion	257
Chapter 11	Politics	259
	The Political Potential of Meta (*Tout va bien*)	259
	Questioning the Efficacy of Political Films and Series (*Colossal Youth*, *Black Mirror*, *I, Daniel Blake*)	265
	Conclusion	279
Conclusion		281
Notes		291
Glossary of Meta-phenomena		317
Filmography		318
Bibliography		323
Index		339

Figures

3.1	*Through the Olive Trees*: the movements of Hossein and Tahereh appearing dot-like	40
3.2	*The Magic School Bus*: the Producer of *The Magic School Bus* receives a phone call from a viewer	50
3.3	*Man with a Movie Camera*: the cameraman passes under a bridge	53
3.4	*The Cameraman*: Buster salutes his diegetic audience	55
4.1	*Sunset Blvd.*: Norma Desmond steals the light from her youthful self on screen	72
4.2	*Sunset Blvd.*: Norma Desmond turns into a spectral image	73
4.3	*Contempt*: auditioning Nausicaa at a live performance reminiscent of shadow puppetry	78
4.4	*Mulholland Dr.*: on the stage of the Silencio	81
4.5	*Jurassic Park*: the T-Rex's jaws burst through the jeep's roof window	85
4.6	*Westworld*: Maeve comes face to face with the theme park's promotional video	87
5.1	*Cinema Paradiso*: Alfredo directs the projector outside the movie theater	98
5.2	*The Purple Rose of Cairo*: Cecilia, bathed in the light coming from the movie screen	101
5.3	*The Purple Rose of Cairo*: Tom Baxter addresses Cecilia before stepping out of the movie/screen	104
5.4	*Rear Window*: Stella, Lisa and Jefferies watch the neighbors	111
5.5	*Blow-up*: projection: Thomas's shadow blots out the figures on the photograph	115
5.6	*Blow-up*: cognition: Thomas connecting two photographs	116
5.7	*Blow-up*: abstraction: the photo loses its figurative properties	117

5.8	*Blow Out*: a split diopter shot combines an owl's look to the camera with the equivalent of a shot/reverse shot	119
6.1.1– 6.1.2	*Fellini Roma*: the diegetic film crew filming the Piazza de Siena	127
6.2–6.3	*Fellini Roma*: the shooting of the film-within-the-film and of *Fellini Roma* are confused offscreen	128
6.4.1– 6.4.3	*Fellini Roma*: discovery and destruction of the frescoes in an ancient Roman household	131
6.5	*Family Viewing*: freeze frame and rewinding before a sitcom son and his sitcom stepmom can kiss	135
6.6.1–6.6.2	*Family Viewing*: Armen's memories of herself and her daughter	136
6.7	*Family Viewing*: Stan instructs Aline to direct Sandra in a hypermedia bedroom	137
6.8	*American Splendor*: Harvey Pekar's epiphany	142
6.9	*American Splendor*: "Who are these people? What's in a name? Who is Harvey Pekar?"	144
6.10	*Black Mirror: Bandersnatch*: our first decision concerns the protagonist's breakfast	148
6.11	*Black Mirror: Bandersnatch*: "I am watching you on Netflix. I make decisions for you."	149
7.1	*The Portrait of a Lady*: Isabel Archer looks to the camera in a silent film pastiche	157
7.2	*The French Lieutenant's Woman*: Anna prepares for her role as Sarah	162
7.3	*Tristam Shandy: A Cock & Bull Story*: Tristram Shandy watches Uncle Toby relating his military exploits to a young Tristram	164
7.4	*Inherent Vice*: Sortilège listens to Doc in a café	167
7.5	*Psycho*: a tour-de-force track-in produces a frame-within-the-frame composition	172
7.6	*Psycho*: mopping the blood off the bathroom floor	173
7.7	*Bram Stoker's Dracula*: keying Jonathan Harker's diary into a shot of a model train	175
7.8	*Bram Stoker's Dracula*: the cinematograph scene turns the Count into a metonym of cinema	177
8.1.1–8.1.2	*Dead Man*: William Blake's train ride to the West	183
8.2–8.3	*My Name Is Nobody*: Jack Beauregard faces the Wild Bunch single-handedly and becomes myth	189
8.4	*Funny Games*: Paul winks at the camera moments before Anna finds her dead dog	192

8.5	*Scream*: Casey crouches next to the TV set	195
8.6.1–8.6.2	*Scream*: Sidney Prescott and Kenny the cameraman watch on the surveillance screen	197
8.7	*Community*: Abed, shooting *ABED*, a metafilm about Abed making a film about Jesus	202
9.1	*This Is Us*: Kevin Pearson shows his nieces the painting he made	211
9.2	*LOST*: Ben Linus is made to watch his daughter's death again	216
9.3	*LOST*: Nikki asks, "Hey guys, what are these other TVs for?"	217
9.4	*The Prisoner*: Number Six (in black) meets Number Six (in white)	220
9.5	*The Prisoner*: Number Six impossibly addresses Number Two	222
9.6.1–9.6.2	*Twin Peaks*: Laura Palmer reveals the presence of the cameraman's motorcycle, reflected in her eye	225
9.7	*Twin Peaks: The Return*: Sam Colby watching the glass box, and waiting	227
9.8	*Twin Peaks: The Return*: the Fireman watches the birth of BOB	229
10.1	*Culloden*: Andrew Henderson, addresses the camera like a news reporter	236
10.2	*Culloden*: the voiceover is silenced, leaving us alone with the images of the massacre	239
10.3	*The Man in the High Castle*: Juliana and Frank watch the second *Grasshopper Lies Heavy* reel	246
10.4.1–10.4.2	*Schindler's List*: while Oskar Schindler watches the exactions in the Kraków ghetto, a little girl in red appears	248
10.5	*JFK*: the falsification of the photograph of Lee Harvey Oswald	250
10.6	*Tony Manero*: Raúl Peralta assesses the competition prior to the Tony Manero lookalike contest	252
10.7–10.8	*No*: the YES campaign parodies the NO campaign	255
10.9.1–10.9.2	*No*: René's presentation of a teaser for the soap opera *Bellas y audaces*	256
11.1	*Tout va bien*: Susan looks to the camera and says that she needs a picture of Jacques at work	263
11.2	*Colossal Youth*: Xana and Ventura imagine they can see turtles, a hen, a cop, a lion and the devil	269

11.3.1–11.3.3 *Black Mirror*: Great Britain watches Prime Minister
 Michael Callow have sexual intercourse with a pig   273
11.4.1–11.4.3 *I, Daniel Blake*: Daniel Blake's "new art installation"   276

Acknowledgments

Thanks are due to everybody at Edinburgh University Press, starting with Gillian Leslie. Your enthusiasm and support came at a complicated time in my life. It's good to know there are people out there who are not only highly competent but human beings at the core. I am also thankful to Eddie Clark and Sam Johnson for their help throughout, and to Anita Joseph for the attention she brought to the manuscript.

Because the scope of this book was much broader than my previous ones, I ended up exploiting my friends and colleagues even more than usual. All kidding aside, this project has convinced me more than ever that research in the humanities is a collective enterprise, an ongoing discussion, a process that depends on exchanges with people we read and meet. I'd like to thank Jean-François Baillon, Zachary Baqué, Eve Benhamou, Vincent Deville, German Duarte Penaranda, Jean-Paul Gabilliet, Gilles Menegaldo, Céline Murillo, Philippe Ragel, Mathilde Rogez, Marine Soubeille and Dennis Tredy for their help with bibliographical material and their expertise on specific points, Daniel Yacavone in particular for pointing the way to both Werner Wolf and Edinburgh University Press. I am especially grateful to Janet Staiger for reading the book proposal, and to Celestino Deleyto, Christophe Gelly, Julien Achemchame, Mehdi Achouche, Claire Cornillon, Sarah Hatchuel, Jules Sandeau, Dominique Sipière and Shannon Wells-Lassagne for reading one or more chapters. This book largely benefited from your comments and insights.

It also benefited from interactions with my students at the University of Texas at Austin, Université Toulouse Jean Jaurès and Université Paul Valéry Montpellier 3. Teaching metafiction and metacinema certainly helped me refine my theoretical and methodological propositions, and my analyses of the corpus.

More than ever, this book is dedicated to my family and friends, to my brother Alain and my sister Stephanie, to my partner Virginie and our children Lisa and Tim, and to the memory of loved ones lost.

Preface

Meta in Film and Television Series grew out of my previous work on Quentin Tarantino. I realized that research on meta-phenomena had mainly been carried out in the fields of literature, drama and transmedia, and that film and television studies had pretty much taken for granted terms such as metacinema and metafilm, and had mainly focused on reflexivity, specific devices such as the mise en abyme, or on a genre like the movie about making movies. *Meta in Film and Television* thus seeks to remedy this lack by confronting the writings on the movie about making movies and reflexivity in film and television (most of which date back to the 1980s and early 1990s) to the seminal works carried out on metafiction in the 1980s and metareference in the 2000s. And though I recognize the value of transmedial approaches, I believe it is equally important to focus on the specificities of phenomena in a given medium. *Meta in Film and Television Series* also seeks to respond to the increasing presence of the term "meta" to designate films and series in the writings of fans and journalists. It assumes its timeliness by analyzing phenomena that have been circulating for years but that seem to have intensified and crossed over into the mainstream in the digital age, perhaps as a response to the audience's increasing awareness of self-conscious works. The book's main thread lies in this convergence between academic and popular discourses. The popular usage of "meta" points to a profoundly entangled set of practices and discourses, and suggests that audiences have somehow sensed this entanglement. It is the scholar's job to untangle and make sense of it.

Meta in Film and Television Series is highly indebted to prior work on metafiction, metareference and reflexivity—the writings of Gérard Genette, Linda Hutcheon and Patricia Waugh, Christian Metz and Robert Stam, Werner Wolf and many others—and the preliminary theory of meta presented in Part I devolves from discussions of these important texts. The purpose of this book is not to invent new terms, and the only terms coined herein, metamoment (i.e., a moment that can be interpreted as meta) and hypermeta (i.e., works whose "meta-ness" is evident and overt), are fairly transparent. Rather, it aims to homogenize the existing terminology, clarify distinctions and gauge their overall relevance and usability to analyze meta. In this respect, my main model in composing this book has been theorist Linda Hutcheon, whose theories of metafiction, parody, postmodernism, irony and adaptation were based on discussions of her predecessors' theoretical propositions. I do not believe that this book will fix these terms once and for all, but I do believe that clear definitions are a prerequisite to analysis, even if one ends up redefining them in the process.

This book is, above all, a study of a certain kind of analysis and interpretation. Meta supposes an interpretive act. And even when it is diegeticized, as has increasingly been the case since the 1990s, it makes demands on its audiences. Meta offers a framework with which to engage a given work and its relationship to its conditions of production and reception, its materials, and to its existence in the world. We are free to ignore this framework, just as we are free to interrogate its functions and intentionality. Although meta can very much be critical, it is always, at heart, a lesson in, and a celebration of, the powers of fiction and art, and of our own capacity for emotional and intellectual engagement. Contra the charge of narcissism and solipsism, I argue that meta is relevant because, by playfully inviting audiences to take on the role of hermeneutists, it develops sensibilities and skills that are relevant in our day-to-day lives. *Meta in Film and Television Series* is a book about making meaning; it recognizes that meaning-making is one of our key activities and pleasures as audiences and scholars. And if the risk of misinterpretation exists, metaphenomena invite us to analyze works, see beyond the surface, and unravel and question the forms and discourses that energize them. The theory of meta-phenomena proposed in *Meta in Film and Television Series* aims to offer a methodology with which to interpret a certain quality in art and fiction—that is, how a work invites commentary on itself and its medium. My final theoretical propositions result, however, from the analysis of the works in Part II because meaning-making of this sort requires rigorous formal analysis.

The films and series studied herein range from the 1950s to the 2010s (silent cinema is only touched on in Chapter 3) and only include works that have been distributed through mainstream channels. Attention is paid in equal measure to art cinema and more popular fare (documentary and the avant-gardes are only broached in Chapter 3 and the Conclusion). Most chapters put the spotlight on several films and at least one series. *Meta in Film and Television Series* revisits some of the most obvious examples of movies about making movies, movies about movie-going and/or reflexivity in film, many of which have received critical attention (*Sunset Blvd.*, *Rear Window*, *Contempt*, *Blow-up*, *The Purple Rose of Cairo*, *Scream*, *Funny Games*, *Mulholland Dr.*, *Adaptation*, the films of Jean-Luc Godard). But attention is also paid to less obvious examples (*Fellini Roma* compared to *8½* or *Intervista*, *JFK* compared to *Natural Born Killers*) and to works that have received less critical attention (*My Name*

Is Nobody, *Family Viewing*, *The Portrait of a Lady*, *American Splendor*, *Inherent Vice*, the films of Pablo Larraín). The book also aims to demonstrate that meta is present in realist works such as the films of Pedro Costa and Ken Loach. In the end, the corpus of films and series was the fruit of a constant negotiation between what seemed to be the most paradigmatic examples and my main areas of expertise (US-American and British cinemas), and thus my own limitations. This explains the presence of works by Jean-Luc Godard (which I had never previously studied), and of David Lynch and Steven Spielberg (which I had studied copiously) in several chapters. It also explains the lack of balance in Chapter 5, which does not focus on a twenty-first-century film or series because the most compelling examples were, to my mind, from the 1950s to the 1990s. Finally, it was easier to step out of my comfort zone for film than for series (those studied are exclusively US-American and British) because I am newer to the field of television studies and had less access to series other than those available on streaming platforms. Because of the breadth of the works explored herein, and even more so because *Meta in Film and Television Series* is ultimately a study of interpretation, my analyses rely on my own insights into the corpus while building on the critical writings devoted to them.

The book is divided into two uneven parts. The three chapters of Part I seek to propose a theoretical and historical framework by answering the basic questions posed by meta. My theoretical propositions emerge from the discussion and confrontation of key theoretical texts from film and television but also literary and media studies. The aim is to formulate a theoretical, historical and methodological framework for the analysis of meta-phenomena in film and series. Many of the observations made in this section remain relevant for the study of meta in other media.

Chapter 1 starts with a consideration of the circulation of the adjective "meta" in the popular media today, before attempting to define meta in light of existing definitions of reflexivity and various meta-phenomena; it concludes that meta can be defined as a high degree of reflexivity in which the work appears to comment on itself and/or its medium: it is characterized by its aboutness. Chapter 2 opens with a discussion of the typological approaches that have heretofore dominated studies of meta-phenomena; it is followed by a series of theoretical proposals that refine the definition proposed in Chapter 1: meta is playful interpretation. Chapter 3 presents a brief history of reflexivity and meta-phenomena before discussing specific points that are taken for granted in writings on the subject; tentative answers are provided based on existing research, but the aim of this chapter is, above all, to raise questions that will be broached in Part II and that will hopefully pave the way for historical-based research by other scholars.

The case studies of Part II are meant to be illustrative of the theoretical framework established in Part I, but it is also from these studies that a more definitive theory of meta will emerge in the Conclusion. The chapters explore the variety of concerns meta-works or -moments can address, moving from the facet of meta that has received the most critical attention—artistic creation in an industrial context and the movie-about-making-movies genre—to the main criticism that has been addressed to all things meta: their solipsism and lack of engagement with social and historical reality. The eight chapters can be organized into three groups: Chapters 4, 5 and 6 analyze films and series that focus on their conditions of creation, modes of reception, and medium and materiality; Chapters 7, 8 and 9 explore how such works engage with their hypotexts, architexts and format; and Chapters 10 and 11 how films and series can address their relationship with the real world both as subject matter and as a target for change. Of course, the cases studies will regularly spill out of the bounds the composition of this book imposes on them, one of my main arguments being that meta inevitably resists such neat categorization because the modes and concerns of meta-phenomena are as entangled as their devices.

Chapter 4 opens with a discussion of the movie about making movies. These films do more than explore the tension between economics, aesthetics and politics; they also reflect on the medium's properties and potential. Similar concerns traverse films and series that function on a more allegorical mode. Chapter 5 follows a similar trajectory as Chapter 4 by taking us from films portraying audiences to metaleptical fantasies of escaping or crossing over into the fictional world, to allegories of spectatorship. These works offer a multifarious view of spectatorship and movie audiences whose various activities and responses confirm, anticipate and counter theories and observations put forth by film scholars. They also reveal how a concern for spectatorship is intimately interweaved with a concern for creation, its materials and its relation to the world. Chapter 6 completes the study of meta from the perspective of the apparatus by focusing on the medium itself—that which connects the creator and the spectator (and thus Chapters 4 and 5). It also pursues two lines of inquiry raised in Chapter 3 by addressing the avant-age concern for the material properties of a given medium. This is often effected through what we now call intermediality or remediation, for instance by confronting film to other arts and media (architecture, painting, video, comics, Internet) to interrogate the ontology of moving pictures and its potential as a synchretic medium. Together, the three chapters demonstrate the entanglement of meta whose concerns regularly spill out of the boundaries of each chapter.

Chapters 7 and 8 both explore what Genette calls "metatextuality." Chapter 7 focuses on instances where an adaptation or a remake engages with its secondary nature, such metamoments often occurring in the opening scenes. It then returns to one of the questions raised in Chapter 3 concerning the influence of literature by assessing the quality of meta in adaptations of famous metafictional novels. Special attention is devoted to what adaptation scholars have recently called "metadaptations," i.e., works that not only consistently engage with the question of adaptation but turn it into an allegory of life or film history. Chapter 8 shows how films and series can also assert their modes of engagement with a given genre in a programmatic fashion, indicating the degree to which a genre's conventions will be subverted and/or its politics revised. It then tries to answer one of the questions raised in Chapter 2—is parody essentially meta?—through an analysis of three Western parodies. Finally, it examines how a surface concern for genre can actually serve as a framework for a more profound metadiscourse on the ethics of fiction. Focusing exclusively on series, Chapter 9 opens with an overview of the modes and functions of meta-phenomena. Eminently metanarrative and sometimes justified by industrial stakes, the discourse on seriality often takes the form of a motif that functions as a metaphorical mise en abyme of the work as a whole. Special attention is paid to how seriality can serve to build up and complexify meta in specific series. Together, Chapters 7, 8 and 9 demonstrate that formal concerns are frequently grounded in profound ethical questions.

Chapter 10 opens with a discussion of "historiographic metafiction," a term coined by Hutcheon to describe works that interrogate "the epistemological and ontological relations between history and fiction." It then seeks to answer a similar question regarding parody in Chapter 6, that is, whether an allohistory (i.e., alternate history) is always meta. Attention is paid to historical movies that address their role in our remembrance and understanding of history, notably through the use of (mock) archive footage, echoing the intermedial concerns explored in Chapter 6. Chapter 11 starts with a discussion of Stam's study of the politics of reflexivity and Christopher Carter's study of the materialist rhetoric of specific metafilms. Grounded in Jacques Rancière's writings on the politics of aesthetics, the chapter then analyzes how meta can question the political efficacy of a given work or medium, that is, its capacity to change the world. Chapters 10 and 11 both contest the assumption (and criticism) that anything meta is fundamentally disconnected from real-world concerns, and pursue the conclusions of Chapters 7, 8 and 9 that meta involves ethical and political questions just as much as formal ones.

Part I

The Theory and History of Meta

CHAPTER 1

What Is Meta and Who Uses the Term?

"That's so meta"

Everyone has been using the word "meta" quite a lot these days. Fans, critics, scholars. So much so that the prefix has graduated to the status of adjective. A book such as this one could even be said to be helping it along its way to the status of noun and, more importantly, autonomous concept. The fact that it's being used so much and in such a carefree manner would suggest that its meaning is fairly obvious and that we all know what we're talking about when we talk meta. And yet, as a student of US-American literature who became a scholar in film and television studies, I, for one, am not at all sure that such a complex word is being used in the exact same sense by all those concerned. And it is the variations—and above all what they have to say about art, media, our contemporary world, and basically what it means to be human—that interest me.

"Meta" is not just a fashionable word used in the restricted circles of academia; it is all over the Internet. Acclaimed Spanish director Pedro Almodóvar's recent venture, *Pain and Glory* (2019), has been described as "all very meta" by executive editor Gordon Bowness for *Xtra*[1] and as a "remarkably mature meta-fiction" by film critic Peter Debruge for *Variety* online.[2] The adjective is regularly used to describe mainstream series and films as well. "For 'Community,' how much meta is too much?" asked UPROXX Senior Television Writer Alan Sepinwall in an online article devoted to the NBC sitcom (2009–15) posted in May 2010.[3] Writing for the AVCLUB in November 2015, Genevieve Valentine stated that "*Scream Queens* [Fox, 2015–16] gets meta as hell with a few 'Ghost Stories.'"[4] "*The Cabin in the Woods* [Goddard, 2011] is about as meta as horror gets," opined Josh Hammond on a blog in October 2017.[5] "Is the show getting too meta?" an anonymous blogger worried about the animated sitcom *Rick and Morty* (Comedy Central, 2013–) in 2018.[6] In December 2020, freelance writer Grant Hermanns posted a list of "The 13 Best Meta Episodes of *Supernatural* [The CW, 2005–20]" on comingsoon.net.[7] And in January 2021 a list of "The Most Meta Episodes in TV History," which basically equates "meta" with "breaking the fourth wall," was published by Xandra Harbet on looper.com.[8]

The word "meta" is being used in a similar fashion in French and Spanish. Cédric Delelée of *Mad Movies* describes the series *Scream Queens* and the film *The Final Girls* (Strauss-Schulson, 2015) as "meta-slashers,"[9] while writer François B. describes *The House That Jack Built* (von Trier, 2018) as "meta," which he defines as "a film in which the characters are aware of the fact that they inhabit a work of fiction and not reality."[10] The movies of Quentin Tarantino have been described as "mas meta" by Kiko Vega on the website espinof.com.[11] This usage has not yet been generalized to other languages (Italian, Russian) where it remains a preposition. Germans tend to use the word "metaebene" (i.e., "meta-level"), a term used by German scholar Werner Wolf whose essential work on "metareference" is discussed below.

Similar usages can be found in the films and series themselves. The season 4 finale of the *Doctor Who* reboot introduces a doppelgänger of Doctor Who called the Metacrisis Doctor (BBC, 2008). In season 2 of *Community*, broadcast in 2010–11, Abed is reprimanded or praised for being "meta" (see Chapter 8). One of the characters of *Scream 4* (Craven, 2011) complains about the *Stab* franchise, "How much more meta can it get?", employing a word that is absent in the first three movies' very similar dialogues (Craven, 1996–2000).

The adjective "meta" has recently found its way into English dictionaries. My well-worn fourth edition of *The American Heritage Dictionary* contains entries for metafiction, metalanguage and metalinguistics, but none for meta. Merriamwebster.com, however, now includes an entry for the adjective meta with two definitions, the first of which corresponds to the popular usage: "*informal*: showing or suggesting an explicit awareness of itself or oneself as a member of its category: cleverly self-referential."[12] The examples provided are of the same ilk as those cited above:

> "The Bar?" she said. "I know the place. Been meaning to drop by. Love the name. Very *meta*."
>
> Gillian Flynn

> The *meta* gift of the year: a picture of a lamp that actually lights up. Designer Finn Magee's trompe l'œil is printed on plastic, embedded with electronics, and equipped with a cord and switch.
>
> Karissa Bell et al.

> A new comedy about fantasy football, which follows a group of armchair quarterbacks as they try to tackle life. How *meta* would it be if people started betting on what was going to happen on the show?
>
> *TV Guide*

Leave it to Larry to contort public desire for a Seinfeld reunion into a *meta* plot that chronicles his not-necessarily-noble struggle to pull off a Seinfeld reunion.

Dan Snierson

The less legitimate dictionary.com includes not only an entry for meta as an adjective, but one for meta as a noun ("a consciously and playfully self-referential story, conversation, etc."), and features a list of examples taken from the web.[13] In January 2019, merriam-webster.com even added an article entitled "That's so meta," which observes that journalist Noam Cohen's 1988 prediction that "meta could follow retro as a prefix that developed its own meaning as a standalone word" has been realized in less than thirty years.[14]

What does this brief overview tell us? It tells us that the prefix's use as an adjective (and sometimes even as a noun) seems to have emerged in the late 2000s (Snierson's remark about *Curb Your Enthusiasm* [HBO, 2000–] dates back to 2009,[15] and Flynn's *Gone Girl* was published in 2012). The word has since earned its own dictionary entry and become a very common term to describe films and series, whether they are popular genre fare or of the art cinema tradition (three out of four of the examples provided by merriam-webster.com relate to popular fiction either as source or object of the commentary). "Meta" is used by a large but nonetheless specific group of people, fans and critics who produce and circulate discourses on comics, films, series, video games, etc. Its usage is a media phenomenon (three of the examples on merriam-webster.com are quotes by journalists). Its presence in the fictions themselves is an instance of self-consciousness that further contributes to the validation and dissemination of the term. So it is likely that a growing number of people who watch series and films, including those who do not bother to write or tweet about them, are familiar with the term from hearing it in the mouths of characters and other fans. Its presence in titles, leads, bulletin topics and fictional conversations implies that it is seen as a central, perhaps even defining, characteristic of the referent it describes. Not only is its meaning generally taken for granted, it is, like retro or camp, an immediately identifiable label, on a level (or almost) with a film or television genre, for instance. "Meta" is associated with cleverness and playfulness (as the four examples from merriam-webster.com seem to suggest), and more implicitly with a highlighting or transgression of the ontological border between reality and fiction (the football comedy and *Curb Your Enthusiasm*), art (Finn Magee's trompe l'œil) or signifier (The Bar). It can—and is quite often—used in a derogatory sense, notably when it is preceded by an intensifier such as "too" or "so." Finally, the term is mainly used to describe works that are self-conscious (of genre and/or narrative conventions, of their status as works of fiction or art), full of references and intertexts, and whose stories sometimes deal with artistic creation. In a nutshell, "meta," in its popular usage, has become a sort of umbrella word for academic terms such as "reflexivity" and "metafiction," or more specific phenomena such as the "mise en abyme" (i.e., the reflection of a given work within the work) or "metalepsis" (i.e., the transgression of ontological borders, see Chapter 5).

METAFICTION, METANARRATIVE, METAFILM, METACINEMA, METAFILMIC . . . AND REFLEXIVITY

It's a whole other story in academic circles. Meta is not an autonomous concept, and each field has more or less conceptualized its own brand of meta: metalanguage, metatheatre, metadrama, metanarrative, metafiction, metahistory, metacinema, metafilm, etc. In his seminal *Metatheatre: A New View of Dramatic Form* (1963), Lionel Abel studies plays in which "the play's the thing,"[16] and Bill Angus (2016, 2019) has since used the term "metadrama" in his studies of the English Renaissance to refer more or less to the same thing—"drama about drama, either implicit in content or form, or where dramatic codes themselves become 'an explicit object of discourse.'"[17] Author/critic William Gass and scholar Robert Scholes coined the term "metafiction" the same year (1970)—though separately—to refer to fictions whose material is their own form.[18] Hayden White's *Metahistory: The Historical Imagination in Nineteenth-Century Europe* (1973) analyzes the "main forms of historical consciousness," that is, the strategies utilized in order to address the historian's representation of historical phenomena.[19] In his study of intertextual phenomena, *Palimpsests* (1982), Gérard Genette defines "metatextuality" as a specific mode of intertextuality: "otherwise known as 'commentary'," it is "the relationship which unites a text with another text which it talks about without necessarily citing it."[20] A term like metanarrative is used in two senses that are only partially related: to describe any work that comments on its own narrative and/or narration; or in a more specific sense, related to French philosopher Jean-François Lyotard's 1979 theory of postmodernism, that of an overarching narrative founded on universal truths. The words "metalanguage" ("a language used to talk about language") and "metafiction" have long made it into the *Merriam Webster* and *Oxford Learner's* dictionaries.

Until recently, film critics and scholars tended to use terms such as metanarrative, metacinema and metafilm(ic) sporadically, and rarely the word metafiction(al). Major writings of film scholarship focus predominantly on reflexivity (Fredericksen 1979; Metz 1991; Stam 1992; Withalm 2007; Connor 2012) or on specific devices such as the mise en abyme (Févry 2000;

Tore and Raus 2019) or the metalepsis (Genette 2004), not on metacinema, metafiction or even metanarrative. In fact, when we organized a conference on "Metafiction and Reflexivity in Cinema" in fall 2019, published as an issue of *La Furia Umana* in 2021, we were surprised to see that the vast majority of the scholars dealt exclusively with reflexivity.

There is, indeed, a long history of studies of reflexivity in film—Robert Stam lists Bruce Kawin, Noël Burch, Martin Walsh, Don Fredericksen, Alfred Appel Jr. as notable precursors.[21] In "Modes of Reflexive Film" (1979), Fredericksen proposes a typology of reflexivity in film based on Roman Jakobson's six functions in any speech event; these are the ironic (emotive), genetic and ontological (referential), communicative (connotative and phatic), metafilmic (metalingual) and formal (poetic). Today, the landmark works in the field are Christian Metz's 1991 *Impersonal Enunciation, or the Place of Film* and Robert Stam's 1992 *Reflexivity in Film and Literature: From Don Quixote to Jean-Luc Godard*. (Daniel Yacavone, in his forthcoming book, *Reflexive Cinema: Rethinking, Self-Consciousness, Affect and Intermediality in the Moving Image*, aims to build on Metz's and Stam's seminal work, in part by proposing a new typology of reflexivity that takes into account its transmedial aspects and the changing mediascape.) Building on Francesco Casetti's 1983 *Inside the Gaze: The Fiction Film and Its Spectator*, Metz focuses on the relationship between enunciation and reflexivity; he argues that film, because it is not a linguistic medium and cannot mark its enunciation through the use of deictics (words such as pronouns which immediately point to the act of enunciation), draws attention to the enunciation through reflexive devices.[22] Metz then proposes a typology of these devices (direct addresses, diegetic screens and frames, subjective shots, voices and sounds, the objective oriented system) and concludes with the bold claim that, in film, even the most neutral enunciation is simultaneously enunciating and commenting on the act itself.[23]

Stam's book remains to this day the seminal work on reflexivity in film. It traces the history of a tradition of anti-illusionist fiction from Cervantes and Shakespeare to Godard and Woody Allen, via Bertolt Brecht and Alfred Jarry. Although Stam's book, unlike Metz's, is not organized according to families of devices but according to themes (spectatorship, production) and functions (allegory, self-consciousness, subversion), both scholars (like Fredericksen before them) identify numerous reflexive devices and their singularities in the context of specific films. Some of these are common to cinema, drama and prose fiction (the thematization of creating art or consuming it; the mise en abyme and in particular the film/novel/play within the film/novel/play; interruptions and narrative discontinuity; intertexuality), others to cinema and drama (breaking the fourth wall; the thematization of acting; diegetic spectators), while others are proper to visual or audiovisual media (the look-to-the-camera; frame-within-the-frame compositions; mirrors and diegetic screens; flattened perspectives; sharp primary colors; unmotivated camera movements; static images; violations of classical narration; the "counterpuntal" use of sound, etc.).

For a long time, metacinema, metafilm, the metacinematic or metafilmic did not seem particularly problematic or interesting to film scholars. Fredericksen defines "metacinema" in passing as "film commenting in some sense and at some level upon itself,"[24] uses the term "metafilm" as quasi synonymous (i.e., a metafilm is a film that resorts to metacinema[25]) and uses the words "reflexive," "metacinematic" and "metafilmic" interchangeably.[26] Writing the same year as Fredericksen, William C. Siska, in an article entitled "Metacinema: A Modern Necessity," ends up equating metacinema with "modernist reflexivity."[27] Even a rigorous semiologist like Metz tended to use the terms "metanarrative," "metadiscursive," "metafilmic" and "metacinematographic" as if they were fairly self-evident.[28] Nor did these scholars look to the numerous writings devoted to similar phenomena in other fields, with the exception, perhaps, of Jean Ricardou's work on the Nouveau Roman (1967) and Lucien Dällenbach's work on the mise en abyme (1977). Robert Stam refers to Linda Hutcheon's and Patricia Waugh's work on metafiction in his introduction,[29] only to sidestep the question of what is reflexive and what is metafiction proper, even though his analyses, as we shall see, often stray into the territory of meta. Metacinema and metafilm are taken for granted, and the real stakes lie in circumscribing the arsenal of reflexive devices in film. Scholars of reflexivity are above all interested in the modes of reflexivity (and their history in the case of Stam), and thus in proposing typologies (this is especially true of Fredericksen, Metz, and Withalm). It makes sense that reflexivity would appear more engaging than metacinema or metafiction in a 1970s–1980s context where structuralism and semiology were the dominant theoretical paradigms. Because of its multimodality, audiovisual media provide, in effect, ideal material for examining how reflexive devices function, differ from their equivalents in other media, are occasionally medium specific, and evolve with the technological developments.

It is only recently that scholars and critics (myself included) have shifted the focus on metacinema and metafilm (Cerisuelo 2001; Chinita 2014; Carter 2018; Stuckey 2018; LaRocca et al. 2021), and explored "filmic" or "cinematic metafiction" in a more deliberate manner (McRoy 2008; Sinnerbrink 2011; Roche 2018; Brammer 2019). Like the popular usage of "meta," the terms are often used as if self-evident, even in such works as the wonderful collected volumes on *Inglourious Basterds* (Tarantino, 2009) and *Django Unchained* (Tarantino, 2012) edited by Robert von Dassanowsky (2012) and Oliver C. Speck (2015); one must deduce from Von Dassanowsky's introduction that he associates "metacinema" with the use of distancing and reflexive devices, and with the disruption (in the aesthetic and political sense) of classical conventions and the postmodern deconstruction of master plots.[30] Even Christopher Carter's stimulating 2018 book, somewhat misleadingly entitled *Metafilm: Materialist Rhetoric and Reflexive Cinema*, never really defines the terms "metafilm" and "metacinema"; the author is clearly more interested in explaining what he means by "materialist rhetoric" (i.e., one that "works to frame a political collective" by offering viewers a "common ground," "a space of negotiation"[31]) than "metafilm," and he ultimately focuses on a specific trend of "reflexive cinema" that delivers a "materialist rhetoric." This is not to say that the works analyzed in these books (Tarantino, Atom Egoyan, Michael Haneke, etc.) do not qualify as meta—they undoubtedly do—but it falls on the reader to figure out what is meant by metafilm or metacinema, and to realize that what these authors have in mind involves a specifically cinematic form of reflexivity associated with aesthetic and political subversion. G. Andrew Stuckey's *Metacinema in Contemporary Chinese Cinema* (2018) is, in this sense, quite exceptional, for although it pursues the trend of ignoring the seminal writings on reflexivity and metafiction (only Stam is cited), it does open with a welcome definition of metacinema—"a specific variety of textual reflexivity that foregrounds, to a greater or lesser extent, the mechanisms involved in the creation or reception of film which is defined as film engaging with the production and consumption of films."[32]

One scholar who proposed early on a very specific definition of the term "metafilm" is Marc Cerisuelo. In *Hollywood à l'écran, essai de poétique historique des films: l'exemple des métafilms américains* (2000), he defines the metafilm as a film genre with specific conventions: a metafilm would be

> a movie that deals explicitly with cinema by representing those responsible for the production (actors, directors, producers, technicians, publicity and public relations agents, studio personnel, etc.) through a strict storyline, regardless of the film genre the movie can eventually be associated with, and that proposes at a given moment in time a better understanding, whether achieved through a documentary style or through realist fiction, of the cinema world which it views in a critical light.[33]

Metafilms, in Cerisuelo's sense, are films whose diegeses center on the industry and the filmmaking process. These would include movies like *What Price Hollywood?* (Cukor, 1932), *A Star Is Born* (Wellman and Conway, 1937), *Sunset Blvd.* (Wilder, 1950), as well as more recent movies like *The Player* (Altman, 1992), *Mulholland Dr.* (Lynch, 2001) and *Once Upon a Time . . . in Hollywood* (Tarantino, 2019). But apart from Cerisuelo and his followers in France (Achemchame 2021), in English, the term metafilm is rarely used in such a restricted sense; scholars such as Christopher Ames (1997) and Steven Cohan (2018) simply refer to such film as "movies about the movies" or "backstudio pictures."

Fátima Chinita (2014) helpfully distinguishes between Cerisuelo's metafilm and the more general phenomenon of metacinema. Metacinema, which she associates primarily with fiction (and not with documentary and experimental film[34]), "reveals a taste for spectacle rather than just entertainment, a penchant for variety instead of narrative formulas, and a propensity for the eulogy of art and artists, connoting film with other artistic endeavors."[35] This broader sense allows her to include some of the "metacinematographic allegories" Cerisuelo's definition sets aside, including *Rear Window* (Hitchcock, 1954) and *8½* (Fellini, 1963), which she discusses in terms similar to Stam's;[36] it also suggests that films can engage with cinema through other arts, such as theatre in a movie like *Birdman*[37] (Iñárritu, 2014). It is obviously a similar understanding of metacinema that informs the collected volumes on Tarantino mentioned above, given that only *Inglourious Basterds* (and not *Django Unchained*) would qualify as a metafilm for Cerisuelo. And it is also in this broader sense that Christopher Carter or Werner Wolf[38] use the term metafilm, and that G. Andrew Stuckey uses the term metacinema. In the introduction to the collected volume *Metacinema*, which was published just as I was wrapping up my own manuscript, David LaRocca defines metacinema as "when film *form* or film *content* calls itself into question" and "makes *awareness* (either internally, i.e., reflexively; or externally, i.e., referentially) a hallmark of its attributes."[39]

For film scholars and critics apparently, the terms metafilm and metacinema are so obvious they warrant little discussion and investigation (another pointed also noted by LaRocca[40]). The general consensus seems to be that a metafilm is an instance of metacinema, and that metacinema is explicitly or allegorically about cinema. It is this lack of attention that explains the variety of definitions, the failure to consider possible relations with metatheatre and metafiction, and, more problematically, the collapsing of metacinematic and/or metafilmic with reflexivity. In *The American Avant-garde*, for instance, P. Adams Sitney speaks of "the absolute reflexivity of a film about cinema,"[41] while Christopher Ames, in *Movies about the Movies: Hollywood Reflected* (1997), follows Stam when speaking of the "self-referentiality" and "self-reflexivity"[42] of Hollywood on Hollywood films and limits his discussion of the "developing metanarrative of Hollywood"[43] to the story that the sum total of these films would create. Film—and with them television—scholars thus find themselves in an epistemological bind similar to that created by the dissemination of the term meta: everybody knows more or less what it means.

This is not the case in other fields. As scholar Werner Wolf reminds us, it is to literary studies that we owe the most detailed studies of metafiction, which is not surprising since the term was coined by a famous author/critic and a literary scholar.[44] Historically, the term metafiction has been constructed as literary metafiction. The seminal books on the subject are Linda Hutcheon's 1980 *Narcissistic Narrative: The Metafictional Paradox* and Patricia Waugh's 1984 *Metafiction: The Theory and Practice of Self-Conscious Fiction*; they served as a basis for later works, such as the collected volume *Metafiction* edited by Mark Currie (1995), as well as Werner Wolf's own work on metafiction (1993) and metareference (2009, 2011).

Hutcheon defines metafiction as works that "transform formal properties of fiction into its subject matter."[45] Waugh provides a more elaborate definition:

> *Metafiction* is a term given to fictional writing which self-consciously and systematically draws attention to its status as an artefact in order to pose questions about the relationship between fiction and reality. In providing a critique of their own methods of construction, such writings not only examine the fundamental structures of narrative fiction, they also explore the possible fictionality of the world outside the literary fictional text.[46]

Hutcheon and Waugh do not limit metafiction to the representation of the creative process (though stories centered on writers or other artists do figure prominently among the works they study), but insist on the formal, linguistic and structural qualities of metafiction. Waugh's definition is particularly helpful in distinguishing metafiction from reflexivity: metafiction resorts to reflexivity ("draws attention to [...] the artefact") to reflect ("pose questions") on fiction. Her implication that metafiction is not just playful but critical seems to align it with deconstruction, but the word "critique" should probably be understood, here, as meaning "analysis" in general. Furthermore, while Hutcheon defends the relevance of metafiction because of the "vital" role of "imaginative creation" for human existence,[47] Waugh recognizes that its scope can be much broader, since metafiction, for her, also deals with fiction's "relationship" to reality within and without the work. Hutcheon's later writings (1988) on "historiographic metafiction" equally emphasizes the real-world relevance of metafiction by showing that novels like John Fowles's 1969 *French Lieutenant's Woman* or E.L. Doctorow's 1975 *Ragtime* can foreground how historiography and literature are both grounded in a history of discourse (see Chapter 10). Both Hutcheon and Waugh focus primarily on contemporary authors (Doctorow, Fowles, John Barth, Donald Barthelme, Italo Calvino, Robert Coover, Gabriel García Márquez, Thomas Pynchon), to which Currie's volume adds the likes of Martin Amis and Julian

Barnes, authors who have often been labeled postmodernists or whose œuvre exemplifies the shift from modernism to postmodernism (Jorge Luis Borges, Vladimir Nabokov). This should come as no surprise given that metafiction has often been seen as a recurrent approach in postmodernist fiction, if not the dominant one, by critics and scholars such as Brian McHale in his 1987 *Postmodernist Fiction*[48] and by Hutcheon herself, who went from devoting a book to metafiction to writing two books about postmodernism (1988, 1989). The emergence of such research in the field of literary studies is thus a logical reaction to an artistic trend in literary fiction that caught the attention of scholars in the 1970s, though Hutcheon admits that "the visual arts and music both have also shown signs of self-reflectiveness" and even cites Godard as an example.[49]

The precision with which the term "metafiction" was defined in literary criticism to address a singular trend contrasts with the vagueness of the popular usage of the term "meta". If we look back on our discussion of popular usage in the light of these definitions, meta appears to be a kind of bastardization of, and umbrella term for, the critical concepts of metafiction, metanarrative, metatheatre, metaperformance, metacinema/metafilm and metalepsis. Perhaps the simultaneously vague and overarching sense of meta could be seen as a reaction to a wider phenomenon that is further ranging in terms of both the media and the genres involved—meta is everywhere (in literature, comics, movies, television, video games) and is no longer an elite concern. Yet I would point out that the vagueness of the prefix meta- and its frequent collapsing with related terms such as reflexivity and self-reference preceded this phenomenon and inhabited scholarly discourse as well, particularly in film and media studies. In 1992, Robert Stam listed "[t]he terms associated with reflexivity [that] belong to morphological families with prefixes or roots deriving from the 'auto' family, the 'meta' family, the 'reflect' family, the 'self' family, and the 'textuality' family";[50] fifteen years later, semiotician Gloria Withalm would likewise note the "plurality of notions used to cope with the various ways a text can evince a relation to other texts."[51]

There is, indeed, a degree of confusion concerning such terms even in the hands of the most rigorous theorists. In Metz's *Impersonal Enunciation*, for instance, "meta-narrative" means a narrative (fictional or non-fictional) that comments on itself as such, "metadiscourse" a discourse that comments on itself; a "metafilmic" marker comments on the filmic, while a "metacinematographic" one comments on the apparatus. Yet I am not certain that the terms "metafilmic" and "metacinematographic" are not just synonyms of "reflexive" and are even entirely appropriate for that matter. Though they seem very specific, they are also quite misleading. Metz does not demonstrate to what extent they lead beyond or are about the "filmic" and the "cinematographic";

as markers, they do not actually comment on, but simply point to, or "remind us" of (*rappeler*[52] in French), the filmic or the apparatus—in other words, metafilmic and metacinematographic markers are quite simple reflexive,[53] a collapsing Cerisuelo also effects.[54] At fault, albeit occasionally, is Metz's usage of the word "comment," which he alternately uses as a synonym of foregrounding (for instance, when he says that "the film, which all of a sudden designates itself, *comments directly on itself*, with visual or sonic signals"[55]) or in the sense that it produces a discourse:

> In this way an autonomous layer of meaning, explicit or confused, is formed, which comes to *double* the story from time to time, to comment on it, to punctuate, contradict, and explain it, as well as to muddle it. As a result, this marginal layer of sound obliges the spectator who wants to access the diegesis to make an always somewhat surprised stop at the *semantic tollbooth*.[56]

What Metz is describing, here, is not solely reflexive; it is an additional layer of meaning that engages with the diegesis, what German scholars like Wolf call a "meta-level."[57] Clearly, Metz does not explain how the previous instances of the metacinematographic commented on themselves in this sense, but merely noted that they drew attention to themselves. If the usage of metafilmic and metacinematographic can be problematic even in the hands of the most astute thinkers, this is, by comparison, less the case of the term metanarrative, probably because a narrative is a form of discourse as such, so one clearly gets the sense that a metanarrative is a narrative about narrative—more precisely about how a story is told—and thus a discourse about discourse.

Perhaps the confusion stems from the prefix meta- itself—or, rather, from the way it has been used in the humanities. This brings us to the inevitable scholarly moment when we jump back in time to the Ancient Greeks. According to etymonline.com,[58] the varied meanings of the Greek prefix ("in the midst of; in common with; by means of; between; in pursuit or quest of; after, next, behind") have been lost. The prefix meta- is now used in the sense of (1) "after, behind; among, between"; (2) "changed, altered"; and (3) "higher, beyond." It is the third sense that was used to coin the term "metaphysics," and that literary criticism, linguistics and the humanities adapted for such concepts as "metalanguage," "metalinguistics" and "metahistory" to evoke a language, a linguistics or history that is situated on a "higher" level than the main term. Ironically, etymonline.com explains, this usage of "meta-" was erroneous from the start, relying on a "misinterpretation"[59] of the field of "metaphysics" as a "science of that which transcends the physical," rather than, as we can read in *The American Heritage Dictionary*, "the branch of philosophy that examines the nature of reality, including the relationship between mind and matter, substance and attribute, fact and value."⁶⁰ The "higher" of metaphysics thus refers to the perspective that is cast on existence itself, apprehended through the disciplines of cosmology, epistemology and ontology. Because of this original misinterpretation, meta has come to mean examining oneself from a distance rather than attempting to examine the cosmos from a distance. The popular usage of "meta" that has now infiltrated merriam-webster.com is thus a derivation from the meaning used by scholars discussing metafiction and metanarrative, which is itself a derivation of the term metaphysics. The solipsistic (or "narcissistic" to use Hutcheon's word⁶¹) implications of meta originate in this derivation.

One scholar, Werner Wolf, devoted a lot of energy to trying to solve the "meta" problem in the late 2000s, an enterprise undertaken in a pair of collected volumes (2009, 2011) that aimed to study what he calls "meta-phenomena."⁶² Wolf's work builds on his own study of metafiction, as well as on recent work on "self-reference" by semioticians like Winfried Nöth (2007), for whom reference is a synonym of reflexivity (for Nöth, "any sign that refers to itself or to aspects of itself is a self-referential sign"⁶³). Unlike Nöth, however, Wolf contests the idea that metareference is exclusive to verbal media, though he admits it may be less obvious in visual media.⁶⁴ He contends that the contemporary mediascape begs for a transmedial understanding of meta-phenomena. He thus calls for an interdisciplinary and pluridisciplinary approach in order to find common ground regarding such phenomena in various arts and media, and elaborate a framework/toolbox/typology that is at least partly transferable from one medium to another.⁶⁵ If he also uses literary theory on metafiction as a starting point,⁶⁶ he opts for the term "metareference," which he feels has a broader meaning than terms such as self-consciousness, self-reflexivity, metafiction, metatextuality, etc.⁶⁷ Wolf argues that metareference is a special case of self-reference, and that the latter terms have often been used indiscriminately⁶⁸ (like reflexivity and the family of words utilizing the prefix meta- in the discussion above). Wolf distinguishes metareference from "heteroreference," the "commonsensical default-function of everyday language" that points to "extra-semiotic reality,"⁶⁹ and alternates between two quasi-synonyms—"metaization" and "metareference"—depending on whether the focus is on the process or the result.⁷⁰ If Wolf uses the word "reference [. . .] as an umbrella term that encompasses a wide range of realizations [. . .] from a simple 'pointing to' a referent to complex cases of relations between sign and referent (or between signifier and signified,"⁷¹ appending the prefix meta- entails that metareference "always is, or at least implies, a metacommunicative statement—this is why it is a special kind of self-reflection or self-reflexivity."⁷² Wolf thus equates reflexivity with mere "pointing to" and "metareference" with a mode of reflexivity that articulates a "statement" on a "meta-level."⁷³

A Theoretical Proposition

A series of problems have been identified in the course of our discussion: (1) the popular meaning of meta is vague and fairly broad, but seems to echo scholarly concepts including reflexivity, metafiction and metanarrative; (2) metafilm and metacinema have not been clearly defined in film and media studies because attention has primarily been paid to the functioning of reflexive devices; (3) confusion between reflexivity and various meta-phenomena (metafiction, metacinema, etc.) is quite frequent in academic studies, and is no doubt caused by the ambiguous polysemy of the prefix meta- and the root "reflect." What follows is a first attempt to theorize the popular usage of "meta" within the framework of academic discourses on meta-phenomena; it expands on my own definition of "cinematic metafiction" (2018) and largely rejoins Wolf's theory of metareference. The rest of the book will then aim at refining the theory of meta, notably through the analyses of films and series in Part II.

Meta "implies a high degree of reflexivity; it is essentially reflexive, but reflexivity does not necessarily make a work" meta.[74] Reflexivity refers to the anti-illusionist practice of drawing attention to the artifice—which is why, like Yacavone, LaRocca and others,[75] I consider the addition of the prefix self- in self-reflexivity to be redundant, given that reflexivity is already a redoubling on itself; equally redundant is the occasional use of "meta-reflexive"[76] in discussions of art or media. Reflexivity is not synonymous with meta, but nonetheless represents the zero degree of meta in the sense that meta cannot exist without it. For though I questioned Metz's usage of the adjectives "metafilmic" and "metacinematographic," and especially of "comment" because mere foregrounding may not exactly be what we have in mind when we use that verb, foregrounding is, in effect, the formulation of a very basic comment: "I am pointing to myself" (hence Metz's contention that reflexivity is the equivalent of deixis in audiovisual media). Reflexivity that reflects in both senses of the word—that explores the reflection and the relation between the reflected and the reflection—is, in effect, meta. In order to be meta, then, the work or scene needs to offer not just a foregrounding, but a discourse that engages analytically with the aspect of the root term that is being emphasized. Thus, meta's relation to the root term can combine proximity and distance (the "among" or "higher, beyond" of the prefix): proximity because it is formally, structurally and intimately connected to the work; distance because it represents another layer that is distancing itself from the work. This remains true when meta is used as an adjective and the form or medium is merely implied. Meta is above all a question of introspection—the "aboutness" brought on by the misunderstanding of "metaphysics"—though

I will later argue that introspection by no means precludes real-world considerations and can simultaneously be outward-looking. While reflexivity often leads to the study of devices (such as the metalepsis or mise en abyme), meta begs us to consider how these devices are used to comment on the work and/or medium.

This distinction is already latent in Fredericksen's and Siska's 1979 articles. Siska's "metacinema" not only represents filmmaking (*Singin' in the Rain*, Donen and Kelly, 1952); it reflects on the creator and the act of creating the film itself (*8½*).[77] Fredericksen's opening analysis of *Wind from the East* (Godard and Gorin, 1970) proves that the film resorts to reflexive devices (commentative sound, the repetition of shots) in order to comment on both itself and cinema; the recycled images, for instance, "manifest and comment on the logics of power and drama at work in another kind of film."[78] Stam's book on reflexivity also contains numerous examples that help clarify the distinction between meta and reflexivity in spite of his avoiding the issue. His entitling the first chapter "Allegories of Spectatorship"[79] is already an avowal that some of the films are doing more than just holding up a mirror; indeed, allegory is, for Hutcheon, and Jean Ricardou before her,[80] one of the forms overt diegetic metafiction may take. Take Stam's remarkable analysis of *400 Blows* (Truffaut, 1959), for instance.

> *400 Blows* orchestrates variations on the theme of *écriture*, in a way that makes little sense except as part of a structural metaphor subtending Truffaut's vision of filmmaking. Antoine, Truffaut's youthful surrogate in an admittedly autobiographical film, "tries on" diverse writing styles in an attempt to become his own man. He complains that his mother's writing is "hard to imitate." His affectionate pastiche of Balzac elicits accusations of plagiarism. [...] The accusation of plagiarism anticipates the frequent charge against new wave filmmakers that their best ideas were borrowed, that their films were merely collages of citations and cinematic in-jokes.[81]

Stam uncovers the meta in a film which, given its naturalistic techniques (handheld cameras, natural light, nonprofessional actors), has, on the surface at least, very little to do with meta-slashers, *Seinfeld* (NBC, 1989–98) or a Charlie Kaufman movie. And yet, its portrayal of the figure of the artist as a young man reflects Truffaut's and even the French New Wave's "attitudes toward the cinema," and is thus a commentary on itself specifically, but also on cinema and more generally artistic creation. This commentary is "structural" and thus foundational: the film is grounded in it. A work that can be read as an obvious or not-so-obvious allegory of spectatorship (*Rear Window*) or of creation (*400 Blows*)—and often both—is fairly typical of meta, as we shall see in Part II.

Positing that reflexivity is the zero degree of meta begs the question: How meta does a work have to be to qualify? Because popular usage tends to equate meta with reflexivity, complaints that a work is "too meta" seem to point to the quantity of reflexive devices more than to the quality of the discourse. However, Wolf's stating that "if meta-phenomena become salient features of work as a whole, one may speak of a 'metatext', a 'metadrama' etc.,"[82] makes it sound like quality is the decisive factor. I would side with Wolf and go somewhat against popular usage by arguing that meta is more a question of quality than quantity—though it is, in effect, a combination of the two. Granted, the quantity of reflexive devices might make meta more noticeable, but it could simply imply that we're dealing with a highly anti-illusionist work. A given work could be reflexive from beginning to end—notably by including an abundance of intertextual references—and yet fail to ever propose an elaborate commentary. This has been my experience when comparing two remakes, *Dawn of the Dead* (Snyder, 2004) and *Halloween* (Zombie, 2007). The many allusions to films in *Dawn of the Dead* (2004) are purely for fun and fail to build up a reflection on horror or the remake as creative process; *Halloween* (2007), on the other hand, revisits specific scenes from *Halloween* (Carpenter, 1978) and refers to other horror movies like *The Texas Chain Saw Massacre* (Hooper, 1974) to align itself aesthetically and politically with the 1974 film against the 1978 one.[83]

Quality would thus be the central criterion to distinguish meta from reflexivity—one that no doubt implies some subjectivity on the part of the viewer or reader (see Chapter 2). Quantity nonetheless remains important. I noted above that scholars use the adjective "metafictional" far more often than the noun it is derived from. This may be because, in practice, few works are metafictional through and through—in literature, for instance, only a handful of postmodernist writers (Barth, Barthelme, Coover, Paul Auster) would qualify as authors of metafiction. The usage of the adjective "metafictional" suggests a limited quantity—that the work may not be metafictional enough to be considered metafiction. Yet not only are there metafictional and metanarrative passages in the most realist works, but the opposite is true as well: even the most diehard work of meta-something is never just meta and can always be received on other terms. It is the use of "meta-" to describe specific passages in a given work (Wolf notes that "'metafiction' can refer to individual passages of a novel"[84]) that lead me to suggest we refer to them as metamoments. A metamoment occurs when the work explicitly or implicitly comments on itself, its form, art and/or medium; a work in which metamoments abound is intensely meta, quantity thus factoring into quality. Metamoments have existed from the early days of cinema and television, but have apparently become a staple—and maybe even a requisite—feature of the digital age (see Chapter 3). It is such metamoments that Part II of this book proposes to analyze in order to argue against more restricted understandings of both "meta" (in popular usage) and metacinema, metafilm or metafiction (in scholarship). Considered as a quality, the forms and scope of meta are as boundless as the possibilities of art and fiction themselves.

CHAPTER 2

How Does Meta Work?

TYPOLOGIES OF METAFICTION, METAREFERENCE, METACINEMA, ETC.

The question "How does metafiction or metacinema work?" has often been understood as, and thus subsumed by, the question "What are the formal devices it resorts to?" It is this question that has justified the typological approaches that have dominated the study of reflexivity and meta-phenomena like the mise en abyme.[1] This can at least partly be accounted for by the history of theory in the humanities. Writing in the 1980s, Metz, Hutcheon, and, albeit to a lesser extent, Waugh and Stam employed a methodology influenced by their structuralist contemporaries or predecessors (Gérard Genette, Michael Riffaterre among others) by attempting to classify common devices or trends in literary metafiction (Hutcheon, Waugh), anti-illusionist cinema and literature (Stam) or cinematic reflexivity in general (Metz). More recent typologies have striven to refine and update our understanding of the various modes of reflexivity, thus consciously or not pursuing the structuralist project. Like many of my predecessors, in this chapter at least, I propose to elaborate a theory of meta based on previous writings, and like Hutcheon, I will attempt to answer the question of how meta operates. But instead of attempting to identify and classify the forms meta-phenomena may take, an approach which tends to collapse meta-phenomena with reflexive devices in general, I would like to build on what I feel is actually one of Hutcheon's most productive insights: the idea that metafiction needs to be "actualized" or "concretized"[2] by an audience. I argue that the answer to the question "How does meta operate?" lies not just in the devices employed, but, more importantly, in how we make sense of these devices, how we interpret them and end up elaborating a metacommentary. Meta is thus, at least in part, a matter of reception. I will first try and elaborate this theory through a discussion of several typologies of meta-phenomena, starting with what I believe to be the two most significant, Hutcheon's typology of metafiction and Wolf's typology of metareference.

In her 1980 *Narcissistic Narrative: The Metafictional Paradox*, Linda Hutcheon presented two sets of binaries—diegetic and linguistic metafiction on the one hand, overt and covert metafiction on the other—which could then be productively combined in a "four-part system."[3] The self-awareness of overt metafiction is explicit in that it is thematized or allegorized, while "[i]n the covert form, this process is internalized, actualized."[4] With diegetic metafiction, "the text displays itself as narrative, as the gradual building of a fictive universe complete with character and action. In the linguistic mode, however, the text would actually show its building blocks—the very language whose referents serve to construct that imaginative world."[5] Hutcheon includes the portrayal of artists at work and the "mise en abyme" as instances of overt diegetic metafiction, while covert diegetic metafiction would involve more subtle processes whereby metafiction is "structuralized," that is, embedded in a model based on the detective story, fantasy, play or even erotics. These models have to do with how the reader engages with the fiction—as an enigma to interpret, a world distinct from our own, a game with specific rules, or a potentially sensual experience of seduction—and are by no means "exclusive."[6] With overt linguistic metafiction, "the formal language issue" is brought "into the foreground, into the thematized content itself";[7] it mainly consists of various forms of direct address and narratorial commentary. Finally, covert linguistic metafiction involves "linguistic play"[8] such as puns and anagrams, which, Hutcheon admits, are "hard to analyze in terms of the devices or models employed,"[9] even though she includes riddles, jokes, anagrams and puns as examples.[10]

In her 1984 *Metafiction*, Patricia Waugh mainly avoids the typological endeavor and suggests, instead, that the texts she discusses be considered on a "spectrum," with those that "take fictionality as a theme to be explored" on one end, those that "posit the world as a fabrication of competing semiotic systems which never correspond to material conditions," on the other, and at the center, "those texts that manifest the symptoms of formal and ontological insecurity but allow their deconstructions to be finally recontextualized or 'naturalized' and given a total interpretation."[11] The structuralist/semiologist project surfaces in her fourth and final chapter, "Fictionality and context: from role-playing to language games," which identifies several strategies common in literary metafiction, organized in similar terms as Hutcheon depending on whether they be diegetic ("role-playing," "script-writing," characters seeking their authors) or linguistic (contradiction, paradox, collage, intertextuality).

Twenty years later, in the introduction to *Metareference across Media* (2009), Werner Wolf proposed an elaborate typology of what he calls metareference, adapted from his previous work on metafiction (1993), and drawing on the work of both Hutcheon and Marie-Laure Ryan. Indeed, in the opening paragraphs of a book chapter published in 2007, Ryan had proposed to consider "self-reflexivity" in the light of three "continuums": explicitness (recalling Hutcheon's overt/covert binary), scope ("how dominant [the self-reflexive elements] are in the global economy of the text"), and individuation (focus on itself or on the genre or medium).[12] Wolf presents four oppositions, each based on a specific criterion,[13] with the first two recalling Ryan's tripartite proposition.

(1) Intracomposition/direct vs. extracomposition/indirect metareference. Here, the criterion is the "scope of the metareference,"[14] which is closer to what Ryan understood as "individuation," that is: does the metareference focus on the work itself (intra) or does it branch out to other works and media (extra)? Wolf concedes, of course, that works often do both to varying degrees.

(2) Explicit vs. implicit metareference. Here, Wolf follows Ryan's discussion of the "degrees of explicitness,"[15] the decisive criterion being the "semantic discernibility of metareference."[16] Does the work resort to an element of the diegesis (usually a narrator or character) to comment on its processes or is the commentary achieved through the devices themselves? Wolf compares this opposition to Hutcheon's diegetic vs. linguistic metafiction, no doubt because diegetic phenomena are on the whole more obvious than linguistic ones, but this is not necessarily always the case; whether effected by a character or a narrator, direct address (an example of overt linguistic metafiction according to Hutcheon), for instance, is potentially more explicit than an underpinning game model (Hutcheon's covert diegetic metafiction). So Wolf's second binary is, in this respect at least, closer to Hutcheon's overt/covert binary.

(3) Fictio vs. fictum (or mediality-centered vs. truth/fiction-centered) metareference. Wolf's third opposition is exclusively meant for metafiction, though perhaps fiction can quite simply be replaced by art. The criterion, here, is "content,"[17] more specifically, how does the work speak about fiction? Its subtlety lies in how fiction is apprehended: "fictio-metareference" is concerned with the fictionality of fiction and with the artificiality of the artefact, while "fictum-metareference" focuses on the relationship between fiction and reality. Wolf's pair is, I would argue, quite useful because it responds, through a neat combination, to both Hutcheon's and Waugh's understanding of the relevance of metafiction: metafiction is relevant because fiction is an essential human activity (Hutcheon); metafiction explores the relationship between fiction and reality (Waugh). Wolf's answer is that it can pertain to both.

(4) Critical vs. non-critical metareference. Here, the criteria, Wolf explains, are the "frequent functions of metareference."[18] Wolf contests the "tendency to overstress such critical 'laying bare of the work's

fictionality so often encountered in scholarly discussions (in particular of postmodernism)."[19] In other words, he goes against the assumption that reflexivity or meta are radical per se and cites, as the most obvious example, a work that celebrates the power of an artist.

The only common criterion in these typologies is the degree of explicitness (which is implicit in Waugh's "spectrum"). The other criteria are not all the same. Hutcheon's mainly have to do with the "modes and forms" of metafiction, as the title of Chapter 1 indicates. Unlike Hutcheon, Waugh is more interested in what I have called the quality of metafiction, more specifically how radical its engagement with the relationship between fiction and the world is. Wolf's typology also aims to determine the quality of metareference, and more precisely the quality of the reference in metareference, so to speak. (Note that Wolf does not carry over Ryan's second "continuum" whose determining criterion is, in effect, quantity.) The questions posed in Wolf's binaries are not "What sort of devices and strategies does metareference resort to?" but: (1) What is its subject? (2) How salient is it? (3) How does it tackle the reality-fiction binary? and (4) What is its attitude? Three of Wolf's oppositions (1, 3 and 4)—the three that are not indebted to Hutcheon, with the third basically reprising Waugh's "spectrum"—concern what meta is about. This rejoins the conclusions made in Chapter 1 whereby meta was defined *contra* reflexivity as a matter of quality more than quantity and based on its aboutness.

By and large, the typologies proposed by most twenty-first-century film and television scholars and critics are variations or expansions of these seminal typologies. Focusing exclusively on the film-within-the-film, Nicholas Schmidt (2007) effects a categorization based on the dichotomy illusion/reality and the authorial expression of the film director. His taxonomy is comprised of (1) film-on-film, in the broad sense of an embedded fiction either in the form of a film projection or a film shooting; (2) mise en abyme, designating the presence of one work inside another of the same nature; (3) metafilm, as the portrayal of filmmaking but endowed with a critical discourse (and thus in the sense Marc Cerisuelo gives to the term).

Authorial "discourse" is equally central to Fátima Chinita's (2021) understanding of metacinema, first articulated in her 2013 PhD dissertation. Having identified metacinema as a specific mode of "reflexive cinema" that is nonetheless broader than "cinema about cinema," she proposes a taxonomy comprised of four main categories: (1) films about the film industry, which "evince the literal meaning in the stories told and the professional universe portrayed"; (2) cinematic allegories, which "deal with the figurative meaning of the films and its cinematic underlying discourse"; (3) hybrid films, "a combination of literal and figurative meaning, to the point of blurring the lines between one and the other"; (4) metanarrative, which "concentrates on narrative and on the goal of drawing attention to the process of fictionalization involved in filmmaking." The "hybrid films" category is then separated into two subcategories (those that focus on production and those that focus on reception) with their own subtypes.

Presented in a 2015 blog article entitled "When Fiction Points the Finger: Metafiction in Films and TV Series," journalist Rune Bruun Madsen's typology includes seven categories, the first four being derived from Anker Gemzøe's (2001) work on written forms: (1) author meta ("where the director draws attention to himself and his ability to manage a narrative"); (2) addressee meta ("in which an entity from the diegetic universe addresses the reader or view directly"); (3) composition meta ("a self-referential emphasis on all variations of composition that defines a work"); (4) inter meta ("intertextual communication that can be formed through references to directors, works, fictional persons, genres, etc."); (5) cinematic language meta (devices that call our attention); (6) genre meta (the play on genre expectations); (7) para meta ("how events outside of the work, but with a connection to it, can make us re-evaluate the work and its link and place in the real world"). Madsen's typology is actually a typology of families of reflexive devices that brings to mind Metz's work. Madsen also tends to equate meta with formal play or subversion, whether structural (3), stylistic (5) or generic (6). The aboutness of meta is nonetheless latent in the names of his categories, whether the focus is on production/creation (1, 3 and 4), reception (2 and 7) or form (3, 5 and 6).

Gloria Withalm's (2007) and G. Andrew Stuckey's (2018) more modest proposals, on the other hand, are exclusively concerned with what self-reflexive or metacinema is about. Withalm advances a thematic distinction between "self-reflexive textual strategies and practices" depending on whether the focus is on the product, production, reception or distribution.[20] Stuckey makes an even more basic distinction between metacinema that emphasizes production or consumption.[21]

There is something to be said for all these typologies, and I certainly do not want to downplay their relevance, nor the intelligence and effort that went into their conception. I believe any typology to be a bold and ambitious enterprise because typologies often provide useful starting points in a given analysis (Ryan's proposal is, in fact, the framework for her study of self-reflexivity in net.art). This is clearly the case of this book, and the theories and analyses it offers were made possible because of the typological approaches that came before.

The validity of a typology resides largely in its usability; in fact, much of the rhetoric in the presentation of any typology involves an intertwined empirical demonstration of how one came up with it and how it actually works. Usability can be partly gauged in relation to a typology's stated ambition. While Wolf conceived his from a transmedial perspective in the hope of making sense of meta-phenomena across media, as the title of the collected volume suggests, Hutcheon and Waugh focused exclusively on literary fiction. Yet if their typologies would appear for that very reason more limited, many of their insights are transferable to other media. Hutcheon's discussion of "diegetic metafiction" is potentially relevant to all forms of fiction (literature, drama, films, series, comics, etc.), devices such as the mise en abyme and especially the allegory operating fairly similarly regardless of the medium. Her most astute proposition—the idea that covert metafictional texts are grounded in structures based on detective fiction, fantasy, play and/or erotics—is equally transferable to narratives in other media. The strength of her proposition is that these structures point to a variety of ways of conceiving fiction: as hermeneutics, as world-building, as a cognitive game, as a sensual experience. However, if these models do play a structural role, the analyses of Part II will demonstrate that they need not be entirely covert to participate in meta. If "linguistic metafiction" is more medium specific, some of Hutcheon's analyses of overt instances are equally transferrable ("narratorial commentary" does occur in audiovisual fictions, although its modalities are complicated by the fact that a voiceover is not a narrator). In order to adapt it to other media such as film, television, music and comics, this mode of metafiction, whether overt or covert, could more generally be called "formal metafiction." The same can be said of the diegetic and linguistic strategies identified by Waugh, the first being directly transferable to other media, the second group requiring some adaptation. So there is much to be salvaged from these typologies, and the analyses in Part II will frequently refer to them.

It is generally more productive to consider binaries and typologies not as strict categories, but rather in terms of degree or the poles of a "spectrum" (Waugh) or "continuum" (Ryan), and the fact that Wolf follows Ryan in her discussion of "degrees of explicitness" suggests that he himself would agree in spite of his use of the preposition "versus." Since Jacques Derrida's deconstruction of binaries and critique of the structuralist project, the tendency in the humanities has been to consider binaries and typologies as a continuum or a topography whose borders are porous—Daniel Sibony (1991), for instance, recuperated binaries through the concept of "entre-deux" (in-between).[22] Chinita ultimately works around the typological impasse—that a category is almost never a perfect fit for a singular work—by positing a "hybrid" category that mixes elements from her three other categories, and which she finds the most compelling in her typology.

If we take Wolf's first binary, it is unlikely, in practice, that a metamoment be entirely "intracompositional," that is literally and exclusively about the scene or work: can a metamoment really engage with its own creation or reception without touching upon creation and reception in general? As Daniel Yacavone suggests, "cinematic reflexivity is no more or less than the conjunction of a film's recognized *reference to cinema via self-reference*, and *self-reference via reference* to cinema."[23] Can a mise en abyme hold up a mirror to the work without investigating it in relation to the medium it is redoubling? Does the play on intertexts, genre and artistic conventions not immediately inscribe a work within the history of forms and instigate a dialogue with other works? It is equally unlikely that a work be exclusively mediality-centered (Wolf's third binary); fiction about fiction does not mean that the fiction it is about is about nothing but fiction. Even an Italo Calvino story such as "The Form of Space" where two men and one woman are falling through space in parallel lines is also, and perhaps above all, a story of impossible love; while the collection it's in, *Cosmicomics* (1965), as a whole can be viewed as a stylistic game, the latter is based on scientific theories of our universe, and thus on our comprehension of reality. Moreover, it remains to be seen whether, in the end, "fictum-metareference" does not always underlie what appears to be "fictio-metareference," and if the attention to *fictum* rather than *fictio* is not a question of degree as well. This is another question the analyses in Part II will attempt to answer.

Finally, any convincing typology—because of its totalizing ambition—can be useful because it is flawed: it is the loopholes, which are sometimes pinpointed by the authors themselves (Genette is particularly brilliant at discussing the limits of his own typologies), that make the latter so valuable. In so doing, these typologies indirectly account for some of the problems raised because of what remains ungraspable from the perspective of the typology, if not because of the typological enterprise itself. It is both the insights and the blind spots of these typologies that provide the foundation for the exploration of how we make sense of meta.

Problems when Doing Meta

The specificity of meta is its aboutness

The confusion between meta and reflexivity, as we have seen in Chapter 1, stems from the fact that meta is a particularly intense form of reflexivity that operates through various modes of reflexivity. This has led many scholars and critics to focus more on the forms metafilm (Schmidt), metacinema (Chinita) and metafiction (Madsen) may take than on how it actually works and what it actually does. As a consequence, such typologies are bound to become typologies of reflexive devices. This was already the case of Hutcheon's early work, since the chapters of *Narcissistic Narrative* are organized according to the devices and structures metafiction resorts to; her analysis of metafiction thus falls back, at least in part, on the kind of discussion of reflexivity that was common at the time she was writing (Riffaterre's classification of mises en abyme, Don Fredericksen's "modes of reflexivity" in film), and she often loses sight of the very specificity of metafiction she pinpoints in the opening lines of her book: that it is fiction about fiction.

Some of the devices Hutcheon discusses (e.g., direct address) do not immediately qualify as meta-phenomena but are, in effect, reflexive devices of a similar kind as those discussed by Metz a decade later in *Impersonal Enunciation*, whose structure is based on these devices (note that Metz is characteristic of the opposite tendency of hastily qualifying the reflexive devices he studies as "metafilmic" or "metacinematic"). And yet, as Wolf argues, if devices like the mise en abyme and the metalepsis have metareferential "potential," "the extent of this potential varies and depends on several further factors."[24] Discussing the film-within-the-film and mise en abyme, which he tends to equate, Wolf concedes that, in performance media at least, a film-within-the-film is always metareferential because of the explicit frame it materializes.[25] Schmidt's distinction between the film-within-the-film and the mise en abyme is quite useful when discussing audiovisual media because it confirms that the two are always reflexive because both redouble the apparatus, but the film-within-the-film does not necessarily reflect the specific fiction or narrative itself, unlike the mise en abyme;[26] the mise en abyme is thus likelier to instigate a metamoment. This is probably even more obviously the case of direct address (notably the combination of look to the camera and speaking to the audience) which, as many scholars have noted, is characteristic of certain genres (comedy, the musical) indebted to the popular stage:[27] the fourth wall may be broken, but that does not necessarily imply that it is driven by a radical Brechtian project, nor that the foundations of a discourse on fiction and/or the medium are being lain in the process. This is equally true of the metalepsis which, depending on the type, need not be reflexive at all (see Chapter 5). In terms of the history of scholarship, it is thus significant that the majority of authors have sidelined the specificity of meta in relation to reflexivity even after asserting it. Thus far, Wolf's typology has been the only proposal that seeks to circumscribe the quality of the discourse of metaphenomena rather than its forms. The structure of this book, of which Part II constitutes over two-thirds, is largely an attempt to remedy this neglect by giving meta's aboutness pride of place.

Reflexive devices can alert to the presence of and express meta

The relation between reflexivity and meta can be reformulated in the following manner: reflexive devices act not as *triggers* (the effect is not automatic as with a startle effect), but as cues or signals (that can be missed or grasped and made sense of through close analysis). When they do more than just point to the illusion, reflexive devices may serve to simultaneously alert to the presence of, and participate in, the elaboration of meta. They operate as recognizable signs in a system. This sign system is open. It has a history and is constantly mutating in relation to cultural, technological and aesthetic shifts; its devices can evolve, and new ones can emerge, as we shall see in Chapter 3. Hence, reflexive devices are particularly suitable material for typological approaches influenced by linguistics and structuralism. And hence, Metz's strong thesis that reflexivity is an audiovisual medium's equivalent of deixis (see Chapter 1). This is why meta-phenomena sometimes appear to be immediately identifiable: meta materializes when its devices (or at least some of them) are identifiable and "readable." The popular usage of "meta" testifies to the ease with which meta-phenomena can sometimes be spotted and interpreted; it suggests that it has become a precise quality and, more specifically, a sign system recognizable by many. Yet it is this which breeds confusion between meta as a discourse and its formal devices (scholars of meta-phenomena, like other audiences, don't just fall back on reflexive devices for no reason), and thus between meta, and mise en abyme, metalepsis, or reflexivity and parody in general. All of these devices will be discussed in Part II in order to foreground not so much their uses as the moment when they contribute to a metacommentary, often in very dynamic ways.

The explicitness of meta is a question of degree

The distinction between overt and covert or explicit and implicit (Hutcheon, Ryan, Wolf) explains another issue brought up in Chapter 1: why meta can seem so obvious as to be considered excessive ("That's so meta.") or, on the contrary, can go completely unnoticed until an insightful analysis has brought it to our attention. As with anything that is allegedly implicit or explicit, it is so for a specific viewer/reader/listener, a group or a community. Whether as fans, students or teachers, we experience on a regular basis the baffling and yet utterly banal truth that what is explicit for us may not be so for others and vice versa. This can even lead to disagreement within a given community such as the humanities. Hutcheon describes the mise en abyme as an overt form of metafiction,[28] whereas for Wolf, the mise en abyme, along with metalepsis, intertextuality and intermediality, are "implicit" devices.[29] Take another of Hutcheon's examples of overt diegetic metafiction: the allegory. It is by no means certain that every viewer finds the allegory of spectatorship in *Rear Window* (see Chapter 5) obvious on a first viewing (I certainly didn't when, as a ten-year-old, I first watched it on TV during Hitchcock week!). I remember recently discussing *mother!* (Aronofsky, 2017) with colleagues who thought the allegory of the artist and his muse was too heavy-handed, but then realized that many viewers had missed the allegory in the first place. As cinephiles/fans/academics/critics/teachers/etc., we tend to forget that we engage with and interpret these works through frameworks that are by no means inherent; they are learned, have taken years for us to build and are still assembling as we speak, write and teach (some of our fellow peer-reviewers are very keen on reminding us of that reality when they vet our work). The degree of explicitness is thus liable to change in time if only because our interpretive frameworks evolve.

It is also liable to change in media history, as we shall see in Chapter 3. The advent of the meta-slasher has taken explicit or overt metafiction to a whole new level. The conversations on genre conventions in *Scream* (1996) and *Community* are by no means allegorical; they are literally textual and do not require the viewer to make sense of them. In fact, even if this is your first slasher movie, the character of Randy Meeks is here to explain the genre's conventions to you as he does to the film's other characters, though clearly part of the fun lies in the recognition of the recognition. Clearly, the explicitness of *Rear Window* is not the explicitness of *Scream* and *Community*, and the fact that such hypermeta works have become popular fare, no doubt, explains the disagreement between Hutcheon writing in 1980 and Wolf writing in 2009 as to whether or not a mise en abyme is explicit. Clearly, overt and covert cannot be treated as two separate categories, but should, as Ryan argues and Wolf seconds, be considered as two poles in a continuum, as a question of degree, of quality and, though less fundamentally, of quantity. Nor should the two be seen as mutually exclusive. Wolf rightly notes that explicit and implicit metareference usually coexist[30] and that the presence of the first may alert us to the potential presence of the second.[31] In practice, overt meta is often doubled by a covert subtext that requires more of an effort on the part of the viewer and that, like any subtext, could very well work to qualify or contradict it. This will be confirmed by many of the analyses in Part II, particularly of movies about making movies such as *Sunset Blvd.* and *Contempt* (Godard, 1963) that are obviously about the film industry, but also, more implicitly, about artistic creation and, more implicitly still, about film as a medium. In Chapter 8, we will even see that there is more to the dialogue-based meta of *Scream* than meets the eye.

Meta is always analytical or has the potential to be so

Wolf's opposition between critical and non-critical is especially useful for distinguishing meta from reflexivity. Meta, unlike reflexivity, is never merely playful—certainly not in the sense that it is just humorous. Its aboutness implies that it is always, at least to some extent, analytical: the implications of the work, fiction, an artform or medium are analyzed from a distance (i.e., a meta-level). This only seems in contradiction with Wolf's critical/non-critical binary if analytical and critical are seen to be synonymous, and if being non-critical disqualifies an analysis. My contention is that meta-phenomena are invitations to analyze fiction/art/medium and its relation to the world; the commentary can celebrate, offer a critique or, as the majority of analyses in Part II suggest, do a little of both to varying degrees.

Meta entails an act of interpretation

Of course, the terms "playful" and "analytical," though common in scholarship, can be a bit misleading, since they tend to attribute the qualities of sentient beings to phenomena identified in objects. A metamoment is not analytical or playful as such; it is only the relation between the moment and the audience that can be so and that makes it meta. Hutcheon rightly distinguished between overt and covert on the basis of whether or not the metafiction needs to be "actualized" or "concretized"[32] by the reader, and Wolf maintained this idea in his discussion of metareference by arguing that it exists as a potential that must be actualized by the recipient.[33] Because meta is an elaborate form of reflexive discourse, it has to be articulated by someone, which also explains why it can often be missed. Thus, if reflexivity, Daniel Yacavone (2021) argues, implies "a relation between film and spectator" based on recognition, this relation is exacerbated in the case of meta-phenomena; in addition to recognition, meta entails an interpretation.

Works like *Scream*, *Adaptation* (Jonze, 2002) or *Community* are again very helpful in this respect; they exemplify that this actualization can be effected on the diegetic or extradiegetic level by a character (Randy, Abed) or a narrator (the fictitious Charlie Kaufman). When the actualization occurs within the diegesis, meta is not just a potential; it is textual. Randy in *Scream* and pop culture aficionado and aspiring director Abed in *Community* inform the other characters (and the audience in the process) that the plot is governed by a killer who plays with slasher conventions or that the characters' behaviors are abiding by the conventions of a given television or film genre; the only effort that is required of the audience is to deduce from this that the work itself is playing with these conventions. The beyondness of meta is thereby made immediate and quasi-nullified; or rather, the meta-level is fully integrated within the primary level of the diegesis, a potential subtext has become a text, and meta is limited to being *about* without being *beyond* (or hardly). This does not mean that it cannot be called into question like any other explicit element, notably by more implicit elements—it is left to the viewer to go for an extra meta-turn of the screw by attempting to further actualize the diegetic actualization proposed in the work. But the aboutness of meta is quite simply there; there is no mistaking that it is overt and "conscious" because the self-conscious discourse has been diegeticized. This textualized form of self-consciousness, in which characters or narrators comment on genre and formal conventions in moments involving metalepses, mises en abyme, direct address and/or parody (the sitcom *Community* offers a myriad of such examples, often mediated by Abed, see Chapter 8), corresponds to what many audiences of the 2010s refer to as "meta" when they laud or criticize a work.

When meta is not diegeticized, however, it requires viewers to activate it, to sense and make sense of it, to delve into the material and uncover a subtext. And as in the case of any subtext, interpreters engage with the content in light of a context—notably their own frames of reference and their understanding of the frames of reference of others, whether cultural, personal or theoretical—to unravel an underlying commentary. As Wolf notes, with implicit metareference, the "meta-quality of the corresponding devices is notoriously questionable and disputable," and it is particularly difficult to distinguish "motivated salient deviations from ordinary deviations."[34] Meta that is implicit—even if obvious for many—can only be a subtext, and thus an interpretation; an allegory, for instance, is a subtext whereby the story stands for the story of something more universal. This implies that you must argue and prove that a given work is implicitly meta (Gian Maria Tore makes a similar claim for the mise en abyme, arguing that it is an "interpretation" that is up for debate[35]).

My understanding of meta as interpretation is very much informed by Stanley Fish's famous theory of "interpretive communities."[36] In formulating his theory, Fish sought a means to recognize the variety of interpretations, their potential validity, their tendency to change, and thus the simple fact of human subjectivity, while attempting to rationalize it to avoid absolute relativism.

> It is interpretive communities, rather than either the text or the reader, that produce meanings and are responsible for the emergence of formal features. Interpretive communities are made up of those who share interpretive strategies not for reading but for writing texts, for constituting their properties. In other words these strategies exist prior to the act of reading and therefore

determine the shape of what is read rather than, as is usually assumed, the other way around.

Fish thus argues that an interpretation does not rely on the stability of a text, but "on the (relative) coherence of interpretive communities which provide the frame for the interpretation of a text."[37] Thus, because meta is a matter of interpretation and because interpretations rely on frameworks that are acquired and shared to various degrees, the demonstration must garner enough support by a given community for a given work or moment not only to be recognized as meta, but for there to be an agreement as to its quality, i.e., the interpretation of what the work is trying to say about itself and/or its medium. In practice, there can be a general consensus that a given work or moment is meta, and more so even that it is resorting to specific reflexive devices (metalepsis, mise en abyme, direct address, etc.), but not necessarily on what it is doing as meta (i.e., on what it is about). This means that metacommentaries—and basically the majority of my analyses in this book!—can be contested, reappraised or (re)interpreted in a wholly different fashion. It also means that a given work may have other subtexts that coexist alongside the meta-level, although I would argue that they tend to be intertwined, as we shall see in Part II.

Meta can be intentional but is not necessarily so

Wolf muses that "the complexity which metareference implies with its characteristic distinction between a meta- and an object-level, renders it highly probable that the actual metaization is the product of an intentional act on the part of an *author*."[38] This may be the case in examples such as *Scream* or even in most allegories or instances of mise an abyme, yet it is not so obvious when meta-phenomena are more implicit. In Hutcheon's words, covert metafiction is "self-reflective but not necessarily self-conscious,"[39] and even Wolf concedes that "there are cases where non-intentional and intentional phenomena are quite similar both in form and in (illusion-breaking) effect."[40] Because implicit meta requires an act of interpretation of form in relation to content, it may, like any subtext, be nothing more than an effect of the work itself (what Umberto Eco calls the "*intentio operis*"[41])—not to mention an effect of the interpretation and its rhetoric. As an interpretation, meta is always at least "intentional" on the part of the reader or viewer (Eco's "*intentio lectoris*"). This does not invalidate the interpretation per se—the validity, in Fish's logic, comes from the adhesion it will eventually garner—but it is nonetheless troubling in the case of the particular kind of subtext that is meta because its combination of beyondness and aboutness seems to posit a higher level, which can easily be perceived as an origin or intention. Meta can equally appear to originate in an *"intentio auctoris,"* even when it is implicit (this certainly has been my experience when studying the works of Vladimir Nabokov and Quentin Tarantino); and this impression has, no doubt, been fueled by the fact that metafiction and other meta-phenomena have largely been theorized through studies of writers (John Barth) and directors (Jean-Luc Godard) who are, if not theorists, at least very much aware of critical, theoretical, artistic, and philosophical debates. In a sense, meta that would devolve not from an *"intentio auctoris"* but exclusively from an *"intentio operis"* would lead to the paradoxical conclusion that the work's self-consciousness emanates from an individual or collective unconscious, thus rendering the very idea of self-consciousness absurd (especially for those who do not adhere to the Lacanian tenet that "the unconscious is structured in the most radical way like a language"[42]).

Meta seems to impose its own framework

Works of metafiction, Hutcheon concluded in 1980, make "demands upon the reader and constitute their own critical framework,"[43] that is, the "theory"[44] with which the work is to be analyzed. In so doing, works that are intensely meta tend to give the impression that interpretations that would not take into account their own discourse on their reflection are bound to devolve into misinterpretation. Hence the impression of narcissism, of solipsism, of folding inwards, even when the work is what Wolf calls "fictum-centered," since its engagement to the world would be limited to its own discourse on its relation to the world. Hence also the previously discussed sense that there is necessarily an intention, an author, a controlling presence imposing an interpretation. And I think this might actually often be the case: that a work has been just so organized as to resist interpretations other than those it anticipates and that meta might be a strategy of cleverly imposing a view and annulling unwanted meanings. Although the work remains "open," an oppositional interpretation must certainly not ignore the discussion the work seems to have anticipated; it must rise to the challenge by taking the meta-level into account and attempting to deconstruct it, and to reveal its limitations and how the work itself exceeds such boundaries and adds up to a lot more than its own discourse on itself. Facing one's "responsibility toward the text" is not just about owning up to one's participation in the co-creation of a "novelistic world,"[45] as Hutcheon would have it; it also implies taking responsibility for one's participation in meaning-making beyond the diegetic, that is, taking responsibility for one's actualization of what may or may not be a text-based interpretation. More generally, I also think that the beyondness of meta—the structural hierarchy identified by Wolf when he speaks of "a higher-level meta-comment on elements situated at a lower object-level"[46]—should not be confused with a hierarchy of meaning and that the other original sense of the Greek prefix ("with") needs to be retained. Some of the metamoments analyzed in Part II (in *No* [Larraín, 2012] and *I, Daniel Blake* [Loach, 2016] in particular) exist alongside other aspects of the film or series, do not necessarily contradict them, and the work can be analyzed without much attention to meta-phenomena.

Meta is play, and play is learning

To my knowledge, no one has insisted on how productive Hutcheon's analysis of the underlying models of metafiction is. Beyond the usability of these models discussed above, her typology implicitly uncovers the very foundations of metafiction. Indeed, the conceptions of fiction implied by her four models—fiction as hermeneutics, fiction as fantasy, fiction as game, fiction as sensual experience—are opposed to the idea(l) of fiction as mimesis, in the sense of fiction as an imitation/illusion of reality, as a window onto another world we passively observe. These views posit, instead, that fiction is an activity in which we engage actively whether intellectually, physically or imaginatively. This commonality enables combinations that can be explained for the very reason that these models reflect the variety of pleasures and needs fiction can provide: the conscious/intellectual pleasure of interpretation, the unconscious/immersive pleasure of fantasy, the physical pleasure of the erotic, and the combination of fun and learning of games.

Furthermore, unpacking Hutcheon's four models, it becomes clear that at the core of all metafiction is an understanding of fiction as play. This point was developed by Patricia Waugh; she offers much insight into the relationship between metafiction and play, to which she devotes a subchapter entitled "Play, games and metafiction."[47] Metafiction, she explains, always implies formal play, "but not all playfulness in fiction is of the metafictional variety."[48] Waugh's defense of metafiction rests on the educational potential of play. Metafiction "suggests, in fact, that there may be [. . .] much to be learnt from setting the mirror of art up to its own linguistic or representational structures."[49] The deconstruction of conventions in metafictional novels "offer[s] extremely accurate models for understanding the contemporary experience of the world as a construction, an artifice, a web of interdependent semiotic systems."[50] Waugh subsequently reminds us that play theory also posits that reality is a construct.[51] By adhering to the idea that fiction is play and that play teaches us how to comprehend the world, metafiction presents itself as "a fictional form that is culturally relevant and comprehensible to contemporary readers."[52] Waugh concludes that critics of metafiction thus contest either the educative function of play or the very idea of art as play (35), a conclusion which ties in to Jean-Marie Schaeffer's (1999) critique of the anti-illusionist discourses inherited from Plato that fail to realize that, as play, fiction has the potential to educate.[53]

I would further Waugh's argument and expand it to meta-phenomena in general. Meta is not just playful; it considers itself to be so because it is grounded in the view that art and fiction are play. This accounts for what it does on a variety of levels. It is meant to be played with: it constitutes a framework which can be seen as a set of rules and calls on the active participation of the viewer or reader to engage with it, and is thus co-created (as much by the audience as by the artist or the work) and interactive; it is an activity that engages not just the recipient in relation to the work, but members of the interpretive community who will ponder the interpretation, validate, qualify and contest it. Meta values play as a means to learn about art and fiction, to embrace our imaginative and creative potential as human beings (Hutcheon), to reflect on the relationship between artifice and reality (Waugh), our imagination and the world. Contrary to what Wolf's binary suggests, "fictum" is never far away from "fictio," as the analyses of Part II shall prove. Meta values play as a means of inhabiting and understanding the world, as well as an activity that can bear on epistemology and ontology, aesthetics, politics and ethics. Meta is a validation of the basic precepts we stand for as students, teachers and fans: analysis, interpretation, theory and a critical mindset have value outside the classroom and beyond coffee-machine conversations. Works that compel us to actualize their discourses should not be feared as works that impose meaning but embraced as works that value our capacity to make meaning. Thus, meta-phenomena should not be considered as a list of illusion-breaking strategies and devices identifiable in a given corpus (and confused with reflexive devices and strategies in the process); rather, they should be considered as the variety of processes by which we accept the invitation to identify such devices and make sense of them, to develop and hone our interpretive skills, to concretize and interrogate what they seem to say about themselves as fiction, as works of art or cultural products, about the potential of fiction, art or a medium, and about how we relate to the world through fiction, art and culture and/or relate to fiction, art and culture through the world.

CHAPTER 3

When, Where and Possibly Why Did Meta Appear?

A SHORT HISTORY OF REFLEXIVITY AND META IN FILM AND TELEVISION

The history of meta begins with reflexivity. Reflexivity is as old as film and television, but its history cannot be limited to those of each medium and industry, for it is inscribed within the broader history of reflexivity in all arts and media. Film historian Tom Gunning has identified anti-illusionism as a central component of the "cinema of attractions," which "displays its visibility, willing to rupture a self-enclosed fictional world for a chance to solicit the attention of the spectator."[1] Films focusing on film-making and -viewing were produced in Hollywood as early as the 1910s.[2] Responding to modernist precepts,[3] the late silent era saw the rise of self-conscious and experimental filmmaking in avant-garde cinemas (Hans Richter, Luis Buñuel, Dziga Vertov, etc.), whose aim was to explore and theorize the new medium's potential. These experiments influenced mainstream cinema to varying degrees, even in Los Angeles,[4] so that reflexive devices found their way into the classical Hollywood cinema, most famously in *Citizen Kane* (Welles, 1941).[5] In mainstream productions, reflexive devices have traditionally been more common in specific genres such as animation (the Felix the Cat short *Comicalamities* [Messmer, 1928] and the Tex Avery shorts of the 1940s[6]), comedy and musicals because of their connection with vaudeville[7] (*Hellzapoppin'* [Potter, 1941] is a case in point), or in a genre like horror in which the gaze is a central motif[8] (*Peeping Tom* [Powell, 1960]). They were present in early television because of the medium's debt to radio and theatre (*The George Burns and Gracie Allen Show* [CBS, 1950–8] is one example). "Self-consciousness" and "commentary" became central features of the art cinema that emerged after World War II,[9] and reflexivity in film proper was associated more specifically with the 1960s European (post) modernist cinema (Ingmar Bergman, Federico Fellini, Jean-Luc Godard),[10] a director like Godard being very much influenced by modernism.[11] The European new waves influenced each other and, in turn, influenced the New Hollywood directors, who aspired to produce art films in the US, reprised some of their stylistic devices, and endeavored to inscribe their work within the history of film.[12]

The dissemination of reflexive devices in 1950s–1970s cinema is, more broadly, symptomatic of what Werner Wolf calls the "metareferential turn," a phenomenon discussed from a historical perspective in his introduction to the 2011 collected volume of the same name. Involving all the arts and media, this turn started in the 1950s–1960s and overlapped with the shift from modernism to postmodernism discussed by literary scholars[13] and reprised by Stam, for instance;[14] Wolf himself describes the advent of postmodernist literature as a "meta-peak."[15] This turn does not correspond to a change of perspective in academic debate, but to an inflection in the arts and media, though academic discussion may ultimately have heightened its presence.[16] What Wolf calls "metaization" has, since, "increased in a *disproportionate* and therefore significant quantity";[17] it has also expanded across media and genres (becoming more present in "non-comic modes," for instance[18]) and found its way into the "popular arts and media."[19] Finally, Wolf notes a change in quality, pointing to the increase of "critical metareference to the detriment of the uncritical variant."[20]

The German scholar is more cautious when it comes to discussing the causes of the turn initiated in the 1950s and proposes three "groups of explanations." First, human beings have, in the long term, evolved (they are cognitively gifted for self-reflexion) and with them their systems (which tend to reflect on the "internal differentiations" they elaborate); this evolution has, in the digital age, been reinforced by our becoming increasingly "media-savvy" and "metatolerant."[21] Second, Wolf follows both Winfried Nöth and Vincent Colapietro[22] (2007) in suggesting that the turn can be explained by a postmodernist cultural context dominated by deconstruction, the questioning of master narratives and a crisis of creative exhaustion (the idea that nothing can ever be absolutely original) or high art (which has become too complex for its own good); the "positive" consequence is that consumers are somewhat empowered: calling on their "expertise" makes them "part-producers."[23] Third, the metareferential turn might be explained by more immediate factors, such as a medium or form that resorts to metareference to promote itself (for instance, when an animated sitcom like *The Simpsons* [Fox, 1989–] refers to "high art") or a movement reacting against a dominant mode (the Nouvelle Vague in relation to Hollywood cinema).[24] Wolf, in this respect, follows Andreas Böhn (2007) who takes it for granted that "media nostalgia" and increased "self-reference" is a consequence of the emergence of new media.[25]

In the case of film and television, scholars often point to cinephilia, telephilia and media-savviness[26] as a fertile ground for meta-phenomena to thrive. The development of new technology—recording devices (VCRs in the late 1970s), Internet with its discussion boards and blogs, streaming platforms—is often cited as a factor for the increasing presence of reflexivity and meta-phenomena;[27] by facilitating the archiving and sharing of such knowledge, it has produced a "new cinephilia"[28] or a "post-classical cinephilia" that may be "more of a hybrid, more diverse, and maybe more self-reflective and self-referential than its classical counterpart."[29] Viewers have become more knowledgeable of the history, technique and even aesthetics of film and television, and their practical knowledge has increased with the emergence of digital cameras[30] and home video editing software. They have also become more conscious of meta-phenomena such as the mise en abyme[31] or breaking the fourth wall (see Chapter 1). In brief, a combination of cultural shifts and technological inventions seems to have fueled the development of features that existed in film and television from the start and which the two media had inherited from other arts and media, and shaped the contemporary media landscape into one where meta holds pride of place. Indeed, reflexivity, Jason Mittell contends, is one of the defining features of twenty-first-century "complex television,"[32] and "hyper-reflexivity," Daniel Yacavone suggests, of contemporary video games.[33] It is likely that, given the increasing presence of meta-phenomena in contemporary productions and the mainstream audience's awareness of "meta," audiovisual works are establishing new norms of self-conscious narration, and audiences are developing cognitive schemes to interpret metamoments in film, television and other media, in a back-and-forth process between production and reception.

Like all received truths, there is probably much truth in this metanarrative about the origins of meta. Four key moments stand out, which roughly overlap with central paradigm shifts in film, art and media history, the first two (the birth of the medium, the modernist avant-gardes) tapping into a potential and the latter two (cinematic modernism and the postmodernist digital age) disseminating and even mainstreaming it. These shifts are tempered, however, by their position within the broader history of reflexivity and meta-phenomena that largely predates the birth of cinema and television. The difficulty for the art or media historian is to determine the significance of these shifts against the more general background of art and media history—to navigate the circulations of transmedia history while pinpointing events and trends specific to a given medium or group of media. This chapter aims not to provide a substantially new account of the emergence of meta-phenomena in film and television (that would require an entire book at the very least). Rather, it discusses some of the main assumptions of this metanarrative, as well as methodological questions raised by studies of meta-phenomena (including this book). So although this chapter will attempt to provide some answers, it will end up, as will soon become clear, raising more questions and pointing to fertile lines of inquiry, some of which will be addressed in Part II, others which will hopefully be pursued by other scholars.

IS META SPECIFIC TO WESTERN CULTURE?

The fact that terms such as metatheater and metafiction were first used by US-American writers, critics and/or scholars (Lionel Abel in 1963, William Gass and Robert Scholes in 1970), metadiegesis and metatextuality by French scholar Gérard Genette, to comment on literary phenomena observed mainly in Western literature, and that nowadays the term "meta" is primarily being used in the US, Canada, the UK and France, would certainly give that impression. This impression is reinforced by the title of a book like Josh Toth's *Truth and Metafiction: Plasticity and Renewal in American Narrative* (2020) or the contents of the volumes edited by Mark Currie (1995) and Werner Wolf (2009, 2011), with Wolf himself observing a "remarkable increase in 'metaization' across media in contemporary Western culture"[34] and admitting that the 2011 volume "miss[es] perspectives on metareference that focus on areas outside Western culture(s)."[35]

Identifying meta and, more generally, reflexivity as Western phenomena would certainly substantiate the chief accusations of narcissism and solipsism—that they are signs of the exhaustion of Western art and culture, which can no longer find any worthy topic other than the forms they produce (this was the charge leveled at the metafictionists of the 1960s and 1970s[36]). The increasing "metaization" of popular Western culture observed by Wolf could even be seen as proof that post-World War II Western and especially US-American societies have been nurturing a "culture of narcissism" ripe for the emergence of narcissistic personality disorders, as per Christopher Lasch's famous 1979 thesis. It may very well be that there is a degree of truth in the claim that the intense form of reflexivity that is meta would be produced by a cultural milieu in which real-world concerns are not as pressing as life-threatening problems such as war and famine. And yet, this view comes with its own problems. First, many Western works that are intensely meta are concerned with history and their own efficacy as political art (see Chapters 10 and 11). Second, attributing reflexivity and meta-phenomena to a Western culture of narcissism may, on the surface, seem like a way of celebrating the authenticity of Third and Fourth World Cinema, but it also runs the risk of upholding and essentializing a colonial binary that positions the West as the sole locus of reflexivity, reflection, theory and thus thought, and the Third and Fourth Worlds as the loci of nature, the primitive, and the body.

In any case, it is important not to posit a binary that probably bespeaks more of our own ignorance (starting with my own) than of a social and historical reality. Reflexivity and meta-phenomena clearly exist in non-Western productions. Literary scholars like Hutcheon, Waugh and McHale do discuss the work of prominent Latin American writers (Julio Cortázar,[37] Gabriel García Márquez[38] and especially Jorge Luis Borges[39]), and metafiction is also an important trend in the works of English-speaking authors studied by postcolonial scholars (Taban Lo Liyong,[40] Ben Okri[41] and Salman Rushdie,[42] to name but a few). Further research would be necessary to determine to what extent the metafictional quality of their work is tributary of Western influences (Borges's well-documented love of Poe, for instance, or more generally, the significance of Cervantes for all authors writing in Spanish[43]) and/or academic education (in the case of Okri and Rushdie who studied in Great Britain), or whether it (also) originates in local forms and traditions. One such attempt (which also proposes much more) is Evan Maina Mwangi's 2009 *Africa Writes Back to Self: Metafiction, Gender, Sexuality*. Although Mwangi notes "the rise of metafictional novels [in Africa] since the mid-1980s," he stresses that "[t]here is no immanent and transhistorical moment in which African literature did not have metafictional components,"[44] and explores the metafictional dimensions of novels of the 1950s in Chapter 2; he also emphasizes how "metafictional elements in the African novel tend to emanate from its connectedness to oral culture," which many authors aim to break away from, and concludes that "African fiction should be read not as exclusively 'writing back' to the metropolis but more meaningfully as writing back to itself,"[45] thereby establishing its own literary history.

In contemporary art cinema, meta-phenomena can certainly be found in works from all around the world. In Poland: *Escape from the "Liberty" Cinema* (Marczewski, 1990) focuses on a film whose characters/actors go on strike.[46] In Iran: Abbas Kiarostami's 1994 *Through the Olive Trees* is a fictional account of the relationship between the cast during the making of his previous film, the 1992 *Life and Nothing More*. In India: Bharathiraja's 2008 *Bommalattam* is a crime fiction in which the director is the prime suspect in the murders occurring during the shooting of a movie.[47] In Japan: *Perfect Blue* (Kon, 1997) tells the story of Mima, a singer who wants to become an actress, for whom reality and fiction become confused;[48] Takeshi Kitano meditates on art in the 1997 *Hana-bi* or on his star persona in the 2005 *Takeshis'*; and three decades earlier, Akira Kurosawa's 1962 *Yojimbo* depicts the eponymous samurai watching two clans fight from atop his perch. In *Metacinema in Contemporary Chinese Film*, G. Andrew Stuckey explores a metacinematic trend in contemporary Chinese cinemas that includes not only art films but blockbusters, and notes that films about production (*An Amorous History of the Silver Screen* [Bugao, 1931]) and reception (*Street Angel* [Muzhi, 1937]) have existed since the 1930s.⁴⁹ It is the presence of meta in more mainstream fare that is, perhaps, more common today in US and British productions, as Wolf observes and as my own quest for academic material on meta-phenomena and reflexivity in films and series tends to suggest, though recent examples can be found in Japan (*One Cut of the Dead* [Shin'ichirô Ueda, 2017]) and South Korea (*Squid Game* [Netflix, 2021]).

Further research of the sort Evan Maina Mwangi has carried out on the African novel would be necessary to identify the aesthetic and cultural specificities of meta-phenomena in the films and series of specific nations. Stuckey, for instance, observes the rise of metacinema in contemporary Chinese cinemas against a background of globalization, arguing that these films express an anxiety concerning a "deracinated 'universality'" that cannibalizes specifically Chinese forms (Chinese opera, ghost stories, martial arts films) in favor of "a pan-Asian mainstream strategy of film production in line with global mainstream standards"⁵⁰ (modeled on Hollywood and Bollywood productions, for instance).

Philippe Ragel's brilliant analysis of Kiarostami's *Through the Olive Trees*, for instance, reveals how the meta quality of the final shot of this movie about making movies can only be deciphered in the light of Persian and Islamic motifs (Figure 3.1) [1:33:28–1:37:14]. The right-to-left movement and the

Figure 3.1 Through the Olive Trees: *the movements of Hossein and Tahereh, appearing dot-like in a very long shot, seem to inscribe a message written in Persian or Arabic calligraphy across the surface of the image.*

two dots formed by the minuscule characters (of Hossein and Tahereh) evoke Arabic writing and, thus, inscribe a written message across the surface of the landscape shot: "it is as if the director, with his camera-reed pen, were writing in calligraphy, in white ink across the green page of the landscape, Tahereh's secret answer [whether or not she will return Hossein's feelings for her], suspended in the mystery of its impossible revelation."[51] Iranian viewers would, Ragel surmises, see the end of the film—materialized by the characters' exiting the frame—in a more hopeful light, because of the symbolism of green (nature and life) and white (purity) in Persian and Islamic cultures. I would further argue that only viewers familiar with Persian and Islamic cultures could interpret this sequence shot as a metamoment wherein two opposing views of film theory—the camera as pen and the film image as plastic matter—coexist within the same shot, reconciled through the art of calligraphy. With its title recalling Lewis Carroll's second *Alice* book, Kiarostami's movie about making movies neatly illustrates how Western and Middle Eastern traditions of reflexivity can be combined, an Islamic symbol like the olive tree[52] supplanting the mirror motif and, thus, operating as what Jean-Marc Limoges calls a "metaphorical" mise en abyme.[53] Clearly, more research needs to carried out to understand the emergence of reflexivity and meta-phenomena in the cinema and television of specific cultures, and to articulate local traditions to the circulation of Western paradigms both from a historical and formal perspective.

Did Meta Come from Literature?

As far as the history of theory is concerned, the answer is mainly yes. The terms metatheatre and metafiction, as we have seen, were first employed by authors, critics, drama and literature scholars, while the term metanarrative was made famous by philosopher Jean-François Lyotard in his 1979 theory of postmodernism. The concepts of metafiction and metanarrative were a response to their immediate context—a postmodernist culture in which numerous authors were producing fictions about fiction and narratives about narrative. The terms metacinema and metafilm, and the adjectives metafilmic and metacinematic, though of less concern to the film scholars of the time than reflexivity (Fredericksen, Casetti, Metz, Stam), emerged roughly contemporaneously, but they were not referring to Hutcheon and Waugh (whom, with the exception of Stam, they had not read) but, rather, to the same linguistic and literary heritage they shared with these literary scholars, and which had bequeathed upon them terms such as metalanguage (Roman Jakobson's term for "[l]anguage when used to talk about language"[54]), metadiegetic (Genette's term for a narrative-within-the-narrative[55]), metatextuality (Genette's word for cases when a text comments on another "without necessarily citing it"[56]) and metadiscourse. In the 1970s and 1980s at least, the terms metacinema (as used by Judith Mayne and William C. Siska) and metafilm were not transferred from studies of similar phenomena in literature, but from the same sources the theorists of metafiction drew on in the fields of drama, literature, linguistics and philosophy. It is only recently that film and television scholars such as Barbara Pfeifer writing on *Stranger than Fiction* (Forster, 2006) in 2009, Henry Keazor[57] on *The Simpsons* in 2011, Patrick Maurer Escobar on *Battles Without Honor and Humanity* (Fukasaku, 1973), Rebekah Brammer on *Birdman* in 2019, and myself on the films of Tarantino in 2018 and 2019 have turned to the work of Hutcheon and Waugh to examine similar phenomena in fiction films and series.

It is highly unlikely, however, that meta in film and television was the result of a direct transposition from literature and drama to cinema and television. For one, few of the works discussed by Hutcheon and Waugh were adapted to the screen, perhaps because they were deemed "too literary" and mainly appreciated in academic and elite circles. The major exception would be Vladimir Nabokov, whose 1955 *Lolita* (Kubrick, 1962; Lynne, 1997), 1932 *Laughter in the Dark* (Richardson, 1969; Papas, 1986), 1928 *King, Queen, Knave* (Skolimowski, 1972) and 1934 *Despair* (Fassbinder, 1978) were made into films, but, significantly, adaptations of his later, more radically metafictional novels, the 1962 *Pale Fire* and the 1969 *Ada*, have yet to see the day. Other adaptations of major works of metafiction include John Barth's 1958 *End of the Road* (Avakian, 1970), John Fowles's 1969 *French Lieutenant's Woman* (Reisz, 1981) and E.L. Doctorow's 1975 *Ragtime* (Forman, 1981), as well as adaptations of the novels of Henry Fielding, *Tom Jones* (1749) and *Joseph Andrews* (1742), directed by Tony Richardson in 1963 and 1977, and Miguel de Cervantes, whose *Don Quixote* (1605–15) has been the subject of many ventures (most famously by Orson Welles and Terry Gilliam). The stories of Argentine writer Jorge Luis Borges have often been adapted in feature and short films or anthology series in his home country, occasionally in other countries (mainly, France, Italy and Spain, but also Australia, Brazil, Greece, Iran, Mexico, the UK, the US and the USSR); *The Strategy of the Spider* (Bertolucci, 1970) and the transnational anthology series *Tales of Borges* (1992–3) are among the better-known adaptations. Compared to the number of film adaptations released every year, such productions are few, and few (*Lolita*, *The French Lieutenant's Woman* and *Ragtime*, and to a lesser extent perhaps *The Strategy of the Spider* and *Despair*) had a major impact upon their release. Many of these films were produced by well-read directors and screenwriters, often associated with European art cinema (Bernardo Bertolucci, Rainer Werner Fassbinder, Milos Forman, Michael Papas, Karl Reisz, Tony Richardson, Jerzy Skolimowski).

In terms of quality, these film adaptations, as we shall see in Chapter 7, tend to dilute and sometimes entirely do away with the metafictional elements of the source texts, reducing a network narrative to a "traditional"[58] one (*Ragtime*), playfully scattering reflexive devices here and there (*Tom Jones*) or reducing an elaborate historiographical framework to a movie about making movies (*The French Lieutenant's Woman*). Apparently, a metafictional novel or story does not necessarily make for an equally metafictional film. A radical experiment like *End of the Road* would appear quite exceptional in this respect—its makers were very much influenced by Sartrean existentialism and European art cinema (Antonioni, Buñuel, Godard),[59] and the film mixes archive footage, theatrical moments and X-rated scenes, and resorts to non-classical framing and editing (blurry images, jump-cuts)—but it was seen by very few people on its release.[60]

The story in France is a bit different because of the well-documented proximity between the Nouveau Roman writers and the New Wave directors. With *Hiroshima mon amour* (1959) and *Last Year at Marienbad*[61] (1961), Alain Resnais worked back-to-back with two figureheads of the Nouveau Roman, Marguerite Duras and Alain Robbe-Grillet, both of whom would pursue their own careers as directors of important films. The exchanges between film and literature, however, go well beyond Duras, Resnais and Robbe-Grillet. In the words of Richard Neupert, "both movements [the Nouveau Roman and the Nouvelle Vague] were loosely organized around youthful searches for new ways to tell new stories that engage the modern world," and a belief that novels and films were powerful cultural artefacts with revolutionary potential.[62] The ambition of these directors and writers, as described by Neupert at least, resonates with Waugh's definition of metafiction as "pos[ing] questions about the relationship between fiction and reality."[63] This commonality of spirit produced a series of films that would qualify as metafiction as much as the works of Robbe-Grillet, Nathalie Sarraute[64] and the other Éditions de Minuit writers: *La Pointe courte*[65] (Varda, 1955), *Paris Belongs to Us*[66] (Rivette, 1961), *Last Year at Marienbad* and *Muriel*[67] (Resnais, 1963), *Trans-Europ-Express* (Robbe-Grillet, 1966), *India Song* (Duras, 1975), arguably all the films of Jean-Luc Godard,[68] and even more popular fare such as *Le Magnifique* (de Broca, 1973).

Though a counter-example on the surface, French film and literary history may actually provide several answers: (1) it substantiates Wolf's claim that the "metareferential turn" can be situated in the 1950s–1960s; (2) it suggests that the turn may be more a matter of cultural zeitgeist than of actual influences or collaborations;[69] and (3) it also suggests that literature and theater's contribution to the incorporation of reflexive devices in film, and more fundamentally to self-conscious approaches of creation, may have been indirect and transited through specific films or film movements. Jean Douchet insists on how "literature dominated intellectual life" at the time and describes the work of New Wave directors as demonstrating "the nostalgia for a missed opportunity with literature."[70] The Nouveau Roman may, then, have influenced world cinema via the Nouvelle Vague, Alfred Jarry through the films of Godard, Bertolt Brecht through those of Godard again, Peter Watkins or Danièle Huillet and Jean-Marie Straub,[71] and Thomas Pynchon through Japanese animation like *Tamala 2010: A Punk Cat in Space*[72] (Tol, 2010).

Oddly enough, the second major turn of the meta screw—that of the 1990s–2000s—did not see a drastic increase in the amount of film and television adaptations of metafictional novels and stories. Notable exceptions include Tom Stoppard's *Rosencrantz and Gildenstern Are Dead* (1990), based on his 1966 play, Resnais's adaptation of British playwright Alan Ayckbourne's 1982 metadrama *Intimate Exchanges* as *Smoking/No Smoking* in 1993, Shari Springer Berman and Robert Pulcini's 2003 adaptation of Harvey Pekar's *American Splendor* comics, Michael Winterbottom's go at Laurence Sterne's 1759 *Tristram Shandy* in 2003, David Cronenberg's *Cosmopolis* (2012) based on Don DeLillo's 2003 novel, P.T. Anderson's *Inherent Vice* (2014) based on Thomas Pynchon's 2009 novel, *The Plot Against America* (HBO, 2020) based on Philip Roth's 2004 novel, and Terry Gilliam's endeavor to put an end to the curse of Don Quixote adaptations with his 2018 *The Man Who Killed Don Quixote*. As in the 1960s and 1970s, such films are of the art cinema variety. More mainstream examples include adaptations of Alan Moore and Dave Gibbons's *Watchmen* into film (Snyder, 2009) and mini-series (HBO, 2019) or of the Marvel comics *Deadpool* (Miller, 2016). If the latter films and series are meta at least to some degree, the tendency to do away with meta remains, for instance in recent adaptations of Duras such as Jean-Jacques Annaud's 1992 adaptation of *The Lover* (1984) and Rithy Panh's 2008 adaptation of *Un barrage contre le Pacifique* (1950), in spite of Duras's legacy as a director as well. Meta is not an inherent quality and can easily be lost in translation; conversely, it can also be added in the process (Genette's "metatextuality"; see Chapter 7).

DID META COME FROM MODERNISM AND/OR THE AVANT-GARDES?

This is no doubt the most common belief. In literary studies, the metafictionists Hutcheon and Waugh study are also postmodernists whose works represent not so much a radical departure from, but an inflection of, the modernist experimentation of T.S. Eliot, William Faulkner, James Joyce, Gertrude Stein and Virginia Woolf. Waugh, however, sees the metafictional trend as a response to "the absence of a clearly defined avant-garde 'movement'"[73] in the 1960s; and Italian writer Paolo Volponi, indeed, pinpointed the "limits" of the "neoavant-garde."[74] In the 1960s and 1970s, literary metafiction would have been at once a continuation of modernist avant-garde practices and a response to its exhaustion. Film scholars also tend to view the development of modernism and the avant-gardes (which should always be plural[75]) as inseparable,[76] although some like Andreas Huyssen have insisted on the need to distinguish between modernism and the "historical" avant-gardes (noting that the former strove to separate high and low culture).[77] They also tend to associate reflexivity with modernism and the avant-gardes. For Bordwell, self-consciousness is a central characteristic of art cinema narration, which emerged after World War II as a reaction against classical cinema as well as an intensification of earlier movements, including German Expressionism, Soviet montage and French poetic realism.[78] Stam's study of reflexivity insists on the influence of the avant-gardes in general (Brecht, Jarry, Dada, Genet) on the use of discontinuity and direct address in film, and on directors like Godard in particular.[79]

What is less clear, perhaps, is exactly how the cinematic avant-gardes influenced the mainstream film industry, and more precisely how this influence might involve meta-phenomena. In spite of the opposition between the avant-gardes and the majority of cinema, which is sometimes made to overlap with an opposition between art and cinema,[80] circulations between the avant-gardes and mainstream film industries have existed from the start. "Vertov's work," Jeremy Hicks claims, "serves as a model for what has been called metacinema, a cinema that questions its own processes of representation."[81] David E. James describes *Citizen Kane* as an "industrial avant-garde film" and reminds us that its director was very much familiar with the European modernists (Brecht, Cocteau, Eisenstein), that his second short film, *The Hearts of Age* (1934), was unapologetically influenced by *The Cabinet of Dr. Caligari* (Wiene, 1920), and that the freedom RKO gave Welles allowed him "to galvanize *Kane* with his concerted repertoire of tropes and reflexive tricks derived from previous avant-gardes; he also played filmic self-consciousness against its opposite, a transparent realism wherein artifice is concealed."[82] For James, a similar ambition would drive *Rashomon* (Kurosawa, 1950) and later *The Last Movie* (Hopper, 1971).[83]

The circulations between the avant-gardes and the mainstream involve films but also the artists who made them. Jean Epstein's 1923 *Cœur fidèle*, which François Albera cites as an example of "narrative avant-garde," was produced by Pathé and exemplifies how welcoming the French film industry was to the avant-gardes in the 1920s.[84] Jean Cocteau's 1946 *Beauty and the Beast* was produced by a small French company, les films André Paulvé, which had previously released a romantic comedy, the 1941 *Premier Bal* (Christian-Jacques). Famous collaborations between directors and avant-garde artists include Hitchcock, whose debt to the avant-gardes is well-documented,[85] hiring Salvador Dalí for the dream sequence of *Spellbound* (1945). An earlier and equally well-known example is *Metropolis* (Lang, 1927), whose set design was influenced by the work of architects, including the avant-garde Erich Mendelsohn and the Futurist Antonio Saint'Elia.[86] Some avant-garde artists worked in the mainstream industry. Born in Brazil, Alberto Calvacanti directed one of the first city symphonies in Paris, the 1926 *Rien que les heures*, before moving to Great Britain where he contributed with John Grierson to the invention of documentary, and went on to direct more mainstream fare like the Gothic anthology film *Dead of Night* (1945). John Cassavetes juggled a career as an independent filmmaker (*Shadows*, 1958; *A Woman under the Influence*, 1974) and a Hollywood actor (*The Dirty Dozen*, Aldrich, 1967; *Rosemary's Baby*, Polanski, 1968). And like Cocteau before them, many contemporary art cinema directors (David Lynch, Peter Greenaway, Atom Egoyan, Takeshi Kitano, Steve McQueen) have divided their career between the mainstream film industry and the art world. These circulations established bridges between avant-garde and mainstream practices over which meta-phenomena, among other things, could be carried over. Such practices may also have contributed to the circulation of meta-phenomena in film and audiovisual media around the world. Although Albera warns that it would be "illusory" to describe the avant-gardes of the 1920s as "transnational and transgeneric,"[87] the exchanges within the avant-gardes are undoubtedly transatlantic. P. Adams Sitney speaks of "[t]he influx of masters of European modernism into America" and their influence on painting and film,[88] and mentions the influence of Cocteau on the American avant-gardes[89] and of Gertrude Stein on Stan Brakhage[90] in particular.

What exactly would the mainstream have derived from the avant-gardes? Specific formal devices? Theoretical views regarding the nature or potential of cinema? The idea that the medium itself could become the central concern of the work? All of these questions would require in-depth historical research to provide a more definitive answer, but I will hazard a few tentative ones and formulate a hypothesis. While commenting on *Stardust Memories* (Allen, 1980), Robert Stam seems to take it for granted that its reflexive devices originate in the avant-gardes:

> the film deploys avant-garde strategies familiar from reflexive films—a constant shuttle between past and present, memory and fantasy à la *8½*; the scrambling of spatial and temporal categories à la *Marienbad*; the sustained utilization of jump-cuts à la *Breathless*; and the metacritical discussion of aesthetic questions à la *Contempt*.[91]

Stam's description prompts a series of remarks. First, his collapsing the avant-gardes and art cinema suggests the influence of the former may have been mediated through the latter. Second, the majority of the devices he cites are not specific to cinema. Formal devices such as the mise en abyme, as Stam shows throughout his book, have existed in drama, literature and painting long before cinema and the avant-gardes, and even more specific devices such as frame-within-the-frame composition existed in painting and had already been used in early cinema. So mainstream and art filmmakers could just as easily have derived their devices from works in other media. Third, such "avant-garde" devices coexist alongside a more "moderate self-consciousness"[92] (to use Bordwell's term) regarding genre and narrative conventions, which could also have been derived from other media. For instance, *Swing Time* (Stevens, 1936) calls attention to "the specific ways in which it expects the viewer to 'read' it,"[93] while Fritz Lang's Hollywood productions *The Woman in the Window* (1944) and *House by the River* (1950) foreground the artificiality of storytelling and genre conventions and reflect the spectator's look[94] without necessarily developing a metadiscourse (see also the discussion of *The Big Sleep* [Hawks, 1948] in Chapter 8). Moreover, James points out that certain scenes (notably of the city) in mainstream Hollywood films of the early 1920s (he cites two movies about making movies, both released in 1923, *The Extra Girl* directed by F. Richard Jones and *Hollywood* directed by James Cruze[95]) evince a modernist self-consciousness" that anticipates the post-war avant-gardes. Finally, the mainstream industry was focusing on itself through narratives dealing with production and reception before the emergence of the modernist avant-gardes (see Chapter 4).

So I would suggest that the avant-gardes' legacy regarding meta-phenomena would be eminently practical and materialist: it would concern the focus on the materiality of the film image and on the political implications of form, and more so even, on the practice of filmmaking as a means to theorize film and art. Sitney says that filmmaking was "essentially a reflexive activity"[96] for artists like Maya Deren and Kenneth Anger, and Nicole Brenez and David E. James contend that structural cinema is fundamentally reflexive since "it is devoted to shedding light on its own processes and thus participates to a description and perhaps even to a definition of cinema."[97] This is furthered by the fact that many avant-garde artists (Germaine Dulac, Sergei Eisenstein, Jean Epstein, Dziga Vertov) were also critics or theorists, and many conceived of their art as a way to explore the potential of the medium, to put theory to practice. Albera reminds us that the circulation of the avant-gardes entails not only the circulation of their films but of their texts.[98] Such avant-garde filmmaking would thus represent an intense, niche variant of meta *avant l'heure*. It may also have provided a model for how to approach pre-existing material, notably intertexts. Indeed, the relationship between mainstream and avant-garde flows both ways. Avant-garde directors borrowed many devices from silent film,[99] and they regularly used mainstream cinema and pop culture as material. Directors like John Baldessari, Kenneth Anger, Joseph Cornell and Jack Smith famously recycled Hollywood images and icons,[100] and Masao Adachi provocatively spoofed popular genres in movies like *Sei chitai: Sex Zone* (1968).[101] Even before them, films like *L'Inhumaine* (L'Herbier, 1924) and *Un Chien andalou* (Buñuel, 1929), Albera argues, engaged with commercial genres like melodrama.[102] The emphasis on practice as theory and theory as practice would lend further weight to the conclusions made in Chapter 2: that meta-phenomena should not be considered as an arsenal of devices but as a heuristics wherein creation is interpretation and interpretation creation.

ARE THE ORIGINS OF META THE SAME IN TELEVISION AS IN FILM?

Television is said to accommodate reflexivity easier than cinema.[103] In her 2004 study of reflexivity in French television, Virginie Spies demonstrates that reflexivity pervades the medium, in the sense that most programs (whether game shows, teasers, or more obviously programs about stars and television) refer to and sometimes discuss their medium quite explicitly, and that television has done so since the beginning.[104] Television historians have often put reflexivity down to the medium's debt to media other than film, primarily theater and radio. Media and screen scholar Joanne Morreale describes *The Donna Reed Show* (ABC, 1958–66) as an example of how "the early self-reflexive television sitcoms adapted from radio [. . .] acknowledged the artifice of the world portrayed on television," and describes *The George Burns and Gracie Allen Show* as a "self-reflexive backstage sitcom," which "was initially a vaudeville act that was brought to radio and then television."[105] The origins of the sitcom's reflexivity would, thus, be similar to those of the Hollywood musical and comedy—vaudeville—but filtered through radio more so than cinema. Reflexivity in television animation was, however, directly transposed from cinema to television, the short films of Hanna-Barbera and Disney having transitioned from the movie theater to television in the 1950s,[106] with *The Flintstones* (ABC, 1960–6) being the first in a series of prime-time animated series, child-friendly adaptations of 1950s adult sitcoms (*The Flintstones* of *The Honeymooners* [CBS, 1955–6]), produced by Hanna-Barbera for ABC.[107] The overt meta of *The Simpsons* and its successors, *South Park* (Comedy Central, 1997–) and *Rick and Morty* (Warner Bros., 2013–), is, thus, both a merging of the reflexive tendencies of the sitcom and animation, and symptomatic of the enhanced self-consciousness of the 1990s onward. Television has also witnessed the invention of many genres in which reflexivity is a part of the basic setup. In game shows, for instance, the host regularly reminds the audience of the rules, recaps each player's situation and draws attention to the format by mentioning commercial breaks. More recently, television scholars have described reality TV as a "meta genre"[108] in which "[p]erformers are acting out, producing meta versions of themselves they assume producers and audiences want to see"[109] (Leigh H. Edwards has even described the documentary on reality TV entitled *Reality T.V. Secrets Revealed* [VH1, 2004] as "meta-reality TV"[110]). The meta of shows that play on the boundary between person and role, like reality TV and *The Colbert Report* (Comedy Central, 2005–14), is, precisely, metaperformance.

Breaking the fourth wall—extradiegetic metalepsis—has long been authorized in sitcoms and animation, as it has in comedies, musicals and animated films produced for cinema. It is coded as non-problematic in programs such as the news, game shows, talk shows and reality TV, in which it is inscribed within the basic setup. In such cases, the dynamic term "breaking" seems inappropriate because there is nothing exceptional about this mode of address, even though a minimum degree of reflexivity, no doubt, remains (on screen, the "real event," Metz would probably have noted, is nonetheless mediated and, thus, "unreal"[111]). In a medium that delivers entertainment in the intimacy of the individual's or family's home, the direct mode of address aims, above all, to create complicity between the anchor, host or performer and the audience—a complicity that is essential to the aesthetic effect since it aims to move us, whether by laughter, tears or contempt. In reality TV, for instance, Edwards says, "[d]irect address [...] tries to relate cast members and audiences, encouraging viewers to identify and sympathize with the cast talking directly to them, modeling behavior, and hailing audiences to join their particular kind of imagined pluralist community."[112] In the sitcom, looks to the camera and canned laughter may draw attention to the artifice, but their main aim is to create a sense of complicity with the characters[113] as would a live performance—the characters/actors, the mock-live or live studio audience, and the audience back home are all laughing together, enveloped in a communal audiovisual setup. Twenty-first-century sitcoms such as *The Office* (BBC, 2001–3) and *Modern Family* (ABC, 2009–20) have "naturalized" direct address by blending ingredients from the documentary and reality TV, with characters casting sidelong looks to the camera in the middle of a scene or explaining their views on the situation in brief sequences (an approach spoofed in episodes S1E6 and S1E7 of *WandaVision* [Disney+, 2021]). Direct addresses in *Modern Family* systematically invite us to interpret one character's reaction to another character or a situation, but by breaking the fourth wall, the look is, at the minimum, redoubled by a comment on the character as a fiction: s/he is behaving outrageously *as* a character. A framework that accommodates copious doses of reflexivity does not, as previously argued, necessarily make for highly intense meta, but it certainly contributes to create the conditions of its emergence.

Another highly reflexive genre is the children's educational program. Here, it is justified by the educator–child relationship the program is attempting to establish, and thus again by a sense of understanding and trust. Mr. Rogers (NET/PBS, 1968–2001), the *Sesame Street* crew (PBS, 1969–), Pee-wee Herman (CBS, 1986–91)—all address their audiences directly and acknowledge the artifice (in the 1969 pilot episode of *Sesame Street*, Ernie points at the camera and says, "Hey, you out there in TV land, everybody wash!"). It is the reflexive tendencies of both animation and the children's educational program that allows an episodic animation show like *The Magic School Bus* (PBS, 1994–8) to thematize the audience's possible reactions in the epilogue of each episode, when diegetic members of the audience call in to comment on the story and the educational material dealt with—an inversion of the traditional direct address by a character of classical animation (Figure 3.2). Thus positioned, the narrative metalepsis operates as a metamoment that fulfills several functions: it invites complicity, which it thematizes through the phone call; it reinforces the episodic show's ritualistic

Figure 3.2 The Magic School Bus: *at the end of episode S1 E3 "Inside Rauchie," a parody of* Inner Space *(Dante, 1987), the Producer of* The Magic School Bus *receives a phone call from a viewer.*

dimension through repetition and the sense of community; it suggests that it can anticipate the target audience's reactions; and finally, it invites the actual child audience to adopt a degree of critical distance vis-à-vis the story and assess its real-world relevance. If each epilogue seems to reveal the artifice, it is also a celebration of the power of fiction to provoke thought, pleasure and socializing through discussion. It is, besides, possible that shows like *The Magic School Bus* and *Sesame Street* before it have contributed not only to the scholastic education of children,[114] but to the increasing media literacy of twenty-first-century audiences and to their capacity to identify and interpret meta-phenomena.

Fiction programs inherited from cinema (drama, crime, Western) are less obvious terrain for reflexivity and meta-phenomena. Apart from notable exceptions like *The Prisoner* (ITV, 1967–8), the appearance of such phenomena in drama or genre fare like *Twin Peaks* (ABC, 1990–1), *The X-Files* (Fox, 1993–2018), *Alias* (ABC, 2001–6) and *LOST*[115] (ABC, 2004–10), or more recently the *Doctor Who* reboot (BBC, 2005–), *Supernatural* and *American Horror Story* (FX, 2011–), however, seems correlated to the 1990s turn of the meta screw. The *Scream* franchise in particular is an obvious model for many slasher series of the 2010s—*Scream: The Series* (MTV/Netflix, 2015–19), *Scream Queens*, *Slasher* (Super Channel, 2016–)—but perhaps also for most genre fare in which characters evince a high degree of self-consciousness. My hypothesis, which Part II and especially Chapter 9 will endeavor to substantiate, is that, in such fictions, the forms and functions of meta-phenomena are largely inherited from cinema but adapted to the serial format and, thus, primarily metanarrative.

CAN SILENT FILMS BE META ANYWAY?

Film historians have insisted on how common certain reflexive devices were during the early silent era. *The Big Swallow* (Williamson, 1901) shows a performer becoming angry at the camera(man), walking up to them and swallowing them, and even a narrative film like *The Great Train Robbery* (Edison, Porter, 1903) concludes with the villain looking and firing at the audience. Looks to the camera were not seen as a destabilizing device, but merely as the logical continuation of vaudeville and, thus, as examples of what we might today call "remediation," i.e., the adaptation of one medium within another (see Chapter 6). It is the eventual dominance of narrative cinema in the 1900s and the advent of classical narration in the late 1910s that made such reflexive devices more exceptional—because they compromised the ideal transparency of classical narration, their usage became more salient. The question is whether certain instances of reflexivity in silent cinema correspond to what is now identified as meta. Obviously, this book approaches pre-1970s films as meta *avant l'heure* even though the terms "metafictional" and "metacinema" had not yet been coined, but how far back can we go and do we run the risk of decontextualizing the work in the process[116]? I will start with three late silent era films, *Man with a Movie Camera* (Vertov, 1929), Keaton's 1924 *Sherlock Jr.* and 1928 *The Cameraman*, whose reflexive devices have received critical attention, before ending on *The Big Swallow*, a famous trick film and exemplar of the cinema of attractions.

Film scholars agree Dziga Vertov's 1929 film is a paragon of reflexivity. Its numerous reflexive devices (the foregrounding of the apparatus, the attention drawn to the surface of the image, the diegetic presence of a cinematographer) have been discussed by the likes of Annette Michelson and Christian Metz.[117] Michelson argued that the film is a "wholly autonomous metacinematic celebration of filmmaking as a mode of production";[118] Fredericksen that its reflexivity is above all concerned with ontological questions;[119] and Stam that it is "a film about film language" that "foregrounds its *own* process of production," and whose "central subject" is "the laying bare of the mechanisms of film within the social context of a continuum of productive forces."[120] The experimental film resorts to staple reflexive devices, such as the mise en abyme (images from the film are consumed by diegetic spectators) and the metalepsis (superimpositions allow the cinematographer to coexist alongside his machine and the image of his film, notably in the famous extreme close-ups of the camera eye which contains both a human eye and the body of the cinematographer with his machine). The film also inscribes itself within the medium's history (the freeze frame of a horse recalls Eadweard Muybridge's invention of the zoopraxiscope to study the movements of horses [21:51], the train in the Lumière brothers' 1896 film, the cameraman in the glass of beer a Méliès trick film [55:03]). Finally, it examines the differences between static and moving images (notably during the scenes with the editor [22:22–24:17]), as well as the political implications of the medium's aesthetic potential: the juxtaposition of moving images enables the expression of the experience of the modern world, but also the evocation of a utopian collective. One of the film's recurrent motifs, the bridge [8:20] (Figure 3.3), can, like Kiarostami's olive tree, be seen as a metaphorical mise en abyme of the medium's potential to connect a variety of energies and experiences. A notable influence on *Contempt*,[121] *Man with a Movie Camera* is clearly meta *avant l'heure*, and an early example of the "reflexive materialism" Christopher Carter studies in his 2018 *Metafilm*.

Robert Stam names "Buster Keaton, the poet-laureate of reflexivity in the silent cinema,"[122] without actually analyzing his work, and David E. James

Figure 3.3 Man with a Movie Camera: *the cameraman passes under a bridge, a motif that operates as a metaphor for the connections the medium can establish notably through editing.*

cites Keaton as an example of "an indigenous populist avant-garde as self-consciously virtuosic as the most advanced cinematic modernism of the time."[123] The scene from *Sherlock Jr.* in which the Projectionist dreams that he enters the moving pictures on screen [17:16–21:35] is often cited as an example of metalepsis (by Gérard Genette himself) and recognized as an inspiration for *The Purple Rose of Cairo* (Allen, 1985) and *Last Action Hero* (McTiernan, 1993) (see Chapter 5). In it, the Projectionist attempts to intervene in a film starring his love interest and his rival; the film momentarily spins out of control, each cut transporting him into another landscape and potential genre, before returning him to the dreamed film in which he appears as Sherlock Jr. [21:35–41:20]. Momentarily at least, immersion is not viewed as a blissful wish-fulfillment—as in later screen theory—but as a brutal threat to the self (the cars, the cliffs, the lions, the train). The scene where the movie goes berserk provides not so much an allegory of spectatorship in the 1920s—that would be *Hearts and Pearls*, the film-within-the-film—as one of program viewing during the early silent era (the Projectionist travels back in time to a period where scenics and trick films outnumbered narrative films). The scene thus presents a history of film genre and film spectatorship, and puts itself on display as a manifestation of the medium's possibilities at this stage in history; it also epitomizes the terms of Keaton's own films: we delight in the protagonists' clumsiness and dire predicaments in a variety of genres, in Keaton's own physical prowess and in the presence of the performer's body in a long shot.[124] Viewed in these terms, the metalepsis corresponds both to Hutcheon's "overt diegetic metafiction" and Wolf's "fictio-centered metareference" (see Chapter 2), but Petr Kràl's interpretation suggests it is also a lesson in heuristics and in our relation to the world: "by demystifying the image in order to alert us of the uncertainty of appearances," "Keaton invites us to constantly try and see more, deeper, with more circumspection."[125]

The famous metalepsis is by no means the only metamoment in Keaton's work. Four years later, *The Cameraman* (Sedgwick and Keaton, 1928) has Keaton in the opposite role, that of cinematographer. If initially Buster has no control over his machine and records a chaos of images [20:36–21:32], which recalls the momentary disruption of *Sherlock Jr.* as well as avant-garde films of the 1920s (Goudet even compares the superimposition of the boat and New York to Vertov[126]), Buster is later seen recording live footage of a Chinatown Tong war [55:34–1:00:50]. Yet again, it is the border between reality and fiction that is at stake here. Although Buster works for the MGM division that produces newsreels, he actually ends up directing the event he is meant to document, moving profilmic objects (notably a body) to improve his compositions. The end of the film shows the MGM division boss, Buster's love interest and his rival, watching his footage of Chinatown and of his saving his love interest from drowning, which actually corresponds to the images we have seen on screen [1:12:18–1:14:33]. Buster is thus endowed with a metanarrative function in an instance of "overt diegetic metafiction" whereby the creation of film is thematized. Yet the film's exploration of the border between cinematic fiction and reality goes beyond the instances of movie-making and -watching. In fact, one of the most striking scenes occurs early on after Buster has failed, the carton tells us, to film anything but "nuts" [17:00–20:34]. When a Yankee Stadium manager informs Buster that the team is playing in St. Louis, the amateur news reporter is momentarily at a loss. He moves away from his camera, steps up to the pitcher's mound and starts acting out a baseball game. Buster becomes performer, director and hero, thus taking on several key roles in both filmmaking and baseball (he single-handedly eliminates three opponents as a pitcher, then strikes a home run as a batter). Buster's performance, which expresses the "fantasy of an ideal and glorious command over space,"[127] makes the game come alive for himself and, partly, for us, the real audience. The analogy with cinema is reinforced by the presence of the camera, which is never completely relegated offscreen (it is even visible on the left edge of a medium full shot of Buster). This is reinforced in the final shot where the man in the right

When, Where and Possibly Why Did Meta Appear? 55

Figure 3.4 The Cameraman: *Buster salutes his diegetic audience after miming a baseball game in an empty Yankee Stadium.*

foreground, Buster in the left midground and the camera form a triangle. The hero—a synecdoche of the fiction film—stands between the camera and the spectator (Figure 3.4).

While the reverse shots of an empty home base or a vacant field (when Buster's up to bat) remind us the stadium is empty, the medium frontal full shot of Buster on the pitcher's mound relegates first and third bases and most of the field to the offscreen and, therefore, would have been quasi-identical in a "normal" scene with a pitcher. The scene thus emphasizes the dramatic power of Buster's performance (which was not scripted and entirely devised by Keaton[128]) and of cinema to make the scene come alive in our imaginations—in this respect, it serves as a model for the bull-fighting scene in *Hollywood or Bust* (Tashlin, 1956) and even the tennis scene in *Blow-up* (Antonioni, 1966) (see Chapter 5). As in *Sherlock Jr.*, the baseball scene comments on Keaton's films in particular, but here it expands into a celebration of the medium and a study of how slapstick differs from its stage predecessor, burlesque. In both media, the mime's performance has the power to turn emptiness into a dramatic spectacle, but the added power of cinema is its capacity to delimit space and call on our imaginations to fill in the blanks created by offscreen space.

The films of Buster Keaton prove that reflexive devices such as the metalepsis and the mise en abyme were used in classical silent cinema long before the avant-gardes potentially influenced mainstream cinema. Many scenes in Keaton's films would now be considered as meta because they comment on themselves and explore the boundaries of cinematic fiction and performance. Further research would, however, be required to determine whether Keaton's work is an exception or whether this meta quality is equally present in the work of his contemporaries, including filmmakers working in genres other than slapstick comedy (James also cites the Marx Brothers and Mae West as resorting to avant-garde devices in mainstream fare[129]). But how far back can we go? Does it make sense to analyze the phenomena at work in the cinema of attractions as meta? *The Big Swallow*, for instance, has been described as "self-reflexive,"[130] and the performer's laughing at the end certainly underlines the knowingness in the "frightening impossibility"[131] of the situation: he has not really been swallowed up by the camera since he is still being filmed, and the camera and cameraman he did swallow are diegetic and disconnected from the apparatus, contrary to what the first shot established. *The Big Swallow* thus draws attention to the impossible terms of filmic enunciation, as underscored by Metz: "showing the apparatus" inevitably means showing a (diegetic) apparatus.[132] The short film can be interpreted as meta if you consider that it is commenting on the specificity of an apparatus that cannot represent itself at work—or that a "pure mise an abyme" would run the risk of annihilating itself, as Gian Maria Tore points out[133]—but it is very likely that the interpretation is, above all, an effect of the gimmick itself. In short, its meta quality would owe more to how we interpret the gimmick in light of contemporary frameworks.

A Series of Tentative Conclusions

This chapter has, perhaps, raised more questions than it has answered, which is why I will conclude by offering a series of tentative conclusions that can be viewed as working hypotheses:

- meta-phenomena are everywhere but seem especially prominent in North American and Western European film and television;
- the impression that they are characteristic and/or symptomatic of Western culture is, at least in part, an effect of a Eurocentric perspective that ignores regional traditions of meta-phenomena;
- the theory of meta-phenomena originates primarily in literary and drama theory, but its practices tap into a multitude of sources;
- the history of meta-phenomena is transmedial, but includes instances that are medium specific;

- meta-phenomena have always been a central characteristic of avant-garde and art films, but were already present in mainstream productions and are increasingly so;
- the influence of modernism and the avant-gardes on the emergence of meta-phenomena in mainstream fare has been direct (Welles, Hitchcock, Godard) and indirect (when the influence has been mediated by the works of such directors), but does not necessarily account for the presence of all meta-phenomena (which can have been derived from other media or more mainstream works);
- indeed, the presence of meta-phenomena must also be considered within a more general anti-illusionist tradition (Cervantes, Shakespeare), a specific form (such as a genre), a technological context (the digital age) and/or the zeitgeist (such as postmodernism);
- meta-phenomena may thus be found in works that were formerly described as reflexive, but such interpretations run the risk of ahistoricism.

Part II

The Aboutness of Meta

CHAPTER 4

Industry and Creation

MOVIES ABOUT MAKING MOVIES

No doubt meta is at its most obvious in films and series that revolve around the film and television industry and depict the workings of its three branches (production, distribution, exhibition), such "thematization" qualifying as "overt diegetic metafiction" according to Hutcheon. Such films have existed since the silent era[1] (*The Evidence of the Film* [Marson and Thanhouser, 1913], *Mabel's Dramatic Career* [Sennett, 1913], *A Film Johnnie* [Nichols, 1914]) and have, accordingly, received sustained critical attention—from Patrick Donald Anderson (1976), Christopher Ames (1997), Marc Cerisuelo (2000) and, more recently, from Steven Cohan (2018) and Julien Achemchame (2021). All these scholars consider these "films about Hollywood and the movie industry" (Anderson), films-about-filmmaking (Stam), "movies about movies" (Ames), "metafilms" (Cerisuelo, Achemchame) or "backstudio pictures" (Cohan) as a full-fledged and primarily Hollywood genre.[2] They also see it as eminently "self-referential,"[3] "reflexive"[4] or "self-reflexive."[5] The first section of this chapter thus draws on their ideas and expands beyond the US to offer an overview of the genre before moving on to the more implicit forms and concerns that may inhabit them, and leading us beyond the confines of the industry and into the domain of allegory.

The degree of aboutness—that is, the extent to which they are really about the industry—varies greatly from one work to another. Often their plots are less concerned with the role and structure of the industry than with problems such as jealousy (*Shooting Stars* [Asquith and Bramble, 1928]), alcoholism (*In a Lonely Place* [Ray, 1950]), psychopathic behavior (*Peeping Tom*), romantic relationships (*Identificazione di una donna* [Antonioni, 1982], *Through the Olive Tree*s), dysfunctional families (*Maps to the Stars* [Cronenberg, 2014]), homosexuality in the face of censorship (*Where the Truth Lies* [Egoyan, 2005]) or genocide (*Ararat* [Egoyan, 2002]). The vast majority of films that do engage with the industry itself concentrate on filmmaking and production. Those that involve the third branch rarely explore the intricacies of exhibition but center on the experiences of specific viewers (see Chapter 5).

An audiovisual fiction that privileges distribution has, to my knowledge, yet to see the day.

Apparently, the experience of creating or viewing a film is considered to offer more dramatic potential than the industry's politics and economics, the industry's artists (directors, screenwriters and especially stars and actors) making for more engaging characters than business people and less visible crew members (the sound technicians of *Blow Out* [De Palma, 1981] and *Berberian Sound Studio* [Strickland, 2012] are notable exceptions). The most compelling, if one goes by the numbers, is the star or performer (*Show People* [Vidor, 1928], *Shooting Stars, What Price Hollywood?* [Cukor, 1932], *A Star Is Born* [1937], *Sunset Blvd.*, *Bellissima* [Visconti, 1951], *Singin' in the Rain, The Star* [Heisler, 1952], *Hollywood Boulevard* (Dante, 1976), *Body Double* [De Palma, 1984], *Through the Olive Trees, Wes Craven's New Nightmare, Scream 3* [Craven, 2000], *Shadow of the Vampire* [Merhige, 2000], *Mulholland Dr., Where the Truth Lies, Inland Empire* [Lynch, 2006], *Tropic Thunder* [Stiller, 2008], *The Artist* [Hazanavicius, 2011], *Maps to the Stars, Once Upon a Time . . . in Hollywood*, not to mention biopics such as *Man of a Thousand Faces* [Pevney, 1957], *Mommie Dearest* [Perry, 1981], *Chaplin* [Attenborough, 1992], *The Life and Death of Peter Sellers* [Hopkins, 2004] and *Blonde* [Dominik, 2022]). Screenwriters (*Sunset Blvd.* [Wilder, 1950], *In a Lonely Place, Contempt, Barton Fink* [the Coen brothers, 1991], *Adaptation, Hunger* [Giese, 2001]) and directors (*Hellzapoppin', 8½, Contempt, Day for Night* [Truffaut, 1973], *Stardust Memories, Identificazione di una donna, Intervista* [Fellini, 1987], *Life and Nothing More, Ed Wood* [Burton, 1994], *Living in Oblivion* [DiCillo, 1995], *Mulholland Dr., Ararat, Reality* [Dupieux, 2014]) seem tied for second place, probably indicating a certain hesitation as to who, in the end, is the film's creator or "auteur." Only the occasional film focuses on the cast and crew as an ensemble (*Trans-Europe-Express, Beware of the Holy Whore* [Fassbinder, 1971], *The State of Things* [Wenders, 1982], *Living in Oblivion, One Cut of the Dead*). Producers, often relegated to secondary roles (*Barton Fink, Mulholland Dr.*), act as embodiments of the corporate interests involved in the creative process and appear as calculating and heartless (*The Bad and the Beautiful* [Minnelli, 1952], *The Player*), unless they are romanticized (*The Last Tycoon* [Kazan, 1976]) or turned into figures of ridicule (*Matinée* [Dante, 1993]).

There are comparatively few series about making series or movies. To this day, *The Dick Van Dyke Show* (CBS, 1961–6), which relates the eponymous screenwriter's life and travails, remains, no doubt, the most famous example. Its twenty-first-century equivalent, the HBO sitcom *Curb Your Enthusiasm*, follows the adventures of real-life showrunner/writer Larry David, who became famous as the co-showrunner/writer of *Seinfeld* (NBC, 1989–98); though not a spin-off per se, *Curb Your Enthusiasm* certainly banks on the success of the highly successful NBC sitcom and even features an episode entitled "Seinfeld" (S7E10) in which David tries to organize a *Seinfeld* reunion. Generally speaking, series seem to favor artists in other milieux (stand-up in *Seinfeld*) or standalone episodes about movie-or-television-making (see Chapter 9), perhaps because the rise-and-fall arc of the star or director would not translate well as a serial narrative, unlike the work of a stand-up comedian whose weekly routines neatly fit the format. The number of series-about-movie-or-television-making does seem to be somewhat on the increase. Recent examples include the British mini-series *Dead Set* (E4, 2008), which focuses on a reality TV show in the midst of a zombie outbreak; *Cult* (The CW, 2013), centered on a TV show (of the same name and broadcast by the same network) with a mysterious and dangerous cult following; *This Is Us* (Fox, 2016–22), in which we witness Kevin Pearson's acting career after he quit his role in the sitcom *The Manny*; season 6 of *American Horror Story*, which centers on the making of a made-for-TV docufiction entitled *My Roanoke Nightmare* (S6E1–S6E5), followed by a reality TV sequel mixing the actual victims and the performers (S6E6–S6E9), and the subsequent media productions that emerged in the wake of the two (S6E10); *The Morning Show* (Apple TV+, 2019–), a backstudio series centered on the production of the eponymous early-morning program; and the 2020 Netflix mini-series *Hollywood*, set in the post-World War II entertainment industry.

Many movies about movies address, as Ames has noted, the tension between two views of film: film as product and film as art.[6] This tension played a central role in Hollywood history, since the question was explicitly tied to film's falling or not under the First Amendment's protection (the 1915 Supreme Court ruling that film was "a business pure and simple" was overturned thirty-seven years later when examining calls to censor neorealist frontrunner Roberto Rossellini's segment in the anthology film *The Ways of Love* [1950]). In many Hollywood movies about movies, this tension is expressed through a dynamic whereby the industry is criticized for its economic, political and essentially moral corruption, while the drive to create film art is celebrated as a thrilling and noble endeavor. The stakes are patent in a title such as *What Price Hollywood?*, which links the economic and moral through polysemy. The underlying question raised is: To what extent can the creation of art redeem the industry's systemic corruption? Anderson, Ames and Cohan agree that the first cycle of Hollywood on Hollywood films (of the 1930s) tends to celebrate success, while the second cycle (of the 1950s) generally critiques the evils of the industry.[7] For Ames and Cohan, the genre is inhabited by a paradox: that of "simultaneously demystify[ing] and mystify[ing] their subject,"[8] of "promulgat[ing] the

Hollywood mystique" as a "brand shared by all studios,"[9] in spite of the more parodic and deconstructive tendencies of the fourth cycle (of the 1990s to today).[10]

Day for Night, Stam notes, is quite exceptional in this respect; an "ode to film craft,"[11] it lacks the critical bent of the majority of such films. The French film, as well as its less-known predecessor *Beware of the Holy Whore*, seems to have inspired the US-American indie movie *Living in Oblivion*, in which the overcoming of a variety of practical contingencies on set are orchestrated to produce humor. Perhaps these films' emphasis on positive energy can be explained by their production contexts. In a national cinema system, Truffaut received funding from the Productions et Éditions Cinématographiques Françaises, which allowed him relative artistic freedom, while the US indie film takes its limited budget as a given and tries to make do. This would explain why the majority of movies about the movie industry are US-American productions set in Hollywood, even when they are filmed by foreigners (Cronenberg, Egoyan, Hazanavicius), and maybe why those that are not usually include some kind of link to Hollywood (the arrogant US-American producer portrayed by Jack Palance in *Contempt*, the discussion involving the securing of US distribution through Paramount or MGM in *Peeping Tom*, the French producer whose ambition it is to win the Oscar for Best Scream in *Reality*).

Although film history would tend to qualify this view (the British production *Shooting Stars* was released eight months before *Show People*), and although it is clear from the titles mentioned above that a nation like Italy has a long history of movies about making movies, and that directors such as Federico Fellini and Abbas Kiarostami have returned to the genre on a regular basis, the genre itself does seem inexorably linked to Hollywood. The difference in tone of *Day for Night* and *Living in Oblivion* may shed light on why. As the only film and television industry in the world (with the exception of NPR) that is managed entirely by the private sector, Hollywood films are governed by the laws of capitalism (or at least are believed to be so), unlike productions in most film industries that receive at least some national or local funding, notably through tariffs and tax incentives. This is not to say that corruption does not exist within national or local funding bodies, but that the economic stakes within these industries are perceived as being incomparable to those within Hollywood. In short, the largely US-American corpus of movies about the industry do not so much reflect an industrial reality as, rather, the concern that moral, political and aesthetic corruption might be far greater in a milieu that is entirely ruled by profit.

Prostitution becomes an apt metaphor, Cerisuelo notes,[12] to evoke not only the sacrifices an actress may have to make (implicit in *A Star Is Born*, more evident in *Inside Daisy Clover* [Mulligan, 1965]), but also the screenwriters' or directors' subordination to various economic imperatives and decision to sell out (*Sunset Blvd.*, *Contempt*, *Mulholland Dr.*). The attempt to reconcile artistic and economic imperatives is represented as a sort of Faustian pact in *Contempt* (where the screenwriter compromises his marriage for a job), *Barton Fink* (whose working-class neighbor, an embodiment of the aesthetic and political principles the playwright has betrayed, turns the hotel into an inferno) and *Mulholland Dr.* (where Adam the director makes a midnight deal with the mysterious Cowboy who informs him he is no longer driving "the buggy"). The capitalist context also comes with implications that are narrative, dramatic and ideological: it is an ideal setting for the upward mobility narrative that is one of the manifestations of the American dream,[13] mediated through the myths of Pygmalion[14] and Cinderella. It may just be that a story about a filmmaking team seeking out public subsidies for a project would be perceived as a less dramatic premise—or maybe as the premise of a film with a more limited audience, directed by Ken Loach or the Dardenne brothers.

Since the 1950s at least, the majority of these films have tended to be critical about the industry itself; they also tend to emerge, as Ames, Cerisuelo, Cohan and Achemchame have shown, in times of crises within the movie world, which can be economic, technological and political, but also aesthetic and even theoretical. All these films inform us on how the industry views itself, its history and its present, and how it tries to market Hollywood as a town, a fantasy and an industry.[15] The rising star narratives of *What Price Hollywood?* and *A Star Is Born* have been read in the light of the Great Depression as upholding "a version of the American dream of self-improvement,"[16] an idea Luchino Visconti's neorealist *Bellissima* transposes more explicitly in the dire context of post-World War II Italy, where a working-class mother is basically trying to get her daughter a job. The investigation of an earlier crisis (for instance, the advent of sound technology) can even be a way to reflect on a current technological crisis, the emergence of a rival media such as television in the 1950s (*Sunset Blvd.*,[17] *Singin' in the Rain*[18]) or the digital age in the early twenty-first century (*The Artist*). For Cohan, the nostalgia for Hollywood's golden age patent in the third cycle "discounts" the industry's economic hardships of the 1970s.[19] *Barton Fink*'s misadventures as a screenwriter in 1940s Hollywood, following the success of his play in New York, echo the concern that Hollywood is going to bleed the creative energy of late 1980s US independent cinema dry, while those of Adam in *Mulholland Dr.* suggest that media conglomerates have transformed the entertainment industry into a labyrinth in which the moneyed minotaur is ever elusive, spectral, like *Inland Empire*'s Phantom, a metaphor for the shameful secrets

Hollywood conceals for the sake of profit. With these movies about making movies, filmmakers and ultimately the industry that supports them express their anxieties, provide their self-critique, sometimes even fueling rumors of Hollywood corruption. But even in the most critical, corruption is at least somewhat redeemed through the defense of art, as epitomized by Barton Fink's sincere admission that he "tried to show" his audience "something beautiful, something about all of us," with his Wallace Beery wrestling picture script [1:44:45].

It is this creative energy that is celebrated in the numbers of *Singin' in the Rain* and *The Artist*, the comedy routines of *Where the Truth Lies*, the actor rivalry of *Tropic Thunder*, the auditions of *The Star* and *Mulholland Drive*, the rehearsal and shooting sequences of *Inland Empire* and *This Is Us*. Such scenes were often ellipticized in the classical era (*The Star* counts among the exceptions) but have now become staple scenes, moments of bravura in which an actor can prove his or her talent by embodying a performer in action and maybe even claim a major industry award (movies about movies are known to do well at the Oscars and Grammys). They are the moments when the positive energy is physically released by the performance and they often constitute high points in the narrative arc (Betty in *Mulholland Drive* and Rick Dalton in *Once Upon a Time . . . in Hollywood* are congratulated by their diegetic audience for their stellar performances, in scenes that take place halfway through the film). This creative energy is celebrated quite physically in the finale of *Blazing Saddles* (Brooks, 1974), when the fiction turns out to be a movie being shot which gets completely out of hand and overruns the entire studio. A similar, albeit more poetic example occurs at the end of *Taste of Cherry* (Kiarostami, 1997), when the epilogue reveals that the depressing story of a man's imminent suicide is nothing but a fiction, director Abbas Kiarostami and actor Homayoun Ershadi sitting side by side near the camera, the radical change in the color scheme (the hillside is no longer the sickly yellowish brown that dominated the movie's color palette but a vivid green) proving that the film's bleak tone is an elaborate illusion. Even films centered on the porn industry manage to salvage some enthusiasm among the economic and moral corruption, in the carefree sex scene of *Boogie Nights* (Anderson, 1997) or the alleged political radicalism of the Mitchell Brothers in *Rated X* (Esteves, 2000).

A common trait of many of these movies is what Cerisuelo describes as their "secondariness," that is how self-conscious they are about being modeled on other films. The most obvious case is the sequel (*Wes Craven's New Nightmare, Scream 3*), the film that is about the making of an existing film (*Ed Wood, Shadow of the Vampire*) or the backstage relationships during a shooting (*Through the Olive Trees*), a remake or sequel of an existing film (*Son of Rambow*

[Jennings, 2007], *Be Kind Rewind* [Gondry, 2008]) or that simply borrows ideas from previous material (the hilarious *Twin Peaks*-inspired dream sequence of *Living in Oblivion*, Kevin's shooting a war movie scene with Sylvester Stallone in episode S2E3 of *This Is Us*). Many films pay homage to earlier films (*Tropic Thunder* parodies the hard-body action movies of the 1980s, including previous films about the industry: *A Star Is Born* is modeled on *Show People* and *What Price Hollywood?*,[20] *Living in Oblivion* on *Day for Night*, *Stardust Memories* on *8½*,[21] *The Artist* on *Singin' in the Rain*[22]; *Boogie Nights* alludes to *Contempt* through a track-in on the camera filming two performers (Amber and Eddie) having sex [51:50]. This secondariness extends to other art forms, including literature and drama (the character of Barton Fink resembles Arthur Miller and W.P. Mayhew, "the greatest living American novelist," a blend of William Faulkner and F. Scott Fitzgerald). The secondariness of many of these films would tend to indicate that they are not solely concerned with the intricacies of the industry or even the filmmaking process; they do not consider cinema as just an apt topic but as a material that is narrative, iconographic and historiographic; they embrace the opportunity to contribute to the elaboration of the Hollywood master narrative and seem to posit a view of creation as recreation. This leads us to the second question that will be addressed in this chapter: can movies that are very explicitly about the industry be meta more implicitly and in other respects?

More than Just about the Industry (*Sunset Blvd.*, *Contempt*, *Mulholland Dr.*)

Here, I would like to look at specific moments when a movie about moviemaking becomes more than just a story about the industry, but develops a subtext on cinema, fiction and/or art that would qualify as meta. I will start with what has, no doubt, become the model of the genre, *Sunset Blvd.*, before focusing on two films that are through and through meta, *Contempt* and *Mulholland Dr.*

A theoretical reflection on cinema that goes far beyond a critique of the industry can be found in *Sunset Blvd.*, although it is more discrete and less systematic than in more recent films and has hardly been noted. The 1950 film contains all the ingredients of the movie-about-movie-making genre. Set in Hollywood, all its characters are movie people, and it allows us to observe various stages of the filmmaking process: writing (the protagonist, Joe Gillis, works with both Norma and Betty Schaefer), shooting (the DeMille scene), and even the complicated task of digging up specific props (Gordon Cole's phone calls to borrow Norma Desmond's car). The movie mentions and features actual studios (Paramount, Twentieth Century Fox) and people (director

Cecil B. DeMille, journalist Hedda Hopper, actor Alan Ladd, producer Darryl F. Zanuck), some of whom (DeMille, Hopper) play themselves.

Hollywood is not just a spatial setting in *Sunset Blvd.*; the plot is very much grounded in the industry's history and investigates one of its most important crises on several levels: technological, economic, and aesthetic.[23] As Wilder biographer Gene D. Phillips remarks, the title evokes not just an actual Hollywood street; "the sun set on their careers when they failed to make the transition to sound films."[24] If the premise centers on a star's artistic exile following the transition from silent to sound cinema, the film also looks back on the golden age of the studio era from a moment in time when cinema is facing a new adversary; it "speaks to," as Stam notes, "the television crisis by referring to an earlier technological crisis—the coming of sound."[25] This is suggested through the reference to Technicolor [17:33], which was to become one of cinema's main assets to compete with television in the 1950s. Viewed in this light, Norma's famous claim that "it's the pictures got small" [16:38] could be interpreted as an indirect reference to television.[26] The golden age is also associated with healthy economics. While Norma is depicted as a spendthrift still living in the Roaring Twenties, Joe turns out to be very much aware of the need for a modest budget during his interview with the producer ("I bet you could make the whole thing for under a million," he says) [6:09]. Unlike Ames for whom *Sunset Blvd.* evinces nostalgia for the 1920s,[27] Stam opines that "[t]his newer, in some ways duller world, Wilder seems to be telling us, is considerably healthier than the bigger-than-life decadence of the old Hollywood."[28] Hollywood history is not just a backdrop; it gives the film its narrative and dramatic drive. The tension between the 1920s and 1940s is dramatized by the pairing of characters separated by a generation gap and spanning three generations (Joe/Norma, Joe/Max, Norma/Max, Betty/Norma, Betty/Joe); the characters represent either the "has beens" or the "never will bes,"[29] and are thus set in a tragic light. The death of Norma's chimpanzee, a reminder of cinema's fairground origins, provides the depressing proof that the past will ultimately be forgotten [26:22].[30]

More implicit are the stakes raised by two consecutive scenes that occur a third of the way into the movie: the private screening of *Queen Kelly* (von Stroheim, 1929), followed by the bridge game [30:56–35:05], offer a framework with which to interpret the rest of the film. The card game prolongs the intertextual play of the screening. After recognizing a younger Desmond/Swanson in a film whose completion was compromised by the advent of sound,[31] we are now invited to identify three other celebrities of the past (Buster Keaton, Anne Q. Nilsson and H.B. Warner), turning the scene itself into a game of Who's Who for the spectator whose recognition will depend on the extent of her/his cinephilia. The stars are no longer to be spotted on the diegetic screen but within the diegetic world itself. In so doing, the scene, like the card game in *Inglourious Basterds* which it no doubt influenced, mirrors the film's intertextual play, including the recognition of the "real" movie people mentioned above. The playfulness is suggested by Keaton when he sadly repeats the word "pass" (which sounds dreadfully like "past"), drawing attention both to his status and the player/viewer's activity (or lack thereof). Even the choice of the game is revealing, since a bridge also connects two points on either side of a chasm. The scene thus suggests that identifying an intertext is an activity which consists in establishing a bridge between the diegesis and the real world (i.e., movies and people that really exist), and that *Sunset Blvd.* itself is a game in which the viewer acts like a player/hermeneutist on the lookout for allusions and citations.

The film wears its palimpsest credentials on its sleeves. Its heroine is named after a silent film actress (Mabel Normand) and director (William Desmond Taylor), who had an affair.[32] It contains several films within the film, mixes real films (the images from *Queen Kelly*, accompanied however by Wilder's intertitle[33]) and invented scripts (*Dark Windows* and *Bases Loaded*), and pastiches scenes from Swanson's career (the tango dance and Chaplin imitation allude to Swanson's movies *Beyond the Rocks* [Wood, 1922] and *Manhandled* [Dwan, 1924][34]). Betty's describing *Bases Loaded* as a "rehash of something that wasn't very good to begin with" [6:29] can be said of all the plots and titles evoked in the diegesis: the title *Dark Windows* rings like a conflation of the titles of two famous noir films—*Dark Passage* (Daves, 1947) and *The Woman in the Window*—and the plot concerning the Oakies Joe mentions to Norma as his credits [18:10] recalls John Steinbeck's 1939 novel *The Grapes of Wrath*, adapted by John Ford in 1940. Not only is Wilder's 1950 film reminiscent of *The Sin of Harold Diddlebock* (Sturges, 1947),[35] it fundamentally inverts the plot of *Queen Kelly*, as Cerisuelo has shown, with Norma in the role of the old queen and Betty in that of Patricia, Swanson's former role; Norma even ends up murdering the man she loves just like Salome, the heroine she means to embody for her big return.[36] Symbolically at least, the films within the film all evoke death (*Queen Kelly* is von Stroheim's last film[37]), and the screenplays end up orphans. Norma's plight is made more tragic still thanks to a dab of irony: while her Salome story seems like the movie pitch of a bygone era, her visit to the studio confirms that DeMille is still making peplums [1:05:55–1:11:54] (the scene actually shows the director shooting the Paramount production *Samson and Delilah*, which was released a year before[38]). Norma's imitation of the Tramp [1:02:34–1:03:03] is not only an homage to an artist/character who, with *City Lights* (1931) and *Modern Times* (1936), famously resisted the advent of sound but ultimately gave in with *The Great Dictator* (1940); it also reflects *Sunset Blvd.*'s debt to the past through a figure who is a paragon of imitation (the famous scene in *The Circus* [1928] where the Tramp imitates an automaton springs to mind). Operating as what Limoges calls a "metatextual" mise en abyme,[39] the card game scene works on a more implicit meta-level by drawing attention to the intertextual play at hand; it also indicates that the former might distract us—as it does Gillis—from much darker metanarrative stakes.

For it is during the card game that Max turns away two thugs looking for Joe Gillis, in appearance to save him from being taken to the gangster he owes money to but in effect imprisoning him. Joe's lack of control over his own fate is expressed visually in a very long shot, Max dealing with the problem in the right background, while an imposing column in the midground emphasizes visually that Joe is cut off from the discussion that is to determine his fate. To further the irony, the only reason Joe notices Max's doings is because he was obeying Norma's order to fetch her an ashtray. This illustration of Joe's subjection to both Norma and Max calls into question his stance as a voiceover narrator who condescends to the "wax works." The scene thus contrasts Joe's apparent control over the narration as a voiceover narrator (he addresses us in the second-person pronoun) and his increasing lack of control as a character. Underlying the intertextual play there lurks a disquieting power play, which was already evident in the previous scene. Indeed, if Joe the character initially appears cool as a cucumber during the screening of *Queen Kelly*, and if his voiceover dominates the first two-thirds of the scene, Norma's overbearing presence becomes increasingly pressing, most explicitly when she squeezes his arm with her talon-like hand. The camerawork insists on the shifting balance in power by singling out elements that point to Joe's loss of control (Norma's hand, Max's presence in the projection booth) and by modifying the center of composition from Joe to Norma, whose medium close-up puts an end to the scene.

The two scenes thus reflect a metanarrative stake: that the characters are vying for control not only over each other within the story (Joe initially believes he can make easy money off Norma) but over the narration. They encapsulate the metanarrative drama that structures the entire film, with each character attempting to control the narrative of his/her life. Framing the flashback structure, the voiceover appears to control the narrative, including his past self whom he refers to in the third person ("Nobody important, really. Just a movie writer with a couple of B pictures to his credit. The poor dope." [2:25]), whereas Joe the character in the story increasingly loses control, a point the narrator makes clear when he ends up describing Norma's mansion as "that peculiar prison of mine" [90:03]. Not only does Joe subject himself to Norma (for instance, when he returns from the party), but from the start, Max takes control of the course of his life (he puts Joe's belongings in the room above the garage) and even the soundtrack (he is playing the "wheezing" organ, significantly, at the very moment Joe realizes Max brought his things from his apartment) [26:55–28:22]. Norma's servant is—paradoxically—still very much the director/screenwriter of her life, as the origin of her fan mail confirms [40:04]. Like Norma, Joe attempts to regain some control over his life by writing a screenplay, this time with Betty, but in Hollywood, the real power, the film demonstrates, is on the side of the star and director. His voiceover is less and less present as the film progresses and disappears shortly after his corpse is revealed.

Stam argues that "[t]he circular structure of the film further underscores the implausibility of the device."[40] In effect, the revelation that the voiceover was a spectre all along turns what was initially presented as based on a true story into a tale of the supernatural. The crime fiction is thus modeled on a fantasy structure, something which Norma's Gothic mansion, "crumbling apart in slow motion" [25:38] like a filmic House of Usher, hinted at all along. *Sunset Blvd.* thus combines at least three of the models (detective, fantasy, play) of diegetic metafiction identified by Hutcheon. The film nonetheless continues after the twist and proposes an epilogue in which the former star (Norma) and director (Max) direct the last scene [1:48:40–1:49:45]. Her final monologue having already replaced Joe's voiceover, Norma's breaking the fourth wall in close-up is the moment when she (and Max offscreen) finally establish complete control over the narration, and thus over what the narratee (that is, us, the audience they had lost) can see: the star's face. Yet they had already taken over as soon as they had gotten their hands on what they were looking for all along: a camera, a stage and an audience. As Norma descends the stairs, the bystanders tend to freeze like "waxworks," and a Gothic chiaroscuro lighting replaces the more realistic high-key lighting in Norma's room [1:46:48–1:48:38], proving that, even before the final shot, Max/Norma had already taken over an essential component of the narration: the staging.

In many ways, the concluding scene is the logical and desired outcome of the *Queen Kelly* screening, which foreshadowed its more explicit transgression of ontological boundaries.[41] A series of dichotomies—past/present, old/young, employer/employee, star/fan, star/critic, silent/sound cinema, painting/cinema—are set up only to be undercut. Norma crosses the line of professional etiquette by giving in to Joe's charms, then behaves like her own greatest fan, and finally speaks out like a film theorist of the late 1920s (Rudolf Arnheim among others) when she laments the passing away of silent cinema. The scene momentarily reproduces the viewing conditions of silent cinema, yet the older Norma violates these terms by delivering a monologue in which she, quite contradictorily, values "faces" over "dialogue." The painting, both an ancestor of cinema and a model of what film as art should be, acts as a curtain for the screen, thus calling on another ancestor of cinema, the theater. Yet the smoke in the painting echoes the smoke from Gillis's cigarette, thus conjuring up the popular 1920s notion of film as a synchretic art (particularly among the Russian formalists,[42] see Chapter 6).

Of course, the hint at the violation of ontological boundaries is an expression of Norma's own longing to step into the screen again and relive her glory days. The figure on screen represents her "ego ideal," but this is complicated by the fact that this ideal is also her reflection. Her plight is tinged with narcissism: Norma loves her past self, but loathes her present self for not being her past self. It is her own mortality that she is struggling with, as the montage sequence of her makeover (which references similar scenes in *What Price Hollywood?* and *A Star Is Born*[43]) will confirm [1:15:56–1:16:34]. By stepping into the light, she attempts to steal the light from her former self and become once again a creature of light, and thus a creature of cinema (Figure 4.1), in a composition that mirrors her younger face looking to the left lit by candles in *Queen Kelly*. Norma rejects the materiality of her body and desires the immortality of what Joe calls "her celluloid self" [30:40]. And yet, as Ames notes, "The situation points up the contradiction of filmic immortality: movies preserve the youthful image while the real self ages, but movies themselves are

Figure 4.1 Sunset Blvd.: *Norma Desmond steals the light from her youthful self on screen: "I'll show them! I'll be up there again, so help me!"*

transitory phenomena, popular for a brief run and then forgotten (especially in the era before television and videotape)."[44] Ironically, her Gothic mansion proves that she is already entombed and has already become spectral, though not in the sense that she desires. At this stage, the film insists on the impossibility of her desire. But the final scene allows her to see her "happy ending" fulfilled,[45] as "[t]he dream she had clung to so desperately [. . .] enfold[s] her" [1:48:10]. As she advances into her close-up, she becomes a creature of light and shadows again, her blurring face (Figure 4.2) expressing not just the loss of her self but, on the contrary, the persistence of her life as a star, as an icon, as a celluloid being, as plastic matter, as the stuff of cinema. With her face once again occupying the frame in close-up and ultimately becoming a light gray blur that draws attention to the surface of the screen, the celluloid ghost has conquered, and silent cinema has bested sound cinema, metonymically represented by Joe's ghostly voice. *Sunset Blvd.* is not just a paragon of the Hollywood metafilm or an example of the increased presence of reflexivity in popular Hollywood cinema; it engages with its star's and its own materiality as film.

Contempt expands on previous Hollywood movies about making movies by providing a translatlantic perspective that is absent from Alberto Moravia's

Figure 4.2 Sunset Blvd.: *breaking the fourth wall as she advances into her close-up, Norma Desmond turns into a spectral image, an abstract figure of light and shadows.*

novel, in which all the main characters are Italian except for the German director named Rheingold. A French writer, Paul Javal, is hired by a US-American producer, Jeremy Prokosch, to doctor the script of an adaptation of Homer's *Odyssey*, directed by none other than Fritz Lang. Like *Contempt*, Lang's *Odyssey* is to be a US–European co-production. Casting the Austrian director as himself enables Godard to call on his translatlantic background, his Hollywood years having often been described as lacking the power of his early career in Germany; when Paul and his lovely wife Camille mention having recently watched *Rancho Notorious* (1952), Lang counters that he prefers the 1931 *M* [22:40–22:54].[46] Scholars like Marc Cerisuelo and Michel Marie have noted how *Contempt* engages with its immediate film history: in 1963 the Nouvelle Vague is losing steam, the Hollywood studio system is coming to an end,[47] and was about to pull out of the Italian industry following the *Cleopatra* (Mankiewicz, 1963) debacle and, more generally, the exhaustion of the peplum cycle.[48] Cinecittà Studios is conspicuously deserted, "haunted by the history of film and production companies, and notably by the shooting of *Cleopatra*"[49]—a destabilizing sight in a genre that tends to depict the hustle and bustle of movie-making.[50] The Mediterranean color scheme (based on blue, white and yellow) is regularly broken by the red of passion and death, announced in the film's title and culminating in Prokosch's Alfa Romeo that will lead the producer and Paul's wife Camille to their deaths.[51] The dying film industry is depicted as lethal to both creativity and love. Prokosch, who mentions recently losing a studio, insists on other people's weaknesses, whether Paul's "need[ing] the money" because he has "a very beautiful wife [10:50–11:05] or Lang's loss of status as an artist ("But this is not '33. This is '63. And he will direct whatever is written, just as I know that you are going to write it." [9:47–9:56]), a comparison that unwittingly aligns the producer with the Nazis Lang fled and turns him into an embodiment of "the fascism of money and its contempt for all values other than monetary ones."[52] "This is the price to pay for hanging out with movie people"[53] is the moral of this film, says Marc Cerisuelo, echoing Camille's own comment that Paul has "changed" since he started frequenting them [49:33:49:44]. *Contempt*'s "real subject" is "artistic prostitution,"[54] which it displaces onto the screenwriter, thus allowing Fritz Lang to play the part of the wise "classical man of culture"[55] who manages to finish his film in spite of it all.

Contempt sports its secondariness proudly and even more explicitly than Godard's previous films, many of the references appearing as explicit citations.[56] Paul and Camille are cinephiles and mention, in the addition to the films of Fritz Lang, *Rio Bravo* (Hawks, 1959) and *Bigger Than Life* (Ray, 1956) [36:52–37:05], and Camille is even shown reading Luc Moullet's 1963 book on Lang and quoting the director's words [53:16–54:26]. Movie posters of

Psycho (Hitchcock, 1960), *Hatari!* (Hawks, 1962) and Roberto Rossellini's *Vanina Vanini* (1961) are used to indicate the time-setting and to pay homage to Godard's mentors [22:06].[57] The character of Prokosch resembles producer Kirk Edwards in *The Barefoot Contessa* (Mankiewicz, 1954).[58] An adaptation of Moravia's novel in which Lang is adapting *The Odyssey*, *Contempt* almost remakes Rossellini's *Voyage in Italy* (1954), a notable influence on the novel,[59] posters of which frame the night-time scene outside the Silver Cine movie theater [1:15:50]. Both films start in Rome and take us to a second location (Naples in *Voyage in Italy*, Capri in *Contempt*); the 1963 statues are shot in a similar fashion as those in the 1954 film;[60] and the character of the translator Francesca Vanini, yet another addition to the novel, is named after Rossellini's eponymous heroine.[61] At the same time, *Contempt* sets itself against other models, notably Michelangelo Antonioni, whose theme of "ennui" resonates with Moravia's novels.[62] Godard famously and provocatively stated that his aim, with *Contempt*, was to "make a successful Antonioni film, that is to shoot it like a Hawks or a Hitchcock film."[63] In a way, the Capri scenes tend to reject any connections with somewhat similar island scenes in *L'Avventura* (1960) by taking us back to *Stromboli* (Rossellini, 1950) via the Rossellinian statues.

Godard's engagement with film history is also theoretical. The films referenced in *Contempt* also happen to be *Cahiers du cinéma* favorites.[64] The 1963 film opens with a quote attributed to André Bazin, which we now know to be Godard's adaptation of an excerpt from Michel Mourlet's 1959 manifesto "Sur un art ignoré." In it, Cerisuelo explains, Mourlet states that "eroticism" is cinema's "supreme" *raison d'être* and advocates "*a politics of mise en scène.*"[65] *Contempt* thus presents itself as the illustration of a theory, a *Cahiers du cinéma* film, and a "reassessment"[66] of the Nouvelle Vague, as much as, if not more so than, an adaptation of a famous Italian novel. Yet what appears on the surface as straightforward allegiance to Bazin signals, in effect, Godard's departure from his mentor in film criticism. While Godard shared Bazin's belief that cinema was the prime twentieth century candidate for a popular artform, and though *Contempt* indulges in the sort of lengthy sequence shots advocated by Bazin, Godard does not adhere to a Bazinian ontology of cinema as an inherently realist medium,[67] a view however upheld by his Lang in one of his final conversations with Paul ("And the beauty of *The Odyssey* lies precisely in this belief in reality as it is. [. . .] And in a form that cannot be broken down. And that is what is. Take it or leave it." [1:14:10–1:14:35]). A quote is only as good as its context. And the Bazin quote warns knowledgeable viewers (and presumably few in 1963 had immediate access to the actual source[68]) to adopt a cautious attitude towards the film's many citations and avoid jumping to conclusions.

The same caution should be exercised regarding Lang's own comments on filmmaking. If Lang, during the screening, more or less "recites" his own words[69] [17:41] from a 1959 *Cahiers du cinéma* interview that is included in the book Camille will later read, Jean-Pierre Esquenazi has shown that the view of cinema put forth by the real Fritz Lang in early 1960s interviews differs from that expressed by the character in Godard's films. Godard, in Esquenazi's words, "has thus chosen a father he has previously reconstructed"[70] and made over into the *"politique des auteurs* made flesh."[71] And yet, Lang is more than just the incarnation of *Cahiers du cinéma*/Nouvelle Vague theory (and ideology). Cerisuelo has brilliantly shown that, during the *Odyssey* rush sequence, in a small movie theater whose stage reads the Italian translation of a quote attributed to Louis Lumière ("Cinema is an invention without a future") [17:57],

> Godard cleverly weaves [...] a discourse centered on the question of the adaptation of connections between Western cultural history and film history. The discourse is elaborated through the construction of two triads of emblematic names: Homer–Dante–Hölderlin on the one hand; Lumière–Lang–Godard on the other.[72]

The words and mere presence of this venerable figure of film history establish an interconnected history and heritage between literature and film, and uphold cinema's potential to rival with poetry, notwithstanding the economic imperatives of the entertainment industry.

Stam says of *Contempt* that it offers a "metacritical discussion of aesthetic questions,"[73] and Cerisuelo identifies one of them as "the possibility of a modern(ist) classicism."[74] The question is raised both on the diegetic level through the characters' discussions and formally through the film's poetics. One of Godard's most conspicuous modifications of the source text is his inverting the positions of the producer and director regarding the problem of adaptation; in the film, Lang is the upholder of fidelity and classicism, in opposition to Prokosch's project of a sensationalist, psychoanalytically inflected update of *The Odyssey*.[75] Yet if Lang's practice corresponds to that of a classical director,[76] the images we are shown from *The Odyssey* are anything but classical cinema. During the screening [11:17–21:36], the shots of the statues' busts and of statuesque actors appear like a succession of moving pictures entirely disconnected from a narrative, with no sense of spatial, temporal or narrative causality; a semblance of drama and classical narration is restored when a performer is shown carrying out specific actions (a woman swimming in the sea, a man climbing a rock). The screening provokes an outburst of rage from the US-American producer, "That's what I think of that stuff up there, Fritz. [...] Yes, it's in the script, but that's not what you have on that screen," to which Lang calmy replies, "Naturally. Because it is a script, it is written. On the screen, it's pictures. Motion pictures, it's called." Clearly, Godard's Lang's quest for fidelity is doomed from the start—he "has difficulty conveying the grandeur of the gods because of distance in time—the modern ethos has no place for Greek divinities—and differences in medium."[77] Nor is his classicism that of classical cinema. *Contempt* might express Godard's desire for classicism, and it might be his "most classical film,"[78] but "the desire for classicism does not evidently transform he who displays it into a classical artist."[79]

Contempt has all the attributes of art cinema narration, starting with its self-consciousness and its play on "intrinsic norms"[80] (norms proper to a given film and body of work). Its famous opening credits [0:58–2:49], accompanied by an anonymous and omniscient Wellesian voiceover, depicts not only the shooting of a tracking shot—the film's prime device—that culminates with the real cinematographer Raoul Coutard aiming the diegetic camera at the viewer (and thus breaking the fourth wall in an "aggressive designation of our voyeuristic position"[81]), but it does so within a sequence shot whose composition exploits the breadth of the CinemaScope image, with the main action situated on the far right. All these features (the tracking shot, the sequence shot, the off-balance composition) are utilized throughout the film. Paradoxically, the individual shots from the diegetic film, which were initially presented as a disconnected assemblage of shots, are then used to link scenes when the characters move to a new place [24:57, 36:39], thus contributing to the classical, place-determined structure[82] of *Contempt* itself. If such instances are reflexive and make *Contempt* a prime example of Metz's self-conscious enunciation, collectively they express both the intentions and limitations of Godard's project. Like his Lang, try as he might, Godard is incapable of making a classical film, let alone of indulging in a classical film-within-the-film—or at least of showing it as such—and is thus drifting dangerously near the Antonionian waters he wanted to avoid.

Contempt abounds with a wide variety of metamoments in addition to the opening credits and the screening scene. The heart of the apartment sequence becomes eminently metanarrative when Paul's and Camille's voices suddenly vie for control of the soundtrack [56:54–57:58:40], a radical departure from the film's narration that is not a return to the stability of the novel's first-person narration. The voiceovers accompany a montage sequence containing new images (of the past and present), as well as two previously seen images (Camille kicking Paul after hanging up the phone [47:40], Paul first introducing Camille to Prokosch at Cinecittà [22:23]) and, quite impossibly, one future image (of Camille and Paul on the roof of the villa [1:33:33]). The sequence seeks to express, through modernist fragmentation, two entangled subjectivities engaged in the acts of memory, introspection and interpretation, and prompts us to interpret these words and images in the light of one another—and possibly to take a moral stance. For either subject—if not the narration itself—could be the source of these images, and some of their comments could just as well refer to the image itself as to another moment in the narrative; for instance, the image of Camille on the bed when the voiceover states that she "had deliberately uttered that sentence with a deep feeling of revenge" suggests that she is referring to her calling Paul "crazy" when she kicked him, but given that the montage sequence also allows us a glimpse of the future, it could just as well be referring to the forthcoming—and eminently more dramatic—revelation that she despises him [1:08:33]. The montage sequence not only draws attention to its artificiality, but raises the question of the possibility of expressing human subjectivity through the film medium.

The casting scene [1:09:46–1:13:00] also explores the ontology of film through comparison to another medium by resorting to what we would now call intermediality; while the five protagonists watch a live performance of a female singer Prokosch would like to cast as Nausicaa, the presence of a white screen, against which the singer's lateral dance movements stand out, and on which the shadows of the extras moving back and forth behind her are projected, invites us to consider whether we are not watching a live performance and moving pictures such as those produced by one of cinema's ancestors, shadow puppetry (Figure 4.3).

The scene paves the way for the Capri scenes in which the boundary between live and recorded is further destabilized and made to overlap with the boundary between (diegetic) reality and fiction. By journeying to Capri, the characters are transported into the world of *The Odyssey*, with its islands

Figure 4.3 Contempt: *auditioning Nausicaa at a live performance reminiscent of shadow puppetry.*

and color scheme dominated by blue. The change of location is marked by a high-angle medium close-up of Camille against the turquoise blue sea [1:16:07] in place of the habitual statue, inviting us to consider the connections between a series of oppositions: Camille and Penelope, *The Odyssey* and *Contempt*, Lang and Godard, Homer and Godard, a human being (Bardot) and a statue, reality and fiction/art, myth and cinema. These connections are reinforced by a reverse shot of Lang's crew's diegetic camera (as if Camille were the heroine of a movie and not just the screenwriter's wife), and driven home by the scene's concluding shot which pans from the film crew to a very long shot of Prokosch's motorboat taking Camille/Penelope away, merging with the blueness of the sea [1:19:59].

These images provide the plastic and interpretive framework not just for the shooting scene but for the rest of the film, as Camille will shortly be seen swimming naked in the sea [1:37:02–1:37:22] just like the character in Lang's film [14:22]. The visual allusions are made explicit in the next scene when they are voiced by Paul who, in conversation with Lang, reinterprets *The Odyssey* in the light of his own failing relationship [1:21:19–1:22:54]. Yet his voicing the analogy ultimately has the effect of questioning its validity, since his interpretation of his own wife's behavior was previously shown to be flawed. The final scene of *Contempt* makes a similar demonstration of the limits of the analogy [1:40:56–1:43:14]. The elaborate track-and-pan not only depicts the artifice of filmmaking, and notably the actor portraying Ulysses sidestepping in order to keep pace with the diegetic tracking shot; it demonstrates, as Stam has argued, that an "antiepic quality pervades both the world of the film and the world of the film-within-the-film."[83] In so doing, it seems to conclude that Godard's/Lang's intentions were doomed from the start. And yet, by panning away from the ludicrous Ulysses, the camera expresses the contrary of Lang's intention (Ulysses is not seeing his homeland) and captures the pure beauty of the sea. Acting as Lang's assistant director, Godard's command for "Silence" is not just the order to be quiet on set; on a more covert meta-level, it recognizes the poetry of the moment. *Contempt* thus celebrates cinema's potential to offer a poetic experience even as it reveals its own economic and technical limitations to do so; cinema's power would lie in this fundamental ambivalence.

Though not included by Cohan in his list of backstudio films, *Mulholland Dr.* is a veritable synthesis of the movie about making movies. It is bookended by references to two of the most famous films of the genre, *Sunset Blvd.* (the close-up of the street sign [7:50]) and *Contempt* (the final word of the movie is "Silencio" [2:22:05]), reprises the sets of *In a Lonely Place*[84] (Aunt Ruth's apartment) and features Ann Miller, who starred alongside Janet Leigh in *Two Tickets to Broadway* (Kern, 1951), the story of a group of performers trying to get on a TV show. It combines a rising-star narrative à la *A Star Is Born* (through the character of Betty, named after the character of Betty Schaefer in *Sunset Blvd.* but maybe also Bette Davis who starred in *The Star* in addition to *All About Eve* [Mankiewicz, 1950], of course) with an art-versus-industry subplot à la *Contempt* (through the character of Adam), thus revisiting the first Hollywood backstudio picture cycle via the European art cinema's take on the second cycle. The parallel narratives promise to merge quite happily through the "This Is the Girl" motif [30:25–33:20]: the producers want to force Adam to cast a young blond actress in his new movie, but the narration's attention to Betty's ambition and talent seems to suggest that she might, in fact, be the girl. The narratives intersect a little over halfway through the film when Betty, following a successful audition for another movie, visits the set of Adam's film [1:22:11–1:27:20]. But although the actress's and the director's gazes meet, as a series of extreme close-ups edited in eyeline match indicate, Adam has already made his "choice" and their paths will not cross— at least not in this part of the film. An anti-*Day for Night*, *Mulholland Dr.* emphasizes the complex economic and political forces working behind the scenes (with studio executive Ray Hott answering to the enigmatic and apparently omnipotent[85] Mr. Roque, who is assisted by a nameless manservant [34:40–36:10]) and threatening to compromise the young director's artistic, physical and moral integrity. The scene on Adam's set only serves to certify that the driving power behind his movie will be money (embodied by one of the Castigliane brothers) and that Adam has given up on the idea that he is the one, in the Cowboy's words, "driving the buggy" [1:08:00]. As in *Sunset Blvd.*, the industry's moral corruption is expressed through film noir conventions (Betty and Rita will discover a woman's corpse [1:35:25]), which culminate in a Gothic final act in which Rita has taken on a name (Camilla) reminiscent of Sheridan LeFanu's famous 1872 vampire.[86]

Mulholland Dr. asserts its fictionality by combining three non-mimetic models typical of diegetic metafiction according to Hutcheon: detective (Betty and Rita the amnesiac's investigation into the latter's identity), fantasy (the first three-quarters of the film are generally interpreted as Diane Selwyn's dream) and play (performance, of course, but also the intertextual play). The three are intertwined—Betty and Rita play at being detectives, the dream is full of signs to be deciphered, the workings of the game remain a mystery—and thereby elaborate the hermeneutic dynamics the film invites us to take part in by making sense of the signs. The film's view of itself as a puzzle is epitomized by the blue cube Betty finds in her bag at the Club Silencio [1:52:14]. Compared to Pandora's box, a Rubik's cube or the cube that serves as an interdimensional portal in *Hellraiser* (Barker, 1987),[87] the blue cube precipitates us into another Hollywood story and thus appears to reveal the subjectivity controlling the narration: Diane Selwyn's unconscious mind. The blue box reappears at the end of the film in the hands of the person behind Winkie's [2:18:10], this time to unleash the forces that will bring about Diane's death (again, presumably originating from her own unconscious mind) and thus the film's ending. In addition to this metanarrative function, the cube also represents the suture between the original television pilot and the feature-length film.[88] Yet another example of what Limoges identifies as a "metaphorical" mise en abyme, the blue box is at the same time a synecdoche[89] of the film (one of its elements) and a metonymy (it contains the film). Its paradoxical nature is furthered by its association with the Silencio. Indeed, the utterance of the Italian word for silence by the Fellini-esque Blue-Haired Lady calls on the same paradox that inhabited *Contempt*: the silence following the lovers' death overlaps with the silence of creation ("silence on the set"), and Betty and Rita will live on as images, as will the film beyond the cancelation of the TV series.

Mulholland Dr. contains one particularly salient metamoment: the Silencio scene [1:44:47–1:52:13]. The scene is not a mise en abyme in the literal sense—it does not reflect the narrative proper—but it does formulate the film's theoretical principles on art and film (thus corresponding to Limoges's "metaphorical reflexivity"[90]). The show Betty and Rita watch opens with a metaperformance in which a magician comments on the illusion of the spectacle he is proposing, and notably of the sounds (a muted trumpet, thunder) that can be heard: "It's all recorded. No hay banda! It is all a tape. Il n'y a pas d'orchestre. It is an illusion." (Figure 4.4). In spite of the anti-illusionist

Figure 4.4 Mulholland Dr.: *"It's all recorded. No hay banda! It is all a tape. Il n'y a pas d'orchestre. It is an illusion." On the stage of the Silencio, a "magician" illustrates his point with some help from a "musician."*

discourse, the performance has a disquieting effect on its audience, and on Betty and Rita in particular. The magician is then followed by what appears to be an a cappella performance by Rebekah Del Rio. The ontological boundary between fiction/performance and reality is further disrupted because the real singer is playing herself—at least until her collapsing on stage reveals that she was actually miming a live performance thanks to a studio recording. The performance further proves the magician's point: Rita and Betty are brought to tears by Del Rio's cover of Roy Orbison's "Crying," which is thus endowed with a perlocutionary effect verging on the performative (it makes the listeners cry).

What is celebrated here is the mysterious power of all fiction/illusion/art (theater, song, mime, cinema) to produce powerful emotions, and it is tellingly celebrated at the margins of Hollywood, in a Latin American theater whose name is a mark of linguistic and cultural otherness, as well as a reference to a famous European art film. The cinema is evoked through its ancestors not to evoke their deaths, but rather the resilience of all art and popular entertainment—the theater and the fairground, Godard and William Castle (the audience's shaking seats)—in spite of the economic forces that control the film industry within the diegesis. This explains the Silencio's paradoxical position within the film, as a sort of Chinese box that is essentially flawed because it fails to fully frame the film. Like the blue box, it is both inside (the Silencio scene) and outside (the epilogue); it is both content and recipient. The Silencio sequence is thus an instance of the Deleuzian crystal-image, an image whose actual image cannot be told apart from its virtual image.[91] As such, it epitomizes (again like the blue cube) the unknowability of the subjectivity governing the film. In spite of its darkness, the sequence is full of light; it is celebratory. And its depiction of a powerful intermedial performance makes a case against Walter Benjamin's "loss of the aura" thesis.[92] Reproducible art forms, whether musical or audiovisual, the scene demonstrates, have an aura of a different nature, one that remains connected to the work in spectral form; they are haunted by a subjectivity (such as the ghost of Mexican lore, the Llorona, Del Rio is compared to[93])—an argument renewed in the haunted film-within-the-film premise of *Inland Empire* and in *Twin Peaks: The Return* (Showtime, 2017) (see Chapter 9). Moreover, part of the power of reproducible art derives from the fact that it offers material that can be refashioned. In this respect, the Silencio sequence upholds a view in accordance with the tenets of postmodernist fiction, themselves inherited from avant-garde practices, which may explain why *Mulholland Dr.* closes with a reference to Godard but opens with images reminiscent of both the audition scene in *Contempt* and of the lesser-known *Global Groove*[94] (Nam June Paik, 1973) [0:22–1:45].

These seminal movies about making movies display a knowingness of cinema that involves the thematization of the tension between economics and art at the heart of the industry as much as their place within film history, and more specifically within the history of the movie-about-making-movies genre. Indeed, each film builds its narrative and representation of the industry by tapping into the conventions and imagery provided by its predecessors, sometimes even referencing them. In so doing, these works not only foreground the artifice, but assert a view of fiction as play that is characteristic of metafiction. The meta-level of such films is bustling with activity and invites further considerations than current scholarship has recognized. The conflict between opposing forces becomes a metanarrative stake through their attempt to control the narrative and sometimes even the narration. The investigation of filmmaking makes way for a reflection on the medium's materiality and ontology, suggesting that the aura of film may lie in the spectral quality of the trace; the underlying question is whether or not film and other recorded media have the potential to become art. What these movies highlight is, then, the contingency of film in spite of its reproducibility, which is not synonymous with immortality—the film and star can only exist with an audience. These films make a case for the continued relevance of the formalist tenet that the power of film derives from its failure to perfectly reproduce the world.[95] And, unlike Ames, they do not view the celebration of art as incompatible with a critique of the industry, for it is film, not the industry, that is redeemed.

ALLEGORIES OF THE FILM AND MEDIA INDUSTRY (*WESTWORLD*)

The tension between art and economics is equally central to works that are not situated within the film industry but within other branches of the entertainment industry, whether theater (*All About Eve*, *Birdman*), music (*A Star Is Born*[96] [Cukor, 1950; Pierson, 1976; Cooper, 2018], *La La Land* [Chazelle, 2016]), reality TV (*The Truman Show* [Weir, 1998], *The Cabin in the Woods*), games (*Battle Royale I* and *II* [Fukasaku, 2000, 2003], the *Hunger Games* franchise [2012–15], *Ready Player One* [Spielberg, 2018], *Squid Game*) and theme parks (*Westworld* [Crichton, 1973; HBO, 2016–], the *Jurassic Park* [1993–2001]/*Jurassic World* [2015–22] franchises). The analogy is grounded not only in the kinship between one medium and another, but in the structural relations between the various branches of the entertainment industry. Such relations have always existed (artists and producers moving from vaudeville to cinema; actors, writers and directors going back and forth between Broadway and Hollywood), but have been exacerbated since the dawn of media conglomerates in the 1960s. In a work of fiction, this structural underpinning establishes metonymic relations that are fertile terrain for metaphor and allegory. Such works raise a series of questions: Do they portray the tension between industry and creativity in similar terms as the movie about making movies? How are connections with other media established? Diegetically, metaphorically, both? What does the allegory allow that the actual representation would not? And finally do their concerns go beyond the state of the industry? I have chosen to focus on the theme park as allegory of audiovisual fiction in *Jurassic Park* (1993) and HBO's *Westworld*.

Jurassic Park chooses a fairly direct tack to construct the theme park as an allegory of cinema. In the age of media conglomerates, the theme park represents a synecdoche of the entertainment industry and coexists in the same ecosystem as film and other media. Technology and economics are intertwined in the basic premise and the subplot, which ultimately takes over the main one: a theme park, run by John Hammond, has succeeded to clone dinosaurs, and its insurance company is having the project vetted by three scientists (Dr. Grant, Dr. Sattler and Dr. Malcolm) in order to assess risks and thus viability, while a sneaky employee (Dennis) conspires to make a killing selling dinosaur embryos to a rival company. The theme park's value turns out to be more economic than scientific. The film (like the novel) establishes a parallel between computer sciences and biology: both rest on a belief in the mastery of codes (whether bits or DNA). The creation of the dinosaurs—and thus of the film's images—is "thematized" within the film, as Alain Boillat has noted, the film's scientist having used computer technology to reconstruct dinosaur DNA, much like the film's special effects team.[97] The theme park and the film are both showcases for technology, and *Jurassic Park* (1993) can, in Boillat's words, be seen as "a mise en abyme of the film industry's uses of technology."[98]

But the theme park mirrors *Jurassic Park* only so far. If the fiction film is likewise an economic enterprise meant to capitalize on the spectacle enabled by modern technology (animatronics, CGI), it proposes to interrogate the ethics of such a fantasy and contests the idea that a fictional world is a perfectly contained ecosystem with which audiences cannot interact. Hammond and his staff make the mistake of treating the scientists like ordinary viewers, expected to sit quietly through the promotional film, observe the private sector scientists at work, and enjoy the self-driving jeep tour. And yet, Grant, Sattler and Malcolm are not neophyte observers, such as the visitors of Grant's excavation site in the film's third scene [5:20–9:10]; they are informed ones, who constantly breach the boundaries of the tour, express intellectual curiosity, and call into question Hammond's project in scientific, logical and ethical terms. At the lunch table, Malcolm delivers a Promethean

Industry and Creation 85

warning ("Yeah, but your scientists were so preoccupied with whether or not they could that they didn't stop to think about if they should" [36:07]), and Sattler criticizes Hammond and his team for making decisions based purely on aesthetics ("I mean you have plants in this building that are poisonous; you picked them because they look good" [37:04]). The informed viewer will not immerse him- or herself so totally as to abandon all rational and moral thinking. The point is driven in when Sattler and Grant examine a sick triceratops [49:52–52:07]: two modes of spectatorship—passive immersion and informed engagement—are distributed between Grant who admits the triceratops was his favorite dinosaur as a child, and Sattler who immediately hypothesizes that Hammond's team did not pay sufficient attention to the creature's environment. The theme park's "target audience" [38:08], the term Hammond uses to describe his nephews Lex and Tim, will not be entirely subjected to the spectacle either. Tim is an intelligent child who has read Dr. Grant's book as well as those of his rivals [39:18], and even his sister Lex, the prototypical naive viewer who knows next to nothing about dinosaurs, turns out to have a trick or two up her sleeve thanks to her computer skills [1:53:00]. The image of the T-Rex breaking through the glass roof of the children's jeep [1:06:00] may encapsulate the power of the technological/realist/Bazinian illusion, but the violation of "spectatorial space" and imposition of a form of passive spectatorship onto the characters[99] is only a momentary horror/delight (Figure 4.5). *Jurassic Park* expresses faith in the audience's ability to enjoy the spectacular ride and respond to its underlying

Figure 4.5 Jurassic Park: *the T-Rex's jaws burst through the jeep's window, assaulting Lex and Tim, the film's target audience, and metaphorically breaking the fourth wall.*

ethical implications; the critique of the industry is thus counterbalanced by a basic faith not so much in technological magic and art as in humanity.

Also a Michael Crichton adaptation, HBO's *Westworld* updates the 1973 film to the age of globalized media conglomerates, digital and transmedia, expanding on the range of the *Jurassic Park* franchise. The series maintains the 1973 premise—all is well in *Westworld*, a theme park in which guests can become the heroes of a "real-life" Western, until the android hosts go berserk—but the perspective is broadened (the 1973 film follows two guests in *Westworld* and a secondary character in Medievalworld) to focus in equal measure on the guests (Logan and especially William/the Man in Black), the hosts (mainly Dolores Abernathy and Maeve Millay), park management (Robert Ford, his assistant Bernard Lowe and company representatives, Theresa Cullen and Charlotte Hale) and other worlds (Shogunworld and The Raj in season 2, Warworld in season 3). The expansion allows the series to explore consumerism, creation and the politics of production in equal measure, as well as the nature of fiction.

Borrowing from Mark J.P. Wolf's terminology,[100] Giulia Taurino and Sara Casoli have described the diegetic park as a "meta-world" (i.e., a narrative based on the building of an imaginary world), but is this enough for the series itself to qualify as meta? HBO's *Westworld* is an elaborate palimpsest, its secondariness as a remake redoubling its secondariness as a movie-based theme park. Like the 1973 film, the series reprises Western tropes and casts Ed Harris, lead actor and director of the 2008 Western *Appaloosa*, in the role of the Man in Black, previously held by Yul Brynner, star of *The Magnificent Seven* (Sturges, 1960). The series also recycles names, lines and shots from classics of the genre and Western folklore in general: Clementine Pennyfeather brings to mind *My Darling Clementine* (Ford, 1946), as does the lateral shot of a villain leaning back in his chair like the 1946 Wyatt Earp[101] in episode S1E3, which is reflexively cued on the phrase "Pretty as a picture" [23:22]; the doorframe shot of Dolores and the Man in Black in S1E10 recalls *The Searchers* (Ford, 1956) [3:51]; episode S1E3 quotes the famous line, "When the legend becomes fact, print the legend," from *The Man Who Shot Liberty Valance* (Ford, 1962) [36:37]; the town of Sweetwater is named after the McBain farm in *Once Upon a Time in the West* (Leone, 1968); and in S1E6, Teddy mows down a group of soldiers with a machine gun, much like the 1966 Django (Corbucci, 1966) [42:09].

Episode S1E6 strays into familiar movie-about-making-movies territory when Maeve goes behind-the-scenes and observes the creation of the hosts, a discovery that climaxes with a mise en abyme when she faces a wide screen promoting *Westworld* with previously seen images of the park's narratives that are also Western clichés (Figure 4.6) [21:15–22:11]. Positioned like the

Figure 4.6 Westworld: *after witnessing the creation of hosts backstage, Maeve comes face to face with the theme park's promotional video, featuring Western cliché images of her life.*

1973 guests who watch promotional material aboard a train on the way to the park, Maeve is thus not only discovering that her reality, she and the other hosts are simulacra, and that these images of their lives are marketing material, but that their world is entirely modeled on a genre that is itself a mythologization of historical reality. And yet, the series's numerous intertextual references also foreground the secondariness of the "real world" itself. Human characters are named after movie characters (Logan after the eponymous hero of the science fiction movie *Logan's Run* [Anderson, 1976]) or historical people related to the West and the Western (the name Robert Ford combines that of the most famous US-American director of Westerns with that of the real-life outlaw who betrayed Jesse James). And if episode S1E1 has a host quoting lines from Shakespeare's *The Tempest*, *Henry IV Part II*, *King Lear* and *Romeo and Juliet*,[102] it is Robert Ford himself who quotes the line from his namesake's *The Man Who Shot Liberty Valance*. These references suggest that potentially everything and everybody is a simulacrum in *Westworld*, whose premise thus exploits the poststructuralist tenet that reality itself is a construct. Theoretical self-consciousness is displayed in episode titles that bear on the history of art and entertainment (S2E10 "The Passenger" recalls Michaelangelo Antonioni's 1975 film and Iggy Pop's 1977 song) and on the concepts it engages with (S1E1 "The Original," S1E4 "Dissonance Theory," S1E7 "Trompe l'Œil," S3E5 "Genre," S3E6 "Decoherence," S3E8 "Crisis Theory"). The HBO series wears both its cinematic and theoretical credentials on its sleeves.

The series's structure is characteristic of what Hutcheon calls diegetic metafiction, with main arcs based on game, fantasy and detective models. The hosts' new behavior is a problem to be solved for the park managers, their identity a mystery to the hosts themselves. *Westworld* is a wish-fulfillment fantasy for its guests, but becomes a horror movie when the hosts turn against them in S1E10; it is a "hideous fiction" for hosts like Maeve who achieve consciousness [S1E9, 4:50]. The semantic field of play is especially present in lines spoken by the Man in Black [S1E4, 25:54], Logan [S1E5, 6:57] and Bernard [S2E4, 12:26], and is explicitly referred to in certain episode titles (S2E4 "The Riddle of the Sphinx," S3E7 "Passed Pawn"). For the Man in Black especially, *Westworld* is a "meta-game"[103] whose maze constitutes its "deepest level" [S1E2, 14:15], and in the season 1 finale, Ford reveals to Bernard that his partner Arnold's creation was, indeed, based on an actual toy maze [S1E10, 1:07:03]. The hosts themselves resemble video game characters made flesh: a "codebase" specifies their character "attributes" [S1E6, 48:30]; their memories are experienced as audiovisual narratives that can be paused [S1E9, 14:31]; and their creators even experimented with a form of "interior monologue" to endow them with consciousness [S1E9, 41:18]. The hosts are not just pawns but "games" (Maeve again [S1E9, 23:14]), fictions and intertexts unto themselves; they are at once synecdoches and metonyms of the theme park—one element of the whole, and some like Kissy even contain the map of the maze [S1E2, 14:03].

In a theme park where ontological boundaries are already precarious—the guests are both users and viewers,[104] while the hosts are performers who are unaware they are performing[105]—season 1 relates the toppling of other dichotomies: between human and robot, guest and host, guest and producer (the Man in Black turns out to be both [S1E10, 32:50]), character and creator (Maeve decides it's "time to write [her] own fucking story" [S1E8, 9:20]). Holding it together (in season 1 at least) is the figure of the auteur/director/showrunner, Ford, whose "new narrative" for the theme park increasingly becomes the underlying backbone: the park managers may be losing control of the hosts, but the company is also losing control of the mad scientist creator who, Cullen confides to Bernard in S1E4, is "creating chaos" [38:07]. An artist whose work is celebrated for its aesthetics (in S1E1, Bernard marvels at the beauty of the hosts' "new gestures, the reveries" [22:13]), Ford is, like Fritz Lang or Adam Kesher, pitted against the economic forces that constrain his work. In S1E6, Cullen tells Sizemore that Ford will lose his position if he fails to pull off his new narrative [27:05], and in S1E7 Cullen's superior Hale asks her to take action against Ford who "is suddenly using half the park's resources to build some new narrative" [11:20]. Confident that he will regain the upper hand as always, Ford eliminates Cullen at the end of S1E7 [52:16]. The dominion of economics is patent in the host's design, which, the Man in Black explains, is "cost effective" [S1E5, 12:58], a state of things that enables the rogue host Maeve, programmed to be an "entrepreneur," to out-negotiate her adversaries [S1E6, 50:10]. Thus, the theme park is the site of a power struggle that has equivalents in other sectors of the entertainment industry: unruly showrunners must be put in their place, and their narratives, like films and shows, must be cost-effective in order to turn a profit (some of the problems originate in the recycling of hosts in other roles). The narrative is based on the very tension that is at the heart of many movies about making movies: the battle between art and capital. This tension is epitomized through the Man in Black's arc: although the "titan of industry" [S1E8, 46:55] enjoys complete mastery of the park economically speaking, its full aesthetic potential, or so he believes, continues to elude him. As in the movie about making movies, the series celebrates art as that which transcends economics in spite of its depending on the latter.

The series also ventures into considerations of the functions of fiction and what makes good fiction in the first place. In S1E2, Ford gives a lesson in narrative building to the younger Sizemore, who is reprimanded by his peer for orchestrating a sensationalistic bloodbath:

> It's not about giving the guests what *you* think they want. [. . .] The guests don't return for the obvious things we do, the garish things. They come back because of the subtleties, the details. They come back because they discover something they imagine no one had ever noticed before, something they've fallen in love with. They're not looking for a story that tells them who they are. They already *know* who they are. They're here because they want a glimpse of who they could be. [55:08–56:11]

The master's lesson suggests that audiences are not seeking sensationalistic formulas to satisfy their baser drives; they are thirsty for layered works of fiction rife with aesthetic and ethical potential—"[l]ies that [tell] a deeper truth," as Ford puts it during his speech in the season 1 finale [S1E10, 1:23:00], and that speak to the intellect and the sensible—and they return not so much for immersion as for the hermeneutic game. A worthy fiction is, therefore, a fiction that invites rediscovery beyond the genre clichés it apparently dishes out. Thus, the tension at the heart of the narrative is not just one between economics and aesthetics: it is ideological and ethical: the producers want a super-product they can control, and that will in turn give them control over the guests, as season 2 will confirm, whereas the artist is driven by a Promethean ambition to create a new world in his image (Arnold "said that great artists always hid themselves in their work." [S1E6, 37:58])—a world that will ultimately become autonomous and outlive its maker—and thus to create the ultimate metafiction in which not only the players but even the characters themselves are invited to contribute to.

Westworld, like *Jurassic Park*, is a metonym for the series itself, as the shared title and logo suggests (Wolf's "intracomposition metareference"); more generally, it is a reflection on contemporary serial fiction (Wolf's "extracomposition metareference"). In the age of digital, Internet and transmedia, the narratives of television series,[106] video games and movie franchises unfold spatially across media and platforms. The Man in Black, Taurino and Casoli argue, embodies the viewer "drawn in by the complex serial narrative" of a series like *Westworld*.[107] The park designer, like the game designer or showrunner, is a "narrative architect,"[108] and the park managers (who resembled workers in a production control room in 1973) are now equipped with 3D maps. Ford's new narratives are like new character or season arcs, and the hosts' identities can be rebooted like a comics or movie franchise. The ethical stakes raised by the series's central theme of posthumanity are thus intertwined with the questioning of the boundaries of the creator's agency, as well as that of his creations and audiences. If season 1 literalizes the metafictional conceit of the characters' emancipation from the fiction,[109] season 2 reveals that the theme park was, for the company at least, more about the guests than the hosts [S2E2, 33:30]. HBO's *Westworld* is thus a cautionary tale regarding the modern audiences' apparently increased agency: the point of the game remains economic control, and the consumer's agency remains illusory. *Westworld*'s puzzle narrative is an allegory of the interconnectedness of both the industry and its products, its ideology and its aesthetics, and both a showcase and a critique of its own efficacy—a precarious, but no doubt strategic, balancing act to say the least.

Conclusion

Movies about making movies are meta at its most obvious. They dramatize the tension between aesthetic and economic imperatives, sometimes on a metanarrative level, and regularly redeem the latter through the former. Such films interrogate the industry and its history, criticizing the industry's founding myths but sometimes promoting it as a brand, all the while inscribing themselves within the history of the genre. They can also invite interpretations that are more covertly meta, offering theoretical insights into the ontology of the medium, and the limits and power of reproducible arts. Such concerns are similarly dramatized in works centered on other components of the entertainment industry that establish an analogical relationship with film and television. The interest of such allegories is threefold: they can

(1) generalize (what is true of one medium or branch of the entertainment industry is potentially true of another), but they can also foreground (2) the differences between media and sectors, and/or (3) the interconnectedness between them (that is, the metonymical relations the allegory is founded on in the first place). Though such structural connections have always existed, they are less evident in the movie about making movies. And they appear particularly potent and dynamic in the age of media conglomerates and transmedia storytelling. These allegories of the film and entertainment industry bring to light certain evolutions of the formal, ontological and ethical questions raised by metafiction: Where does the fiction end? Where does the frontier between creator and consumer lie? And wherein lies agency? Such questions, we shall now see, have always been central to works that thematize or allegorize questions of spectatorship.

CHAPTER 5

Apparatus and Spectatorship

MOVIES ABOUT MOVIE-GOING

Movies about movie-going are less common than movies about filmmaking, and even in famous instances such as *The Purple Rose of Cairo* and *Cinema Paradiso* (Tornatore, 1988), going to the movies is often the premise to something else (an adventure, a relationship). Unlike movie-making, it does not appear to provide a self-sufficient plot. There are, however, plenty of movies and series featuring scenes in which characters watch movies or shows in a movie theater or on TV.

Such scenes are common in movies about making movies, as Christopher Ames has noted,[1] whether screenings of finished films or series (*Sunset Blvd.*, *The Player*, *Barton Fink*, *Once Upon a Time . . . in Hollywood*) or of unreleased material (*Contempt*, *Day for Night*, *Blow Out*, *The Player*, *A Cock & Bull Story*). They frequently dramatize the two competing views of cinema as consumer product or art, already discussed in Chapter 4, a dichotomy that often overlaps with Hollywood versus art or independent cinema. In *The Player*, producer Griffin Mill goes to a screening of *The Bicycle Thieves* (De Sica, 1948), which he concedes is a "great movie," but he is more interested in tracking down his would-be stalker among the members of the audience than in enjoying the Italian neorealist classic's final scenes [28:14–30:10]; as for the last film-within-the-film, this one an invention, the screening of the final edit of *Habeas Corpus* [1:46:49–1:50:48] reveals that British screenwriter Tom Oakley gave in to the producers and accepted the stars (Julia Roberts and Bruce Willis) and happy ending he so adamantly rejected when pitching the film in the first place [1:14:04]. Such scenes also illustrate Rick Altman's point that film producers act as critics, analyzing the movie in order to improve their product and sometimes to reproduce an earlier success.[2] In *Barton Fink*, the eponymous playwright is required to study the rushes of a wrestling movie to get a better grip on the film genre whose conventions he is expected to abide by [56:33–57:47]. Watching rushes is generally presented as an active type of spectatorship, an integral part of the creative process, in which members of the audience discuss the film's merits or defects (*Contempt*, *Day for Night*, *Blow Out* and *A Cock & Bull Story*).

The two other staple movie-about-movie-making scenes that dramatize spectatorship are the audition and shooting (*Sunset Blvd.*, *The Star*, *Contempt*, *Day for Night*, *Body Double*, *Living in Oblivion*, *Ed Wood*, *Mulholland Drive*, *Inland Empire*, *One Cut of the Dead*, *Once Upon a Time . . . in Hollywood*). Such scenes particularly trouble the border between creation and reception. Many insist on the magic—and its precariousness (you only have one shot at an audition)—that can occur during moments when the performance seems to become "real," that is, gives birth to a distinct fictional world in spite of the diegetic audience's presence within the same space. Such scenes not only highlight the artifice but are rife with metaperformative and metafictional potential. Unlike screening scenes, the focus generally remains on the performance itself, while the diegetic audience mainly reflects our own position; Betty, in *Mulholland Dr.*, is congratulated for her performances, even if a more critical viewer like Bob Brooker the director offers a word of advice. It is, yet again, the power of fiction that is celebrated in such scenes. And even a movie like *Ed Wood*, which presents counterexamples with numerous upsets on the set that prevent the fictional world from coalescing except in the diegetic director's overenthusiastic imagination, seems to suggest that there is poetry to be found in these embarrassing moments.

In works that do not belong to the movie-about-making-movies genre, movie- and television-watching scenes are often justified by the presence of a character that is a projectionist (*Sherlock Jr.*, *Goodbye, Dragon Inn* [Tsai Ming-liang, 2003]) or, more frequently, a cinephile and/or television fan: the film critic and *Casablanca* (Curtiz, 1942) lover of *Play It Again, Sam* (Ross, 1972); the young cinephile of *The Long Day Closes* (Davies, 1992); the martial arts movie fans of *True Romance* (Tony Scott, 1993) and *Augustin, roi du kung-fu* (Fontaine, 1999); Tony Soprano, the Gary Cooper-lover, in *The Sopranos* (HBO, 1999–2007); the boy who wants to own a movie theater in *Cinema is a Miracle* (Başaran, 2005); the *Saturday Night Fever*-obsessed protagonist of *Tony Manero* (Larraín, 2008); aspiring director Abed Nadir in *Community*. They also occur in countless films and series in which the act appears less central to the plot: *Amarcord* (Fellini, 1973), *Taxi Driver* (Scorsese, 1976), *Halloween* (Carpenter, 1978), *Coup de torchon* (Tavernier, 1980), *Gremlins* (Dante, 1984), *Arizona Dream* (Kusturica, 1993), *In the Mouth of Madness* (Carpenter, 1995), the *Scream* movies (Craven, 1996–2011), *Au-delà de Gibraltar* (Barman and Boucif, 2001). If watching movies or TV is not necessarily central to television drama—notable exceptions include *Twin Peaks* (ABC, 1990–1) and *The Sopranos*—I doubt there is a single family sitcom, from *All in the Family* (CBS, 1971–9) to *Married . . . with Children* (Fox, 1987–97), *The Simpsons* and

Community, in which these activities are not presented as important pastimes that merit their own standalone episodes (S2E13 of *The Simpsons*, S9E12–13 of *Married . . . with Children*, S1E15 of *Community*).

If case studies of the above-cited films and series exist and occasionally touch on the movie/television-watching scenes, no book-length study on the subject currently exists. Spectatorship has, however, been one of the central concerns of film studies, at least since Hugo Münsterberg's 1916 *The Photoplay: A Psychological Study*. The effect watching a movie has on its spectator has regularly been compared to a dream (Baudry 1975) or hypnosis (Bellour 2009). Screen theory (Baudry 1970, Mulvey 1975, Metz 1977) posited a passive spectator subjected to the film on screen and, more disquietingly, to its underlying ideology, which was presumed to be capitalist and patriarchal in the majority of narrative and especially Hollywood films. Influenced by a diversity of approaches (cultural studies, feminism, history, sociology, cognitive psychology), theories of spectatorship of the 1980s countered the tenets of apparatus theory by demonstrating that viewers were anything but passive. The spectator actively participates in the establishing of space, time and action, and in the interpretation of basic plot elements (Bordwell 1985). While cognitive studies emphasized the universal activities involved in spectatorial response (Tan 1996), identity politics and sociology have insisted on the diversity of possible responses and interpretations, and on how actual reception depends on many elements outside the film itself (Bobo 1988, Staiger 1992). Recent studies have foregrounded the "perverseness"[3] or "unpredictability"[4] of audiences' reactions and insisted on how they could "negotiate"[5] meaning in unexpected ways. The idea(l) of a lone spectator has further been disproven by studies that shed light on the social and sometimes even ritualistic functions fulfilled by movie-going, proving that going to the movies involves much more than just watching a film (Stokes 2012). As Judith Mayne put it, historical studies have proven that "the experience of film viewing has involved a unique and specific combination of individual fantasy and social ritual."[6] The emphasis on ritual and group behaviors led to the emergence of fan studies in the 1990s, with seminal works by Camille Bacon-Smith and Henry Jenkins in 1992.[7]

This chapter explores how certain metamoments invite us to theorize questions of spectatorial response and audience reception. It mirrors the trajectory of Chapter 4 by starting with the explicit thematization of spectatorship before moving on to more allegorical approaches; it also spotlights the more specific case of metalepses in which characters from the "real" world and the film-within-the-film come to meet. It aims to show how the analysis of scenes that thematize or allegorize movie and television consumption may uncover views on spectatorship that echo and sometimes anticipate the theories of spectatorship formalized by film and media studies, and even illustrate the way such theories can contest or complement each other. In so doing, such metamoments confirm one of the fundamental features of metafiction according to Hutcheon and Waugh:[8] that the blurring of the boundary between creation and reception, reader/viewer and artist, demonstrates that consuming fiction is by no means a passive activity, thus rejoining the arguments of contemporary film theory. In an audiovisual medium, the blurring between the figures of the director and spectator is exacerbated. The hesitation between creation and reception is patent in the central concept of 1970s film theory, the "apparatus" (*dispositif* in French), which was theorized as a situation whereby a spectator is watching moving images captured by a director's camera. The collapsing of reception and creation was an effect of the pride of place given to the gaze, in which the human gaze (of the director and the spectator) came to be confused with the technological gaze (of the camera or projector). If film scholarship has since disproven many tenets of apparatus theory, the metamoments studied below suggest that the analogy between making and watching audiovisual fictions, or between filmmaker and spectator, was relevant long before the 1970s and continues to be so today.

MOVIE-GOING AS RITUAL (*CINEMA PARADISO*)

The majority of movies seem to cultivate the view of movie-watching as a dream-like state of immersion (the projectionist's dream in *Sherlock Jr.*; the rapt fascination on Allan's face while watching *Casablanca* in *Play It Again, Sam*) and of fandom as obsession and delusion (*Play It Again, Sam*'s Allan seeks counsel in love from Bogart; *Arizona Dream*'s Paul Leger tries to mimic Cary Grant's and Al Pacino's performances in *North by Northwest* [Hitchcock, 1959] and *The Godfather Part II* [Coppola, 1974]; Augustin believes he has mastered kung fu from watching kung fu movies; and in *Cult*, the eponymous TV show's fans confuse the performers with their characters and partake in dangerous games). Not including more exceptional cases in which the protagonist is a film critic or censor (*Play It Again, Sam*, *Escape from the "Liberty" Cinema*), many viewing scenes portray active viewers who analyze, provide context for, and sometimes even critique the film or show they have watched (the man waiting in line criticizing Fellini's previous films in *Annie Hall* [Allen, 1977]), are going to watch (Clarence Worley shares his encyclopedic knowledge of Sonny Chiba films with his date in *True Romance*) or are watching (the eponymous director and Bela Lugosi in *Ed Wood*; the protagonists leading an investigation in *Ring* [Nakata, 1998] and *Cult*; Doctor Darcy Lewis studying the eponymous sitcom in S1E4–6 of *WandaVision*). Emphasis is sometimes put on the social dimension of movie-going and on the group behaviors it elicits (in *Amarcord*, it is the teenage boy's approach of a mature woman that warrants ten shots against one of the movie hero on screen [38:31–39:34]; the 1984 Gremlins behave like a hyper-enthusiastic crowd, keen to consume popcorn and soda and trash the movie theater while singing along to a screening of Disney's 1937 *Snow White and the Seven Dwarfs* [1:22:49–1:26:23]; the prologue of *Scream 2* [0:08–11:40], with its loud, costumed audience, depicts the ritual of watching cult movies as popularized by screenings of *The Rocky Picture Show* [Sharman, 1975] in the 1980s and 1990s). Watching television is represented along similar lines—as solitary immersion (Paul in *Arizona Dream*, Don Grga Pitić watching *Casablanca* [Curtiz, 1942] in *Black Cat, White Cat* [Kusturica, 1998] or Tony Soprano watching *Rio Bravo* in episode S4E1 of *The Sopranos*) or social event (the party at Stuart's in the 1996 *Scream*, the get-together in Abed's room to revel in exploitation fare like *Kickpuncher* in episode S1E15 of *Community*), but its central position in domestic space also allows it to function as a backdrop, with dramatic and ironic potential, even in the absence of a diegetic audience (in *Halloween*, *Scream* and *Funny Games* (Haneke, 1997), the TV sets remain on throughout the violence). Recent series (*Supernatural*[9], episode S3E1 of *Sherlock* [BBC, 2010–17], *The Flash* [The CW, 2014–]) have thematized their own fandom by representing fan communities.

Cinema Paradiso may be the most memorable example of a film whose movie-going scenes focus as much on the audience as on an individual spectator. And this in spite of its canonical narrative centered on the relationship between a boy named Totò, whose father, we (and he) eventually learn, died in World War II, and the local projectionist, Alfredo. The two come together because of their shared loved of movies (Totò cannot imagine a more idyllic occupation than working as a projectionist), and the father–son relationship that ensues is couched in cinephilia, much of Alfredo's worldly wisdom coming from Hollywood films, which he cites on two occasions (Spencer Tracy in Fritz Lang's 1936 *Fury* [48:39], John Wayne in Henry Hathaway's 1941 *The Shepherd of the Hills* [1:08:45]). Yet the eponymous movie theater is shown to be not just the heart of their relationship; it is a central locus in the life of the Sicilian town of Giancaldo. The emphasis on audience as community and movie-watching as ritual is evident in the *Cinema Paradiso*'s location—right on the town square—and in the repeated portrayal of screenings (nine in all, including a five-minute-long montage sequence [18:31–23:08] and a seven-minute-long one [58:07–1:05:15]).

The first [9:38–12:14] and especially last [1:58:09–2:01:25] movie-watching scenes are centered on Totò (the boy and the man) and frame the bulk of the narrative; the frame is reinforced by the concluding scene's pointing back to the earlier scene, as both involve the viewing of images censored by the village priest. Yet if Totò's love of cinema is emphasized through the repetition of Woody Allenesque close-ups of him reveling in movie magic, the child increasingly becomes one spectator out of many, while other members of the audience become familiar faces through the repetition of these scenes and of shots that single them out. The shift is partly determined by Totò's change of social status and viewing position; graduating from member of the audience to assistant projectionist and finally sole projectionist, he comes to occupy a central role in the mechanics and economics of exhibition.

Like the more recent *Goodbye, Dragon Inn*,[10] *Cinema Paradiso* has logically been interpreted as a nostalgic portrayal of the "lost communities of cinemagoers."[11] The narration singles out individual responses in close shots (one man goes to the cinema just to take naps [19:54], while another utters lines of movie dialogue before the actors [1:15:20–1:16:40]) and group reactions (laughter, tears, boredom, teenagers masturbating) in very long shots and tracking shots, revealing how individual and group reactions can overlap but occasionally diverge (one bourgeois spectator finds *Stagecoach* [Ford, 1939] hardly engaging [19:44]). The extent to which the immediate social and political context affects a movie's reception is suggested through the fact that the Sicilian audience clearly favors escapist entertainment whether from Hollywood or Europe; the second montage sequence highlights how engrossed and amused the majority of the audience is while watching *Stagecoach* and Chaplin in *The Knockout* (Sennett, 1914), whereas the harsh neorealism of Luchino Visconti's *La terra trema* (1948) only inspires a torpor of sorts, its Sicilian setting presumably striking a little too close to home.

With its separation of the middle-class in the mezzanine and the working-class on the lower floor, the *Cinema Paradiso* is in itself a social space, a metonymy of the town and, as Alizera Vahdani[12] has argued, of post-World War II southern Italy. It is a place where future couples meet, the local prostitute does her business, and class tensions are played out among members of the audience (the bourgeois who regularly spits on the working-class audience below gets his comeuppance when a soiled diaper hits him square in the face during the second montage sequence [1:04:59]). Watching *Cinema Paradiso* is, for us the actual viewers, all about watching the movie theater's audience, and in this respect, the film is very much indebted to the movie-going scenes in another Italian director's portrait of his childhood town: Fellini's *Amarcord*. *Cinema Paradiso* thus celebrates the power of cinema not only to provide the orphan boy with a calling and a surrogate father,[13] but also to provide a sense of ritual to the community. The movie theater's role in the town's life is as central as the church's, so much so that it is not only presented as being contiguous to the holy institution—the narration elides the transition from one space to another [9:18]—but its being ruled by the local priest and the Virgin

Mary (present in both spaces) testifies to the potential threat the cinema poses to religious mores. The emotional, imaginary and social significance of the movie theater in Totò's and the town's life is further confirmed by the fact that the church itself is only shown in two scenes that are narratively and symbolically related to cinema: Alfredo the projectionist's funeral, of course, and before that, Totò's declaration of love to Elena, which takes place in in a confessional that, because of its screened window separating the two teenagers, recalls the cinematic apparatus [1:20:58–1:23:00].

The narrative's turning point encapsulates how intertwined the social and imaginative powers of cinema are. It occurs when Alfredo gives in to a crowd of frustrated viewers who have not been able to get in to watch *The Firemen of Viggiù* (Mattoli, 1949), by projecting the comedy on one of the town square's walls [49:11–53:00] (Figure 5.1). *The Firemen of Viggiù* operates as a mise en abyme of *Cinema Paradiso* (it features the Italian star Totò, who plays himself, and the premise involves theatrical performances in a village). The moving pictures spill out of the movie theater and thus momentarily escape their capitalist *raison d'être* (the villagers refuse to pay for the tickets even if they're 50 per cent off); it becomes, instead, the beacon at the center of the village, which it always was and will continue to be. Its powers serve to re-enchant town life, especially the lives of those hardest hit by the economic strife of post-World War II southern Italy.

Figure 5.1 Cinema Paradiso: *confronted by some upset townspeople who have been denied access to the screening of* The Firemen of Viggiù *(Mattoli, 1949), Alfredo directs the projector outside the movie theater, projecting the film onto a wall in the village square.*

Cinema Paradiso thus depicts an audience very much in line with the arguments put forward by film historians to contest the foundations of apparatus theory—noisy, and comprised of members who value the social dimensions of movie-going just as much as the movies themselves. It also endows the projectionist with a sense of agency that contradicts Alfredo's own opinion of his role: "This is no kind of job for you," he tells his young disciple, "You're like a slave ... and always alone. [...] I'm a nitwit. Who else around here could run a projector? Nobody. It takes an imbecile like me" [33:05–34:00]. Alfredo's subversive act of aiming the projection machine outside, which will, in melodramatic fashion, lead to the instigator's losing his sight, is both political and aesthetic. First, it leads to the foundation of the Nuovo Cinema Paradiso (the film's original title), a symbolic rejuvenation of both Italian society (the upper-class sitting on the balcony will no longer be safely separated from the working class below) and of Italian cinema, metonymically evoked through the projection of Fellini's 1953 *I Vitelloni*, with which Tornatore's film asserts its legacy, as Alizera Vahdani astutely points out. And yet, recalling the fairground origins of cinema and especially magic lantern shows, Alfredo's act is also creative, aesthetic and perhaps even sacred: his act simultaneously reconfigures the diegetic film, the town square's architecture, and the actual film itself, which are both fashioned into something else—a properly cinematic space on which the shapes, colors and textures playing across the surface of the image are as important as the diegetic space represented. The projectionist's creative potential is confirmed in the concluding scene when Totò enjoys Alfredo's posthumous gift, a Proustian *madeleine* comprised of images censored by the village priest, which Alfredo, like an avant-garde artist, had spliced together and refashioned into something else—we are invited to recognize these "clips *as* clips,"[14] as material that has been shaped into a work of art. Although centered on individual and group viewers, *Cinema Paradiso* celebrates not only the wealth of functions provided by movie-going, but suggests that the line between reception and creation is a thin one indeed.

ADVENTURES IN METALEPSIS (*THE PURPLE ROSE OF CAIRO*)

Many works that are commonly referred to as "meta" feature what Ames calls "screen passages,"[15] moments when "real" characters enter a film, show or fiction, or, conversely, movie or television characters cross over into diegetic reality; Fátima Chinita classifies this specifically cinematic instance of the metalepsis in her "Permeability of Worlds" category of metacinema.[16] In an attempt to refine Gérard Genette's (2004) rather tenuous proposals on metalepsis in cinema,[17] Alain Boillat (2012) and Jean-Marc Limoges (2012) have specifically defined cinematic metalepsis as a passage between a fictional and an extrafictional world, that "seems" impossible but is not since it remains a representation.[18] Limoges distinguishes between "extradiegetic" and "intradiegetic" metalepses. The former involve the violation of the boundary between diegesis and narration, and are basically instances of direct address or breaking the fourth wall.[19] The main criterion for crossings within the diegesis to qualify as "intradiegetic metalepses" involves, for Limoges, how unrealistic and thus transgressive they are within the scope of the diegesis[20] (arguably, they are less destabilizing in a work that allows for time or interdimensional travel). Boillat concludes that metalepsis "operates at once as a world-creating device and as a descriptive category to analyze certain (meta) fictional productions,"[21] notably because it can foreground the "fictional contract."[22] In other words, a metalepsis is not essentially meta but potentially so.

Less radical and more "realistic"[23] than their "extradiegetic" siblings, intradiegetic metalepses are rife with dramatic potential and often function as inciting events (*Escape from the "Liberty" Cinema*, *Last Action Hero*, *Pleasantville* [Ross, 1998], episode S6E15 of *Supernatural*), complicating actions (*Sherlock Jr.*, *The Purple Rose of Cairo*, *Inland Empire*, the end of S1E3 of *WandaVision*) or climaxes (S1E3 of *The Prisoner* [ITV, 1967–8], *In the Mouth of Madness*, *Wes Craven's New Nightmare*). They are, in effect, of the same order as staple science fiction or fantasy premises involving time-travel, multiple dimensions or the confusion between reality and dream (Boillat cites David Cronenberg's *eXistenZ* and the Wachowskis' *Matrix*, both released in 1999, as examples of metalepsis[24]). They rarely go unexplained for that matter: a dream does the trick in *Sherlock Jr.* and *The Prisoner*, a magic ticket or remote in *Last Action Hero* and *Pleasantville*, madness or supernatural phenomena in *In the Mouth of Madness*, *Wes Craven's New Nightmare* and *Inland Empire*, interdimensional travel in *Supernatural* and *The Man in the High Castle* (Amazon Prime, 2015–19), Wanda Maximoff's superpowers in *WandaVision*. *The Purple Rose of Cairo* is quite exceptional in this respect because the transgression goes unexplained[25] and is implicitly provoked by sheer desire (*Escape from the "Liberty" Cinema* follows suit). Such metalepses—and perhaps all metalepses in the end—are grounded in a fantasy structure, which, Hutcheon argues, often underlies literary metafiction, quite overtly when the transgression is diegetically justified. Regardless of whether the diegetic spectator penetrates the fiction or the fiction spills out into her or his reality, the majority of these metaleptic narratives seem to thematize the view of spectatorship as immersion, dream state, delusion or denial. They also play on another trope of science fiction and supernatural stories, one that can also be linked to the theory of relativity: the idea that each world is governed by its own laws, which may be irrelevant in another world.

By primarily focusing on an individual spectator, a Depression-era waitress named Cecilia, *The Purple Rose of Cairo* presents movie-going as an escape from economic and marital hardship,[26] with the eponymous film-within-the-film representing just the kind of screwball fare Hollywood dished out to distract the working classes of the time.[27] The film's second shot introduces the heroine in frontal close-up, gazing with quiet intensity at the poster of the week's feature movie [3:35–3:57]. As early as the second scene where she talks about cinema with her sister at the diner they work in [4:15–4:55], we find out that she attends her local movie theater, The Jewel, every week, watches her favorite movies several times, and is knowledgeable about the private lives of stars; her constant chatter about movies and stars annoys her boss, who eventually fires her when, daydreaming about a movie character, Tom Baxter, she drops the dishes one time too many [17:33]. Cecilia, like Allan Felix in *Play It Again, Sam* (written but not directed by Woody Allen), very much seems to embody the "passive" spectator subjected to the cinematic apparatus as defined by Baudry[28] and, more specifically, the "enraptured" female film-viewer.[29] The four movie-going scenes centered on Cecilia [7:32–11:52, 12:34–13:05, 17:54–20:53, 1:18:51–1:21:06] repeatedly show her watching the screen in rapt fascination (even when she is accompanied by her sister or is eating popcorn), the three-quarter angle highlighting her expression (her parted mouth and tears in the third and fourth such scenes), her gleaming skin and the white glint in her eyes produced by the screen itself, as much as the direction of her gaze (to the left and slightly upward) (Figure 5.2).

Figure 5.2 The Purple Rose of Cairo: *Cecilia, immersed in* The Purple Rose of Cairo *and bathed in the light coming from the movie screen.*

The repetition of such shots (twelve in all) demonstrates that the power of classical cinema is such that, blinded by the fiction on screen, Cecilia forgets her abusive husband Monk and, at the end, the two-timing Gil Shepherd. Although the narration offers just three shots of the other members of the audience in these scenes (all three during the first one), they are shown to be just as quietly focused on the film as Cecilia. More attention is paid to them when Tom and Cecilia exit the picture, so to speak, and the audience and film-within-the-film characters bicker; their last exchange confirms the view that movie-watching fulfills a fundamental lack when a woman explains that her husband, "a student of the human personality," is interested in movies because he has "trouble with live humans" [29:40].

Ames rightly notes that "[t]he variety of responses [in these scenes] reminds us that we cannot treat 'audience' as a unitary, easily knowable entity,"[30] and that the opening movie-going scene indicates that "the movie will include Cecilia's gaze but will not be consumed by it."[31] However, like *Play It Again, Sam*, in which the ambivalent Allan laps up an imaginary Bogart's advice while expressing doubt as to its real-world relevance ("Who am I kidding? I'm not like that. I never was, I never will be. That's strictly the movies." [4:25]), *The Purple Rose of Cairo* also suggests that immersion and obsession are not incompatible with critical distance. As early as the third scene, Cecilia proves that the cecity, or blindness, evoked in her name is by no means absolute; she is fully aware of the escapist pleasures of cinema when she invites her husband to come with her so he can "forget [his] troubles" [6:57]. Later in the film, when spending some quality time with Gil Shepherd, it turns out she can act out dialogue from a film and take on the role of film critic or agent when commending the actor for his talent: "And you're not just a pretty face, you're also a peach of an actor. Really, I've seen you, I've seen you a lot. You've got something. [. . .] You've got—oh, how can I describe it—you've got a magical glow. [. . .] I was thinking you should play some of the more heroic parts" [51:35–52:30]. And when interacting with Tom Baxter, Cecilia constantly reminds him of the difference between his fictional world and the real world—"You don't find that kind [of consistent and reliable person] in real life." [31:38]—till the very end when she turns him down: "You'll be fine. In your world, things have a way of always working out right. See, I'm a real person. No matter how tempted I am, I have to choose the real world" [1:14:06–1:14:25].

Although *The Purple Rose of Cairo*'s famous metalepsis has often been compared to *Sherlock Jr.*,[32] the two are, in fact, polar opposites: the 1924 picture starts with a projectionist's nightmare (granted on a slapstick mode), the 1985 film a fan's dream come true. The 1985 metalepsis is justified by a romantic comedy conceit and redoubled by a metafictional one: it is the combined power of Tom Baxter's love for Cecilia, desire for freedom and ambition to be the main character of the film-within-the-film that enable him to break free—although the fact that the other characters and the other Tom Baxters on screens across the US remain prisoners of their diegetic world suggests that Cecilia's "magical glow" is, in effect, the prime catalyst for this Tom Baxter's liberation (Cecilia will later confess that "[her] eye did always go to [Tom] up on the screen" [24:24]). By highlighting the trajectory of her gaze, the three-quarter close-ups of Cecilia the spectator express her intensity as much as her blindness.

The film's title and the 1935 time setting call attention to the significance of color in the film (RKO released *Becky Sharp*, the "first" feature-length color film[33] just two months before *Top Hat* [Sandrich, 1935], the movie Cecilia watches in the final scene). As in *The Wizard of Oz* (Fleming, Cukor and Leroy, 1939) and *A Matter of Life and Death* (Powell and Pressburger, 1946), the two worlds' distinctness is expressed chromatically—the black-and-white fantasy of *The Purple Rose of Cairo*, the drab colors of Cecilia's New Jersey—a use of color that, Stanley Cavell would say, "unif[ies] the projected world"[34] (in this case the two diegetic worlds), but that is not at all in keeping with classical Hollywood practice whereby color usually signified fantasy and black-and-white realism.[35] The irony, as Ames points out,[36] is that the black-and-white world of *The Purple Rose of Cairo* is more colorful and desirable than Cecilia's. And yet, Tom cannot find the "purple rose" in a black-and-white world because the flower turns out to be Cecilia. Tom manages to chromatically integrate the real world by becoming color, and Cecilia later comes to aesthetically inhabit the world of the diegetic movie (not just by becoming black and white, but by becoming an image that can be superimposed with others, as during the night-on-the-town montage sequence); Gilles Menegaldo even suggests that "the black-and-white film is vampirized by the colour film which appropriates one of its characters, feeds on its substance diegetically (through the agency of the escaped Baxter) and narratively (the adventure motif is transferred)."[37]

Tom's and later Cecilia's screen passages destabilize a series of ontological boundaries: between black-and-white and color, fiction and reality, character and actor (Shepherd and the RKO lawyers are worried the character's actions are going to ruin the actor's career), celluloid and flesh-and-blood being. Not only do the characters of the film-within-the-film break the fourth wall and converse and argue (with the audience and the RKO people) in shot/reverse shot [21:27–22:50, 25:46–26:44, 29:06–29:42, 39:16–40:40], but the positions are eventually reversed[38] when the characters, sitting in a row and facing the movie theater, end up attending their own boring show or screening, letting out such comments as: "Anything happening out there?" "Not a thing." "Life is amazing, isn't it?" [1:02:21]. The "madcap" topsy-turvy situation caused by Tom Baxter's breaking through has everything to do with the fact that he is not just a character but also a spectator. Tom remarks that he has "seen" Cecilia "before" and, later at the theme park, admits that he was "looking" at her out the corner of his eye when proposing to his romantic interest in the movie, the glamorous singer Kitty [23:45–24:13]. In effect, the metalepsis starts when Tom looks at Cecilia in the movie theater (Figure 5.3). The narration constructs the metaleptic moment not through a look to the camera, but through eyeline match and a decrease in shot size (the close-ups of Tom and Cecilia), and it is ultimately Tom's voice that drives in the transgression (Tom: "You've been here all day. And I've seen you twice here before." Cecilia: "You mean me?" Tom: "Yes, you."). The narration, more so even than the diegesis, suggests the impossible: that it is not the implied spectator Tom is looking at (and thus the whole audience), but one viewer in particular—the other characters in the audience are immediately aware that it is Cecilia who is being singled out even before he breaks out of the screen. It is as if the character and the audience already inhabited the same space in spite of the ontological boundaries imposed by the cinematic apparatus, thereby foreshadowing the fact that they will shortly share the same world. Activated by her gaze, Tom is logically Cecilia's double, a spectator who desires and idealizes the world beyond the screen. As the spectator of a spectator, Tom is also our double, that of the audience who's been watching Cecilia watching *The Purple Rose of Cairo*, which effectively positions the spectator-character at the heart of the movie.

Figure 5.3 The Purple Rose of Cairo: *Tom Baxter, "explorer extraordinaire," addresses Cecilia, "You've been here all day. And I've seen you twice here before," before stepping out of the movie/screen.*

But the self-proclaimed "explorer extraordinaire" also points to a more active form of spectatorship, that of the hermeneutist, so that underlying the film's overt metafictional fantasy is not so much a detective plot as one of exploration. Tom discovers that the laws that govern the real world are not the same, but he makes the more precise discovery—mainly because he takes his time to think about it—that there are, admittedly, some similarities; he thus reflects on the analogy between God and author on the one hand, and fiction and magic on the other, for instance when he muses to a group of prostitutes that the "miracle of birth" is what makes the real world "magical" [55:58]. As the film's metaleptic operator, Tom does more than physically bridge reality and fiction; he connects reality and fiction through his interpretations of the relationship that unites them. The metalepsis is meta because the device produces a commentary on fiction. Granted, the impact of Tom's destabilization is a fairly limited one, since the ontological separateness of reality and fiction is ultimately asserted, as Cecilia's parting words to him prove, but the movie character nonetheless succeeds in fulfilling his role—that of re-enchanting a dreary real world—even from within.

Subsequent film and television adventures in metalepsis propose variations on *The Purple Rose of Cairo*, sometimes explicitly referring to the 1985 film by including excerpts (*Escape from the "Liberty" Cinema* features a metalepsis wherein Allen's Tom Baxter penetrates the Polish film-within-the-film) or casting an actor from Allen's film (Jeff Daniels in *Pleasantville*). The Polish film reprises the basic premise of *The Purple Rose of Cairo*—the actors of the cast of a film go on strike—to formulate a critique of the Polish film industry in the 1980s, in which art films such as Woody Allen's could not see the light of day due to government intervention embodied by the protagonist, Censor Rabkiewicz;[39] the defense of artistic freedom is driven in by the ontological confusion introduced between the characters and the actors who portray them. *Last Action Hero* first inverts the premise of *Sherlock Jr.*— Danny, a young fan, is transported into the Arnold Schwarzenegger vehicle *Jack Slater IV*, his knowledge of the franchise and movies in general enabling him to be more than just a "comedy sidekick" and spoil the film from within; its final act then revisits *The Purple Rose of Cairo*, with Jack Slater discovering that his very existence is a matter of economics ("You cannot die until the grosses go down." [1:05:28]) and that his mourning his son had no higher purpose than entertainment, thus experiencing the traumatic revelation of his fictionality (a typical trope of metafiction[40]) as trauma and quasi-Shakespearean tragedy (hence the reference to *Hamlet*[41]). In *Pleasantville*, two teenage siblings, Betty and David, enter the comforting black-and-white world of a 1950s sitcom whose characters, through contact with real people, come to long for something more than their usual routine and become colorful in the process; as in the 1985 film, both worlds are re-enchanted through their impossible encounter. And in *WandaVision*, it is the superheroine, Wanda Maximoff, who, traumatized by the loss of her lover, Vision, has turned the town of Westfield into a sitcom world modeled on the sitcoms of her youth (S1E8); again, fiction is a means for the spectator-turned-creator to, first, escape hardship and, ultimately, negotiate loss.

Ames concludes that *The Purple Rose of Cairo* and *Last Action Hero* demonstrate that "the construction of meaning is a two-way screen passage: audience members complete the meanings initially constructed in an individual film, but films as a whole pass into the consciousness of viewers and shape how they watch and interpret."[42] If these cinematic adventures in metalepsis tend to dramatize the power and limits of fiction to re-enchant the world, they very much emphasize the spectator's role in making the fiction come alive—and thus in enchanting the fictional world in turn. Although the premises initially confirm the view of cinema/television as escapism and alienation, the diegetic spectators turn out to be more active and layered than meets the eye, revealing a knowledge of formal conventions and a critical sensibility, that allows them to participate in the creation. Such works posit, in effect, that the author is dead and that a fiction cannot exist without its audience; such metalepses thus dramatize the relation between fiction and reality as fundamentally intertwined. But the diegetic spectators are not the only figures of the spectator in these films. The transgression of boundaries also positions the characters of the film-within-the-films as sensitive and critical subjects who respond to the world and attempt to interpret it. Self-consciousness is thus dramatized and expressed through a model of active—and thus creative—spectatorship. The existential crises experienced by the characters of film-within-the-films also carry political and ethical implications, whereby the fictional world becomes a darker allegory of the limits of freedom.

ALLEGORIES OF SPECTATORSHIP REVISITED (*REAR WINDOW*, *BLOW-UP*, *BLOW OUT*)

There is something obvious about allegory apparently. Hutcheon lists allegory among the strategies of "overt diegetic metafiction," while Stam's *Reflexivity in Film and Literature* starts with a chapter entitled "Allegories of Spectatorship." In Chapter 2, I contested the idea that an allegory is explicit per se. What I would now like to demonstrate is how complex such allegories can be, by insisting not only on their multi-layered discourse on spectatorship, but even more so on the fact that they are not just allegories of spectatorship but of creation as well, and of the cinematic apparatus, thus confirming metafiction's tendency to draw parallels between creation and reception. Like the three movies about movie-making discussed in Chapter 4, the films analyzed—*Rear Window* (Hitchcock, 1954), *Blow-up* (Antonioni, 1966) and *Blow Out* (DePalma, 1981)—build on and respond to their predecessors and will thus be analyzed in chronological order.

Many scenes from Hitchcock's movies (*Rebecca*[43] [1940], *Vertigo* [1958],[44] *Psycho* [1960][45]) have been analyzed as reflections on spectatorship, and everybody knows that *Rear Window* is a movie about cinema. Hitchcock even admitted to Truffaut that it was his intention to "make a purely cinematic film."[46] Accordingly, the film has been received as such by critics and scholars. Writing about *Psycho* (1960) the year of its release, Jean Douchet briefly returned to the 1954 film, which "exposed Hitchcock's conception of cinema (cinema within cinema)."[47] Three decades later, Stam described the 1954 film as a "a brilliant filmic essay dealing with the nature of the cinematic experience."[48] For Douchet, Jefferies is a "Peeping Tom" who represents the double of the "Hitchcockian spectator," watching "his projection of himself."[49] The space the characters inhabit mirrors the cinematic apparatus: "Stewart is like the projector; the apartment building is the screen; the distance that separates them, the intellectual world occupied by a ray of light."[50] Stam follows Douchet by describing Jefferies as a "hidden spectator" and the diegetic setup as a mirror of the cinematic apparatus.[51] For Stam, *Rear Window* represents a paradigmatic example of an "allegory of spectatorship." The windows across the courtyard offer a variety of Hollywood genres (social realism at Miss Lonelyhearts', the musical comedy at Miss Torso's, the musical biopicture at the composer's, murder mystery at the Thorwalds');[52] Jefferies has also been compared to a "typical television viewer" switching from one channel to another.[53] Stam notes that Jefferies is also a figure of the director, who "orients the gaze, frames our vision and imposes his interpretation";[54] not only do certain POV shots reproduce the viewfinder of his camera, but he also acts like an editor when he examines the pictures he has taken [1:25:50], like a screenwriter when he writes a letter to Thorwald [1:27:59], and like a stage director when he gives instructions to his actress Lisa and his assistant Stella [1:34:30].

Rear Window has systematically been framed in discussions of reflexivity; Jean-Marc Limoges cites the movie as an example of "metaphorical reflexivity,"[55] and Daniel Yacavone as one of "environmental reflexivity" whereby "literally non-cinematic spaces metaphorically connote the spaces and conditions of filmmaking and/or film viewing."[56] And yet, it deploys strategies characteristic of both overt diegetic metafiction (the allegory, the mise en abyme) and covert diegetic metafiction (the allegory of spectatorship relies on a detective plot, while the artificiality of the decor and the thematization of sleep liken the plot to a fantasy). More so than the strategies it deploys, it is the film's discourse that makes *Rear Window* meta *avant l'heure*. What Douchet's analysis brings to the surface is an examination of the boundary between fiction and reality, the central concern of metafiction according to Waugh. Indeed, a series of ontological boundaries are proven to be problematic, including those between spectator and creator, and between creation and projection.

Following the raising of the curtains during the opening credits [0:30–1:45], the opening track-and-pan [1:46–2:24] marks the entry into fiction, one reflexive device (the theatrical curtains) erasing another (the frame-within-the-frame composition created by the window frame) and eventually dissipating as it mimics the plunge into immersion (the following shot is, in effect, a high angle). By inviting us to both identify with, and distance ourselves from, Jefferies' perspective, the elaborate camera movement not only signals that the narration's point of view will not always be aligned with the hero's,[57] but warns us against the seductions of what Metz called secondary cinematic identification (identification with the represented).[58] In this respect, *Rear Window* foreshadows *The Purple Rose of Cairo*. The film's allegory will also warn us against the temptations of primary cinematic identification (identification with the apparatus). The plot, in effect, dramatizes the difficulty of maintaining distance. The diegetic setup on which the allegory of spectatorship is founded collapses during the climax when Thorwald penetrates Jefferies's apartment [1:47:19]. Jefferies struggles in vain to uphold the apparatus by turning the lights off and plunging the room in movie-theater darkness.[59] His failure to keep the perpetrator at bay with his camera flash is foregrounded by the scene's sole POV shot from Thorwald's perspective [1:48:52]. Pointedly, the only POV shot not marked by a viewfinder, it is redoubled by a look to the camera from the perpetrator. The villain who has stepped out of the crime movie momentarily disrupts the ontological border between diegetic and real spectator, between the spatial setup and the actual cinematic apparatus through which we experience the film. The border between fantasy and reality is thus not just a theme; it is translated into an experience. *Rear Window*, like *Jurassic Park* with its T-Rex breaking through the children's jeep's window forty years later (see Chapter 4), offers a naturalized intradiegetic metalepsis, wherein the crossing of thresholds is diegetically justified but metaphorically evokes the same implications as the metalepses of *Sherlock Jr.* and *The Purple Rose of Cairo*.

More impressive, perhaps, is how relevant *Rear Window*'s allegory of spectatorship remains to this day. Not only does it propose a view of cinema that is very much of its time, it anticipates, in many respects, contemporary theories of spectatorship and reception studies. Manifest in Douchet's analysis and in my own recourse to Metz's concepts, *Rear Window* proposes an allegory of the cinematic apparatus that is largely influenced by psychoanalysis, which is logical given the presence of Freudian ideas in Hitchcock's films[60] and classical Hollywood cinema. Confined to a wheelchair, Jefferies is the spitting image of the spectator who passively consumes films or TV shows. Like *Vertigo*, *Psycho* and *Peeping Tom*, the film equates movie-watching with voyeurism as early as its first act. Jefferies's nurse Stella comments that "our species has now become Peeping Toms" [8:48] before calling her client a "window-shopper" [15:30], and Lisa compares the spectacle across the courtyard to a "premiere" requiring "tickets" [17:48]. Jefferies only belatedly comes to question his own behavior, "I wonder whether watching a man is ethical," to which Lisa replies the titular line, "I'm not an expert on rear window ethics" [1:21:10].

The nature of the spectacle is also circumscribed by a psychoanalytical framework. Each window represents a projection of Jefferies's fantasies and anxieties, each inhabitant a potential double. A young couple's probable night of lovemaking draws attention to the male protagonist's physical but maybe also psychological impotence [14:27–15:31].[61] Jefferies is moved by Miss Lonelyhearts, who, unlike him, is dining alone, and compares his fiancée Lisa to Miss Torso whose romantic interests are, he believes, motivated by economics [21:38–24:27]. And his suspicions concerning the murder of Mrs. Thorwald stem from his own "latent desire" to "get rid of" Lisa,[62] and thus to his reluctance to commit himself to their relationship: "[t]he central trajectory of *Rear Window*," Stam says, "consists in the progressive shattering of Jefferies's illusion of voyeuristic separation from life and the concomitant rendering possible of mature sexuality with Lisa."[63] The film is clearly underpinned by the logic of fantasy: Jefferies's desires come true. This logic reaches its climax when the protagonist utters a quasi-performative statement: "A man is assaulting a woman," he tells the police on the phone [1:39:42]. The use of the progressive form indicates that the event is already happening in Jefferies's mind, and it is only after this utterance that Thorwald starts pushing Lisa around. Recalling the title of Freud's 1919 article on sadomasochism, "A Child Is Being Beaten," the line encapsulates the film as a whole and neatly illustrates the polysemy of the word "projection" (i.e., the possible confusion between images projected on a real screen and a viewer's unconscious projections). It is this collapsing and questioning of the boundaries between both reality and fiction, and creation and reception, that are foundational to metafiction.

The film draws on another commonplace idea about cinema—the analogy between cinema and dreams—latent in the writings of silent cinema directors like Germaine Dulac and Jean Epstein and eventually theorized by Baudry.

Dreams are evoked in the song titles ("Many Dreams") and lyrics (of "To See You (Is to Love You)" [21:38–23:31] and "Mona Lisa" [1:51:40]). Four scenes show Jefferies sleeping at crucial moments in the plot: the incipit [2:21], Lisa's arrival [16:05], the murder [32:02, 34:38, 36:07] and the beginning of the epilogue [1:41:41]. The repetition of these scenes establishes a clear link between the cinema-as-dream analogy and the subject voyeur, indicating that the dream/movie is precisely Jefferies's. The incipit depicts the place (the apparatus) in an establishing shot, then the sleeper (spectator) in close-up, and finally the neighbors (the movies) in long shots. The epilogue inverts this structure by showing first the neighbors, then the happy dreamer. The incipit and epilogue thus form a frame that tends to reinforce the sense that the whole film is Jefferies's dream. The scene that will effectively trigger Jefferies's suspicions utilizes a similar frame and ends with a pan that recalls the film's opening [36:07–36:32]. The cinema-as-dream analogy thus endows *Rear Window* with a fantasy structure and reinforces the film's discourse on cinema as a projection of the unconscious.

The three instances of sleep during the crime scene provide us with the key to the analogy: Jefferies's awakening marks both the end of his absence *and* the event he has missed and that has been elided following a fade-out. The concomitance of dream and ellipsis suggests that it is Jefferies's unconscious mind that may be filling in the gaps. However, his waking moments are full of activity: Jefferies is going to identify a series of events (Thorwald's comings and goings), which he will then organize, compare and interpret in the light of an interpretive framework that happens to be the event that preceded his falling asleep (the sound of glass breaking and a woman screaming, "Don't!" [31:50]). The third segment, of which we are the sole audience, plays a function that is at once similar and different: it invites us to distance ourselves from the diegetic spectator and include him among the elements to be studied and analyzed. The film encourages us to remain active and distanced spectators, and to reconsider the moments of awakening in the earlier part of the film. With the Thorwald sequence in mind, Lisa/Grace Kelly's first apparition is basically a nightmare for Jefferies, introducing yet another gap between the diegetic spectator and the real audience; but it is also important to take into account what precedes his first awakening: an accident which, unlike Scottie Ferguson's in *Vertigo*, is not depicted and could (like Scottie's phobia) provide an interpretive framework for the narrative as a whole, and which we can only reconstruct thanks to the bits and pieces of information gleaned from the narration.

Thus, in spite of its debt to psychoanalysis, *Rear Window* qualifies the view, later theorized by apparatus theory, that the spectator is a passive dreamer entirely subjected to his unconscious and the film's ideology. Projection is equated to creation, and desire prompts viewer activity (the investigation). The cinematic apparatus, *Rear Window* suggests, is not just a matter of scopophilia, and a film is not an "imaginary signifier," "a semi-dreamlike instance"[64] opening "onto the transparency of the signified."[65] Spectatorship is also a cognitive, intellectual and collective activity. A more active and collective view of spectatorship is staged in the scenes in which Jefferies, Lisa and Stella watch their neighbors together and interpret the scenes they witness. The turning point wherein other characters are contaminated by Jefferies's paranoia occurs halfway through the film and marks the beginning of the third act. Lisa, in spite of her annoyance with Jefferies's obsession, utters a sentence that sums up the film as a whole: "Tell me everything you saw and what you think it means" [49:23]. The final scenes (act four) then depict the abundance of activities the diegetic viewers indulge in (Figure 5.4): they comment on other characters' behavior ("the music stopped her [Miss Lonelyhearts]" [1:39:12]), question their actions ("What is she doing? Why hasn't she denounced him?" [1:41:51]), judge them ("She's a smart woman." [1:41:53]), address them ("Come on, come on, get out of there!" [1:38:26]), formulate hypotheses ("Miss Lonelyhearts has just gone out to purchase something that looks like sleeping pills." [1:30:20]), disprove them ("Stella was wrong about Miss Lonelyhearts." [1:36:55]), imagine the moments they missed ("[The blood] must have splattered all over the place." [1:25:18]), feel empathy for the people they are watching (the close-ups of Jefferies's fearful face when Thorwald finds Lisa [1:40:05–1:41:00]).

Figure 5.4 Rear Window: *Stella, Lisa and Jefferies watch the neighbors and interpret their every move.*

Rear Window also dramatizes the diversity within a given audience and its interpretations, notably based on variables including gender and occupation. If Mulvey cited Hitchcock as a prime example of the voyeuristic male gaze of classical cinema,[66] Rear Window insists on the differences between male and female subjectivity. Lisa "demonstrates a sensibility quite distinct from that of the male."[67] She contests the stereotype Jefferies imposes on Miss Torso by hinting that the young neighbor is looking for love and not money and by telling Jefferies that her interpretation is legitimized by his own comparison of Lisa and Miss Torso ("You said it resembled my apartment, didn't you?" [24:38]); it doesn't even occur to Jefferies that his ignoring Lisa while she prepares their candlelit dinner makes her an apt double of Miss Lonelyhearts instead, a parallel that is confirmed in a later scene when the lonely neighbor is associated with Lisa through the song "Mona Lisa."[68] Tania Modleski argues that Rear Window does more than simply deconstruct the hero's masculinity: "Lisa and Jeff have very *different* interpretations about the woman's desire in this scene fraught with erotic and violent potential, and it is *Lisa's* interpretation, arrived at through identification, that is ultimately validated."[69] The film thus dramatizes the politics of the gaze via the star couple. Not only is Lisa Freemont an "overwhelmingly powerful" and "extremely self-possessed"[70] presence, but she is "able to provide the missing evidence [the wedding ring which a woman would never have left at home] because she claims a special knowledge of women that men lack."[71] The film thus concludes on a medium shot of Lisa sporting pants, more "masculine" in comparison to her fiancé who is recovering from having been put in the shoes of the victim, Mrs. Thorwald.[72] The film's gender trouble was already implicit during Detective Doyle's second visit. Embodying patriarchal law and logic, the officer pokes fun at Lisa's "feminine intuition" and delivers a misogynistic speech which even Jefferies picks up [1:12:28–1:18:45]; ironically, Doyle's comments are at least as true of Jefferies who has similarly based his hypotheses on intuition. The patriarch's demise is thus effected symbolically not only by the arrest of the woman killer, but also by the validation of (Lisa's, Stella's and Jefferies's) so-called "female intuition."

Similarities between *Blow-up* (and its source text, Julio Cortázar's 1959 short story) and *Rear Window* have been noted by Antonioni scholars.[73] Like *Rear Window*, *Blow-up* is a meditation on cinema, an allegory of creation and spectatorship. José Moure calls it a "fable,"[74] whose subject is "representation" and "poetic perception,"[75] and that demonstrates that the "readability" of an image is a question of scale, focus, distance."[76] Thierry Roche describes the process of reframing as an allegory of interpretation as recontextualization, and goes so far as to compare it to the methodology of anthropology.[77]

Following a photographer named Thomas, whose daily routine appears to randomly take him from a doss house to his studio to an antique shop to a city park to his agent, back to his studio, followed by two more visits to the park, Antonioni's first non-Italian venture is the portrait of the artist as a young man in Swinging London. Arrogant, jaded, yet apparently talented and unquestionably energetic, Thomas represents the epitome of the tyrannical artist, deriving pleasure from his power over his models, whether aspiring (the blond and brunette portrayed by Gillian Hills and Jane Birkin) or professional (Veruschka von Lehndorff who plays her own role). The film immediately and explicitly suggests that the pleasure he derives from his work is of a sexual nature. During his first photoshoot of the day [5:28–9:50], which also provides the basis for the movie's poster, he straddles Veruschka, orders her to "really give it to [him]" and "make it come," kisses her neck frantically twice, and snaps away with his camera, until he shouts out "yes, yes, yes!" and walks away with utter indifference. At the end of the second photoshoot [11:10–15:14], this time a group session, he asks the five models to "Close your eyes and stay like that!" apparently just for fun, denying them the use of the sense his own talent depends on, and thus reducing them to the status of living mannequins. Thomas's abuse of his models can later be put down to a contempt for fashion photography when we find out that he is also working on a book of art photos. Yet if he is a bit more enthusiastic when talking about his personal project to his agent, stating that he's "got something fab for the end—in a park" [36:13], he is just as unpleasant with a stranger, Jane, he takes pictures of in Maryon Park, and even ends up comparing the logic of fashion and art photography to justify his refusal to leave her "in peace": "You know, most girls would pay me to photograph them" [29:03]. Whether as a consumer (he purchases a helix in an antique shop "just because it's beautiful" [53:37]), lover or artist whose talent resides in his capacity to capture specific moments, Thomas is driven by impulse.

This view of the creative act as impulse is voiced early on, in a scene that is rarely commented on by Antonioni scholars, by one of Thomas's friends, Bill, a painter who admits that his work only acquires meaning for him after the fact:

> I must be five or six years old. They don't mean anything when I do them. Just a mess. Afterwards I find something to hang on to, like that—quite like that leg. Then it sorts itself out—and adds up. It's like finding a clue in a detective story. Don't ask me about this one, I don't know yet. [16:00–16:36]

Echoing Alan Davie's views of the artist as "two separate beings – the intuitive creator and the intellectual spectator,"[78] Bill's words end up being prophetic, heralding the film's turning point (some would say the plot's actual beginning) when Thomas becomes, like Bill, the spectator/analyst of his own work—and thus when the film moves beyond the portrayal of the artist to a reflection on art, fiction, and their creation and interpretation.

It is at this moment that *Blow-up* reprises *Rear Window*'s witness-to-a-crime premise. Equipped with a magnifying glass [56:44], Thomas, the amateur detective, stumbles upon a mystery contained in one of his photos and proceeds to investigate it. Thierry Roche, one of the few scholars who insists on Thomas's status as a spectator,[79] interprets the protagonist's attempt to fill in the blanks of the crime in the light of Wolfgang Iser's theory of reader response—the spaces between the photos on the wall are so many "blanks" the viewer must fill in.[80] Thomas not only steps out of his position as artist, his gaze transforms from one that is exclusively concerned with "aesthetically translating social reality" into that of a scholar who would like to "understand" it.[81] The image's ambiguity forces him to analyze it in the light of others, going back and forth between his lab and his living room, between production and reception, the catwalk in his loft materializing this "passage between two worlds"[82] [57:47, 1:14:23]. Piecing together his photos and blowing up certain elements (the figure in the trees) [58:05–1:06:36], Thomas then (re)constructs the events leading up to a murder and ends up creating a sequential narrative reminiscent of a comics or a still-image-based film such as *La Jetée* (Marker, 1962). The scene, Sandro Bernardi suggests, seems to thematize "*the crisis of the cinematic sequence* and the hiatus between different forms of representation that are revealed to be mutually incompatible."[83] Relayed by the narration and accompanied by the windy soundtrack that resounded throughout Thomas's first visit to the park green, this visual narrative ends up filling the frame and becoming the film we are watching. Or almost. Indeed, it is by no means certain that the images we see are all equivalent to Thomas's blown-up images. Marie-Claire Ropars-Wuilleumier, and José Moure after her, have noted how the enunciation constantly introduces a gap between Thomas's subjectivity and the narration throughout the film.[84] Thierry Roche has further insisted that it is ultimately the intervals between the images, between seeing and not seeing, understanding and not understanding, that are foregrounded.[85] This metanarrative scene thus emphasizes the artist's lack of authority over his material by representing active spectatorship and the limits of interpretation.

Thomas then calls his agent to share the "fantastic" story he's uncovered in which he happens to be the hero who unwittingly saved a stranger's life [1:06:03]. As a reflection of and on a previous event in the film, the sequence is a mise en abyme of a particular kind. Because of the ontological and epistemological gap it draws attention to—the uncertainty concerning the event

Figure 5.5   Blow-up: *projection*: *Thomas's shadow blots out the figures of Jane and her lover on the photo.*

in the park (did Thomas witness a man's murder?) and the event in Thomas's studio (is Thomas fabricating the murder plot?)—the "fictional mise en abyme" makes way for a "metaphorical" one.[86] This hesitation is visually conveyed when Thomas suddenly advances to study the photograph of Jane and her lover from up close and the camera tracks right behind the photo to reveal his shadow blotting the human figures out: the photo is thus presented as a screen the artist/spectator is potentially projecting his unconscious desires onto (Figure 5.5) [58:40].

The allegorical potential of the mise en abyme—that the sequential photograph-based narrative stands for cinema—is foregrounded through two specific devices: lateral pans and zoom-ins (three in all) and frame-within-the-frame composition (the majority of shots of Thomas). The pan/zoom-in combination mimics Thomas's own active look, but also operates to edit (the pans) and (re)frame (the zoom-ins) the images; for instance, the camera's moving back and forth between the photo of Jane looking off-camera to the right and that of the figure in the trees invites us to relate the two as if they were edited in shot/reverse shot. Frame-within-the-frame composition highlights Thomas's paradoxical position as spectator/creator and indicates that he is the one who is framing, positioning and connecting the photos (Figure 5.6). Through these devices, three key elements of film narration (staging, camerawork, editing) come into play. Thomas's activity suddenly energizes the narration, which jumps back and forth between his lab and his living room without depicting his walking to and fro, thus eliding

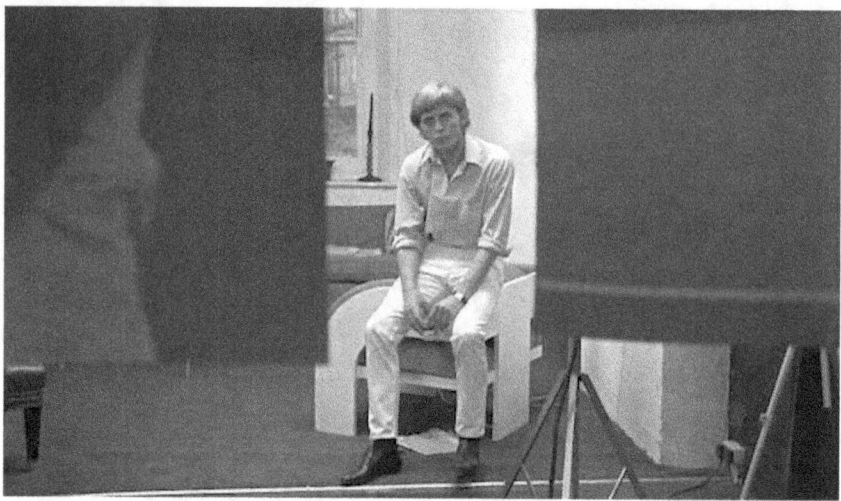

Figure 5.6 Blow-up: *cognition: frame-within-the-frame composition expresses visually the spectator's activity as he establishes connections between the images.*

actions the rest of the movie takes its time to relate [1:01:20–1:04:45]. The narration ultimately reproduces Thomas the spectator's interpretation as an audiovisual narrative by allowing his photos to fill up the frame, cutting from one to another, reconfiguring shot scale, and accompanying the montage with the sounds of the wind in the trees [1:04:46–1:05:34].

The film's central scene is thus a metamoment that dramatizes interpretation as an attempt to resolve a fundamental lack: the mystery, of course, but more generally speaking, the invisible. Because what the title of the film points to is that the invisible lurks not only offscreen; it can inhabit the onscreen and, thus, paradoxically, the visible. In effect, the more Thomas blows up the image of the suspected murderer, the more the image becomes abstract [87] (Figure 5.7), an assortment of blotches that come to resemble Bill's paintings. The painter's comments were thus equally prophetic in terms of Thomas's aesthetic discovery of the abstract potential of the photographic image. Thomas's adopting the gaze of the analyst thus brings about a shift from epistemological concerns to ontological ones. The question posed is not so much, "Did the murder actually happen?" but, "What are photography and film?" Like Cortazar's story, the film questions the truth value of the photographic image, which is sometimes taken for granted in writings on photography and film (Bazin's "mummy complex," Barthes's "that-has-been," Sontag's "trace,"[88]), and engages with the early-twentieth-century debate between realist and formalist views of cinema (that cinema is a reproduction or a transformation of the real[89]).

Apparatus and Spectatorship 117

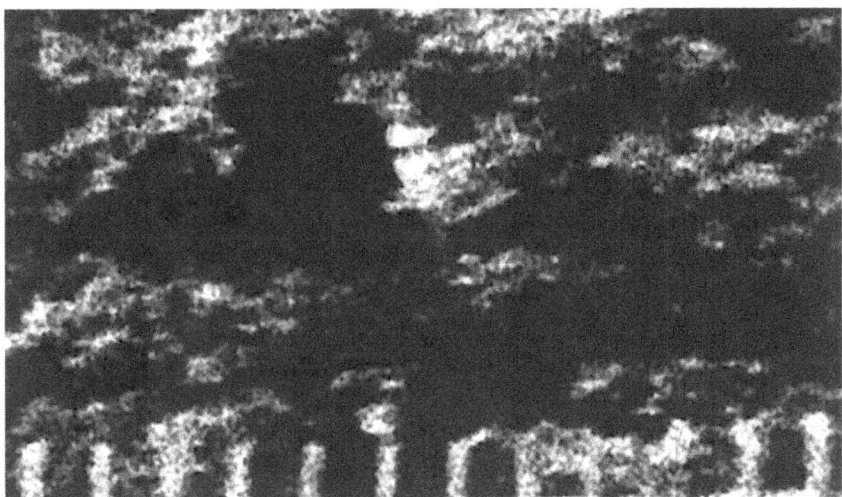

Figure 5.7 Blow-up: *abstraction: blown up out of all proportions, the photo loses its figurative properties and becomes an array of shapes.*

The witness-to-a-murder plot seems to leave the debate open: the blow-up sequence provides an illustration of the formalist precept that art makes reality strange, but Thomas's discovery of the corpse tends to confirm the truth value of photography.

However, the film's concluding scene, Thomas's last visit to Maryon Park during which he watches a group of mimes imitating both the players and the public of a tennis match, offers a new metamoment that tends to side with the formalist view [1:42:32–1:46:20]. Drawing on the art as play model evoked by Bill who compared himself to a child (a model Hutcheon sees as characteristic of diegetic metafiction), the final scene functions like an expanded version of the baseball scene in Keaton's *The Cameraman* (see Chapter 3). In effect, the invisible comes alive through the power of performance, which both the camerawork and editing enhance by cutting between the individual players and spectators, or tracking across the lawn to follow the invisible ball. The ambivalent ending has produced opposing interpretations, Moure viewing Thomas's interaction with the mimes as indicative of his seeking refuge in illusion,[90] Thierry Roche as his social integration into a group.[91] I would argue that this metamoment is particularly exalting because it celebrates the power of all art, however popular or unrealistic (hence the mimes), to make us see and feel the world anew. But it remains a cautious celebration—Thomas's furrowed eyebrows express a degree of worry, until he eventually looks down, and the film ends on a high-angle very long shot of him as a lone figure lost in a green expanse, a mere blotch in a photographic image, the color version of the one he blew up. The transformative power of film affects the portrait of the artist himself, whose status as raw material is ultimately asserted.

Blow Out proposes to merge the witness-to-a-crime premises of *Rear Window* and *Blow-up*[92] and integrate them within a political thriller framework indebted to 1970s films such as *The Parallax View* (Pakula, 1974) and *The Conversation* (Coppola, 1974).[93] It also shifts *Blow-up*'s focus on the tension between moving and still image to a focus on the relationship between sound and image. Because *Blow Out* is a movie about making movies, the line between creation and reception is blurred more explicitly than in *Rear Window* and *Blow-up*, and more rapidly (its prologue opens with an excerpt from the film-within-the-film, a slasher flick entitled *Coed Frenzy* [0:24–3:36]). It is this which leads Thierry Roche to conclude that, unlike *Blow-up*, the 1981 film offers "a metadiscourse that is exclusively concerned with cinema."[94] Chris Dumas argues, more precisely, that *Blow Out* is a "self-reflexive" film, influenced by Brecht and Godard,[95] that "is literally about the responses – critical, activist, feminist, academic – to *Dressed to Kill* [1980]."[96]

The protagonist, Jack Terry, is immediately introduced as a sound man and a critical spectator ("God, that scream is terrible.") [3:38–5:48]. He is then shown at work labeling his stock of recorded sounds during the opening credits [6:17–9:34], and recording new sounds in a park at night, using a condenser microphone [9:35–14:10]. In this famous scene, the narration allows us to see what Jack can only or mainly hear—the sounds' sources in close-up (a couple, a toad, a great-horned owl). Jack's microphone, as the extreme close-up inserted between these images and the shots of Jack suggests, seems to operate, from our perspective at least, like a camera. Or does it really? Instead of resorting to shot/reverse shots, which would unproblematically align point of view with Jack's, the film uses split diopter shots (a trademark De Palma device[97]) that become increasingly ambiguous. While the first such shot (positioned over a couple's shoulders) suggests that, contrary to what the young woman thinks ("He's staring right at us."), it is actually they who are looking at Jack (who is, however, listening in on their conversation), the subsequent shots involve a toad facing the camera and a sign reading Wissahickon Walk—in other words, things which cannot possibly be looking at Jack. The next split diopter shot impossibly blends the antithetical logics of the previous shots: a great-horned owl is facing us, but its super-flexible neck enables it to gaze in Jack's direction (Figure 5.8). The subsequent shot (also split diopter) emphasizes the perceptual impossibility by proposing an improbable deep focus composition whose artificiality is heightened by the bird's look to the camera. Thus, the image of the owl calls into question the status of the previous images, which originated not from Jack's environment, but either from his subjectivity or a highly artificial narration.

Figure 5.8 Blow Out: *a split diopter shot impossibly combines an owl's look to the camera with the equivalent of a shot/reverse shot that is justified aurally but not visually.*

The fact that Jack can picture what he hears—and that we are shown what he hears—is confirmed approximately ten minutes later in a scene where Jack listens to the sounds he recorded [23:05–26:12]. The narration, here, leaves little room for doubt: the shots of the couple and the animals are aligned with the position Jack would have occupied standing on the bridge and are edited in shot/reverse shot, a spatial–temporal impossibility that is exclusively justified by Jack's memory. Jack is thus simultaneously audiovisual spectator and creator, the perceiver and recorder of the sounds and images we are allowed to perceive. And yet, if the film's narration seems to relay the concomitance of Jack's visual memory and actual recording, it nonetheless introduces distance and epistemological doubt. As Ronald S. Librach has astutely noted,

> the key image of blown tire and plunging car, for example, is presented from greater proximity than Jack's own original, and other images complement the audio cuts with slow-motion visuals. The technology at the disposal of the narrative, therefore, usurps but is also telescoped with the technology at Jack's disposal. It is thus enlisted in a hermeneutic enterprise subject to the vagaries of reason, insight, and error—an enterprise which is supposed to hold a mirror up to Jack's experience but which is actually manipulated from an omniscient point of view that ensures at once both Jack's access to the truth and his submission to ambiguity.[98]

The questioning of the sound man's subjectivity makes way for an exploration of the nature of the audiovisual image, psychological concerns for material ones, epistemology for ontology. The narrative hinges on the observation that, culturally speaking, the truth value of sound appears lesser than that of the photographic image: it takes a sound man like Jack to distinguish between the sound of a gunshot and that of a tire blow-out. Like his totem animal the great-horned owl, Jack's sense of hearing is at least as developed as his sense of sight, and he is at his most powerful when, standing on a bridge, he is able to associate both senses; for the night owl, sounds seem to have as much truth value as images. Aware that the gaze is overvalued compared to the sense of hearing, Jack attempts to get his hands on the photos taken by a hustler named Manny Karp. With them, he creates an audiovisual sequence of the events he believes he witnessed that is even more complete (since it includes sound) than Thomas's sequence in *Blow-up* [33:03–35:31]. And yet, it remains, as the sign on the door to the room reminds us, an animated movie, one that mobilizes another one of De Palma's trademark devices, the split screen. The more Jack seeks to put together evidence, the more he transitions from witness to director (like Jefferies, he enlists people to perform in his plot), and the less like a newsreel and the more like fiction (and a De Palma film) his audiovisual project becomes.

Powerless to unravel the conspiracy (he will kill Burke "without ever knowing who he is"[99]) and save his performers (both Freddie and Sally are murdered when they venture off [Jack's] screen), the sound man ends up losing control of the narrative. It is, then, quite ironic that after relaying Jack's audiovisual sequence which existed materially within the diegesis, the narration seems to reproduce the mental images of his performers' deaths that signify his subjection to a metanarrative, be it the political conspiracy, his own unconscious fantasies or the killer's (the film's last split screen expresses Burke's "consciousness"[100] when he listens to a prostitute conversing with a sailor [1:24:14]). A quintessentially postmodernist film, *Blow Out* "starts from the assumption that the truth is *not really* out there"[101]—and ends up almost where it started: Jack has failed to dismantle the conspiracy but has found a good scream (Sally's) for *Coed Frenzy* [1:44:15], thus divesting this formal element of any political content whatsoever. Cinema has failed to illuminate reality, and its power to transform is trivial; both realist and formalist theories are thus undermined. Released in 1981 at a time when apparatus theory dominated film studies, *Blow Out*, however, tends to confirm or anticipate its main tenets: that sound cannot make sense without images (Chion 1990[102]), that cinema is historically a narrative medium (Metz 1968[103]), that the apparatus is fundamentally alienating and that it is in service of the viewer's unconscious and dominant ideology (Baudry, Metz, Mulvey). More than just a response to the reception of *Dressed to Kill*, *Blow Out* is film theory in practice.

Conclusion

Resorting to a variety of meta-phenomena, most notably the mise en abyme, metalepsis and allegory, the films and series discussed in this chapter offer a multivarious view of spectatorship that goes far beyond immersion, whereby this activity is both an individual and a collective affair, a space of projection and of conscious deliberation. These works juggle views that film and media scholarship has tended to separate, sometimes even anticipating them, and keeping alive the cinema-as-dream analogy which is shown to not preclude agency. Moreover, the question of spectatorship is not limited to the portrayal of diegetic spectators but also involves figures of the artist themselves. By portraying the crossing of boundaries, such works debunk the creation/reception dichotomy and posit, on the contrary, a dialogical relationship by foregrounding the creative potential of reception (viewers participate in the elaboration of the fictional world), as well as the artists' own critical view of her/his work. This suggests that spectatorship is a fundamental activity, one that pertains to our apprehension of the "real" world around us and mobilizes similar cognitive and imaginative skills. The analysis of spectatorship thus presupposes a valuation of the act, and thus ultimately of the "vitality" (to use Hutcheon's term) of fiction itself. The distinction between creation and reception, which I have separated in Chapters 4 and 5 for convenience's sake, is routinely called into question by these works that only appear to focus principally on one or the other. Moreover, the positing of a dialogical relationship brings to the surface the modes through which the relationship is materialized: that is, cinema and television as media, and audiovisual images as the material of creation and interpretation, leading to questions that are epistemological (How do we know these images? What is their relationship to reality?), ontological (What are they and what is reality?) and ethical (How do we engage with them?), and that resonate with the discourses of film and media theory.

CHAPTER 6

Medium and Materiality

Synchretism, Intermediality, Remediation

The analyses of *Sunset Blvd.*, *Contempt*, *Blow-up*, *Blow Out* and *Mulholland Dr.* have already shown how meta can engage with the ontology and materiality of film. The exploration of the medium via film is as old as cinema itself. It was one of the prime concerns of the avant-gardes of the 1920s and probably one of their most enduring legacies to art and popular cinema. It has long been one of the prime concerns of film theorists and critics, from the Russian formalists' 1927 *Poètika kino* to André Bazin's 1945 "The Ontology of the Photographic Image" to Stanley Cavell's 1971/1979 *The World Viewed* and, more recently, to scholars writing on digital cinema. What are the boundaries of a given medium? And in the case of cinema and television, what is the specificity of a medium that is reproducible and whose material is the world? This questioning is often effected, as in film theory (again, the Russian formalists come to mind), through comparisons with other media—mises en abyme in particular regularly solicit other media[1] (photography and painting in *Blow-up*, theater and music in *Mulholland Dr.*). Whereas theorists of the 1920s insisted on the "synchretic"[2] quality of cinema, its capacity to blend the arts of the past (Boris Kazanski, for instance, described cinema as a "graphic drama"[3]), today such phenomena might fall under the concepts of intermediality or remediation.

Although early writings on metafiction and reflexivity predate the "intermedial turn," the exploration of the medium is evoked on occasion. Hutcheon, for instance, speaks of "a two-way pull of contradictory impulses" within metafictional texts, one that "treat[s] language as a means" and another as "an artifact," thereby treating "the medium as an end";[4] what she calls "linguistic metafiction" focuses on language as fiction-building material and/or as material in itself.[5] Waugh tends to emphasize the first aspect, her central argument being that metafiction evinces how language constructs both fiction and reality; accordingly, she analyzes the "language games" of "radical metafiction" as indications "that 'reality' as well as 'fiction' is merely one more game with words."[6] Among the early writings on metacinema or reflexivity in film, William Siska alone evokes the exploration of the materiality of film in *Persona* (Bergman, 1966) and *Le Départ* (Skolimowski, 1967), but he puts it on the same level as the representation of film production.[7] Although Stam seems content to state that movies about making movies "make us aware [. . .] of the medium,"[8] his studies of Godard's "systematic exploration of the cinematic parameters"[9] inevitably bring to light the director's consistent questioning of the medium. He notes, for instance, that the "experimentation with variable speeds" in *Sauve qui peut (la vie)* (Godard and Miéville, 1980), influenced no doubt by *Man with a Movie Camera*, "promotes reflexivity" by highlighting "the normally obscured process of '*défilement*'" and disrupting "[t]he appearance of 'natural' movement"; Stam concludes that "[t]he experience of the film, in these privileged moments of altered velocity, coincides with its own analysis, as if the film were looking at itself on the Steenbeck [editing machine]."[10] The general lack of interest in how meta-phenomena engage with the medium and materiality of film may be put down to the dominance of typological approaches (that insist on the devices utilized more than on the works' aboutness), as well as to the defense of metafiction as being not just about itself and its medium.

More recent writings have logically taken into account the intermedial turn. Werner Wolf, who spoke of such a turn as early as 1992,[11] identifies intermediality, which he defines as "any transgression of boundaries between conventionally distinct media," as an implicit device which, like metalepsis and the mise en abyme, has metareferential potential;[12] works that resort to intermediality can thus "expos[e] medial materiality."[13] Terms such as "intermedia reflexivity" (Szczepanik 2002), "intermedial self-reference"[14] (Nöth), "intermedial spectacularity" (Chinita 2021) or "'trans-art' and intermedial" reflexivity[15] (Yacavone 2021) have emerged since the 2000s. Petr Szczepanik, whose brief article is largely based on the ideas of other theorists, defines "intermedia reflexivity" as "a strategy of visualising structural differences between distinct media in hybrid forms of images"[16]: it "represents a process of mutual reflecting and self-reflecting of two or more media forms, correlated within one single image or the diegesis."[17] He then identifies two forms of intermedia reflexivity, one that focuses on the image and pursues the legacy of modernist experimentation (as per Yvonne Spielman's analysis of *Prospero's Books* [Greenaway, 1991]), and another that operates by "allegoris[ing] collisions of different media or technologies by narrating a conflict between diegetic forces"[18] (as per Vivian Sobchack's analysis of *Terminator 2: Judgment Day* [Cameron, 1991]). Szczepanik advances that reflexivity is a "fundamental feature of all kinds of intermediality."[19] Daniel Yacavone, whose understanding of "'trans-art' and intermedial" reflexivity is fairly similar to Szczepanik's, disagrees; for him, reflexivity and intermediality are related processes, but "intermedia incorporation" of "other arts and media" "need not" reflect "back in some notable fashion on *cinema's* artistic and medial nature."[20] This question will be explored in the analyses below.

Szczepanik also notes that "hybrid images" could emerge from the collision of visual media.[21] In her typology of metacinema, Fátima Chinita similarly remarks that "intermedial spectacularity" presents "cinema as an artistic vehicle among others," whose power lies in its capacity to "contain other art forms and match them."[22] Both Szczepanik and Chinita, thus, rejoin observations made in defense of cinema by the Russian formalists notably—that one of cinema's defining characteristics is its synchretism. I am by no means suggesting that synchretism and intermediality are synonyms. Synchretism means that the medium in itself incorporates features from other media (performance and staging from theater, composition from painting and photography, structure from the novel or music), whereas intermediality, if we follow Wolf, is not an essential feature but a case of "transgression." While recognizing the synchretism of cinema, Boris Kazanski also noted that other art forms "are not directly integrated within the art of cinema; they are subjected to a series of transformations so radical that the initial stage seems to disappear in the passage from one creation to another."[23] Recast in the parlance of twenty-first-century media studies, Kazanski's words could describe the medium's "hypermediacy" (the mixing of media and styles within a given work[24]) as much as its capacity for "remediation." Jay David Bolter and Richard Grusin define remediation as "the representation of one medium in another,"[25] and thus as an overt instance of intermediality. Remediation is an attempt to assert the relevance of old and new media by "presenting themselves as refashioned and improved versions of other media."[26] This can be achieved by erasing the other medium (for instance, when a Hollywood film absorbs computer-generated effects in order to create the semblance of a live-action film) or, on the contrary, by emphasizing the differences between media.[27] The meta potential of intermediality would seem to be negated in the first case, exploited in the second. These opposing tendencies recall Szczepanik's own distinction between the diegeticized "intermedia reflexivity" of contemporary popular cinema and the formal experimentations of modernist cinema, but with one significant difference: diegeticized "intermedia reflexivity" nonetheless produces an allegory of intermediality—and sometimes maybe even of remediation—that would qualify as meta.

With this theoretical framework in mind, I would like to formulate two working hypotheses. First, when it comes to the relationship between intermediality and reflexivity, I would tend to agree with both Szczepanik and Yacavone by insisting, once again, on the distinction between reflexivity and meta: intermediality and remediation are reflexive because they make apparent the mediality of a given medium through its encounter with another;

intermediality has meta potential, however, when it appears to comment on the medium and its materiality "in some notable fashion," to cite Yacavone. Remediation, however, tends to be reflexive because as, Mathilde Arrivé notes, it "dramatizes 'its own phenomenology'"—"a 're-medium' is always a commentary on another medium, i.e., a meta-medium of sorts."[28]

Second, a given work need not resort to intermediality to engage with its medium on a meta-level, but there is a definite tendency to do so for two reasons. The first is analytical: intermediality makes a medium's properties apparent through contrast, and, in so doing, represents the aesthetic equivalent of some of the argumentative strategies film and media theorists have resorted to. Here we rejoin the distinction between reflexivity and meta made in Chapter 1: intermediality is at the least a device (reflexivity), but it can potentially become a mode of theorization (meta). The second reason has to do with media ecology: tackling other media is also the best line of defense, a way to assert and even celebrate one's endurance in an ever-changing mediascape.

These hypotheses will, in the analyses that follow, be tested and supplemented by a series of other, perhaps more obvious questions: What can meta tell us about the ontology of the film or audiovisual image? About the difference between moving images and still images, photographic and drawn images, film and video, movie and interactive movie? Finally, is it possible to trace a history of the discourse on the materiality of audiovisual media through meta? Given that the intermedial turn of the 1990s more or less overlaps with the mainstreaming of meta-phenomena, have such practices and discourses crept into more popular fare, as the examples Szczepanik uses to illustrate his typology suggest? Is it even possible to explore the boundaries of a medium without resorting to intermediality, thereby confirming Bolter and Grusin's claim that "[n]o medium today, and certainly no single media event, seems to do its cultural work in isolation from other media"[29]? In this chapter, emphasis will be put on the materiality of the medium, understood as a "means of communication,"[30] since the other components of the apparatus have been explored in Chapters 4 and 5. The case studies that follow pay attention to film's relation to architecture, the fine arts, video and comics, and to the television medium's status in the age of streaming platforms.

CINEMA AND THE FINE ARTS (*FELLINI ROMA*)

Many films have explored their medium through the pictorial arts: the eponymous painting that ages in *The Picture of Dorian Gray* (Lewin, 1945); the colorful exploration of the eponymous character's engravings in *Andrei Rublev* (Tarkovsky, 1966); the frame on an easel that reconfigures diegetic space in *The Draughtman's Contract* (Greenaway, 1982); the audiovisual pastiche of a famous painter's work in *Caravaggio* (Jarman, 1986) or Eugène Delacroix's *Raft of the Medusa* in *The House That Jack Built*; the juxtaposition of the painting and the model within the same shot in *Portrait of a Lady on Fire* (Sciamma, 2019). Hava Aldouby, author of *Federico Fellini: Painting in Film, Painting on Film*, notes that studies of the "film/painting interface" mostly focus on the "clash" between the stillness and motion of the two "alien systems of representation," wherein cinema, according to Frederick Jameson, asserts its superiority over its competitors; tropes such as the "tableau vivant" become reflexive in works that tend to (Jameson again) "assign the film-painting hybrid a metadiscursive function."[31]

One film that seems to tackle all cinema's predecessors all in one go—photography, the performance arts and the fine arts, namely painting and architecture—is *Fellini Roma* (1972). Perhaps less obviously meta than the movies about making movies *8½*, *Toby Dammit* (1968) and *Intervista*, *Fellini Roma* certainly hasn't received much attention from scholars of reflexivity and metacinema, though its reflexive qualities have been noted by Fellini scholars (Peter Bondanella includes it among the director's films that evince a "preoccupation with the nature of cinema," Frank Burke among Fellini's films about films, Rebecca West describes it more specifically as a film about "how to make a film about a city"[32]). Aldouby notes that Fellini's incorporation of painting in his later period has also received little critical attention from scholars studying encounters between painting and film.[33] She argues that the "transmedialization of painting into or, rather, onto film" in Fellini's later period (from the 1965 *Juliet of the Spirits* to the 1976 *Casanova*) produces "sensual excess"[34]: "painting fulfills a role of origin, a core of 'real-ness' whence the experience of meaning originates. In a way, then, Fellini plays the postmodern trope of intertextuality against the grain, employing contemporary form in the service of an essentially romantic project, which he never tires of pursuing."[35] Carnivalesque palimpsest notwithstanding, Fellini's cinema would remain modernist (according to Brian McHale's argument that modernism's dominant is epistemological[36]) because it belies a faith in origin and meaning.

Although Aldouby pays little attention to *Fellini Roma*, her study provides a framework with which to approach it. An audiovisual whirlwind of movement and noise, the Italian director's eleventh feature film orchestrates, on a meta-level, a crescendo in terms of both quantity and quality. The first minutes alone depict a group of children viewing slides of Roman monuments [5:05–6:18] and a family watching a peplum followed by fascist propaganda at the movies [7:04–10:21], before an eighteen-year-old character named Federico is introduced getting off the train [12:00]. The near juxtaposition of these two mises en abyme asserts the nature of the film's material:

Rome is full of movie images and is also a compilation of images; a cinematic city, it is prime material for film. Of course, the Roman architext largely pre-dates cinema and photography and has a long history in the fine arts; it is this specificity that the film tries to capture.

The second act wanders into familiar Fellini territory: the movie about making movies. It introduces a film crew that is setting out to do exactly what *Fellini Roma* is doing: make a film about Rome [30:24–42:17]. If a parallel is established when we see them driving past the ruins of the tomb of Cecilia Metella [35:54], previously shown in a more favorable light in the slides [5:26], the narration mostly keeps its distance from the film-within-the-film. The shots of *Fellini Roma* do not mimic the high angles presumably recorded by the diegetic crew until the concluding scene at the Piazza de Siena (Figures 6.1.1 and 6.1.2) [39:03–42:17]. The blurring of the line between the

Figures 6.1.1 and 6.1.2 Fellini Roma: *the diegetic film crew filming a high-angle shot of the Piazza de Siena, which is then reproduced by the narration.*

film-within-the-film and *Fellini Roma* is, however, evoked from the outset by the soundtrack when we hear a disembodied voice stating, "And what about Rome today? How does it affect someone who visits it for the first time? Let's try and enter the expressway by car and take the inevitable ring that forms circles round the city like the rings of Saturn" [30:29], an intention that is just as much that of the diegetic crew as that of the voiceover/stand-in for the director. The voice alerts us to the possibility that the actual director is lurking offscreen, a potential presence that is evoked in two other instances which, significantly, frame the sequence: when a man's hand can be seen waving at the truck carrying the crane, drawing the crane operator's attention in the process (Figure 6.2) [31:50], and when an anonymous character suddenly appears from the right and looks right at the camera (Figure 6.3)

Figures 6.2 and 6.3 Fellini Roma: *potentially metaleptic intrusions suggest that the shooting of the film-within-the-film and of* Fellini Roma *are confused offscreen.*

[38:00]. If the border between the film-within-the-film and *Fellini Roma* is largely maintained onscreen, offscreen both films potentially coexist within the same space.

Fellini Roma's final scenes clearly identify the roving camera with Fellini [1:42:06–1:49:44]. During the last night-time scene, looks to the camera (a staple device in later Fellini[37]), which were already numerous in the prelude to the Vatican fashion show [1:29:15–1:31:54], become the norm. They culminate in the film's penultimate scene when the voiceover introduces Anna Magnani, star of *Rome, Open City* (Rossellini, 1945), who addresses not the camera but whoever is beside it as Federico: "Federico, go get some sleep. [. . .] No, I don't trust you. Bye. Good night" [1:49:18–1:49:44]. The ontological barrier between fiction and reality is destabilized when a cinematic icon, "a symbol of the city," interpellates another film icon making a movie about that very city. With Fellini thus positioned next to the camera, *Fellini Roma* suddenly becomes a "pseudo-documentary"[38] or making-of, a possibility that was suggested, five minutes before the Magnani scene, with the interview of writer Gore Vidal, a friend of Fellini's [1:45:10–1:46:08]. We are, indeed, in territory already explored in *8½*, as analyzed by Metz: "*The film within the film is the film itself.* The mise en abyme structure reaches its full paradoxical force when there is no longer an included film, that is, when the two films, which are *avowedly* distinct, are physically totally confused. This is the symbiotic type."[39]

The meta becomes more explicit as soon as the film-within-the-film makes its entry; it is even voiced through dialogue. Comments concerning the film-within-the-film and the subsequent live performances echo Fellini's own aesthetic project. A group of youths questions the diegetic director's attempt to capture the city of Rome while neglecting "dramatic" social issues [41:35–42:00]. The talent show that follows is described by a member of the audience as a mix of circus and brothel before referring to Marcel Proust [45:55]. The comment suggests that the later brothel scenes [1:15:47–1:24:41] should, conversely, be approached as yet another spectacle, just like the Vatican fashion show [1:32:33–1:41:31]; it accounts as much for the film's carnivalesque aesthetics as for its Proustian structure (the alternation between images of the present and the past, in which the young Fellini appears). *Fellini Roma* simultaneously acknowledges the social and intermedial complexity of its material (architecture, performance, cinema, streets, people, food, history), celebrates the archeological (Elena M. Past would say "geological"[40]) power of a synchretic medium such as cinema to capture the layers of spectacle/life, and points to its limitations to conjure up an "idea"[41] of the city's multifariousness, its smells and tastes, for instance, which can only be evoked through a poetics that mimic synesthesia. Clearly, Fellini's "self-reflexivity," as Frank Burke contends, is not mere "self-indulgence" but "self-critical."[42]

The exploration of the medium's synchretic potential culminates in the film's central metamoment: the exploration of the city's underside, the Roman catacombs [1:01:57–1:08:51]. The famous scene has been analyzed as dramatizing Fellini's attempt and failure to penetrate the feminine city (Bondanella), and, more recently, from an environmental perspective, as displaying "the massive material footprint left behind by industry and by media"[43] (Past). The catacomb's guide takes a film crew on a visit of the construction of the Roman subway while dishing out information about the city's history. In a metanarrative moment, his voice is endowed with quasi-performative power, as the narration then shows shelves filled with archives representing the city's past. He explains that the transition to modernity could compromise the city's cultural roots, but is also an opportunity for archeologists. The sequence opens and ends on the unearthing of such findings: a mammoth tusk; the ruins of an ancient Roman house [1:08:52–1:13:50]. The ruins are inhabited by superbly preserved statues, tiled mosaics and frescoes on the columns and walls, a neat illustration of Bazin's famous "mummy complex" whereby the visual arts serve to preserve the memory of the past.[44] A member of the film crew remarks that they almost look alive. Indeed, the dust blowing and flashlights playing over the murals seem to endow them with movement (especially since one of the murals shows the characters walking up a staircase that is not painted but created by stones), while the crew's shadows also dance across the walls (Figure 6.4.2). In a film in which movement plays a central role, the animation of the inanimate finds its polar opposite when the animate becomes inanimate (namely when people become akin to sculptures in the Vatican sequence).

The scene goes further than *Andrei Rublev*'s famous epilogue by complicating the exploration of texture (the flat surface of the photographic image and the layered surface of an engraving or a mural) through the presence of other profilmic materials (starting with lighting). The introduction of an audience in this underground abode has suddenly turned it into another one of the film's many showhouses (the church, the movie theater, the bordello, etc.), and more specifically a movie theater (with the drill as a projector letting light in through an aperture that produces light and shadows on the walls). But even before their arrival, the narration contributed to making the murals look alive by showing them before the characters have access to them, even singling them out as if the figures on the mural felt threatened by the intrusion (Figure 6.4.1), a sentiment dramatized by the use of a push-in followed by a zoom-in. The painted figures' looks to the camera cause, in effect, the allegorical cinematic apparatus and the narration to overlap.

One of the characters suddenly notices that the air is damaging the frescoes, and single shots show the artwork whitening and vanishing (Figure 6.4.3). The

Figures 6.4.1–6.4.3 Fellini Roma: *discovery and destruction of the frescoes in an ancient Roman household, whose figures seem to momentarily come alive.*

damaging of these images suddenly calls to mind another prominent theory of the image, Benjamin's loss of the aura: these non-reproducible works of art are now lost forever. The film crew and contemporary capitalist society are indirectly responsible for this destruction, and its memorialization through the film image is meagre consolation. At what price has the camera captured the disappearance of the auratic object?! It might preserve the memory of what it destroyed, but it has potentially commodified it in the process. The sequence seems to monolithically side with Benjamin against cinema. And yet, the act of destruction also brings to mind the precariousness of celluloid—the irretrievable loss of negatives before they have been developed and reproduced—since the artwork is threatened by exposure in what is also an allegory of a darkroom. More shocking, perhaps, this tragic moment of loss is also one of creation, endowed with poetry, as the murals unveil a new potential beauty through the chromatic shifts that occur across their surface. At the moment of their discovery and death, when they have glimpsed the future of visual media, the murals have momentarily become moving pictures, cinema. This moment of loss is thus paradoxically a celebration of cinema's potential because it is both a reproducible and synchretic art, one that can capture, assimilate, reconfigure—today we might say, remediate—its ancestors. In this respect at least, cinema truly is equal to Rome.

FILM, TELEVISION, VIDEO (*FAMILY VIEWING*)

Cinema has equally been prone to interrogating its limits by incorporating the media that have emerged since its invention. The integration of television and video in particular would appear to be facilitated by their similarities with cinema: they are all audiovisual media (as opposed to painting, literature and architecture). This integration need not be transparent and can have reflexive potential. Analyzing *Numéro deux* (Godard and Miéville, 1975), Robert Stam notes that "many of the revolutionary innovations in Godard's films come from television";[45] devices such as "the designation of the apparatus (cameras, monitors, switchers); the commercial 'interruptions' of the narrative flow; the juxtaposition of heterogenous slices of discourse; the mixing of documentary and fictive modes"—"would seem to typify television as well."[46] Stam's remarks suggest that the relationship between old and new media is not teleological (as per Paul Levinson's theory of remediation[47]) but "dialogic"[48]; they also suggest that the process of remediation is potentially reflexive because the presence of the other medium (or of its past forms) cries out to us (this ties in to observations made in Chapter 7 regarding the reflexive potential of silent cinema devices in sound film). Moreover, while Godard's intermedial experimentations certainly work to explore and destabilize the boundaries of cinema, they also demonstrate its potential to assimilate and reconfigure new media. In a sense, the work of Godard represents the nexus between past conceptions of cinema as a synchretic art and contemporary understandings of remediation. It celebrates, more specifically, the plasticity of all audiovisual material—a potential that is as much aesthetic as it is political, since this expanded view of cinema opens a space where a variety of forms can coexist (this point will be furthered in Chapter 11).

The boundaries between cinema, television, video, surveillance footage, video games and other moving images have, since, been explored in art and mainstream films like *sex, lies and videotape* (Soderbergh, 1989), Michael Haneke's *Benny's Video* (1992) and *Funny Games* (1997), and *Alexandra's Project* (De Heer, 2003). One artist whose films and art installations have consistently interrogated these boundaries is Atom Egoyan. His second feature, *Family Viewing* (1987), qualifies as meta because it is intimately concerned with the relationship between fiction, media and human identity. It opens with a series of three metamoments, which roughly correspond to the prologue [0:06–1:19], the opening credits [1:26–2:40] and the "first" scene [3:54–5:38]. The prologue starts with a close-up of two tray racks being emptied; the removal of the trays in the middle creates a form of "natural" split screen, so that we see a medium shot of a very young man standing to the left, and a medium close-up of a television screen to the right. The composition draws attention to the plasticity of the film image—which can morph from close-up to split medium shot through basic staging and a slight zoom-in—and constructs an asymmetrical relationship between a human subject and a screen. It is the relationship between the image/screen and the human subject—as well as the mutations it engenders—that the film means to explore.

A high-angle medium shot then depicts an old woman in bed, while a zoom-out reveals the same young man standing at her side and looking at her. He steps out of the frame, then reappears in close-up, looking to the camera. It is only then (though we might already have guessed from the generic male voice describing polar bear hunting practices on the soundtrack) that we realize that the shot originates from a television screen (as if the retirement home television could equally be a surveillance device of the type found in science fiction fare such as *The Prisoner* and *LOST*). The look to the camera is thus founded on an intradiegetic metalepsis that blurs a series of ontological boundaries: between projecting and recording, diegetic and nondiegetic, nonfiction (the wildlife documentary) and fiction (Egoyan's film). The metaleptic potential is heightened when the young man's switching channels triggers the film's opening credits; channel hopping translates into editing, and the narration alternates between the close-up of the young man and the images of the main characters associated with the names of the actors playing their parts. The metalepsis is sharpened by contrasting distinct ontologies: on the one hand, the characters' belonging to a fictional world is asserted, but on the other, one of them is endowed with the power to affect the narration of the actual film. This metalepsis confirms the interest in the relationship between images and human subjects, already established by the opening shot, and raises the stakes by dramatizing it through a metanarrative and metafictional paradox: if the fiction is fiction, how can it control the narration?

The opening credits are followed by a staple family sitcom scene: the young man is watching a comedy program on TV when a woman (presumably his mother) comes home. The generic quality is reinforced by their remaining nameless throughout the scene. The sitcom setup is reinforced by the soundtrack, as their dialogue is punctuated by canned applause and laughter; if these sounds are justified diegetically (they are coming from the TV set), they systematically occur on cue with the characters' lines and are inexplicably louder than those of the performers, whose voices we cannot distinguish. The effect is jarring in several respects. The doubtful origin of the laughter (diegetic or nondiegetic? canned or live?) casts doubt on the status of the images we are watching. The scene thus renders salient the characters' fictionality by calling on a genre whose central unit is often the family and central space often the living room, and thus by making apparent the film's underlying game and fantasy models. It also complicates the meaning of what we are seeing, as the sitcom scene turns into something resembling incest. The connection between these ontological and epistemological questions (Are these characters characters? What is the nature of their relationship?) is materialized through another metalepsis (this one extradiegetic): a freeze frame of the image occurs right before they kiss as if to censor it (Figure 6.5), and the footage we have been watching is then rewound and paused on yet another freeze frame, this time of the teenager holding a remote control. The narration has not only confirmed the fictionality of the scene and cast further doubt on the narration's origin (is Van the controlling instance, just like *Funny Game*'s Paul will be nine years later?); it has revealed the nature of the image (video not film). The first five-and-a-half minutes of *Family Viewing* are programmatic, with meta being orchestrated through a build-up, each metamoment building on its predecessors. We are invited not only to be vigilant regarding the meaning and nature of the sound and images we perceive, but to participate actively in their interpretation.

Although *Family Viewing* abandons this fairly overt metafictional mode, the damage has been done. The three subsequent shots of the teenager, Van, looking to the camera and switching channels in the retirement home [17:00, 30:36, 39:47], or the many scenes of Van, his father, Stan, and stepmother, Sandra, in their condo, are marked by our memory of the opening scenes.

Medium and Materiality 135

Figure 6.5 Family Viewing: *freeze frame and rewinding right before a sitcom son (Van) and his sitcom stepmom (Sandra) can kiss.*

More generally, these scenes have established a framework with which to interpret the utilization of reflexive devices throughout the film. Many of them are intermedial, involving the insertion of television images (from wildlife documentaries [5:48, 19:48, 38:07]), surveillance footage (of Aline at work [16:54] or her sexual encounter in Toronto [38:47–39:33, 43:20–43:48]) and home video images (of Van's family [28:09, 32:57, 59:07, 1:03:34, 1:06:14, 1:11:48, 1:24:06]). These contribute to the representation of a hypermedia society in which we consume and produce media, and are ourselves transformed into audiovisual material. The images' sources are usually identified and justified diegetically, but their functions seem to vary according to their degree of subjectivity and, in a sense, humanity. In the last third of the film, the narration makes clear that the home video images are subjective inserts from Stan's [50:39], Aline's [59:07] and Armen's [1:11:48] perspectives (Figures 6.6.1 and 6.6.2). However, while we know that Aline can only be remembering the home video since she missed her mother's funeral, we are by no means certain that this is equally true of Stan and Armen (are they remembering the footage itself or the event recorded by the footage? Has the footage come to replace the event?). Unlike the surveillance images that

Figures 6.6.1 and 6.6.2 Family Viewing: *Armen's memories of herself and her daughter (Van's mother) are expressed as, or based on, home video footage.*

convey a sense of reification and potential dehumanization, the home video images can compensate for, replace and/or express human memory, fulfilling functions that are existential, psychological and aesthetic.

One scene in particular thematizes the use-value of video [55:50–58:29]. Stan and Sandra are sitting on their bed, their backs turned to each other, waiting for a phone call, with cameras ready to record their sexual role-playing games and screens ready to display them in real time. The bedroom is at once a studio set, a TV room and even an editing room (since Van realizes his father has been taping his sexual trysts over the family videos). The scene is set in motion by Aline's phone call. After disregarding her admission that she feels "lonely" and had a "strange day," Stan prompts her to get into character, forcing her to shift from her true self to a role. Aline is then required to direct Sandra's movements, and the zoom-in on Sandra's image on a monitor records both Sandra's erasure by Aline whose voice replaces her own, and her distress at being persecuted in such a fashion (Figure 6.7). The scene thus evinces a patriarchal hierarchy in which the man imposes roles on his two female partners; Stan, as Elena Del Río brilliantly argues, "orchestrat[es] the split between image and sound along technological lines" and "effects a split upon the female subject as well"[49] in an instance of "video fetishism."[50] The scene also demonstrates that he is powerless to proceed (and possibly sexually impotent) without Aline's directions. Underlying the role-playing and the images are essential questions of power relations and how they affect our identities. Metaperformance is, here as in the metadrama of Jonson and Shakespeare,[51] eminently political.

Figure 6.7 Family Viewing: *Stan instructs Aline to direct Sandra in a hypermedia bedroom.*

The meta intensifies in *Family Viewing*'s final act. Van's abandoning the family nest leads to a fragmentation of both narrative and narration, one that Stan attempts to counter by hiring a detective to uncover the identity of the person Van is hiding (Armen, whom Stan believes passed away). As is characteristic of diegetic metafiction according to Hutcheon, the detective plot provides a structure to the quest for meaning. The technology Stan's economic power grants him access to initially seems to give him the upper hand, as the detective's videos enable him (and us) to view what the narration had elided—an image of Van, Aline and Armen leaving their apartment [1:12:13–1:12:54] or hiding in a hotel room [1:17:40–1:17:55]. Yet even so, Van, Aline and Armen manage to elude the various surveillance cameras [1:18:31–1:22:35]. This escape is dramatized through intercutting, as Van and Aline conceal Armen, while Stan only finds an empty room with a television screen, on which his wife's face magically appears, in an homage to *Videodrome* (Cronenberg, 1983). The tables are turned in the metanarrative quest for control, as Van, Aline and Armen manage to both slip through the cracks of the patriarchal apparatus and trap Stan within a setup of their own, which, curiously, resembles his own.

Family Viewing proposes a highly complex view of moving images in the age of television and video, and reflects on both its potentials and dangers, avoiding "technomaniac and technophobic positions alike."[52] It confirms the ubiquity of media in contemporary society: the characters are portrayed as producers and consumers of images, but also as their prime material, as images themselves. The film also identifies, as Del Río has analyzed, "the double facet of the image as a vehicle for both the fetishistic and the auratic dimensions of seeing."[53] *Family Viewing* makes manifest the subjection and dehumanization produced by surveillance society and the society of spectacles—the omnipresence of surveillance cameras that are typically utilized when Aline is working at the phone sex company, and the perversion of basic human relations within the family (the bleak albeit parodic pornographic scenes featuring Stan and Sandra, or the fact that Stan, who doesn't even know how old his son is, enjoys watching TV with him); Stan, the patriarch, incarnates the instrumentalization of image technology to police others.

Conversely, *Family Viewing* argues that the democratization of moving pictures enabled by video technology is yet another stage in the Bazinian "mummy complex" or Barthes's "that has been"—such images enable us to preserve the memories of the past. In the end, the film both confirms and contradicts Benjamin's loss of the aura theory: these images threaten to erase our own memories, but they are also powerful connections and welcome material for one's identity as a son and grandson or a mother and grandmother. Even the surveillance camera, as Del Río argues, is somewhat rehabilitated in the epilogue, when it "has taken full account of the auratic charge of the moment, becoming a benevolent witness that presides over the encounter of grandmother, mother, and son."[54] Clearly, *Family Viewing* shifts its interest in the moving image away from the ontology of images to their meanings and uses: "no technological apparatus is inherently suited or unsuited to stage a fetishistic or auratic program. Rather, it is in the intersection between the apparatus and the discursive and affective modalities through which users engage with it that we may be able to sketch a certain course of viewing effects."[55] Armen, whose name evokes Armenia, and thus Egoyan and actresses' Arsinée Khanjian and Selma Keklikian's heritage, is also a link to an ethnic past marked by genocide, which, in *Family Viewing*, goes unspoken, much like Van's mother's fate. However fallible, then, recorded images, in a diasporic context notably, can provide a link to an event that one (like Aline) may have missed, a theme that will be further explored from a diasporic perspective in Egoyan's 1993 *Calendar* and 2002 *Ararat*. In a hypermedia world in which subjects and images are confused, interrogating media ontology, *Family Viewing* demonstrates, implies and enables an exploration of human identity, and thus an attention to the ethical and, albeit more implicitly, political stakes raised thereby.

FILM AND COMICS (*AMERICAN SPLENDOR*)

Contemporary comics adaptations increasingly utilize devices that recall the medium of their source material. Early attempts to integrate such devices into film and television include *Batman* (ABC, 1966–8), of course, *I Want to Go Home* (Resnais, 1989) and *Dick Tracy* (Beatty, 1990). Such "comics effects," as Alain Boillat calls them, can be achieved by resorting to split screens to mimic the layout of a comics page (as in *Hulk* [Lee, 2003]) or by varying the speed of the image and bringing it to a quasi-standstill (as in the opening credits of *Watchmen* [Snyder, 2009] and the fight scenes of *300* [Snyder, 2006]).[56] They are reflexive because, through them, "the movie puts itself on display as a composite artifact"[57]; they also "involve a self-reflexive treatment of filmic expression with contemporary digital technologies."[58] In particular, the sequences that play with the speed of moving images, Boillat argues, inscribe the encounter between digital cinema and comics within media history by pointing to a "common ancestor: chronophotography"[59] (photography is actually a central motif in the *Watchmen* opening credits). Though not remediation proper, intermedial moments such as these, that, like the famous scenes from *Blow-up*, both materialize the ontological borders of visual media and refer to media history, potentially qualify as meta.

An adaptation of Harvey Pekar's autobiographical comics series *American Splendor* (1976–91), with additional material from *Our Cancer Year* (1994), co-written with his wife Joyce Brabner, *American Splendor* (Berman and Pulcini, 2003) does triple duty as comics adaptation, biopic and documentary. The biopic provides the overarching structure: the film relates the coming of age of Harvey Pekar as a comics artist who couldn't draw and continued to work as a file clerk even after the success of *American Splendor*. Scattered across the film, the documentary moments include three classical interview scenes of the real Pekar and Brabner (conducted by the real director Shari Springer Berman); two making-of scenes in which we see the real Harvey Pekar and his friend and colleague Toby Radloff, and the actors playing their parts, Paul Giamatti and Judah Friedlander; and the film's epilogue which depicts Pekar celebrating his retirement (as a file clerk) with family and friends. While the bulk of the film adapts the comics in which Pekar adapted his own life, panels from the original comics are reproduced visually in specific moments in which the creative act takes center stage. Pekar's launching himself into the comics enterprise is narrated in a montage sequence [23:44–25:24], which juxtaposes a series of "actual" events and their comics rendition. The use of the dissolve expresses the transformation of everyday life into the raw material of art as a fluid process, but the causal chain is complicated by the fact that the film images are themselves modeled on the comics images, thus inverting the model–copy relationship—we are actually being presented the copy of a model that is itself a sort of copy. Clearly, this intermedial metamoment materializes at least two ontological questions regarding the similarities and differences between two media, and those between life and art.

These problems had already been raised in the opening credits [1:20–3:40]. The camera tracks along the pages of a comic in which the panels are alternately static drawn images, black-and-white photographs and color moving images, with the photos morphing into moving images or vice versa, except in panels featuring Pekar incarnations other than actor Paul Giamatti's. We are made to navigate between several Harvey Pekars—images of Giamatti portraying the artist, imitations of the various faces different artists (Robert Crumb, Greg Budgett and Gary Dumm, Gerry Shamray[60]) gave him, and a real photo of Harvey Pekar in 2003—and thus to consider "Harvey as always in a state of simulation."[61] Thus, the question of medium identity is intermeshed with questions bearing on the subject's identity: a biopic based on an autobiographical work in another medium, the opening credits suggests, implies a remediation of a character that was already the mediatization/fictionalization of a real person in the first place. Like many of the works analyzed in this book (*Blow-up*, *Fellini Roma*, etc.),

American Splendor seems to demonstrate that cinema's synchretic quality makes it an ideal medium with which to interrogate medium specificity, since the film image can also be a drawing or a photograph (as in animation or Marker's *La Jetée*). But what the opening credits also reveal are the limits of synchretism. The comics layout prevents the moving images from being just cinema; it is an overarching frame that organizes our perception of the material. However, it is itself subjected to the camerawork which, though it seeks to mimic the back-and-forth movement of a comics reader's gaze, nonetheless imposes an order that a comics does not (comics artist and theorist Benoît Peeters insists on the idea that comics are read in a "tabular"[62] fashion). Like a Chinese box comprised of disparate pieces, the film narration constrains the potential of the comics layout which, in turn, constrains the moving pictures in the panels. Synchresis and/or remediation, the film demonstrates, are not without hierarchy, and the medium of choice nonetheless imposes constraints upon the media it integrates, which lose some of their potential in the process.

An adaptation of a highly self-conscious comics that "encourage[s] intertextual or meta-textual commentary,"[63] Julia Round says, the movie contains scenes full of "meta-significance" and a "typically reflexive" finale. It is also paradigmatic of how potentially reflexive intermedial strategies tend to be. The live-action scenes make use of some of the most characteristic comics devices (captions that provide spatial and temporal information; speech balloons [18:32]) or their filmic equivalents (freeze frames [18:35], split screens [19:49, 40:37]). The supermarket scene in particular [18:17–20:22] employs several of these to dramatize Harvey's stumbling for the first time on prime material for his very own comics: the risky business of waiting in line behind a Jewish lady. Speech balloons appear depicting Harvey's thoughts in two close-ups of Giamatti's Pekar; the actor resorts to histrionic facial expressions (furrowing his eyebrows, then raising the right one) to evoke the facial expressions of a drawn character, and the image momentarily freezes and takes on the texture of a comics page (Figure 6.8). Once it becomes clear he's made a bad decision and is going to be stuck behind the Jewish lady who has gotten in an argument with the cashier and asked to see the manager, a drawn Harvey pops up in a thought balloon in the upper part of a long shot of the scene, and starts complaining while looking to the camera. A split screen then juxtaposes yet another drawn Harvey, this time facing the right and addressing Giamatti's Harvey; it is followed by a medium close-up of Giamatti's Harvey with yet another drawn Pekar advising him like a voice of conscience or cartoon devil. This dramatization of an artistic epiphany—it is here that Pekar will find his calling as a comics artist of the mundane, and more specifically realize "the ways in which triviality and profundity intertwine"[64]—is

Figure 6.8 American Splendor: *Harvey Pekar's (as portrayed by Paul Giamatti) intermedial epiphany: everyday life is prime material for comics art.*

also the origin tale of superhero narratives, a genre alluded into in the film's prologue: it is the moment when the "real" Pekar discovers his alter ego, himself as a comics character, and, more profoundly, that his superpower lies in his capacity to transform life into art.

Yet even in the scenes that do not resort to such salient intermedial devices, the characters inhabit a filmic world that is underpinned by the comics medium. Specific strategies are employed to suggest that the actual Pekar, his friends and acquaintances are comics characters, or that their potential to become so resides in everyday life situations and images. These include: tracking shots of Harvey walking the streets of Cleveland, combined with jump-cuts that function like gutters marking the movement effected between one panel and another [1:24, 6:07]; and more frequently, frame-within-the-frame composition (the library bookshelves framing Pekar and his colleagues [7:58]; a closed bus stop Pekar and Crumb are sitting in [14:42]; a window through which Pekar observes some delivery men [25:06]; the multiple frames fragmenting Pekar and David Letterman as they bicker during the show [1:16:04], etc.). These images act as reminders of what has already been stated in the opening credits—that what we have access to is not the real Pekar but the film adaptation of the cast of characters created by Pekar and his collaborators. Together, such devices create an underlying fantasy model characteristic of what Hutcheon calls "covert diegetic fiction," indicating that the film is haunted by Pekar's comics' fictionalization of his own life.

The formal concern with medium specificity ultimately serves to express the existential concern with human identity and the human condition that are at the heart of comics.[65] The blurring of ontological boundaries is complicated when Pekar realizes that, like his friend Crumb, he has become "famous" in the eyes of an acquaintance from college named Alice [33:58]. Centered on the couple, the second half of the film also relates the emergence of a "third" Harvey Pekar, a star whose "image"[66] is, in semiotic terms, based on a multitude of texts and paratexts (*American Splendor*, interviews, *Late Night with David Letterman*, etc.). The split Pekar has engineered between himself and his character, over which he has a degree of control as an artist, has spawned a trinity that escapes him. With the intermedial devices becoming less frequent, the evolution of this situation is dramatized through more classical metamoments based on mise en abyme and metalepsis. Harvey and Joyce fly out to Los Angeles to watch a stage performance of *American Splendor* in 1990 [57:29–59:16]. The real Pekar concludes in direct address, "If you think reading comics about your life seems strange, try watching a play about it. God only knows how I'll feel when I see this movie," overtly admitting his lack of control over the film he is participating in and proving thereby that a voiceover is by no means the equivalent of a first-person narrator in literature. When Pekar is invited on NBC's *Late Night with David Letterman* from 1986 to 1993 (though the last clip shown is actually from 1987), actress Hope Davis's Joyce Brabner and Pekar's friends are shown impossibly watching the real Pekar and Letterman on television on three occasions [1:03:42–1:17:12]. Pekar's lack of control over his star image is tragically redoubled by his lack of control over his bodily self when he is diagnosed with cancer. Ironically, the DSM-III-savvy Joyce, who excels in diagnosing everybody's pathologies including her own, sees comics as his salvation and presents art not as sublimation but as denial: "You'll make a comic book of the whole thing. You'll document every detail. And that way, you'll remove yourself from the experience until it's over" [1:19:53]. This is soon followed by a montage sequence depicting the events related in *Our Cancer Year* [1:24:46–1:26:38]. In spite of its similarity with the montage sequence of Pekar's development as an artist, the main contrast established in this instance is between the ironic tone of the comics and the pathos provoked by images of Giamatti's Pekar's physical condition.

The adaptation of *Our Cancer Year* also pursues the source's exploration of Pekar's identity, "Is he author and character, or just character?" brought about by his body's betrayal of his mind.[67] The 2003 film climaxes with a dream sequence [1:28:14–:31:11] that is a textbook example of metafiction. In it, Giamatti's Pekar delivers an existential monologue while strutting around an empty white space that morphs into drawn space, a comic panel, a

Figure 6.9 American Splendor: *Giamatti's Pekar demands to know, "Who are these people? What's in a name? Who is Harvey Pekar?"*

live-action setting; he finally steps out of the panel back into the white space and concludes: "Who are these people? What's in a name? Who is Harvey Pekar?" (Figure 6.9). The three questions set up a series of binaries—ontology and epistemology, signified and signifier—only to deconstruct them, much like the unholy trinity that Harvey Pekar has become. For although the final question seems modeled on the first, the use of a "name" connects it to the second and evokes the idea that "Harvey Pekar" is not just a person (who?) but a signifier (what?). The questions insist on the contingency of language, images, sounds (Pekar's raspy voice) and reality within the context of a work that has striven to formalize, order and comprehend all four. Thus, the question raised by the film *American Splendor* is not so much "Who is the real Harvey Pekar?" (the film never claims to answer it), but "Who or what is this character?" (based on a real person, performed by an actor, and so forth). The final metamoment thus depicts a creation calling out its many creators (Pekar but not only) and pointing to their moral responsibility in the existential crisis the character is undergoing, a solitary figure fashioned and consumed by multitudes.

The film will conclude on this question. In effect, its epilogue—the retirement party scene—ends on a close-up of Harvey and Joyce's latest work, *Our Movie Year* [1:37:22], revealing that the making of this film has already provided material for a comic, again blurring the ontological line between the model and the copy, and thus leaving the question as to who has authority over *American Splendor* and its characters dangling. The exploration of these ontological concerns goes far beyond questions of medium specificity and authorship; it intimately weds aesthetics and ethics. A postmodernist biography, *American Splendor* (2003), as Jason Sperb superbly writes, "is a film about painful life experiences," "about the impossibility of representing those experiences," about "the representation of something that necessarily cannot be represented."[68] If it foregrounds the attempt and failure to represent (Pekar as a person, the experience of cancer), it also emphasizes "the sense of a lived experience."[69] Yet again, the questions of creation, reception and medium ontology raised by meta are grounded in profound ethical questions of how we relate to art, fiction and the world.

DIGITAL AND INTERACTIVE MEDIA (*BLACK MIRROR: BANDERSNATCH*)

It is probably not entirely surprising that the concept of remediation has emerged concomitantly with digital technology. Several twenty-first-century films have attempted to address, on a meta-level, the material distinctions between analog and digital and/or the role of digital platforms. Ohad Landesman, for instance, has recently analyzed *Holy Motors* (Carax, 2012) as "a metacinematic work about both the death of cinema and its concurrent rebirth"; a prime example of remediation, the film "puts *the old and the new together*—it treats digital cinema not as a historical point of rupture and crisis, but as a necessary and evolutionary stage that is merely extending the past indefinitely into the future rather than altering the present completely."[70] The boundaries between analog and digital cinema are also a prime concern of David Lynch, patent in *Inland Empire* (where the metaleptical inclusion of the web series *Rabbits* troubles the ontological boundaries[71]) and in *Twin Peaks: The Return* (see Chapter 9).

The digital age has also witnessed the emergence of interactive audiovisual media. The latter would seem to be fertile terrain for the interpretive act that is meta. Digital games, for instance, are "naturally [. . .] *self-referential systems*," Bo Kampmann Walther concludes, but are not necessarily meta (that is, "self-referential on a content related or cultural level").[72] In her analysis of self-reflexivity in net.art, Marie-Laure Ryan observes varying functions of self-reflexivity in digital media. She concludes that computer games develop "self-reflexive features" to balance their own immersive potential and "promote themselves as an art form to be taken seriously," much like the novel before them (this partly rejoins J.D. Connor's "industrial self-reflexivity," see Chapter 9); net.art, on the other hand, is trying to counter the fact that the technology it relies on is trying to "fool us into believing that we fully control it, when in fact our agency is restricted to what the system was programmed to let us do."[73] Net.art would thus draw attention to the constraints of so-called interactive media and reflect on our relation to them (becoming meta in the process). Ryan thus points to two conceptions of interaction, the first modeled on the apparatus, the second emphasizing reception and interpretation. Interaction is not the sole domain of so-called interactive media, and metafiction, according to Hutcheon, certainly celebrates reader participation (see Chapter 2).

It is questions such as these that are raised by the interactive TV movie, *Black Mirror: Bandersnatch* (Netflix, 2018). In the late 1970s, "interactive" television fiction might take on the form of a hybrid sitcom/talk show like *The Baxters* (WCVB, 1977–8; Syndication, 1979–81), whose first half focused on the eponymous family dealing with a hot topic of the day and whose second half proposed a discussion with the live studio audience on that topic. In 2018, such interaction is likewise achieved though hybridity, but this time by remediating the video game and literature. In many ways, the interactive TV movie is also the digital platform equivalent of the movie about making movies, a parallel that is made explicit in one of the endings when the protagonist finds himself on a film set. In 1984, a young video game artist, Stefan Butler, meets Mohan Thakur, the head of a burgeoning video game company named Tuckersoft, and star designer, Colin Ritman, and pitches his idea for an interactive video game, *Bandersnatch*, adapted from a mammoth choose-your-own-adventure novel of the same name. Thus grounded in the history of reproducible media from print to video games, the diegesis foregrounds the interactive film's own place as a mass entertainment product inscribed within media history and economics: the interactive TV movie is a remediation of the TV movie through cross-pollination with the video game, which is itself, within the diegesis at least, an adaptation of a literary model.

Although its retro aesthetics initially seem to nostalgically celebrate geek culture in a fashion reminiscent of the simulated 1980s of episode S3E4 ("San Junipero") of *Black Mirror* (for instance, with fetishistic close-ups of a record player when Stefan and Colin take hallucinogens), *Bandersnatch* actually downplays the apparent technological abyss between 1984 and 2018 and emphasizes, rather, continuity regarding our uses of, and views on, technology. When Colin shows Stefan the new game he's working on, the amateur video game designer marvels at the smoothness of its graphics; in a later scene, Stefan's father Peter gets annoyed at his microwave. Technophobic and -philic attitudes pre-existed the twenty-first century, and there is nothing new, *Bandersnatch* admits, about *Black Mirror*'s exploration of these discourses, a point the 1984 time-setting drives in through the reference to George Orwell's novel. Such scenes suggest that emerging technologies have always brought their lot of options and anxieties, that our relations to technology are context-dependent, and that any technology is destined to fall into limbo.

By making Colin the inventor of the video games "Nosedive" and "Metalhead", both of which are titles of previous *Black Mirror* episodes (S3E1 and S4E5), attention is drawn to the episode's artificiality—Colin cannot have been influenced by a twenty-first-century television series, just as showrunner Charlie Brooker cannot have been influenced by a game designer who never existed—and to how its own discourse pertains to the rest of the series. A show that moved from one medium (television) to another (Internet) for its third season, *Black Mirror* predicts the newer technology's demise (or at least the end of its dominance) while betting on its future relevance, since the issues it addresses were already relevant thirty years ago and even in 1949 when Orwell published *1984*. With its depiction of a media ecosystem whereby new media turn out to be not-so-new media and older media affirm their relevance by incorporating new media, *Bandersnatch* is, whether deliberately or not, a neat illustration of the concept of remediation.

The interactive film, which allows us to make some of Stefan's decisions for him, also presents itself as an intermedial experiment. The difficulties of adapting the book as a video game thematize the film's own difficulties in striving for video-game-like interaction, in spite of the fact that video games have, since the 1980s, remediated cinema by incorporating filmed scenes (the first to use animated full-motion video, Data East's *Bega's Battle*, was released in 1983, a year before the events depicted in *Bandersnatch*). In the third scene again, Thakur notes that the mammoth book needs to be "streamlined," after Stefan has presented his prototype and explained how he wanted to program pathways so that the game could "be like the book." In effect, what the interactive film immediately emphasizes are the limited spaces of interaction within the film and, possibly, within any form of interactive narrative. The first two questions posed to the player/viewer (should Stefan choose between eating Sugar Puffs or Frosties (Figure 6.10), or listening to Thompson Twins or *Now 2*) hardly affect the immediate course of the narrative; these trivialities merely serve to indulge in 1980s nostalgia and color the soundtrack, and remind us of the long-standing practice of product placement and crossmedia promotion. These options are followed by the more fundamental question as to whether or not Stefan will accept Thakur's offer to finish the video game with a team in the Tuckersoft offices. Yet answering "Yes" leads directly to the end of the movie: Stefan's video game is demolished by a television critic, leading him to tell his father he will start over; the interactive film is then rebooted to the third scene. Some decisions lead to dead ends; others are not even submitted for our consideration. The limits of our interaction with the narrative become more salient in later scenes: we are invited to select one command, "No," during the flashback featuring Colin's mother and "Destroy Computer" when Stefan's frustration reaches breaking

Figure 6.10 Black Mirror: Bandersnatch: *our first decision concerns the protagonist's breakfast.*

point while he is coding, or two options that are basically the same, "Tell him more" or "Provide more details," when Stefan asks about Netflix. The negation and repetitions preclude interaction. An interactive film, *Bandersnatch* acknowledges, is a dubious proposal; at best, it is a maze in which the viewer/player's movements, like the Man in Black's in HBO's *Westworld*, are highly determined.

And yet, these impasses also reveal the possibilities that lie within these constraints. When the interactive film takes us back to Stefan's job interview, the scene is not replayed identically (we are shown a similar scene with the characters uttering lines previously spoken by another) until the decisive question concerning the job offer. This uncanny repetition with difference is noted by the characters, who express their astonishment at the other characters' "newfound" knowledge ("We've met before?" and "How did you know that?" Colin asks Stefan; the latter asks the former, "You've read *Bandersnatch*?"), which borders on awareness of their own fictionality. The modifications bid us to be alert, positioning us as hermeneutists in a quest for meaning. In addition to play and fantasy (*Bandersnatch* is, after all, a work of science fiction about a video game), the interactive film is thus underpinned by another model (detective fiction) that is characteristic of diegetic metafiction according to Hutcheon. The protagonist himself will shortly take on the role of hermeneutist; during his second appointment with his therapist, Dr Haynes, he shares his anxiety that he's "not in control," even of "little things," such as what he eats for breakfast. The above-mentioned trivial options were, then, not so trivial; or rather, it is their trivial quality that makes them revealing of the fiction's building blocks.

The modifications are not just playful; they have existential and ethical implications. The interactive film demonstrates that a decision is not limited to its immediate effect (as in the case of Stefan's accepting Thakur's offer); it is inscribed within a context. The slight changes made to the third scene suggest that, for Stefan to reject Thakur's offer, he has to be a different person ("I need to write it how I know. I mean, just me, at home."). Conversely, some elements (Stefan's memories) cannot be changed, as the flashback reveals, and very much determine the course of the narrative (the breakfast scene makes it clear that Stefan's obsession with the choose-your-own-adventure book is intimately connected to the loss of his mother). Like some of the metafictional novels discussed by Waugh,[74] the dramatizing of *Bandersnatch*'s protagonist's realization of his fictionality becomes a meditation on freedom. In one ending, Stefan the video game designer revels in the fact that the player only has the "illusion of free will" for "really [Stefan] decide[s] the ending." At the same time, Stefan's limited control over his life reflects how constrained our options are as viewers/players of the interactive film. As meta, *Bandersnatch*'s scope is primarily metanarrative, which is typical of television series (see Chapter 9). But it also calls into question the so-called freedom to choose that the streaming platform allows, made most evident in the scene where Stefan is on the verge of discovering his own fictionality and the options that are proposed to us are "Netflix" and the *Bandersnatch* logo; either way, the same answer is revealed on Stefan's computer screen: "I am watching you on Netflix. I make decisions for you" (Figure 6.11). Stefan's prison (one of the film's possible outcomes) is our own, the 1984 computer mirroring its twenty-first-century spawn that we are now utilizing. The limited options refract the limited range of a platform determined primarily by economics, the limited effect of our decisions, the limited freedom we are granted by the algorithms that attempt to preconstruct our way through the

Figure 6.11 Black Mirror: Bandersnatch: *"I am watching you on Netflix. I make decisions for you,"* appears on Stefan's 1984 computer screen.

platform's already limited maze and that nonetheless convey the illusion of a vast space. *Black Mirror*'s sole salvation lies, so to speak, in meta: that is, in its directing a critical gaze on itself and the very media that support it (to be continued in Chapter 11). Its salvation lies in its hope that, though viewers/players might be constrained on the surface, they will remain free to interpret the work.

Conclusion

More than just illustrating the mainstreaming of meta and, more specifically, the avant-garde concern with the materiality of the medium in contemporary film and television series, the chronological order these case studies were presented in was, above all, meant to trace the exploration of audiovisual fictions in relation to art and media history, from the fine arts to comics to television and video to digital and Internet. But while such works evince a concern for medium specificity, what mainly emerges from these analyses is a degree of continuity. The materiality of a medium is regularly interrogated through intermedial devices that are endowed with reflexive potential when they foreground the artifice, and with meta potential when they invite a commentary on the media. The exploration of the medium's properties and its evolution highlights the potentials and limitations of a given medium and/or the boundaries between old and new media, but ultimately celebrates the relevance of new media and the endurance of old media. The synchresis of audiovisual media such as cinema and television accommodates a space for such negotiations and affirms or maintains its own legitimacy and relevance in the process; ultimately, the power of audiovisual material lies in its plasticity. The space created thereby can also allow opposing discourses to cohabit, for instance techno-phobic and -philic attitudes. Meta establishes a dialogue with film and media theory, as was already the case with questions of spectatorship (see Chapter 5), illustrating it, responding to it and sometimes even anticipating it. *Fellini Roma* and *Family Viewing*, for instance, qualify and update the Benjamin thesis that denied reproducible arts an "auratic" quality, and insist both on their capacity to memorialize (siding with Bazin in the process) and on their material precariousness. In spite of the apparent postmodernism of these hypermedia works, the faith that some kind of origin or aura remains points to the persistence of modernist ideas, and tempers Brian McHale's thesis on postmodernist fiction: the epistemological concerns of modernism continue to underlie the ontological concerns of postmodernism—there remains something to excavate. Such continuities beg film and media scholars to gauge the usability and potential cohabitation of old and new media (*Fellini Roma* proves that intermedia reflexivity is nothing new), as well as the possible commonality between concepts such as synchresis, intermediality and remediation and their emergence in history in relation to each other; synchresis and remediation, for instance, both insist on the evolution of media, but the early-twentieth-century concept as applied to film was grounded in a more essentialist perspective and focused on the birth of the new medium rather than on its survival within an ecosystem. The precariousness of media and their material echoes the precariousness of human existence; the focus on the ontology and materiality of the medium, in these studies at least, has been revealed to be bound in questions of human identity and/or of a city that is personified. The chapters that follow will confirm that, even when meta is primarily concerned with form, it ends up raising ethical and political questions.

CHAPTER 7

Adaptation and Remake

ENGAGING WITH THE ORIGINAL: STATEMENTS OF INTENT PART I (*THE PORTRAIT OF A LADY*)

The metatextual, metafilmic or reflexive features of film adaptations and remakes, which recent scholarship has identified as adaptations within the same medium,[1] are regularly discussed in case studies and are touched upon in more theoretical works. Adapting Genette's typology of intertextuality to film, Stam labels adaptations that critique their sources as "metatexts,"[2] and cites *El otro Francisco* (Sergio Giral, 1974) as an example of a film which "self-reflexively explores adaptation as demystificatory critique."[3] In his groundbreaking *Film Adaptation and Its Discontents*, Thomas Leitch describes one of the possible relationships a film adaptation can have with its source as "*(meta) commentary or deconstruction.*"[4] His associating both terms is intriguing, for a commentary need not be deconstructive and deconstruction need not produce a commentary; what's more, the specificity of each term rejoins, to a certain extent, the distinction between meta (production of a discourse) and reflexivity (deconstruction of the illusion) developed in Chapter 1. Of course, Leitch may not be equating the two terms so much as suggesting that they are sibling concepts that (again like reflexivity and meta) are often associated. "The most characteristic films of this sort," he says, "are not so much adaptations as films about adaptations, films whose subject is the problems involved in producing texts."[5] He includes fiction films like *Jane Austen in Manhattan* (Ivory, 1980), *The French Lieutenant's Woman*, *Shadow of the Vampire*, *Adaptation* and *Tristram Shandy: A Cock & Bull Story*, as well as documentaries like *Looking for Richard* (Pacino, 1996) and *Lost in La Mancha* (Fulton and Pepe, 2002), and inscribes them in the tradition of literary metafiction.[6] If these examples also happen to be movies about movies, a film adaptation can also engage with the adaptation process on a more implicit level; indeed, Leitch shows that *Romeo + Juliet* (Luhrmann, 1996) adopts such a position in its prologue when a newscaster, featured on a television in a black void, utters the play's opening lines.[7]

Such metamoments are quite frequent in contemporary adaptations and remakes which, at the very least, acknowledge their secondariness and sometimes even comment on it. These scenes seem to occur primarily in the early stages (prologue, opening credits, opening scenes).[8] A common device found in classical adaptations of classic literature is the book opening before the credits appear on each page and shutting at the end (*Jane Eyre* [Stevenson, 1943]), displaying a cover without the author's name (*The Canterville Ghost* [Dassin and McLeod, 1944]) or skipping directly to the first chapter (*Great Expectations* [Lean, 1946]), a device which has its modern equivalent in the flipping comic book pages during the Marvel Cinematic Universe credits. Thus positioned in the vicinity of the opening credits, such scenes redouble the opening credits' function of creating a portal between two worlds—the film's or series's diegesis and reality.[9] They resemble metalepses whose transgressions are somewhat mitigated by the opening credits. The film or series is acknowledging the book's material existence in the real world and is presenting itself as its offshoot. The authority conferred on the story can even be transferred onto the production company (for instance, Charlotte Brontë's *Jane Eyre* is "presented by" Twentieth Century Fox in the 1943 film). This device is not properly meta insofar as it does not necessarily provide a framework through which the adaptation process should be considered; it merely points to the ontological gap between the book's material existence and the filmic rendition of its diegesis. It does, however unwittingly, draw attention to a fundamental difference between film and literature, that is, that the sounds and images experienced in a reader's mind—what Wolfgang Iser calls the process of "ideation"[10]—differ from one person to another, while the material existence of the film's sounds and images ensures that all viewers are provided with the same audiovisual material (which does not mean that their experience of it is the same). Or in the case of comics, for instance, that the static images can be read in a "tabular"[11] fashion, a possibility that the rapidly flipping pages in the MCU opening credits denies in order to privilege the stability of the brand name.[12]

More elaborate variations of this device can be found in more recent film adaptations. The 2005 *Pride & Prejudice*, as I have shown elsewhere,[13] opens with a scene depicting Elizabeth Bennet reading a book as she walks through a field [1:17–3:03]; she closes the book with an amused chuckle, then heads back home where she witnesses a conversation between her parents that happens to be the novel's first dialogue. A digital enhancement of the close-up of the book's pages reveals that Elizabeth is actually reading the last page of Austen's novel with a different cast of characters. Her closing the book with an amused chuckle works as a declaration of intent that the film is going to playfully depart from its source (and maybe even that actress Keira Knightley is going to approach the role with a touch of sarcasm). The subsequent scene confirms this, as the Bennet house is depicted as dirty and rowdy—in short, vital—inhabited by a couple who enjoys teasing each other. Standing outside so that her parents are framed by the window, Elizabeth is momentarily positioned as the spectator of the staging of the book's opening. Quickly absorbed into the film's overall realism, this metamoment is a mere expansion of the classical opening book device. But in the twenty-first century, it presupposes not only a viewer that is quite familiar with the novel and its previous adaptations—the rowdiness and cheekiness suggested here is, no doubt, meant to set the 2005 film apart from what was at the time the benchmark adaptation, the immensely popular 1995 BBC mini-series starring Jennifer Ehle and Colin Firth)—but also a viewer endowed with the curiosity and the technical know-how to pause and explore the pages of Elizabeth's book.

Less normative, perhaps, are examples in which the threshold between the source text and the adaptation altogether dispenses with a book or writing tools such as ink (*Mansfield Park*, Rozema, 1999) or typewriter (*Atonement*, Wright, 2007). Examples can be found in the classical era. *Hamlet* (Olivier, 1948), for instance, starts out with a very classical title card, including nine lines authored by Laurence Olivier himself, which is followed by the film's rendition of Act I Scene 1 with an additional line from the end of Act I Scene 4 [2:22–9:23]. As if set in motion by the famous "Something is rotten in the state of Denmark," the camera pans right and plunges into the bowels of the castle; the shot dissolves into another tracking shot that passes over the empty seats of the people the spectre of King Hamlet will later identify as being those guilty of his death (Claudius and Gertrude), tracks down the corridor leading to Ophelia's quarters, only to pan right, track down another corridor and finally end on a long shot of the king and queen's bed; by dissolving to a lateral close-up of Claudius, the narration immediately identifies the culprit [9:24–10:30]. The elaborate tracking shot's immediate function is, of course, to set the stage spatially speaking, but it is also metanarrative: it sums up the plot of a play many viewers would be familiar with—Hamlet's attempt to avenge his father's death at the hands of his mother and father-in-law and his thus compromising his love affair with Ophelia (the roving camera also expresses Hamlet's desires). Olivier thus proposes a three-step entry into the film: from a frame text which provides the director's interpretation of the famous source, to the play's filmed performance, to a purely cinematic form—a more concise, discrete and perhaps cinematic equivalent of Olivier's baroque experiment in *Henry V* (1944), which depicts a fictitious performance of the Shakespeare play at the Globe Theatre in 1660, before becoming a full-fledged film (or ideation of the text) from Act II (the events in Southampton) until the final scene. These opening scenes do more than just reflexively point to the familiarity of their sources; they are meta because they reflect on what it means to adapt Shakespeare and interrogate the boundary between film and theatre,[14] filmed theatre and film adaptation, theatrical space and cinematic space, and perhaps even between metatheater and metacinema.[15]

A political variation of the programmatic opening strategy occurs in *The Portrait of a Lady* (Campion, 1996) [0:13–2:44], which Nancy Bentley has analyzed as "a movie about movies."[16] While the names of the cast roll, the voices of several women can be heard talking about a common topic, which shifts from the eminently cinematic motif of kissing[17] to love. This is followed by a series of sensual images of women, some of whom are interacting playfully (lying down in the grass, caressing each other's hair, dancing), while others look right at the camera thoughtfully, harboring expressions that vary from happiness to sadness. The title of the film then appears written in ink on a woman's left hand, which the camera tracks across. The prologue is a clear statement of intent: not only is a woman director going to adapt a renowned male author's classic novel, but she is going to address contemporary women and engage with feminist concerns to do so. The emphasis on voices first, then on gazes, inverts the history of feminist film theory, taking us back in time to Kaja Silverman's 1988 *Acoustic Mirror* whose study of the female voice in classical cinema pursued Laura Mulvey's 1975 thesis on the male gaze; the emphasis on plurality echoes Teresa de Lauretis's call for movies about women and not Woman.[18] Recalling the intertwining female voiceovers of *India Song*, the chorus of voices also evokes a session of group therapy or a series of interviews in a documentary, in either case marking the ontological boundary between the prologue and *The Portrait of a Lady* (novel and film) as works of fiction. These women clearly do not belong to the same world as Isabel Archer—nor even to the world of Hollywood filmmaking (they all have Australian accents, while the cast is exclusively British and US-American and Nicole Kidman plays an American[19]).

The homage to James's novel nonetheless remains. For what the sounds and images also suggest is that this story about a lady—one that is apparently limited in terms of race, class and nationality—can be relevant for modern women regardless of their background, that it has the power of a fable, an idea conjured up by the bucolic environment and composer Wojciech Kilar's sensual flute melody. The position of the hand combined with the lateral tracking shot operates a movement that, like an arrow, takes us effortlessly from the frontal medium close-up of an anonymous late-twentieth-century woman to a frontal close-up of Isabel Archer/Nicole Kidman. And yet, the quasi-avant-garde prologue immediately makes way for a fairly classical period drama; it does not provide a model, but grossly provides us with the framework with which to interpret the adaptation, and notably that the central Jamesian figures of the voice, the look and the young US-American woman will be reinterpreted in the light of feminist film theory—for instance, the scene in which Isabel fantasizes that Ralph Touchett is watching Caspar Goodwood and Lord Warburton caress her [17:13–19:11] has been analyzed by Bentley as a thematization of the tension between female desire and the male gaze,[20] and thus as yet another metamoment.

The prologue is also a statement of intent regarding the film's approach to the costume drama genre and, more specifically, its position vis-à-vis the perceived conversative politics of the British heritage movies of the 1980s and 1990s.[21] For instance, the utilization of Dutch angles and salient camera movements in the Italian scenes not only departs from the genre's habitual postcard cinematography, it invokes the expressionist tradition and turns *The Portrait of a Lady* into an exemplar of the female Gothic (Osmond's declaration of love visually triggers an aggressive track-in more suited to alert the viewer of an imminent attack than a kiss [55:09]). The costume drama is more brutally disrupted almost halfway through the film when Isabel's 1873 travels are narrated in an overtly reflexive montage sequence, which resembles the projection of a silent film, an idea Campion may have borrowed from *Bram Stoker's Dracula* (Coppola, 1992) [58:33–1:00:12]. The sequence is an intertexual palimpsest comprised of "disparate film styles" presented "in quick succession," conjuring up memories of "Valentino-era silent film (recalling the exoticism of *The Sheik* [Melford, 1921]),"[22] *Sherlock Jr.*'s famous metalepsis, Werner Herzog's 1979 remake of *Nosferatu* (Murnau, 1922) because of the images of Osmond enlacing Isabel, *Vertigo* because of the spiral. A close-up of Isabel looking to the camera (Figure 7.1), like the women in the prologue, is followed by a reverse shot that tracks in on an evil-looking Osmond, expressing the hypnotic power of the character's gaze and voice. Positioned almost halfway through the movie, the scene acts as a secondary frame; it reveals the film to be a fantasy about fantasies, points back to the prologue both aesthetically and politically, further asserts the adaptation's inscription within a framework informed by feminist film theory and the female Gothic, and goes beyond adaptation to inscribe the film more generally within the history of representations of female bodies and sexuality in film.

Similar statements of intent can be found in the incipits of remakes and reboots both in film and television. *Planet of the Apes* (Burton, 2001) [3:17–4:40] and *Prometheus* (Scott, 2012) [8:09–12:33] reprise the opening scenes of Franklin J. Schaffner's 1968 film and Ridley Scott's own 1979 film (a spaceship is crashing or navigating through space), but the similarity turns out to be a red herring (the 2001 crash is actually a simulation conducted by a chimpanzee, and the 2012 crew already knows that the pilot is a cyborg). In so doing, the films invite audiences to expect a narrative based on repetition

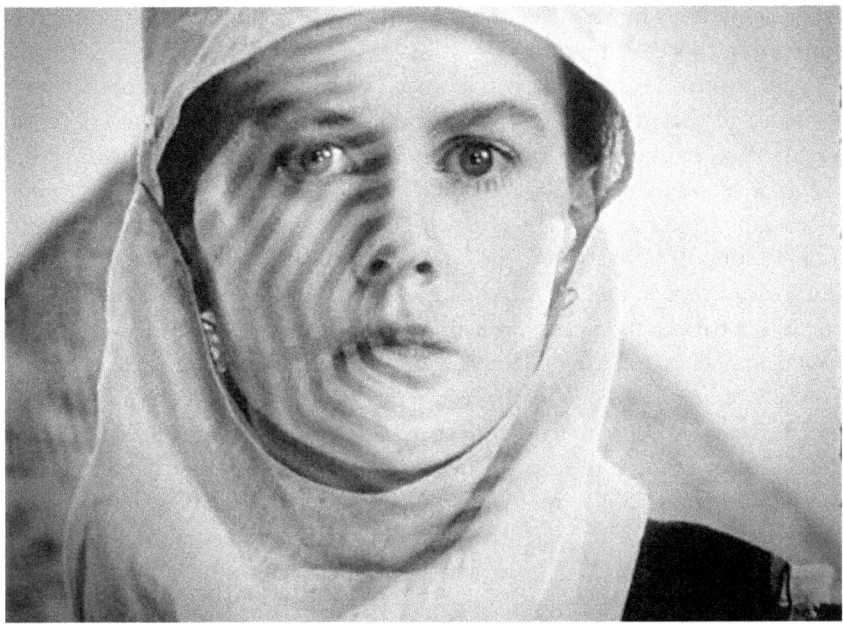

Figure 7.1 The Portrait of a Lady: *Isabel Archer looks to the camera in a silent film pastiche that inscribes the film within the history of cinema from a feminist perspective.*

with variation and to engage with the remake on a playful mode, Burton cheekily making the spectator surrogate a primate in a flight simulator and thus reminding audiences of their own apish nature! Something similar, but perhaps more ambiguous, occurs in the prologue of *The Texas Chainsaw Massacre* (Nispel, 2003) [0:45–2:40]. The remake, as I have demonstrated elsewhere,[23] acknowledges the 1974 *Texas Chain Saw Massacre* by reprising its "based on a true story" conceit (the remake's producers even went so far as to cast John Larroquette whose voice featured in the 1974 prologue, which is then followed by a sample of the conspicuous "zigging" sound from the original soundtrack). The elaborate prologue thus reads like a clear homage, and yet it is also the promise of something more. The additions to the original text, combined with the images from the police archive and found footage, suggest that this *Texas Chainsaw Massacre* really is going to give us, if not the true story, then a more developed one, i.e., one whose production value is greater than that of the independent film (more gore, CGI, and stars from television and even a Stanley Kubrick film). The statement of intent is thus made in bad faith and is more in keeping with what Thomas Leitch has noted about the remake: that it promises to be "*just like* its model" only "*better*,"[24] to improve on the qualities of the original, with the underlying assumption that modern technology and film conventions are inevitably superior to those of the past.

Such moments are similarly positioned early on in series where they tend to occur in the first episode and sometimes even in the opening scenes. Eight or so minutes into the 2003 mini-series that launched the *Battlestar Galactica* reboot (Sci-Fi, 2004–9) [8:23–8:48], the recycling of the original spaceships from the ABC series (1978–9)—and thus the Sci-Fi series's retro look in spite of its reliance on CGI—turns out to be humanity's salvation (the Cylons couldn't take control of the older ships because their computers weren't networked). Faithful to its model, *Scream: The Series* (MTV, 2015–19) includes a character named Noah, who, during a classroom discussion on Gothic literature that occurs thirteen minutes into the pilot episode [13:00–13:50], states, "You can't do a slasher movie as a TV series. [. . .] Slasher movies burn bright and fast. TV needs to stretch things out. You know, by the time the first body is found, it's only a matter of time before the bloodbath commences," the images of the discovery of the first victim's body floating in a swimming pool (which are intercut with the classroom scene) apparently confirming that remaking *Scream* as a series is a challenge because of the film's genre. *Bates Motel* (A+E, 2013–17) opens with Norman Bates and his mother purchasing a motel after Mr. Bates's death and pondering the difficulties of "starting over," Norman's remark that "Maybe some people don't get to start over" suggesting that rebooting does not necessarily imply a change in characterization [5:34]. Throughout the series, Norman's hallucinations, as Sarah Hatchuel has shown, can be interpreted as the spectres of previous works haunting the series. "The gap between the television series and its filmic model,"[25] Hatchuel notes, is likewise foregrounded in *Hannibal* (NBC, 2013–15) through Will Graham's visions. The pilot's opening scene asserts its approach to its source material through its portrayal of Will Graham's talent for empathizing with serial killers. Unlike the first adaptation of Thomas Harris's 1981 novel *Red Dragon*, *Manhunter* (Mann, 1986), which merely shows Graham speaking into a Dictaphone, the narration makes us experience Graham's reimagining the crime in an attempt to determine the killer's "design" [0:00–4:18]; he is then shown expounding his method to a diegetic audience in a university classroom. With its images of the traces of the crime vanishing and Graham moving backwards, the scene as a whole becomes an allegory of the series's intention to reimagine the Hannibal Lecter franchise (as promoted by the series title) by starting with a prequel of *Red Dragon* (as indicated by the episode title, "Apéritif"). The motifs of going back in time and/or repetition with variation have become quite common in reboot series (*Battlestar Galactica*, *Bates Motel*, *Hannibal*, but also *Westworld*).

Adaptations and remakes of well-known works tend to open with some sort of statement of intent that acknowledges the source, recognizes its significance in order to legitimize the adaptation itself, and sometimes presents the adaptation approach proposed in terms of fidelity, updating and/or deviation—a relationship that is more or less always founded on the paradox that the secondary work is the same but different, and, if not better, at least more suitable to contemporary audiences. Such scenes provide a generic and/or theoretical framework through which the rest of the work is meant to be interpreted, and seem to have become more systematic and more elaborate over the years. This relationship is often expressed through motifs including objects associated with the source's medium (books, film reels), as well as audiovisual motifs that express erasure, repetition and/or rewinding. Viewers (or some of them at least) are thought to be familiar with the source material and are thus expected to compare similarities and differences, whether narrative, thematic, aesthetic or political—this is particularly the case in works such as *Ed Wood*, *Shadow of a Vampire* or *Be Kind Rewind*, that remake specific scenes from their sources. If all such openings are reflexive, they are not always meta; they become meta when they have more to say than, "This is based on pre-existing material," and interrogate how they mean to engage with it. The rest of the chapter explores adaptations that are based on metafictional novels and/or are themselves highly meta.

ADAPTING THE METAFICTIONAL NOVEL (*THE FRENCH LIEUTENANT'S WOMAN*, *A COCK & BULL STORY*, *INHERENT VICE*)

Metafictional novels or stories have rarely been adapted, as we have seen, but what happens when one is? Is its metadiscourse about literary fiction discarded, made more or less explicit, or transposed and/or generalized? In 1992 Stam argued that "[w]hile [most adaptations of such works, including *Tom Jones* and *The French Lieutenant's Woman*] incorporate certain reflexive devices, they do not metalinguistically dissect their own practice or include critical discourse within the text itself,"[26] unlike *El otro Francisco* which he would cite as a counter-example in 2005. *Tom Jones* and *The French Lieutenant's Woman* would thus be reflexive but not necessarily meta. What follows is a study of these two well-known and fairly successful adaptations, based on novels written by one of the eighteenth-century metafictionists (Henry Fielding) and a frequent example of postmodern metafiction (John Fowles), along with two more recent endeavors to adapt similar writers (Laurence Sterne and Thomas Pynchon).

Adapted by the playwright and director of *Look Back in Anger* (1959), the Woodfall production that launched the trend of angry young men films influenced by documentary and European art cinema, *Tom Jones* abounds in reflexive devices borrowed from slapstick comedy (addresses and looks to the camera), the French New Wave (jump-cuts, freeze frames) and especially silent cinema (intertitles, irises, wipes, fast-forwarded chase scenes and trick shots that have become markers of artificiality in color and sound film). The omniscient voiceover, like the novel's narrator, foregrounds the protagonist's fictionality by calling him "our hero," acknowledging the viewer's presence through the use of the inclusive pronoun. Tom and his main romantic interest, Sophie Western, look knowingly to the camera on several occasions; Tom even asks the audience if "you" have seen the George Inn Landlady steal his £500 note [1:07:27], while his supposed mother Jenny Jones details the contents of his true mother's letter [1:57:46–1:58:05], proving that they are very much aware of being characters and thereby violating the ontological boundary between fiction and reality. Not only is a gleeful parallel drawn between Tom the bastard's irreverent attitude toward social conventions and that of the protagonists of previous Woodfall productions (notably *Saturday Night and Sunday Morning*'s [Reisz, 1960] Arthur Seaton, also played by Albert Finney), but the cumulative effect of these reflexive devices, together with the film's carnivalesque approach (basic instincts such as hunting, drinking, eating, and having sex are emphasized, and a parallel is ultimately made between human and animal behaviors), mounts a systematic assault on the conventions of the costume drama and classical film adaptations of classic novels (for instance, when Tom covers the camera with his hat to censor a potential sex scene [1:12:48]). The film is actually faithful in spirit to its source text and finds relevance in Fielding's own parodic stance to playfully mock the social and formal conventions that govern the classical film genre. Content to play for laughs rather than establish a framework with which to critically interpret the source text (like *The Portrait of a Lady*) or engage with the process of adaptation (like *Tristram Shandy: A Cock & Bull Story*), *Tom Jones* proves that excessive reflexivity can be deconstructive without offering a "metatextual commentary"[27] other than to say that such conventions are ludicrous.

Stam concludes that *The French Lieutenant's Woman* likewise "retreats from the reflexivity of the John Fowles source novel."[28] The 1981 movie, written for the screen by Harold Pinter, adapts Fowles's reflection on the similarities between history and fiction (their open-endedness and constructedness[29]) as a movie about making movies which parallels the romance experienced by the characters (Sarah and Charles) and the actors (Anna and Mike). The adaptation of the novel as such is never mentioned until the very end of the movie when Anna's fiancé David asks Mike which of the novel's two endings the filmmakers are going to opt for [1:46:49]. Once the opening scene has established that *The French Lieutenant's Woman* is a film being made by director K.Q. Rogers (no confusion with the actual director Karl Reisz, although the first and last name initials are the same), the narration rigorously cuts between the Victorian costume drama (which, though it is revealed to be a cinematic construction, is by no means parodied like the Victorian novel is by Fowles[30]) and the actors' personal lives. Ontological boundaries are preserved throughout; apart from the momentary confusion introduced by the "Three Years Later" title, which follows the party at Mike's place but is immediately clarified by the scene it introduces [1:50:32], we never hesitate between the two worlds depicted, and the actors never wonder whether or not they are characters. The narratives are made to criss-cross quite ironically, the complicated web of emotions experienced by the Victorian characters contrasting with the simple affair Anna and Mike seem to be enjoying. The narration dwells primarily on the fiction (the present-day scenes amount to approximately twenty-three minutes of the film's total run-time, roughly 18.5 per cent) until the actors' story comes to dominate the final scenes, following Anna's announcement that, unlike Sarah, she is going to be reunited with her French lover. The film's structural irony is thus inverted, as the Victorian fiction is given a happy resolution—presumably, because of film conventions—while the contemporary love affair is doomed.

The novel's discourse on the power of social and aesthetic conventions makes way for a romantic plot based, in appearance, on the eternal power of love but, more profoundly, on the power of romance as fiction on the one hand, and of "the permeability of the realms of life and art" on the other—in R. Barton Palmer's astute analysis, "the inseparability of what we might call the performance product (such as the actor's transformation of himself into a signifier) from the existential physical reality of performance (such as acting as a form of work for which the actor is rewarded and paid)."[31] The actors' identities are, in effect, troubled by their roles, as demonstrated by the opening shot (a close-up dominated by Anna's black hood in which the left side of her face appears in the mirror the make-up artist is holding up for her [Figure 7.2] [0:31]) and the concluding scenes (when Mike the actor calls Anna "Sarah," before sitting down and, the final images seem to suggest, fondly remembering the final and happy scene of the film-within-the-film [2:01:07]). Anna is as ungraspable to Mike as Sarah is to Charles because she is, through no fault of her own, a fantasy, an image in which the actress is confused with her character; "[h]er flight from Mike *is* the flight from real reality, the act that defines fiction, [. . .] as a presence with no substance, as a discourse grounded finally in nothing but itself."[32] In this respect, the film cleverly turns the novel's tension between two different readers[33] (Sarah and Charles) into one between a spectator (Charles) and an actress/director (Sarah) in the diegetic film, and especially between an actress (Anna)

Figure 7.2 The French Lieutenant's Woman: *in the opening scene, Anna prepares for her role as Sarah, the eponymous heroine, whose face is reflected back at the actress and audience, announcing the quasi-metaleptical confusion between both women in the mind of Mike, the actor turned spectator.*

who is anything but a manipulative director figure and an actor (Mike) whose professionalism should enable him to avoid becoming a member of the audience his performance is meant for—a spectator in love with an image. Yet the metaleptic and metafictional implications are downplayed because, ultimately, the boundary that is breached is not ontological but unproblematically located in Mike's psyche, a confusion foreshadowed in the cut from Anna and Mike rehearsing a scene to the actual scene of Sarah falling into Charles's arms [26:37–28:08]; it is not the diegesis that is underpinned by a fantasy but the protagonist's subjectivity. Stam might not give the film enough credit, but his general assessment remains valid; "the slippery connections between art and life are not analyzed but dramatized,"[34] as Palmer demonstrates, and the meta remains a surface affair.

Unlike its predecessors, the subject matter of *Tristram Shandy: A Cock & Bull Story* (2005) is quite explicitly adaptation, and more precisely how difficult it is to bring to the big screen a 600-page-long novel in which the eponymous hero doesn't broach his own birth until Volume III (the fact that lots of material had to be cut out is brought up on several occasions). The 2005 film initially combines the approaches *Tom Jones* and *The French Lieutenant's Woman* took to their sources. Like the 1981 film, it is a movie about making movies[35] that is centered on the actors and that (initially at least) alternates between moments where the actors are in character and moments where the actors are "themselves"; as such, it reprises the theme of the permeability between life and art. As in Richardson's *Tom Jones*, the scenes from the film adaptation they are shooting utilize direct address to the camera, freeze frames, wipes, irises and trick shots (e.g. the Brobdingnagian hand intruding in the middle of the battlefield as if it were a model [16:03]). But there are notable differences.[36] First, *A Cock & Bull Story* includes an interview with a Laurence Sterne scholar named Patrick Curator, portrayed by British comedian Stephen Fry, who provides an interpretation of the novel's meaning ("The theme of *Tristram Shandy* is a very simple one. Life is chaotic, it's amorphous. No matter how hard you try, you can't actually make it fit any shape." [59:53–1:00:42]); this parody of interviews, such as those conducted by Al Pacino in *Looking for Richard*, recall the parodies of academic discourse the adapters of Fowles's *French Lieutenant Woman* chose to leave out. Second, in keeping with the novel's first-person narration, Tristram Shandy, unlike Tom Jones, does not compete with a voiceover narrator. His presence in the flesh, however, renders problematic his status as narrator and character, especially since Coogan also plays Tristram's father Walter. In an early scene, Tristram the narrator depreciates the young Tristram's attempt to reproduce the "emotion" produced by the traumatic accident with his penis [6:44–7:44], thus metaleptically crossing the temporal, spatial and ontological line between narration and diegesis which, given the film's approach, the performers can only pretend is there since they are both there at the same time. All this is complicated by the fact that Coogan and Brydon are allegedly playing themselves, thus creating uncertainty as to whether these sections are the actual making-of or a fictional one.[37] If the film is closer in tone to the Woodfall production, including the carnivalesque aesthetics (the costumes, parties and, more generally, the emphasis on the grotesque body whether teeth, nose, penis or uterus, present in Sterne's novel), its dynamics is similar to *The French Lieutenant's Woman*, as the subject of the film increasingly becomes the relationship between the two actors.

The shift, however, occurs much earlier and much more brutally than in the 1981 film (roughly a third of the way into *A Cock & Bull Story*). In place of an actors' romance, we have a story of male rivalry that is itself based on the uncertainty as to who the novel's and film's hero actually is: Tristram, Walter or Uncle Toby. This uncertainty is essentially linked to the problems of adapting a first-person novel into film. As narrator, Sterne's Tristram Shandy is inevitably the heart and lungs of the novel in spite of his quasi-absence on the diegetic level. But a narrative film not only risks displacing Tristram for the benefit of Uncle Toby (in an early scene, the latter momentarily takes over in voiceover to narrate the battle of Namur [15:44–16:00]), its narration englobes Tristram the narrator's interventions, visually highlighting his presence at the margins of the action in terms of both composition (Figure 7.3) [8:59] and narrative (Toby's battle scene and potential romance with the

Figure 7.3 Tristram Shandy: A Cock & Bull Story: *Tristram Shandy the narrator is marginalized as he watches Uncle Toby, positioned next to a model battlefield, relating his military exploits to a young Tristram.*

widow Wadman which Coogan dreams up [1:09:17–1:11:56]). The power struggle between the two actors is overtly metanarrative, with Coogan trying to influence the film's staging by demanding boots with augmented heels [33:46], or unwittingly handing over the lead role to Brydon by suggesting the widow Wadman subplot be incorporated [1:00:44] (an idea he lifted from a journalist in an effort to make people believe he read the novel! [37:40]). Coogan's and Brydon's rivalry is rife with sexual undertones, with the latter expressing concern about the former's libido, so that Coogan himself loses confidence. Is he the "leading man," and thus the alpha male, capable of servicing both Jenny, the mother of his child, and Jennie, the production assistant, unlike Tristram's father's bull [1:29:08–1:30:20]? This hesitation, and the sexual anxiety that it provokes, are expressed in the film's subtitle, the cock and the bull being symbols of virility.

A Cock & Bull Story initially elaborates on the adaptation strategy of *The French Lieutenant's Woman* by turning the adapted work into a mise en abyme of the adaptation, inverting the habitual hierarchy between adapted and adaptation; it is the source text, reduced in the later film to a mere 26 per cent of the total run-time, that comes to mirror the secondary work and not the other way around. In the end, the 2005 film radically departs from the 1981 film because the making-of of an adaptation of *Tristram Shandy* ultimately becomes the "making-of of the making of"[38] *Tristram Shandy: A Cock & Bull Story*, the movie we are watching, when we, like the producers (who voice their alarm that the emotional scene between Walter and his son has been replaced with one between Coogan and the baby girl meant to play baby Tristram [1:22:35–1:26:29]) realize that the making-of we thought we were watching is actually the film itself. The narrative thus becomes about the cast and crew's decision to adapt the novel in such a manner, but several clues (the womb prop Coogan tests on the set of the *Tristram Shandy* adaptation [30:50–32:10], which is later featured in a dream Coogan has [1:11:16], or Gillian Anderson's impossibly accepting the part of the widow Wadman in less than five minutes, which is then recounted in an impossibly energetic flashback [1:03:38–1:04:26]), some of which significantly work in pairs, in keeping with the film's title and the theme of rivalry (Tristram and Coogan quote Groucho Marx [4:07, 51:04], Coogan's two love interests have quasi-identical names), testify to the fact that the film we have been watching was the finished product. Although the diegetic director insists that it remains "true to the original story" [1:27:42], Sterne's novel has been turned into the mise en abyme of a mise en abyme, while the approach of the 1981 *French Lieutenant's Woman* has been made relevant in a digital age where everything is recorded and can potentially become a DVD extra.[39]

If Coogan repeatedly states that a film that is funny is in itself a worthy enterprise, and if *A Cock & Bull Story*'s main ambition is just that (and is thus the same as that of the 1963 *Tom Jones*), the 2005 film nonetheless proves far more ambitious than mere parody (in spite of its spoofing the music from *8½*, *Barry Lyndon* [Kubrick, 1975] and *The Draughtman's Contract*[40]) and qualifies as a "metadaptation."[41] A film adaptation of a novel that is about the conventions of the novel should, it contends, be a movie that is about the intricacies of adaptation as a practice that, in film at least, is at once artistic and industrial. The two are neatly combined in the discussion of the battle scene and the last-minute casting of Gillian Anderson; a dramatic battle scene would align the film with Hollywood conventions (*Braveheart* [Gibson, 1995] is cited as a worthy model [53:05]), while casting a Hollywood star ends up attracting further investment to finance an expensive battle scene. It is during the screening of the rushes that the question of what kind of a movie they are trying to make is raised—a big action film (one of the producers), a comedy (Coogan), an art film (Jennie, the Fassbinder fan), a historically accurate production (production designer David Ingoldsby)—and which audience they are trying to reach. In a previous meeting, in which the production designer vows to give every single character the name of a soldier that was actually on the battlefield that day, Coogan voices his shock that realism should even be a concern in a film in which "a grown man [is] talking to the camera in a fucking womb" [31:42]. Apparently, the production designer profoundly misunderstands the anti-illusionist novel because the criterion of historical verisimilitude is so deeply ingrained in contemporary filmmaking that it goes well beyond adaptations of British classics (*Cold Mountain* [Minghella, 2003]) and includes historical films based on original material like *Braveheart*. For all their mockery of Merchant Ivory productions and the heritage movie craze[42] (they joke that the giant womb Coogan has to crawl in is a "womb with a view"), some of the cast and crew, at least, abide by the same standards (even Coogan can't help point out that "real wombs don't have a window like that" [30:25]).

P.T. Anderson's approach to adapting Thomas Pynchon's *Inherent Vice*, reputedly the most accessible of his novels, couldn't be more different. The film maintains the storyline, much of the dialogue, a dab of allohistory (in a *Forrest Gump* spoof, one character, Coy Harlingen, is seen on TV crashing a "Vigilant California Rally" where Nixon is giving a speech [55:48]), and Pynchon's recurrent themes and features: conspiracy, paranoia, altered states, chaos, sex, linguistic polyphony (the various lingos, languages and accents, which are made more prominent by the performances), the instability of words and signs (notably the swastika which, one character explains, is a Hindu symbol of good fortune [1:34:35]). The film also carries over the novel's parody of hard-boiled/noir conventions that provides a structure typical of diegetic metafiction. Doc makes for a dubious PI, capable, like Philip Marlowe, of navigating various social circles, but seemingly floating in a sense of confusion because of his drugged state; he uses a magnifying glass to decipher a postcard [1:13:30], jots down "Something Spanish" in his notebook after another character (Clancy Charlock) has just given him the name of a place in the desert he should look into ("Arrepentimiento") and translated it into English [1:08:59], and answers "Good question" when a man he's looking into (Adrian Prussia) asks why he's here [1:57:10]. If Doc somehow saves the day, he is at best a very confused Sherlock, and we are often in a better position to retain certain bits of information.

By incorporating some of the novel's dialogue, the film also preserves some of its source's metanarrative commentary (Sortilège saying that Doc is "doing good" with his investigation [1:31:15], Doc and Crocker Fenway working for a "peaceful resolution" in one of the final scenes [2:07:05]). But what is perhaps most striking is the addition of a voiceover (spoken by a secondary character named Sortilège) a viewer unfamiliar with the novel might have believed to be lifted directly from Pynchon. The voiceover operates simultaneously as a marker of literariness and a distancing effect: that is, it distances the film from the source text in which Sortilège is merely a character, and it creates an enigmatic connection between Doc, the protagonist, whom we mostly follow, and Sortilège, which is enhanced by her gender. Sortilège's appearance in close-up as early as the second shot [0:38] in no way clarifies her position in time and space or the communication context of her story (who exactly is she telling the story to?). Nor does her presence at Doc's side in a bar in the fourth scene elucidate the nature of

Figure 7.4 Inherent Vice: *Sortilège, the character speaking in voiceover, listens to Doc in a café, even though her actual presence and even existence is by no means certain.*

their relationship (Figure 7.4) [8:47], which her subsequent appearances (in his car on the way to Chick Planet Massage [16:22] and the Straight Is Hip mental facility [1:30:48–1:31:24], during the Ouija board flashback [1:13:49–1:14:43], and in an indeterminate room [1:51:55–1:53:12]) do little to clarify. She is clearly a confidante ("What's on your mind?" she asks Doc [1:52:03]), but is she a figment of his imagination or does she really exist? Both possibilities lead to aporias: is the film being narrated by a figment of Doc's psyche or by someone who impossibly knows everything in spite of the fact that she did not witness any of these scenes, presumably because Doc has confided in her? Is the voiceover a case of intradiegetic or extradiegetic metalepsis? And is the narration a coherent modernist experiment in subjectivity or a metafictional setup meant to heighten the artifice? The narrative leaves these questions dangling, and the narration thus creates a sense of alienation on two levels: it reflects Doc's complicated rapport with the world, and likewise complicates our engagement with the protagonist and the world he inhabits.

The artificiality of the voiceover participates more generally in a highly artificial narration. Its contrivedness is brought to the fore when it takes over during lulls in conversations to explain the characters' thoughts (Doc's and Shasta's in the third scene [4:57–5:11]), so that it becomes quite obvious that the characters/performers are waiting for the voiceover to be done to carry on their discussion. The status of the voiceover is made even more problematic when another voiceover inexplicably takes over (Jade's voice reading her own letter [43:27]), rendering artificial a well-worn cinematic convention (something which is also effected in *Bram Stoker's Dracula*), or, more daring still, when it comments on a close-up that is utterly disconnected from the protagonist (such as the photo of Coy Harlingen which links two scenes without being handled by a character and thus originates exclusively from the narration [56:42]). Other conventions of audiovisual fiction are parodied, such as when the narration has Doc and Sauncho Smilax talking on the seaside, then in a café, though Doc's question in the seaside diner ("Burke Stodger, the actor?") is a direct follow-up to what Sauncho was saying outside [48:42].[43] Thus combined, this array of narrative devices troubles the ontological boundary between diegesis and narration in a far more subtle (but just as artificial) manner, say, than a look to the camera or direct address. The status of the images—and of this fairly straightforward neo-noir fiction—is called into question throughout. Regardless of the exact nature of the voiceover, the images we are shown are not those of the actual event but images whose content is virtual, constituting the whole film as a Deleuzian "crystal-image," an image in which it is impossible to tell the actual image apart from its virtual image.[44] Given the ontological instability of both voiceover and images, and basically of the narration, what are we to make of the images that are provided as evidence? The photographs of Coy Harlingen or in the newspaper articles on Wolfmann [12:52, 1:38:39]? Or the programs on TV (Coy crashing the Nixon rally and Detective Christian "Bigfoot" Bjornsen's presence in an episode of the NBC cop show *Adam-12* [1:39:25])? These photographic images are proof of nothing more than the inherent untrustworthiness and fictionality of everything we are being shown. In *Inherent Vice* (2014), meta is thus also a means of expressing (and adapting) the kind of paranoia-eliciting world of simulacra that has made Pynchon's work famous.

Adaptations of metafictional novels can be highly reflexive but not necessarily meta, so that there is little correlation between the quality of meta in a source and its adaptation. Meta seems to be easily lost in translation. It appears far easier to deploy reflexive devices that are as playfully scandalous and deconstructive of genre and narrative conventions as in the source text, or to tap into the dramatic potential of the overtly meta movie about making movies, than to rethink the relationship between fiction and reality in another medium on a more covert mode. Such an endeavor may be informed by previous attempts to adapt similar material, thus blurring the line between remake and adaptation. Meta can also be heightened by the introduction of metanarrative and metaperformative concerns, in particular by displacing metafiction's concern with authority onto the relationship between actors, their characters and their personas. In the age of digital and surveillance technology, everyone is potential material for some kind of audiovisual production, and the world is more than ever a stage.

Metadaptations (*Adaptation*, *Psycho*, *Bram Stoker's Dracula*)

Film or television adaptations or remakes in which the status of the adaptation is an ongoing concern throughout are comparatively rare. Works that do so fairly explicitly—that is, whose plots are centered on the difficulties of adapting a specific work—have been dubbed "metadaptations" and include the likes of *Adaptation, Tristram Shandy: A Cock & Bull Story* and the ITV mini-series *Lost in Austen* (2008).[45] *Psycho* (Van Sant, 1998) and especially *Bram Stoker's Dracula* (Coppola, 1992) will provide us with examples of metadaptations that operate on a more covert mode.

Adaptation in particular has drawn much critical attention. Frank P. Tomasulo describes it as "a conscious metatext that critiques the Hollywood system (and itself)."[46] For Thomas Leitch, the film, which "chronicl[es] the fictional attempt to write a screen adaptation that was never really undertaken," "satirizes both the misbegotten quest to bring [Susan] Orlean's decidedly uncinematic story [*The Orchid Thief*] to the screen and the debates about fidelity" that informed a movie like *Jane Austen in Manhattan*.[47] *Adaptation* overtly thematizes questions that are at the heart of the practice and theory of adaptation. The orchid—a synecdoche of the source text—ultimately becomes a metaphor for adaptation as mutation[48] and a symbol of the screenwriter's fetishization of the source text.[49] A whiny Charlie Kaufman voices his worry that the book is unadaptable because "no narrative really unites these passages" [49:10] and that he will "disappoint" Orlean who has "written a beautiful book" [54:10].

This is redoubled by an interest in the practice and theory of screenwriting (which in many cases is adaptation) through a subplot centered on his twin brother, Donald, who has enrolled for a seminar hosted by screenwriter Robert McKee—Donald even posts McKee's "Ten Commandments of Screenwriting" in his brother's work area to help [50:42]! By valuing readymade recipes over originality (and by enjoying the sort of personal life Charlie can only dream of), Donald acts as his brother's doppelgänger; on a meta-level, however, he (with McKee in the background) functions as the voice of the normative framework Charlie is trying to escape but ultimately gives in to out of sheer desperation. The twins thus represent two sides of US-American cinema: Charlie the independent, Donald the mainstream.[50] An annoyed Charlie ends up providing a counter-framework—granted, in jest—when he suggests to his brother that he make his serial killer an academic named The Deconstructionist whose MO is cutting up his victims into little pieces [37:17]. In so doing, Charlie reflexively draws attention to the puzzle film structure of *Adaptation* itself, inherited from the postmodern metafictional novels of the 1960s and 1970s—significantly, when Charlie suddenly decides to turn the adaptation into a script about his failure to adapt, the words he uses to criticize his own autobiographical endeavor ("It's self-indulgent, it's narcissistic, solipsistic" [59:19]) are those used by critics of 1960s–1970s metafiction.[51] The apparent hierarchy between the two brothers is undermined by Charlie's selling out, but it was already foreshadowed by the fact that Donald's screenplay of *The 3* [58:38] is already a mise en abyme of *Adaptation*, with its three voices (Charlie, Orlean and John Laroche).[52]

The hierarchy between the different stories, which is based on the relationship between each text (Kaufman's story frames Orlean's which frames Laroche's, with each character taking charge of the voiceover track), appears like a prime candidate for a fairly straightforward Chinese box structure. Yet the shifts in the narration are by no means crystal clear. Not only are we uncertain as to which text (Kaufman's screenplay or Orlean's book) is the source of the "ideation" the narration is attempting to reproduce, but the human source (Kaufman, Orlean) and their activities (reading, writing) are regularly confused. Sometimes what we believe to be an instance of "ideation" turns out to be a dream sequence, so that a stable indicator such as a character reading a book becomes unstable when it turns out the scene we have just witnessed was a dream or a nightmare. One such instance occurs when Kaufman wakes up from a sex dream with a waitress who's into orchids, thus suggesting that the woman herself is a fantasy, and that the previous two scenes, the one in the diner and the one at the orchid festival never happened [29:15–30:32]. And yet, in the next scene, the waitress and the diner turn out to be very much real [32:40]. All this confusion could, of course, be explained away by Kaufman's mental state, as the moments where Charlie imagines Susan is talking to him or the rapid montage sequence of him dreaming he is writing the screenplay in a frenzy [47:58–48:18] tend to suggest. But if the fictionality of Orlean is problematized fairly explicitly (Kaufman turns her into a "character" just as she turns Laroche into one), that of Kaufman himself can only be deduced from the film's central conceit.

Like other films and series that feature real-life cameos, *Adaptation* plays on the ontological boundary permitted by the act of make-believe inherent in performance: pretending you are or someone is somebody else. This is thematized as early as the opening scene, which introduces Nicholas Cage as Charlie Kaufman, the successful screenwriter of *Being John Malkovich* (Jonze, 1999), on the movie's set, alongside the "real" John Malkovich and Catherine Keener [1:59–2:48]. This staple movie-about-making-movies sequence thematizes the question of (mis)recognition that was already at the heart of Kaufman's previous script: while most of us will recognize Nicolas Cage, the cast and crew ignore Charlie Kaufman, but then the "real" Charlie Kaufman they might know is not there anyway. It is because the movie is about a real-life screenwriter we know to be portrayed by an actor that the main narrative is rendered ontologically unstable and cannot function as a bedrock for the stories-within-the-story. Charlie's attempt to turn the script into more autobiographical material halfway through the film—in particular his dictating lines that describe events [57:44–58:25] reminiscent of the film's fourth scene, his meeting with executive Valerie Thomas [4:04–6:07]—retrospectively calls into question all the images we have seen so far: all are potentially ideations of his script, meaning that we have, from the beginning, been watching Charlie's final adaptation and not the actual process. Released three years earlier, *Adaptation* might be where Winterbottom and his team got the idea for a making-of the making of an unadaptable work.

Adaptation engages with writings on metafiction perhaps more implicitly by demonstrating that a fiction that is about its own making is not necessarily (and maybe even never) just about itself. Kaufman and Jonze's second collaboration is not so much about film adaptation as it is about adaptation as a metaphor for the human condition—just as Orlean's book is not just about orchids but about life. "The book isn't like that," Charlie tells a producer, "And life isn't like that" [5:57]; later Susan's voiceover can be heard saying, "Change is not a choice, not for a species of plant, not for me. It happens" [1:19:27]. What initially seems to be an aesthetic concern turns out to be an ethical one; if the problem of adapting *The Orchid Thief* seems to be technical and aesthetic, it soon becomes clear that Charlie's anxiety is, above all, moral and psychological. Unlike *Scream*, as we shall see, the metaphor is fairly overt and, like a flower, grows out of the premise. It is clear that Kaufman's Orlean and Kaufman the character are not just struggling with their writing but with their personal lives; each writer seeks in their subject (Orlean and Laroche) a model not so much for writing as for making sense of their existence and, perhaps, living a good life.

Cited by Leitch as an example of adaptation as "celebration" and "fidelity as fetish,"[53] *Psycho* (1998) pushes to the extreme the idea that remaking is an exercise in technical and technological updating. It reprises the bulk of the 1960 film's dialogue, shots, music and editing techniques, and merely seems to deliver the same movie in color, with different actors, in a contemporary setting. Gus Van Sant's claim to fidelity[54] invites viewers familiar with Hitchcock's masterpiece to compare the remake with their cinematic memories or a personal copy of it. The 1998 opening shot immediately positions us in this role, thereby operating as "onscreen meta-commentary"[55] [2:29–3:50]. We can notice that (1) the intertitles are identical apart from the addition of the year 1998; (2) the cityscape of Phoenix has somewhat changed; (3) the helicopter shot is more elaborate than the 1960 pan-and-zoom-in and penetrates seamlessly (without a cut) into the hotel room; and (4) the track-in

Figure 7.5 Psycho: *a tour-de-force track-in produces a frame-within-the-frame composition that visually expresses the remaking of the 1960 opening scene.*

through the window with the blinds evokes not just the theme of voyeurism and the voyeurism of cinema, but visually frames the image of a couple in bed as a remade one (Figure 7.5). *Psycho* (1998) is a prime example of the kind of self-conscious enunciation Metz theorized in 1991; because it is so evidently similar to the original, the slightest modification becomes reflexive: a camera movement, a cut, a shot (the shots of the sky and the naked woman during the two murder scenes), an extra event (Norman masturbating while spying on Marion) or scene (Lila's discovery of Norman's room).

It is this self-consciousness that leads Philippe Roger to conclude that color in a remake is "necessarily reflexive and referential."[56] Reading "Color TV," the 1998 Bates Motel sign advertises the remake's main asset [22:50].[57] Based on pastel pinks and green, the 1998 color scheme does more than change the mood from "dark" and Gothic to "rosy" and kitsch;[58] the human bodies' pink hue seems to take Hitchcock's claim that "actors are cattle" quite literally,[59] while the color green operates a "deliberate uglification of the world,"[60] and a disfigurement of a monument of film history in the process. If the use of color is upheld as a marketing asset, in terms of aesthetics, the coloring of a masterpiece is a deliberate commodification of, and violent assault on, a master's "heritage."[61] The 1998 film's irreverence is not just aesthetic; it is also political, as it tends to queer the film by emphasizing male bodies and masculinizing the female characters.[62]

Psycho (1998) is highly self-conscious through and through, but its most overt metamoment may be the famous shower scene and its aftermath

[42:13–45:25]. Contained within a motel dominated by a combination of browns, greens and reds, the bathroom appears conspicuously white, so much so that even the pale-skinned Marion's figure stands out. The shower scene thus becomes the moment the 1998 remake attempts to stick to the 1960 film as closely as possible by returning to a quasi-black-and-white aesthetic—an approach that is marked, like the opening scene, by frame-within-the-frame composition (this time the bathroom door). The attack scene thus becomes the brutal return of color in an oasis of whiteness (in place of a different shade of gray in the original), soiling both profilmic and filmic spaces (Marion's back, the tiles, the water spiralling down the shower drain). The sexual subtext of the original remains relevant, of course—Norman's cleaning the bathroom (Figure 7.6) [48:51–50:20] is not only a means of erasing the traces of his crime, it marks the repression of the filthy desires he believes his mother would disapprove of—but it is also meta: the killer, who, during the first murder, enacts an assortment of filmic roles (spectator/director spying through the peephole, performer in drag, stage designer returning the room/set to its original state), is desperately trying to preserve the black-and-white sanctity of the original scene, and thus his "original" creator's legacy.

The title *Bram Stoker's Dracula* makes a promise that the film immediately breaks by providing the Count with a backstory that is a radical departure from the novel [0:21–5:44]; thus contradicted by the prologue, the title that follows appears in an ironic light, and the statement of intent is particularly

Figure 7.6 Psycho: *by mopping the blood off the bathroom floor, Norman Bates is attempting to eliminate not only the evidence, but also the primary color soiling the original black-and-white film's most famous scene.*

ambivalent. A tale of love lost and reborn, in which the Gothic eventually mutates into a tale of Beauty and the Beast, Coppola's *Bram Stoker's Dracula* is not to be Bram Stoker's *Dracula* after all. And yet, the prologue is, in effect, a celebration of adaptation, a practice that has led to some of Coppola's most accomplished work (*The Godfather*, 1972; *Apocalypse Now*, 1979). The tale of immortal love that diegetically justifies the birth of the vampire can be seen as an allegory of the immortality of the Dracula myth as such: the triangle constituted by Dracula–Elisabeta–the Bishop in the "warlike days" will effortlessly make way for a new triangle, Dracula–Mina Harker–Abraham Van Helsing, portrayed by the same cast of actors (Gary Oldman, Winona Ryder and Anthony Hopkins). The potential to readapt or remake is thus mirrored within the narrative by the possibility of returning from the dead and loving once again. In Tom Whalen's words, *Bram Stoker's Dracula* is "not a film of Dracula, but of Draculas."[63]

What follows the prologue is a highly self-conscious film that abounds in anti-illusionistic devices (toy trains, cardboard streets, vivid color schemes, superimposition, an arsenal of techniques borrowed from silent cinema including irises and trick shots, and my personal favorite, an insert of a harp being strummed between two scenes that underscores a musical and editing cliché [21:01]). It is also with great self-consciousness that, eight minutes into the movie, *Bram Stoker's Dracula* returns to its avowed source and attempts to take into account the novel's epistolary form, thus addressing the problems of adapting the source material [8:18–9:50]. Not only does the narration resort to the traditional voiceover and depict the characters writing letters and diary entries or taking notes with a pen, typewriter [18:51–19:15] or gramophone [23:19–23:40; 39:37–39:51], but some diary entries and letters are superimposed over and/or keyed in to the images, creating a sort of split-screen effect.

Instead of picturing an instance of ideation, such images serve to identify the writer's physical situation (Jonathan writing on a train) (Figure 7.7). They also highlight the differences between word and image, of course, and, more importantly, those between the reader's or the viewer's activity: whereas the stasis of words requires the reader to activate them and create the world through the process of "ideation," the film overwhelms us with its depth and dynamics, forcing us to choose between reading the text or watching the train roll by and listening to the voiceover. The opposition not only points to an awareness of the specificity of each medium, a central concern in adaptation studies,[64] but, thus remediated, the written page is also recognized as a plastic material, a component of the film image on the same level as other props.

The film also plays on the spatial and temporal gaps between the textual and verbal narration and the film narration that encompasses it. Slight

Figure 7.7 Bram Stoker's Dracula: *the keying of Jonathan Harker's diary into a shot of a model train not only foregrounds the artifice; it problematizes the difference between a verbal medium and an audiovisual one, while emphasizing the diary's transformation into plastic material through the process of remediation.*

rifts provoke tears in the narrative fabric. Jonathan's first letter and Mina's first diary entry are both dated from 25 May, yet her voice accompanies his nocturnal journey in a stagecoach when he was previously seen on the train. Twenty-six minutes into the film [26:02–26:19], Jonathan's 30 May entry, accompanied by his voiceover, is visually associated with a later event (his realization that he is Dracula's prisoner and subsequent exploration of the castle) instead of the writing or the event related orally (Dracula's reaction to Mina's picture).[65] These spatial–temporal discrepancies between word and image foreshadow the fatal moment when Mina receives Jonathan's letter shortly before Dracula's arrival in London [36:40]. In effect, the letter- and diary-writing also dramatizes that, in the scope of the film at least, Dracula's power is eminently metanarrative. Not only do his actions largely determine the plot (he purchases real estate in London, imprisons Jonathan, subjugates Renfield, assaults Lucy and seduces Mina), but he also influences the narration. On two occasions when the protagonists are traveling (Jonathan Harker by train to Transylvania, Dracula by boat to London [37:35]), his eyes appear in the heavens in superimpression, and during a social event at the Westenras' his shadow washes over Mina as his voice whispers to her in Romanian [22:50–23:13]. Philippe Ortoli astutely notes that editing cuts are facilitated by motifs associated with the Count, and sometimes even by the vampire himself.[66] Dracula's movements affect the editing (the shadow of his cape blackens the screen in Jonathan's room, triggering an iris-out centered on the Englishman's face [18:45]), and his spectral quality upsets both the rules of nature and the norms of classical narration (he startles Jonathan when he appears from the right though his shadow was in the left background [16:00]). Dracula's narrative power appears to diminish when Van Helsing enters the picture and increasingly occupies the voiceover track, yet the Count's actions repeatedly contest the doctor's authority (for instance, his claim that vampires are weak during the day [44:07–44:22]); even the Beast's death, in the arms of Beauty, turns out to be his own desired outcome and redemption.

The film's most overt metamoment occurs at its midpoint when, running into Mina Murray in the streets of London, the Count expresses his desire to see the cinematograph, "a wonder of the civilized world" [46:18]. Significantly, the cinematograph scenes [51:12–54:33] are announced by a combination of two transgressions: a deviation from the usual vampire myth (since Dracula is perfectly able to walk about in broad daylight so long as he sports a top hat and a pair of John Lennon sunglasses) and a blending of silent film aesthetics (the grainy, sped-up image which opens on an iris-out) and color, created with a real hand-cranked Pathé camera [44:23–48:04]. The subsequent scenes at the fair recall the medium's history in terms of exhibition and technology. Dracula's awe ("Astounding. There are no limits to science.") reminds us that cinema was invented by scientists, not artists, and exploited by showmen like Thomas Edison whose name is visible on a poster in the background. The films screened include a Méliès-like trick film (with a man coddling two scantily clad young women who turn into his wife) that recalls the 1896 *Vanishing Lady*, followed by what appears to be footage of a royal jubilee such as those of Queen Victoria shot by R.W. Paul in 1897, and finally a shot of a train recalling Lumière brothers' 1896 *L'Arrivée d'un train en gare à La Ciotat*. The clips illustrate the variety of approaches that dominated the medium's early years and set the historical context in the process. As pastiches that are spliced together in a continuous loop, they also encapsulate the 1992 film's palimpsestic approach to its material, with its borrowings from its predecessors (Murnau, Dreyer, Browning, the Hammer films, the 1979 *Dracula* directed by John Badham[67]), as well as from Anne Rice's romantic take on vampires that was popular at the time. Finally, the images playing over diegetic screens (including the shadow puppets) point back to the Transylvania scenes (Jonathan's train ride, encounter with the Count and magical orgy with the vampiresses), and thus reframe his travels as a voyage into the history of cinema, and notably its special effects (matte painting, upside-down interiors, shadow puppetry). Jonathan's earlier comment, "I've seen many strange things already. Bloody wolves chasing me through some blue inferno" [28:45], can retrospectively be seen as a comment on the film's aesthetics.

The cinematograph scene thus provides a framework with which to interpret the many instances of reflexivity that preceded it, as well as the romance that will progressively take over the narrative. Not only is the story of Dracula contemporary to the invention of cinema, but this creature of the shadows is a metonym of the medium, as the close-ups of the Count with a blurry movie screen in the background suggest (Figure 7.8). In Whalen's words, "this creature of celluloid and light who has been with us for so long, this master seducer, here is emblematic of the magic and seductive power of film itself."[68]

Dracula's invitation to Mina to pet the wolf is an invitation to sexual release, of course, but it is also one to accept her role and status as an image in *Bram Stoker's Dracula*. This is made obvious by the metafictional implications of each of their meetings. On their second, in which they drink absinthe and talk of the past [1:03:41–1:08:09], they are surrounded by images from the prologue, keyed-in and/or superimposed (movie-like, Elisabeta appears in a framed mirror, while the note that drove her to commit suicide is singled out, recalling the metanarrative power of text within the film), so that the question facing Mina Murray is whether or not she will take on the role of Elisabeta, and thus support this Beauty-and-the-Beast version of Dracula. Her recognition of the Prince is evoked in an extreme close-up using rack focus, which recalls the famous shots of the actresses' faces competing for filmic space in *Persona*, while her acceptance is signified by her waltzing with her Prince in images that recall those of Cocteau's 1946 *Beauty and the Beast*[69] and even the Disney production released a year earlier. The point is driven home in the final scene in which Dracula and Mina's situation holds up an inverted

Figure 7.8   Bram Stoker's Dracula: *the cinematograph scene integrates the figure of the vampire within the medium's history, turning the Count into a metonym of cinema.*

reflection of the image of Dracula and Elisabeta painted on the chapel ceiling, an image which is the last thing Mina is shown looking at and which is also the last one we see [1:58:14–2:01:00].

Petting the wolf, however, is equally an invitation to turn their backs on the visual pleasures offered by the cinematograph. An image made flesh, the Count encourages Mina to abandon the comfort of a visual perspective, such as the one provided by the illustrations in Richard F. Burton's *Arabian Nights* which excited her and Lucy so in an earlier scene [19:22], and to indulge in tactile pleasures instead. In so doing, Dracula goes against the postmodern aesthetics the film seems to revel in and rejects the role of metaphor for the "impotence of cinema"[70] that visual and literary representations of his parasitic nature seem to have cast him into. If Dracula is an image, he is one that is meant to be touched and licked, as when Mina willingly drinks his blood [1:38:49–1:41:47]. The Count's taste for fashion, his capacity to transform into beast or vapor, and his independent shadow make him a highly plastic figure, one that can be endlessly remade and readapted, like the grotesquerie two of the female vampires turn into [34:23]. The film's palimpsestic aesthetics is thus justified not only by the vampire's presence throughout film history, but by the vampire's shadow nature. The Count's tragedy is that he exemplifies both the powers and contradictions of the medium: believing that the photo of Mina Harker is indisputable proof that she is the reincarnation of Elisabeta, this embodiment of the formalist precept that the film image does not reproduce but transforms falls victim to the realist siren. Set against the birth of the medium, the romance plot allegorically dramatizes the historical tension between the formalist and realist views of cinema, less obviously perhaps than in *Blow-up* (see Chapter 6). Engaging with the history and historiography of Dracula (and vampires) on film thus comes down to engaging with the history and historiography of film and film theory (see Chapter 10).

Conclusion

Adaptations and remakes of famous or cult works have a vested interest in reflexivity: self-consciousness is a marketing strategy, an instance of "industrial reflexivity" (see Chapter 9); it is also a justification of the legitimacy of adaptation and remaking as a creative process based on pre-existing material. The assets (such as technological advances) and problems (such as medium specificity) are quite often foregrounded in the opening scenes; these provide an interpretive framework, stating the adaptation's aesthetic, political and ethical terms, which viewers are invited to take into account in order to comprehend the adaptation. Opening metamoments have thus become a staple feature of adaptations and remakes (no doubt because, in the age of Internet, the most obscure source can now be consulted), and heightened their intricacy. Although (and maybe even because) they present a challenge for adapters, metafictional novels tend to make for highly reflexive adaptations that are not necessarily meta. The fact that the formal devices utilized are lifted from previous films that are not necessarily adaptations (such as the Nouvelle Vague) would tend to confirm the hypothesis outlined in Chapter 3—that meta in film and television does not originate in the metafictional novels of the 1960s and 1970s. Less frequent are adaptations that take adaptation and remaking as an underlying concern and sometimes even a theme. They can cast a new, sometimes critical light on the source—films like *Mansfield Park*[71] (Rozema, 1999) and *Halloween*[72] (Zombie, 2008) engage with their sources in critical ways, contesting and revising their politics—and/or interrogating the creative possibilities, implications and limitations of remaking and adaptation as creative processes in a profit-driven entertainment industry that imposes its own set of economic, aesthetic and political limitations. Such works are equally reflections on cinema itself as an industry and medium, recalling observations made in Chapters 4 and 6. Consciousness of the source work—and in some cases of the myth it may have spawned—turns into consciousness of its history and historiography, as we shall see in Chapter 10, and of the genres it engages with.

CHAPTER 8

Genre

THIS IS A GENRE FILM/SERIES AND YOU KNOW IT: STATEMENTS OF INTENT PART II

The association between meta and genre seems fairly obvious in 2022. The adjective "meta," as we have seen in Chapter 1, is often used in reference to popular genre films and series, whether horror (the *Scream* franchise, *Goodbye, Dragon Inn*[1], *The Cabin in the Woods*, *Scream Queens*), science fiction and fantasy (*Doctor Who*, *Supernatural*, *Deadpool*), or comedy (*Community*, *The Good Place* [NBC, 2016–20]). Genres that are not predominantly comedy usually contain a healthy dose of humor and rely on parody, a practice that is regularly associated with metafiction. Like adaptations and remakes, genre films and series, and more generally works that engage with specific genres, often assume their secondariness. (Metz even goes so far as to suggest that "[i]n an extreme sense, all genre films [. . .] contain within themselves all the previous films of the same genre, so they share a very broad lineage of 'films within a film,' which do not present themselves as such but whose traces may be found everywhere."[2]) The recognition of this secondariness can include specific hypotexts, as in the case of adaptations and remakes, but it implies, more broadly, an "architext." Gérard Genette understood "architextuality" as "the entire set of general or transcendent categories—types of discourses, modes of enunciation, literary genres—from which emerges each singular text."[3] Genre is but one form of architext (in film, classical narration would be another), and in the case of mainstream productions, it may perhaps be the most central (again, alongside narrative conventions). It is thus the elaboration of an overt or covert discourse on the relationship between the film or series and its raw material—a hypotext in the case of an adaptation or a remake, an architext in the case of a genre film, oftentimes both, as we have seen in the case of *The Portrait of a Lady* and *The Texas Chainsaw Massacre*—that qualifies as meta.

Both Hutcheon and Waugh have shown how literary metafiction foregrounds the codes of a given genre such as the novel. Literary metafiction assumes that the reader shares these codes with the writer,[4] is able to "draw on his or her knowledge of traditional literary conventions," and is thus capable of recognizing them in order "to construct a meaning for the new text."[5] Much literary metafiction displays not only a consciousness of the conventions of the novel, but reprises specific genres, often in a parodic mode: the Victorian realist novel (Fowles's *The French Lieutenant's Woman*[6]), the epistolary novel (Barth's *LETTERS*), detective fiction (the work of Alain Robbe-Grillet[7]), the thriller (Pynchon, Muriel Spark, Italo Calvino[8]), science fiction (Calvino, Pynchon, Kurt Vonnegut[9]). This raises the question of whether parody is intrinsically meta, which will be addressed below. For Waugh, it is the constraints of genre themselves—the genre's codedness and its historical baggage—that make it worthy material to engage with fiction more generally. "Metafiction," Waugh argues, "is in the position of examining the old rules in order to discover new possibilities of the game."[10] In effect, it is because genre is conceived as a "game" with a set of "rules" that genre fiction can come to epitomize an idea(l) of fiction as game per se, one which is supported by authors like Lewis Carroll,[11] Vladimir Nabokov[12] and Julio Cortázar,[13] and theorists like Jean-Marie Schaeffer (see Chapter 2). The idea that genre fiction does not constitute the margins of fiction but its very essence may explain why two of the underlying structures Hutcheon identifies in literary metafiction are the detective plot and fantasy, and that their playfulness would, in effect, make them subgroups of the "game structure" category.

In film, genre fare regularly points to its generic architext on a mode similar to that with which an adaptation or remake points to its hypotext: the opening scenes offer a statement of intent of sorts. Moreover, the work's relationship to the genre is often established through references to paradigmatic instances or famous models—in other words, to specific hypotexts. This was the case of many slashers long before the release of *Scream* in 1996. The opening scene of *The Funhouse* (Hooper, 1981) [2:40–7:17], for instance, mixes the opening scene of *Halloween* (1978) with the famous shower scene from *Psycho* (1960), which Carpenter's film already alluded to through the theme of sexual voyeurism and a close-up of a knife slashing the air; *The Funhouse* even adds a musical theme partly inspired by John Williams's "Main Title" for *Jaws* (Spielberg, 1975). The narration intercuts between a roving POV shot that penetrates a bedroom, while a teenager, Amy, is shown getting ready to take a bath. As in *Halloween* (1978), the subject associated with the POV shot picks up a mask and covers his or her face/the camera with it, then goes into the hallway and peers into another bedroom before heading for the bathroom. The assailant's silhouette then appears through the shower curtain in the left background of a lateral close-up of Amy, a reprisal of one of the 1960 *Psycho*'s most famous shots. The subsequent attack likewise mimics the editing of the shower scene, until Amy fights back, and the knife is revealed to be a toy and the assailant (as in *Halloween*) her kid brother, Joey. The scene thus clearly banks on the audience's cinephilia: it is only through our recognition of these allusions that the scene can inscribe *The Funhouse* as a whole within the history of a genre, and indicate its knowing and playful attitude vis-à-vis its rules (the childish prank is yet another staple slasher trope). Cluttered with carnivalesque horrors, Joey's bedroom is already a funhouse (the opening shot singles out a poster reading Carnival on his door), which foreshadows the film's main locus and reflexively connects his space to the premise and title. Thus mirrored, the funhouse and bedroom are identified as metonyms of the film itself and the slasher genre, and posit a view of genre as material that is fun to play with and be scared of. Such a scene operates on the assumption that its audience knows the rules of the game; it is minimally meta insofar as its statement of intent merely asserts a degree of self-consciousness about its play on slasher conventions.

Such knowingness, as Metz noted, has long been a staple feature of genre films. Take, for instance, the opening scene of *Once Upon a Time in the West* [0:32–15:11]; by depicting the arrival of three gunmen, as in the opening scene of *The Good, The Bad, and the Ugly* (1966), and replaying the ending of *High Noon* (Zinnemann, 1952), the film, shot in Europe and the US and featuring both Hollywood and Italian stars (Charles Bronson, Claudia Cardinale, Gabriele Ferzetti, Henry Fonda, Jason Robards), promises to be both a mix of, and a variation on, both the classical Hollywood Western and Leone's own Dollar trilogy. Even before Leone's hyperreferential Western, sometimes described as the first postmodern film,[14] a classical Hollywood movie like *The Big Sleep* (Hawks, 1946), for instance, referred to its literary and filmic heritage as early as the third scene, when Vivian Sternwood expresses her surprise at Philip Marlowe's getup in these terms: "So you're a private detective? I didn't know they existed except in books, or else they were greasy little men snooping around hotel corridors" [10:26]. The lines, not present in Raymond Chandler's 1939 novel, are doubly reflexive, uttered as they are in what is actually the second film adaptation of Marlowe's adventures (after Edward Dmytryk's 1944 *Murder, My Sweet*) and addressed to an actor whose breakthrough role five years earlier was that of another famous literary sleuth, Sam Spade in John Huston's 1941 adaptation of Dashiell Hammett's 1930 novel *The Maltese Falcon*. For a 1946 audience, Bogart's Marlowe looks exactly like a hard-boiled sleuth should.

Of course, such statements of intent seem to qualify as reflexive but not particularly meta because the play on genre expectations is fairly limited in scope: the scene or character type does not quite fit the architext/hypotext. A more elaborate statement of intent regarding a film's stance vis-à-vis its genre can be found in the prologue of *Dead Man* (Jarmusch, 1995), which relates, in eight minutes, the protagonist's train ride to the frontier community of Machine [0:21–8:16]. Narrative and metafictional, the journey is one from East to West as well as one through the history and historiography of the genre, with a mostly mute William Blake in the role of the spectator observing the changes in scenery (and genre tropes) within and without the coach. The landscape evolves from hills and forests to rocky mountain, plains and Fordian desert (shot in frame-within-the-frame composition [Figure 8.1.1]), the passengers ranging from businessmen to farmers to bison hunters. Permeated with death (the abandoned band wagons and teepees, the insane bison massacre instigated by the federal government, which, the Train Fireman reminds us, is historical fact,[15]), the Western imagery creates an atmosphere in tune with the film's title and also expresses its ideological view of "civilization" as a "technology of death."[16] But the imagery also evokes the genre's demise in the 1980s following the *Heaven's*

Figures 8.1.1 and 8.1.2   Dead Man: *William Blake's train ride to the West establishes the avant-garde framework through which the historiography of the Western genre will be approached.*

Gate (Cimino, 1980) debacle and rebirth in its environmentally aware or "twilight"[17] variant following the success of *Dances with Wolves* (Costner, 1990) and *Unforgiven* (Eastwood, 1992). The prologue of *Dead Man* clearly indicates that it is leaving all this behind—the town of Machine is "the end of the line," the Train Fireman says. The film's knowingness regarding the genre is redoubled by a highly self-conscious narration, which insists on duration (the slow pace of the action and dialogue) and repetition (of visual and aural motifs like the train wheels, the oil lamp, Neil Young's riffs, the fade-outs [Figure 8.1.2]), promising that it will be adapting the poetics of Jarmusch's previous films, notably the fade-outs[18] of *Stranger than Paradise* (1984) and *Mystery Train* (1989), to this Western, and thus destabilizing the genre through a poetics that is indebted to writer and painter Henri Michaux, cited in the film's epigraph,[19] as well as to the avant-gardes (the allusions to the train ride in Abel Gance's 1923 *La Roue*[20]), thereby invoking the critique of the mechanization of bodies in films like *Metropolis* and *Modern Times* (Chaplin, 1936).[21]

If genre films and series are habitually self-conscious, works that consistently engage with the genre throughout the movie are less frequent. Less frequent still are those that establish a framework with which to explore the political and ethical implications of a given genre. *Once Upon a Time in the West* is one such film. A palimpsest of films including *The Iron Horse* (Ford, 1924), *Shane* (Stevens, 1953), *Run of the Arrow* (Fuller, 1957), and *The Magnificent Seven* (Sturges, 1960) among others,[22] its narrative is underpinned by a metanarrative in which two views of the mythical West, redoubled by two versions of the American dream, compete. This is dramatized through the conflict between the archetypal figures of the hired gun and the saloon girl: Frank is driven by the promise of social mobility implicit in a Rooseveltian virile conquest of the West, Jill McBain by a Turnerian view of the pastoral as a collective enterprise.[23] The 1968 film offers a variation on the ending of Ford's first Western, *The Iron Horse*, by celebrating the US-American melting pot not through the redemption of the West(erner) brought on by the school marm, but through the saloon girl turned universal mother portrayed by Claudia Cardinale. Thus, it is through the Italian star, the death of the classical Hollywood star—and thus implicitly through Leone—that the Western and the myth of the West are reimagined and rehabilitated.

Robert Stam observes similar discourses in the films of Godard, who, beyond the recourse to anti-illusionist strategies of generic hybridization and multiple citations ("*Pierrot le fou* [1965], especially, constantly highlights its character as generic cocktail."),[24] seek to bring to the fore the political ambiguities of a given genre. *The Riflemen* (1963), for instance, "systematically denies us the satisfactions" of the war film ("drama, spectacular battles, vicarious games of strategy"), but also "demystifies the antiwar film" by rejecting the "conventions of dramatic realism" and depriving us of "the suspect pleasures of la bonne conscience" in the process.[25] A contemporary example (and avowed heir to both Leone and Godard) would be Quentin Tarantino, whose films consistently engage with the politics of genre films and the historiography of cinematic and cultural representations (see Chapter 10).[26] In what follows, attention will be paid to three examples of works that interrogate the ethics of a genre from beginning to end—*Scream* and *Funny Games*—or on a regular basis—the sitcom *Community*, but first I will attempt to specify the relationship between parody and meta by examining three Western parodies: *Lemonade Joe* (Lipský, 1964), *My Name Is Nobody* (Valerii, 1973) and *Blazing Saddles*. I deliberately selected examples from genres that are perceived as readily identifiable.

Is Parody Essentially Meta? (*Lemonade Joe*, *My Name Is Nobody*, *Blazing Saddles*)

The popular usage would certainly suggest that it is, given that "meta" is frequently employed in reference to exemplary instances of parody such as *Scream* and *Community*. The literature on parody, reflexivity and metafiction would also tend to answer in the affirmative. In *A Theory of Parody*, Hutcheon defines parody as "a form of repetition with ironic critical distance"[27] and identifies it as "one of the major forms of modern self-reflexivity; it is a form of inter-art discourse."[28] Cécile Sorin, in *Pratiques du pastiche et de la parodie au cinéma*, follows Hutcheon by stating that parodies should be considered reflexive because they "refer to other films" and "produce a certain form of discourse on cinema."[29] Robert Stam identifies parody as a key anti-illusionist strategy in the works of Cervantes, Jarry, Nabokov, Kubrick and Godard.[30] In her 1979 *Parody//Metafiction*, Margaret Rose went so far as to equate "parody with self-reference," a position Hutcheon would contest: "[p]arody is certainly one mode of auto-referentiality, but it is by no means the only one."[31] In *Narcissistic Narrative*, Hutcheon identified parody as one of the forms "overt diegetic metafiction"[32] can take and even conjectured that the "self-centeredness" of the novel—and perhaps even the novel itself—may have started with parody.[33] The function of parody is to "invite a more literary reading, a recognition of literary codes";[34] it can reveal both the generic norms of fiction as well as fiction's existence as language,[35] and thus concerns both style and structure.[36] As a "game"[37] based on pre-existing forms, parody can be seen as the more overt version of the implicit play model Hutcheon sees as fundamental to metafiction. Waugh tends to follow Hutcheon's argument that parody is one of the main strategies employed (by authors like Fowles, Spark, Vonnegut and Doris Lessing[38]) to reveal how literary conventions "malfunction";[39] the specificity of parody in metafictional works is that it is "meant to disturb, not affirm, satisfactions are always undermined."[40]

It has already been noted that one of the problems with Hutcheon's typology is that it takes for granted that allegory and parody are immediately identifiable (not surprisingly, one of Hutcheon's prime examples is Barth's 1968 short story collection *Lost in the Funhouse*, in which genre conventions are spelled out).[41] Parody is assumed to be overt because it posits knowledge of the framework (the hypotext or genre) it defamiliarizes; the work is meant to be interpreted in the light of this framework. Parody can also make this knowledge readily available by having characters voice the framework (as in the *Scream* franchise or *Community*). And even when it doesn't, the ironic tone may be enough to draw attention to the fact that something is being parodied (the slapstick comedy of *Blazing Saddles* is certainly enough for any viewer to realize that the Western is being mishandled). Thus, parody is probably less likely to be missed than allegory; its specific target may be ignored, but not the assault. Waugh also contends that parody fulfills a didactic function: "In reading metafiction, then, where the literary norm(s) become the object of parody, the reader is educated in the relationship of historical and cultural to literary systems."[42] In this respect, parody is characteristically meta insofar as it criticizes and educates through play (see Chapter 2).

Parody is also central to film, television and literary genre studies, and has often been used to substantiate theses based on organic or anthropomorphic models "whereby genres are regularly said to develop, to react, to become self-conscious, and to self-destruct"[43] (Rick Altman cites Jane Feuer's study of the musical as one such example[44]). Stam's view that parody "emerges when artists perceive that they have outgrown artistic conventions"[45] tends to rejoin this view. The evolutionist model has since been countered by scholars like Altman. Parodies emerge when—and not after—a genre is born since they are modeled on recent hits, otherwise they would be liable to miss their mark (*Zombies on Broadway* [Douglas, 1945] was released two years after *I Walked with a Zombie* [Tourneur, 1943], *Scary Movie* [Wayans, 2000] five months after *Scream 3* [Craven, 2000]). Contra the parody-as-exhaustion thesis, Hutcheon emphasizes the positive energy of parody, which has the potential to re-energize forms.[46] Waugh agrees that metafiction's interest in genre is not a sign of the novel's exhaustion:[47] "it is precisely the fulfillment as well as the non-fulfillment of generic expectations that provides both familiarity and the starting point for innovation."[48] On this view, parody would be a strategy by which art and fiction celebrate their own relevance in the face of impending irrelevance. The critical potential of parody would paradoxically be founded in a more optimistic ethics of art and fiction whereby hackneyed material can always be used anew—a central precept of the avant-gardes, modernism and postmodernism. In parody, we thus find energies similar to those traversing the film-about-filmmaking and the allegories discussed in Chapters 4 and 5: a formal system (in this case, genre) redeemed, so to speak, by its own critical recycling. It remains to be seen how meta an overt parody can be—that is, how elaborate a metacommentary it may invite.

Three famous Western parodies from roughly the same period (*Lemonade Joe*, *My Name is Nobody*, *Blazing Saddles*) will be analyzed in an attempt to answer this question. All three borrow imagery and situations from famous predecessors: *Lemonade Joe* alludes to the famous leaning-back-in-a-chair-with-one's-boots-kicked-up-against-the-railing shot from *My Darling Clementine* [41:39], and models the character of Hogo Fogo on Hatfield the gambler from *Stagecoach*[49]; *My Name is Nobody* reprises the opening scene and the final duel of *Once Upon a Time in the West* and the watch motif from *For a Few Dollars More* (Leone, 1965), in addition to numerous allusions to classical Hollywood Westerns;[50] *Blazing Saddles* draws its railroad-centered premise from *The Iron Horse* and *Once Upon a Time in the West*, centers on a sheriff and an ex-sharpshooter drunkard who end up bonding as in *Rio Bravo* or any Wyatt Earp and Doc Holliday Western for that matter, and includes a Marlene Dietrich number à la *Destry Rides Again* (Marshall, 1939) or *Rancho Notorious*. All three films mock the genre's conventions: *Lemonade Joe* pokes fun at the singing cowboy figure and the gunfighter's ludicrous invincibility; in *My Name Is Nobody*, Jack Beauregard practically defeats a gang of outlaws all by himself; and in *Blazing Saddles*, the Waco Kid makes Sheriff Bart's chess king disappear [36:19] and bests eight gunmen without batting an eye [1:06:40]. Western action scenes are staged on a slapstick mode, with bodies and structures collapsing, *Lemonade Joe* speeding up a saloon brawl to evoke silent cinema [2:35–4:16]. *Lemonade Joe* and *Blazing Saddles* draw on comedy and musical conventions by including direct addresses to the camera (having tricked the townspeople, Sheriff Bart says to the camera, "Baby, you are so talented. And they are so dumb!" [30:17]). The two films also foreground the artificiality of their representation of nineteenth-century history through the use of anachronisms (Joe's song is accompanied by a keyed-in image of Tower Bridge [38:06], the construction of which began in 1886 a year after the film's time-setting; the Waco Kid brags that "he must have killed more men than Cecil B. DeMille" [37:00], and Bart uses the word "groovy" on a regular basis); diegetic screens (a group of dancing saloon girls are reflected in a mirror in *Lemonade Joe* [33:30]); staging (Sheriff Bart has the townsfolk build a Western town movie set [1:16:32]); and metalepsis (an elaborate crane shot reveals *Blazing Saddles* to be a movie within the diegesis itself [1:22:56]).

These Western parodies are certainly reflexive insofar as they draw attention to the artifice of filmmaking and mock the genre as a hackneyed form; they are equally critical of the genre's ideology. *Lemonade Joe* reveals the Western's complicity with capitalism (the righter of wrongs is actually promoting a soft drink called Kolaloka, a name that is reminiscent of Coca-Cola but means "Crazy Cola" in Spanish). With its African American hero who continuously outwits the white characters and even disguises himself as a member of the KKK, *Blazing Saddles* blatantly foregrounds the racism, homophobia and misogyny underpinning the Hollywood West (the Marlene Dietrich song parody, "I'm tired," [53:09–57:55] can even be said to call into question the "visual pleasure" of Hollywood cinema Mulvey would theorize a year later). *My Name Is Nobody* also criticizes the Hollywood Western's representation of racial history, albeit less systematically than *Blazing Saddles*, its eponymous hero knocking out the entertainer whose stand invites its customers to peg two African American men with food [42:55–43:50]. The three parodies are thus meta to the extent that they deliver a critique of the formal and political conventions of the genre, which they inscribe within film and cultural history to varying degrees. *Blazing Saddles* in particular systematically debunks the racist stereotypes that have dominated US-American cultural history—Sheriff Bart knows how to play the Uncle Tom for effect, for instance when he dresses up as a bellhop to deliver a bomb to stop a big lug from ransacking the saloon [47:50].

These three Western parodies tend to confirm that parody is essentially meta, but it can nonetheless vary in profundity and "meta-ness" (to use David LaRocca's term). The story of a Hollywood Western fan who wants to direct the final chapter of his favorite star's life, *My Name Is Nobody* qualifies as particularly intense meta because it is about the transnational history of the Western genre. The 1973 film is not the first spaghetti Western parody but capitalizes on the success (which Leone resented) of the Trinità movies of 1970 and 1971, directed by Enzo Barboni and also starring Terence Hill.[51] For this story of a young gunslinger who wants his favorite gunslinger, Jack Beauregard, to consolidate his position in history, Sergio Leone, who came up with the idea and produced the film, hired his former assistant director Tonino Valerii to direct Leone's own parody of the brand of Western he had contributed to creating. The film recycles well-known scenes and situations from Leone's films (the hat-shooting scene from *For a Few Dollars More* [33:40–35:15]); composer Ennio Morricone delivers a goofy score, with echoes of his other Western soundtracks (most obviously the watch melody from *For a Few Dollars More*); and many scenes pastiche the excessive silence of Leone's Westerns, with characters merely observing each other and grunting. The silence also works to reinforce the debt to slapstick aesthetics. Indeed, the 1973 film features staple Terence Hill fare such as a slapping scene and a cream-pie scene, but slapstick was already present in Leone's films (for instance, when Tuco custom designs his own revolver in *The Good, The Bad and the Ugly*). Indeed, Nobody actually conflates characteristics of The Man with No Name and the trickster figures of Tuco, Cheyenne and Homer's Odysseus, on which he was initially modeled.[52] *My Name Is Nobody* is thus self-parody (of Hill the performer, Leone the director,[53] Morricone the composer), and sometimes even parody of parody (since the earlier films parody the conventions of the spaghetti and Hollywood Western).

This comic version of The Man with No Name is also a nobody who wants to be somebody—Nobody is to Beauregard what Eve is to Margo in *All About Eve*, albeit on a gentler mode. A talented gunslinger himself, Nobody is portrayed as a spectator who willingly limits himself to that role: he watches (over) Beauregard who needs glasses because his eyes are failing, sits down to watch Beauregard perform (in the town and from atop a train),

Figures 8.2 and 8.3 My Name Is Nobody: *Jack Beauregard (Henry Fonda) waits to face the Wild Bunch single-handedly—with a little help from his number-one fan Nobody (Terence Hill), that is. The inserts of the history book pages suggest that the act is quasi-performative in its own mythologization. We are witnessing (film) history in the making.*

and uses mirrors, like his mentor in the opening scene, to identify assailants behind him (one POV close-up of a rectangular pocket mirror creates a frame within the frame that turns the object into a screen [57:20–57:57]). But Beauregard's number-one fan also intends to write and direct the Western narrative he desires. As we (and Nobody) witness Beauregard's feat, inserts show us the black-and-white illustrations (or those imagined by Nobody) that will mythologize it (Figures 8.2 and 8.3) [1:31:33–1:42:48]. *My Name Is Nobody* inscribes this allegory of spectatorship within the history of the myth and film genre. Nobody's plot to force Jack Beauregard to face the Wild Bunch can be seen as a young fan's desire to celebrate the classical Hollywood Western through one of its major stars and have him best the 1969 creation of New Hollywood director Sam Peckinpah, whose name features on a grave [32:23] and whose trademark slow-motion aesthetics are utilized during the Wild Bunch shootout, before besting him in turn. Thus, a classical Western situation, the Last Stand, is made to dramatize not US history but the history of the Western.

The stakes are by no means exclusively US-American (the film was shot in Spain, Italy and the US[54]). The European presence is evoked within the diegesis, since Jack Beauregard, whose last name is French and first name is pronounced "Jacques," ends up sailing for the Old Continent. In this respect, Terence Hill's star persona is just as important as Fonda's; Hill was not only associated with Trinità, but also with more "serious" spaghetti Western fare like *Django! Prepare your coffin!* (Baldi, 1968), in which he had the lead role. Nobody is thus the embodiment of Italian Hollywood Western fans of the likes of Leone himself: "[t]he film would show how Italian nobodies, who 'needed something to believe in' when they watched American movies in their childhood, had become somebodies after all."[55] *My Name Is Nobody* may be parody, but it is also self-promotion, asserting Leone's fundamental role in the history of the genre. It is Nobody/Leone who creates this battle between classical Hollywood and the New Hollywood, and who thus ensures his position as an intermediary between Fonda (and through him John Ford[56]) and Peckinpah in film history. Nobody/Leone's plot is all about ego and all about the history of his art. It contributes to the claim that *The Wild Bunch* would not have existed had Leone not come along.[57] Through Nobody, the gunslinging clown, the Italian director asserts his place alongside the masters of the genre. *My Name Is Nobody* confirms Hutcheon's argument that parody can operate "as a method of inscribing continuity while permitting critical distance."[58] For all its slapstick antics, the film is as much a historiography of the genre as *Once Upon a Time in the West*. And by self-consciously presenting itself as the story of a page in the history of the genre, it corresponds to what Hutcheon calls "historiographic metafiction," metafiction that engages with the writing of history, a point that will be further developed in Chapter 10.

THE ETHICS OF GENRE PLAY (*FUNNY GAMES*, *SCREAM*, *COMMUNITY*)

As a work whose metadiscourse aims to assert its producer's place in film history, an exemplary case of what Wolf calls "fictio-centered metareference" (i.e., the focus is exclusively on fiction as fiction), *My Name Is Nobody* would tend to confirm that critics of "meta" are right in deeming all things meta narcissistic. It also raises the question whether parody and, more broadly, "genre meta" are at all capable of addressing concerns beyond form, since the connection with real-world concerns would be less obvious than in works engaging with creation and spectatorship. As a work in which parody is intimately linked to revisionism,[59] *Blazing Saddles* already provides some answers to this question, since it demonstrates that genre can provide a framework with which to address the politics of the cultural representations it contributes to circulate. This is also what my study of gender, racial and ethnic issues in the films of Tarantino demonstrates.[60] What follows is a study of a fairly obvious example of a genre movie (*Funny Games*) that questions the morality of its genre, followed by analyses of two works (*Scream* and *Community*) that appear to delight in genre play and nothing more. I argue that, in all three cases, the genre play characteristic of metafiction is not just formal but ethical.

Funny Games (1997) has received much attention as a reflexive work and/or metafilm. In *Metafilm: Materialist Rhetoric and Reflexive Cinema*, Christopher Carter takes it as an example of a genre film that "know[s] our expectations as spectators," "flatly refuse[s] to fulfill them,"[61] interrogates the safe distance genre spectators benefit from,[62] and introduces "a meta-perspective that questions the ethics of spectators."[63] *Funny Games* opens with scenes and images that are immediately identifiable to any horror movie fan and that inscribe it within the home-invasion subgenre, with particular reference to Wes Craven's *The Last House on the Left* (1972), aligning our potential sympathies with the family.[64] The first indication of a disruption occurs as early as the opening credits [0:00–3:50] when a nondiegetic heavy metal song replaces the classical music the family has been listening to on their CD player, producing a distancing effect as the narration stubbornly flows on with the same sort of images, as if nonplussed by the change—the close-up of the car stereo in particular underscores the fact that the characters are not listening to the same music. The film's statement of intent is brutal both sonically and reflexively, alerting us, through its use of what Chion calls "anempathetic"[65] music (i.e., music whose emotional tone contrasts with that of the images), to a non-correspondence between diegesis and narration.

Funny Games's diegesis quickly thematizes its playful attitude toward the genre. Eighteen minutes into the movie, it is, quite ironically, a victim-to-be, Anna, who first uses the word "game" when speaking of the family dog, giving Peter a chance to mutter, "Funny game," the singular form ominously contrasting with the series of games Peter and Paul will impose on their victims. Paul proposes they play a variety of games, notably of the Q&A sort, and proceeds to outline the rules; his later pursuit of Schorschi resembles a game of hide-and-seek, the pursuant making no effort whatsoever to be stealthy (unlike the typical slasher killer). Paul's attitude toward Peter is equally playful, as they compare themselves to cartoon duos Tom and Jerry (Hanna-Barbera, 1940–) [43:38] and Beavis and Butthead (MTV, 1993–2001) [1:01:50]. Such references foreground the gap between their horrific actions and their childish attitude and, on a meta-level, between the genre's content (torture and murder) and form (play). As in HBO's *Westworld*, the play model of diegetic metafiction is absolutely overt. And the title of the film turns out to be as literal as they come, spelling out the tormentors' sole discernible motive—Paul's account of Peter's past [38:10–40:05], an assortment of psychokiller clichés based on childhood trauma (divorce, drug abuse, incest, etc.), are but excuses to get on with the show.

A metanarrative dimension is introduced quite explicitly through Paul's privileged relationship to the narration. He winks at the camera/us right before Anna finds their dead dog Rolfi (Figure 8.4) [29:30], asks us if we think the family will survive [42:27], and, having stepped inside a neighbor's house, gives us one last knowing look in the film's final close-up (which is freeze framed) to let us know that the show will go on [1:46:45]. The wink, Carter

Figure 8.4 Funny Games: *Paul winks at the camera moments before Anna finds her dead dog.*

notes, highlights the constructedness of the narrative and the genre audience's inability to predict events.[66] This is true of all Paul's addresses to the camera, which function very much like theatrical asides (the other characters, including Peter, never seem to take notice).

And yet, Paul reveals himself to be much more than a stage performer; he is a *deus ex machina*, capable of rewinding a scene when, towards the end of the movie, he loses control of the situation and Anna blows Peter away [1:39:45–1:40:25]. His use of the family's remote control (a diegetic device that didn't even belong to him in the first place) indicates that his control of the narration is an ontological impossibility, an "extradiegetic metalepsis" more typical of animation[67] (hence the above-cited references); this could already be deduced from his absence in many scenes (the opening scenes as well as the twenty-two-minutes' worth of screen time in which Paul and Peter leave Anna and Georg on their own). Paul's privileged relationship to the narration had already been confirmed, vaguely more subtly, when he inserted a CD into the neighbors' stereo and played the same song as in the opening credits while looking for Schorschi [59:12–1:00:40], pointing to yet another ontological impossibility: that Paul had been in control of the soundtrack as early as the opening credits, maybe at the time when he started harassing the family next door [3:56–8:41]. Because he exists within the diegesis and yet controls the narration, Paul is the rough equivalent of a homo- and extra-diegetic narrator in prose fiction, but he is ontologically impossible because he violates the border between diegetic and nondiegetic. Thus, it is not just the house that is an apparatus controlled by the killer (that is the case in *Scream*, as we shall see), but the diegesis as a whole. *Funny Games* thus renders explicit the genre's metanarrative stakes, that point of view and presumably pleasure are aligned with the sadistic director/spectator, and thus with what Carol Clover theorized as the "assaultive gaze,"[68] but unlike the majority of horror films, refuses to reverse these terms (Paul and Peter make fun of Anna's failure to become the Final Girl[69]).

If *Funny Games* makes its genre terms explicit, it refuses, as Carter has argued, to cater to the horror audience's baser appetites: "By focusing on loss and grief, Haneke opposes the dulling of affects that attends the circulation of violent imagery, [. . .] That principle is to resuscitate horror as a visceral and ethical experience rather than consent to its status as a predictable genre."[70] Anna's private parts remain offscreen when her tormentors force her to strip, the close-up of her face insisting on the humiliation she is experiencing [48:47–50:33]; the murders of Schorschi and his father Georg occur offscreen, the camerawork relaying Paul's indifference or Anna's despair [1:04:15, 1:36:05]. *Funny Games* is a lesson not only on the codedness of the genre and the reactionary ideology it may purvey (such as a "deeply embedded" "logic of revenge"[71]), but on the audience's willful complicity in its sadism. And as Carter suggests when he discusses the presence of the television set and the image of its screen splattered with Schorschi's blood,[72] the horror genre itself becomes one example among many of the violence of the contemporary mediascape.

In the Gothic and horror tradition, the killers are symptoms, allegories of a social context, but *Funny Games* seems to refute the idea that they could provide any emotional or psychological release for the audience, including the possibility of enjoying a sense of righteous justice by having the victims return the violence on their tormentors. In so doing, the film delivers the unequivocal moral message that violence should not be game/fiction material, thus going against centuries of philosophy and theory concerning the cathartic function of fiction and art. More problematic, perhaps, is the fact that *Funny Games*'s refusing to turn the tables on the killers leads it to abandon the progressive critique of the middle-class family of *The Last House on the Left*, as analyzed by Robin Wood;[73] Anna and Georg may appear weak and pathetic, but they never become monstrous like their tormentors, and their tormentors never become weak and pathetic in turn. *Funny Games* is quite rigid and haughty in sticking to its Manichean MO in order to call out the moral flaws of producers and consumers of popular horror. I would thus qualify Carter's claim that "the director endeavors to foreclose recourse to aesthetic enjoyment, pressing us to experience horror as an intensity that exceeds its commodified form."[74] Quite perversely, by denying us the pleasures of genre fare, and notably the shift from assaultive gaze to reactive gaze as theorized by Clover, *Funny Games* runs the risk of offering "aesthetic enjoyment" to the sadist.

It is widely accepted that the *Scream* films are "self-reflexive parody"[75] which "take the previously subtle and covert inter-textual reference and transform it into an overt, discursive act,"[76] offer "a knowing and reflexive commentary on the generic logic of the 'slasher' film"[77] and deconstruct it,[78] critics and scholars mainly disagreeing on the extent to which this approach should be considered novel,[79] "emblematic"[80] or just "dull postmodern cynicism."[81] The 1996 movie opens with a statement of intent that is clearly voiced by its killer. In a scene that remakes the first act of *When a Stranger Calls* (Walton, 1979), itself inspired by the pre-slasher *Black Christmas* (Clark, 1974), the stalker proposes to determine a teenage girl's boyfriend's fate and her own by playing a Q&A game involving the names of the killers in *Halloween* (1978) and *Friday the 13th* (Cunningham, 1980). Throughout the film, the stalker's calls and guessing games, which are restricted to the first third of the narrative, reflexively foreground the film's playful approach to genre as repetition with variation, and to *Scream* itself as a filmic palimpsest à la *Once*

Upon a Time in the West. The first of the phone harassment scenes [0:19–12:54] is comprised of several phone calls, and all three scenes include the same or fairly similar questions ("What's your *favorite* scary movie?", "Where am I?"); the stalker even explicitly lists certain rules of the genre ("You should never say 'Who's there?' Don't you watch scary movies? It's a death wish."). The stalker's playful attitude toward the murders/numbers he orchestrates mirrors the movie's own attitude toward genre conventions. *Scream* proves, like, and before, *Funny Games*, that the game model of diegetic metafiction identified by Hutcheon need not be covert.

Less obvious, perhaps, is the opening scene's debt to *Rear Window*. The 1954 premise is turned inside out: the person being watched is not a murderer but the Peeping Tom's victim, and the narration aligns us with her. Casey, who believed she was going to spend a good time watching *Halloween* (1978), turns out to be a character in a horror movie directed by the stalker, a transformation that is expressed visually when she crouches next to the television set whose screen is blank because her VCR is not playing her movie—pointedly, because she *is* tonight's entertainment (Figure 8.5). As in *Rear Window*, the positions of spectator, director/screenwriter and actor/character are confused, the stalker initially presenting himself as a mere viewer ("Who am I looking at?") and Casey believing herself to be one as well. Casey is thus forced into occupying another, unwanted, position within the cinematic apparatus, trapped within a terrifying (fun)house that becomes, as in Hooper's 1981 film, a metonym of the film and genre itself. Significantly, she momentarily reclaims her position as spectator when she manages to get out of the house and observes the stalker, framed by the window, creeping about inside—and thus momentarily alone in his movie. But the latter puts an end to it by breaking through the window/screen and assaulting the teenager, like

Figure 8.5 Scream: *after seeing her boyfriend roped outside, Casey crouches next to the TV set she was supposed to watch Halloween on.*

the T-Rex in *Jurassic Park*. Casey's transformation into a horror movie victim is completed when a diegetic audience arrives on the scene, tragically made up of her parents, who witness her death on the phone as if she has been sucked into the killer's prime stalking device.

The opening scene acts as a blueprint for the whole movie. Ghostface's command of the situation—that is, his capacity to impose his own generic terms on reality—confers upon his comments a metanarrative dimension. When on the phone, he functions as what Chion calls an "acousmêtre," a character whose command of the soundtrack endows him with the gift of ubiquity and omniscience.[82] In Final Girl fashion, Sidney turns the tables when she confiscates both the costume and the voice changer [1:38:19–1:40:13] before neutralizing both killers, slaying one with a TV featuring Jamie Lee Curtis as Laurie Strode in *Halloween* (1978), and thus imposing her ending on the narrative (with some last minute help from Randy Meeks and Gale Weathers).

As the narrative progresses, it turns out that the horrific acts are treated by most everyone as staple genre material rather than actual traumatic experiences: Sidney's friend Tatum says Casey and her boyfriend were murdered "splatter-movie style" [18:10] and later compares Sidney's imaginings to a "Wes Carpenter flick" [54:28]; Stu and Randy are even less tactful when they discuss the gendered terms of the practice of disembowelment [19:50–21:42]; Randy cites *Prom Night* (Lynch, 1980) as a precedent of a slasher in which the killer is actually the heroine's boyfriend [55:46], and reminds the other characters of the genre's rules during a party where they watch the model of the genre, *Halloween* (1978) [1:12:50–1:13:56]; and even Principal Himbry, who reprimands his students for donning the killer's costume, fools around with the Ghostface mask [51:16] shortly before getting murdered. Sidney's boyfriend, Billy Loomis, compares their relationship to an R-rated movie that has been "edited for television" [14:45], leading Sidney to admit that she would rather "be a Meg Ryan movie" or "even a good porno" [1:11:34]. Like Casey, Sidney is thus turned into a movie (character) by both her boyfriend and the stalker (hence the final reveal). As early as the eighth scene [24:49–29:48], the killer attempts to repeat the film's opening, this time with Sidney, trapping her not only within the film genre of his choice but within the cinematic apparatus itself. The killers, it turns out, repeat the attempt on a grander scale by organizing a party in Stu's house while his parents are away (yet another staple slasher situation). Throughout the movie, various physical thresholds (doors, windows, fences) mark the ontological boundary between the killers' horror movie narrative and the "real" world, the killers and the Final Girl being, significantly, the most accomplished at breaking through these barriers.

But it turns out the killers are not alone in attempting to exert overarching control over the narrative of Sidney's life. So is the media. In the 1996 film, it is embodied by local journalist Gale Weathers, who has exploited Sidney's past in her book about the murder of Sidney's mother Maureen and made her the subject of infotainment of the crassest sort. (The sequels will expand on this idea by introducing the *Stab* franchise and inscribing Sidney's story within the entertainment industry.) The indirect complicity between the killers and the media is confirmed when the journalist's spying on the students unwittingly plays into the killers' own enterprise, as Gale and Kenny the cameraman suddenly become directors/projectionists/viewers turning the teenage party into a spectacle. The setup does more than just introduce a mise en abyme and add to the film's ironic "metatextuality."[83] For it is at this moment that Stu's farmhouse/funhouse properties are exacerbated and that ontological borders within the diegesis are the most explicitly blurred. Not only are the audience and the diegetic spectator Kenny watching the teenagers watch *Halloween* (1978), but the model and the copy (the killers' narrative and *Scream*) end up overlapping [1:22:23–1:23:50]. Randy tells Jamie Lee Curtis to look "behind" her, knowing full well as a fan of the cult movie that she will not and, more ironically still, when he should actually be looking over his

Figures 8.6.1 and 8.6.2   Scream: *Sidney Prescott and Gale Weather's cameraman Kenny watch on the surveillance screen as Ghostface creeps up on Randy—with a thirty-second delay.*

own shoulder (Figure 8.6.1). *Scream*'s imitation of *Halloween* (1978) (the 1996 film's original score incorporates some of Carpenter's music for *Halloween* all the way through to the climax) is then complicated by a second movie within the movie. In effect, the surveillance footage proposes a mix of the copy with its model—like Laurie Strode, Randy is being stalked by a killer, and like Randy, Sidney and Kenny urge him to look behind him (Figure 8.6.2). The mise en abyme explicates what was latent in the opening scene: the spectator has metamorphosed into a movie character. Paradoxically, then, *Halloween* (1978), the model, has become a mise en abyme of the copy (or copies)—the surveillance footage and *Scream*—but the surveillance footage is an imperfect copy of *Scream*; it is static, unlike the dynamic camerawork employed when Ghostface is about to strike Randy, and it is viewed with a 30-second delay (leading to Kenny's demise). The repetition of the same images reveals major differences, and the narrative does not perfectly coincide with the generic expectations it raises.[84]

The killers, like those of the later *Funny Games*, are merely symptoms of a postmodernist worldview à la Jean Baudrillard, one in which the dissemination of simulacra has led to the collapsing of various ontological boundaries:[85] between their lives and the movies, Ghostface and his vessels (Ghostface's return with each new installment implies he is, in effect, a performance), actors Jamie Lee Curtis and Anthony Perkins [1:30:39] and their characters, talk show host Ricki Lake (1992–2004) and an actual psychiatrist or psychologist [46:14]. In our hyperreal consumer society where the killer's costume, itself inspired by Edvard Munch's famous 1893 painting which gives the film its title, can easily be purchased [35:04], the desire to "see what your insides look like" fails to reveal an inner truth and ends up producing just another horror movie image. Play is not just the organizing principle of fiction but that of reality.

The genre play of *Scream* is not only grounded in a philosophical worldview; it enables an exploration of its ethical concerns that are just as central as in *Funny Games*. The hyperreal view in which the world is nothing but a genre movie fails to take into account the reality of Sidney's trauma. Given the killers' allegorical function, the words Sidney directs at her sex-obsessed boyfriend are equally valid for the world as a whole: "I am sorry if my traumatized life is an inconvenience to you and your perfect existence" [44:30]. Sidney's trauma is the premise of the genre and of the figure she incarnates, but it is also that which resists the generic framework. Indeed, the incompatibility between slasher and trauma involve their differing relationship to a common structure: repetition. With genre, repetition provides formal pleasure; with trauma, it expresses profound pain.[86] Yet *Scream* ends up exploring potential commonalities. Sidney's first encounter with Ghostface occurs shortly after an intimate scene in which she dozes off after looking at a photograph of her mother and her. The second time she interacts with the stalker (this time exclusively on the phone), he asks her if she's worried she hasn't "fingered the wrong guy again" [37:57], thus tapping into her increasingly guilty doubts as to whether the man (Cotton Weary) she sent to jail is innocent. The final reveal—that Billy and Stu actually murdered her mother, her boyfriend perhaps out of anger that she broke his parents up in order to make his girlfriend experience his own sense of loss—confirms the connection: the horror movie events in *Scream* are, in fact, a celebration of the one-year anniversary (yet another horror movie cliché) of the event that traumatized Sidney in the first place. The emotions Sidney (and Billy) are dealing with align *Scream* with another genre, melodrama, which, for Linda Williams,[87] has, as a body genre, much in common with Billy's two favorite genres, horror and pornography. In a sense, blood keeps getting in the way of tears, or, in Billy's case, has, perhaps, become a way of dealing with them. That grief is a core emotion in *Scream* is brought to the fore through an allusion to *Twin Peaks*, a series that is centered on the traumatic death of a teenager, when Sidney, like Laura Palmer's best friend Donna Hayward in the pilot episode, notices the victim's (Casey's) empty seat in her classroom [18:43]. This traumatic void is what the repetitious pleasures provided by genre cover up.

The story of Sidney is thus a drama of resilience in the face of repeated assaults not so much by patriarchy, though a degree of sexism remains (Stu's comment that no woman could have murdered Casey, and the fact that the killers are men in the first installment), as by a hyperreal genre movie world that is emotionally and ethically disconnected from life and death (most of the teenagers seem unaffected by Casey's death and are excited at the prospect of seeing their principal's gutted body [1:16:18]). Sidney's boyfriend Billy never appears so perverse as when he changes the conversation topic from her mourning her mother to her lack of a sex drive, basically inviting her to trade the pain of melodrama for the delights of pornography (or of horror as it turns out in the end).

The difference between *Scream* and *Funny Games* is ultimately not aesthetic; it is one of attitude. The 1997 film leaves no room for anything but the condemnation of the genre, its aesthetics and morals; the 1996 film, on the contrary, sees the genre as a viable form to address those very concerns, not only because of the allegorical function of the killer/monster, but because it expresses a belief that playing games and creating or consuming fictions are also, as in Jean-Marie Schaeffer's line of reasoning, activities that enable the subject to learn how to deal with life. Sidney's plight—between Final Girl and melodramatic heroine—ultimately points to the value of genre; it is by repeating the game that we learn to deal with our fears (by *Scream 4* [Craven,

2011], she has become a writer and a strong woman). The end of the 1996 movie hints not so much at the economic possibility of a sequel; it makes the cynical observation that, though Sidney may have evolved, the world has not, and Gale Weathers is already back in action transforming the narrative she contributed to into "the plot of some scary movie," her look to the camera revealing itself to be an instance of extradiegetic metalepsis as she moves away and her crew enters the shot [1:43:06–1:43:52].

Community is also a work that was regularly cited as being "too meta," in addition to being a show in which the prefix-turned-adjective is employed within the diegesis as early as season 2 in fall 2010 (by Shirley when referring to pop-culture fan and aspiring movie director Abed in S2E1 and S2E5). *Community* neatly illustrates what is currently understood as "meta": self-conscious allusions to genre, specific movie and television references, metaleptic moments (the characters become animated characters in S2E11 and S5E11), and a good dose of parody and self-parody. In academic writings, Saul Austerlitz described the sitcom as a "dazzling metafiction" which "sum[s] up the history of television"[88] and interrogates "the unspoken clichés of the medium,"[89] and Shannon Wells-Lassagne has demonstrated how the sitcom "embrac[es] the stereotypical, unrealistic nature of the sitcom" and "turn[s] it from traditional comedy to metacommentary on the format."[90]

The premise—six very different individuals (Abed, Annie, Britta, Jeff, Pierce, Shirley and Troy) form a Spanish study group and become friends ("Look at this group having some kind of meeting and being so diverse," Dean Pelton says in S1E6, "There is just one of every kind of you, isn't there?")—knowingly relies on the conventions of the college or high school movie, and the main hypotext, *The Breakfast Club* (Hughes, 1985), is referred to on two occasions in season 1 alone (in S1E1 when Abed recites John Bender's monologue,[91] and in S1E16 when Abed, Jeff and Troy dance to "We Are Not Alone"). Abed regularly notes the sitcom-like quality of the situations they find themselves in (in S1E16, he explains to Jeff that the latter "shifted the balance like in a sitcom when one character sees another one naked," an allusion to *Friends*[92] [NBC, 1994–2004], a sitcom Abed references more directly in S1E23 when he says "Jeff and Britta is not Ross and Rachel [. . .] ironically, and hear this on every level, you're keeping us from being *Friends*."[93]) or prompts such self-consciousness in his friends (in S2E1, Jeff asks Abed to "stop mining [his] life looking for classic sitcom scenarios."). Many episodes are parodies of popular works (*Dead Poets Society* in S1E3 [Weir, 1989], *Mad Men*[94] (AMC, 2007–15) in S1E17, *Spaceballs* [Brooks, 1987] in S2E4, *Pulp Fiction* [Tarantino, 1994] in S2E19, *GI Joe* in S5E11), genres (the war movie in S1E23, the zombie movie in S2E6) or media (role-playing games in S2E14 and S5E10, video games in S3E20), frameworks that are regularly noted by the characters themselves. The prologue of episode S1E9 even includes an intradiegetic metalepsis when the characters realize that "all of Abed's films are about" them (the excerpt shown remakes S1E8) but are impossibly posted online before they occurred, an idea that is regrettably never fully exploited thereafter. The series's self-consciousness increases with every season, with episodes thematizing film criticism (S1E3, S2E19), fandom (Abed invites friends over to watch exploitation movies in S1E15 and attends the Inspector SpaceTime Convention in S4E3), and especially filmmaking (S2E5, S2E16, S3E8, S4E6, S6E8); it climaxes, much like the intensely meta *Moonlighting* (ABC, 1985–9), with an episode (S6E13) in which Abed encourages the other characters to imagine a pitch for season seven of their own show. The series, Wells-Lassagne shows, increasingly gives Abed a metanarrative function as predictor and "metacritic," and sometimes even constitutes him as the subjectivity in which the narration originates (Abed's Claymation fantasy in S2E11).[95] *Community* is clearly a highly reflexive show that flaunts its artificiality and occasionally ventures into the territory of the series-about-making-film/series. Meta appears to be predominantly exploited for its comic potential and its capacity to establish a bond with the actual audience's own references.

Yet, on many occasions, the parody of genre conventions serves to dramatize moral concerns. Episode S2E5, for instance, is comprised of two interwoven plots, one of which centers on Abed and Shirley, who asks the aspiring director to make a "viral video" to be posted on "Christian YouTube" to promote Christianity among kids [2:20] ("It needs to be cool and addictive, like that video of the kitten falling to sleep." [4:44]). Abed only accepts once he comes up with an idea that satisfies his aesthetic credo "I'm a storyteller, not a preacher" [2:35]:

> We need a Jesus movie for the post-postmodern world. [. . .] I want to tell the story of Jesus from the perspective of a filmmaker exploring the life of Jesus. [. . .] See, in the filmmaker's film, Jesus is a filmmaker trying to find God with his camera, but then the filmmaker realizes that he's actually Jesus, and he's being filmed by God's camera. And it goes like that forever in both directions, like a mirror in a mirror, because all of the filmmakers are Jesus, and all their cameras are God. And the movie is called *ABED*. All caps. Filmmaking beyond film. A metafilm. My masterpiece. [4:51–5:27]

Shirley is appalled by this "Charlie Kaufman"-like scenario. The disagreement leads to the usual movie-about-making-movies scenario whereby the producer tries to shut down the director's project, although the disagreement here is not economic but ethical (neither Shirley nor Abed can betray their values). The economic impasse is immediately resolved because Abed benefits from the equipment furnished by Greendale Community College and has an epiphany, "This is the movie," which he addresses to us through a look to the camera [5:52].

The episode then thematizes the reflexive aesthetics that the series as a whole exploits. Abed's project impresses the multitudes that frequent the college ("This is totally meta," Troy says, "I want to watch this." [8:05]), turning the director into a modern Messiah with a cult following (Figure 8.7). The arc, however, ends up bringing to the fore the familiar negative connotations attached to "meta"—its elitism (the setting is, after all, a college), ageism (Shirley is not into "meta," and the second plot concerns Pierce momentarily integrating the elderly students' group) and, of course, narcissism. Abed will have another quasi-religious epiphany: "Dear God, my movie is the worst piece of crap I've ever seen in my entire life. How could I have been so blind? It's a self-indulgent adolescent mess. I can barely sit through it" [16:05]. Shirley, who has witnessed this scene, then proceeds to demolish Abed's equipment, doing double duty as religious righter of wrongs and friend who will save Abed from embarrassment (his unmade film will go down as "a movie so good it could never exist" [19:20]). More importantly, her act saves their friendship (Abed "finishes" the cool Jesus movie she had imagined, and

Figure 8.7 Community: *Abed, shooting* ABED, *a metafilm about Abed making a film about Jesus, impresses his audience and especially his best friend Troy who admits: "This is totally meta. I want to watch this."*

both characters admit to "humbl[ing]" each other [19:59]), the study group they have formed, and thus *Community* the show itself.

The formula whereby an alien genre or hypotext threatens the fabric of the friends-as-family sitcom is employed several times in season 2 alone. In S2E2, Abed frames the main premise—Jeff takes to hanging out with an ex-lawyer buddy aptly named Connor—by comparing this relationship to the toxic one portrayed in the appropriately named *Bad Influence* (Hanson, 1990), so that the saving-Jeff-from-abandoning-his-real-friends plot is equally an attempt to counter the hypotext and preserve the sitcom's formula. In S2E18, it is Jeff who establishes the intertextual framework by preparing a surprise *Pulp Fiction* birthday party for his fan friend, but his plan is offset when Abed meets him in a fancy restaurant, an ideal setting for an intimate dinner and "real conversation." Abed's narrative of authenticity turns out to be modeled on yet another film, *My Dinner with Andre* (Malle, 1981), so that each character has negotiated their friendship through an intertext (Abed regrets that they had been recently drifting apart). The entire group is reunited when the *Pulp Fiction* birthday (during which they parody cult scenes) is relocated in the *My Dinner with Andre* setting, the mixing of hypotexts and genres asserting the group's cohesion and the sitcom's viability. The self-conscious parody is thus underpinned by the sitcom's moral core, but whereas the status quo in classical sitcoms tended to safeguard the patriarchal family, the values celebrated herein are those of inclusion, diversity and, as the title goes, community. Notwithstanding the overt meta-phenomena it mobilizes, the series, as Lisann Anders suggests, offers a utopian social model for the contemporary US: it "shows the audience that they can still be individuals in a group—after all the study group consists of members of various ethnicities and religions—but as soon as you belong to a group and identify with it (and its shared values), you are exposed to change as the group dynamics start to shape and influence you."[96]

CONCLUSION

Genre works tend to be self-conscious of their material—of the architext or specific hypotexts—and to assert their place in the genre's history and the singularity of their approach—whether authorial, parodic, poetic and/or political—early on in statements of intent (*Dead Man*). A favored device of metafiction, parody establishes a bond with the audience, who is potentially aware of its target. Parody is meta because, at the very least, it foregrounds the conventionality of conventions and how they can be reinvented through sheer genius (*My Name Is Nobody*), but it can also participate more radically in an exploration of the history, politics and ethics of a given genre, and even of the ontology of fiction. The increasing presence of genre-savvy characters in contemporary films and series draws attention to the multiple uses genre as a category can be put to, echoing the evolution of film genre theory, which, since Rick Altman's 1999 *Film/Genre*, has drawn attention to the pragmatics of film genre. By asserting, sometimes quite explicitly, that genre conventions function like "rules," genre fiction tends to epitomize the view of fiction as game. But the concern with genre need not be solely formal; the attack can be directed at a genre's politics and, more generally, at how the genre exemplifies and perpetuates hegemonic power relations through the history of cultural representations (*Funny Games*). Such relations can also be evoked on a more allegorical mode; for instance, the dramatization of the characters' subjection to, and resistance against, these rules becomes a plea for the recognition of what the genre prompts us to overlook—that they are not just pawns in a game but are modeled on human agents (*Scream*)—and thus speaks to our own complex dealings with the structures of power. Meta takes genre as a framework to explore genres and frameworks in general, and more poignantly the relationship between such frameworks and basic human experiences such as friendship and trauma (*Scream, Community*). Therein lies the salvation of genre—in its usability as a heuristic framework that, contrary to what Waugh contends,[97] offers both satisfactions *and* their undermining, a template to dramatize the political and ethical struggle against constricting systems of power. And in saving genre, it is the relevance of popular fiction that meta ensures.

CHAPTER 9

Seriality

Metamoments in Series

Series present many opportune moments for meta that are specific to the format. We have seen that metamoments often occur during beginnings, and in Chapter 7 in particular, how serial adaptations and remakes such as *Bates Motel* and *Hannibal* are prompt to address their relationship to their source material. But the specificity of the serial form is that it has a multitude of beginnings: the beginning of the series as a whole, the season opener, the episode prologue. For instance, S3E1 of *Sherlock*, a series whose meta quality has received sustained attention,[1] struggles to resolve the season 2 cliffhanger (Sherlock jumping off a building with Moriarty) by integrating several fan theories, voiced within the diegesis by a group called the Empty Hearse, whose name is also the title of the episode. In so doing, the episode playfully evokes its own complicated genesis and ensures the series's survival through that of its eponymous hero, brought back to life by its fans,[2] partly (at least) responsible for rewriting Arthur Conan Doyle's original story entitled "The Adventure of the Empty House." Sitcoms habitually celebrate their own return in the first scenes of their season openers. The opening of S8E1 of *Married . . . with Children*, for example, has Bud remarking that, if his mother Peg leaves, she will "miss Dad's latest episode of A Fat Woman Came into the Shoe Store Today" [1:55]. Season 2 of *Community* opens with Abed exclaiming, "And we're back!" followed by a lateral tracking shot that quite artificially takes us from one character's bedroom to another, and a shot of Britta walking around campus while Dean Pelton, on the PA system, recaps her humiliating ordeal in the season 1 finale and announces a "fresh start" [0:00–1:10].

Metamoments are frequent in endings as well, whether the series's, a season's or an episode's. One famous example is the metaleptic finale (S5E13) of *Moonlighting*. The protagonists, Maddie Hayes and David Addison Jr., are informed by Walter Whitebread of ABC TV that they have been "canceled" and, consequently, that "in six minutes and fourteen seconds [they] will cease to exist as television characters," a situation a secondary character (Agnes), who hopes she'll get her own spinoff series, blames on Maddie and David's inability to "figure out [their] nitwit relationship" [36:51–40:25]. They then visit Cy, the producer, in a movie theater, who, while moving images play over Maddie and David's faces, admits that his godlike powers are limited to the diegetic world: "Hey, even I can't get people to tune in and watch what they don't want to watch anymore" [40:57]. Maddie and David then desperately attempt to give the audience what it wants by getting married. The season 11 finale (S11E22) of *The Simpsons* proposes a metaleptical episode-about-making-a-television-series, in which it is revealed that the show was Homer Simpson's idea all along; the season closer thus points back at the entire series (we are invited to compare the filming of staple scenes to earlier episodes), potentially terminating it or announcing something new (which is probably why some fans consider it would have made for an ideal ending). Such phenomena are especially common in sitcoms which, like comedy in general, easily accommodate reflexivity. Every episode of *Seinfeld* ends with the protagonist's stand-up scenes, which reflect on the contents of the episode and on how the comedian utilizes the stuff of reality for his show; it further plays upon the relationship between fiction and reality, since Jerry Seinfeld is apparently playing himself and really is a comedian. And in episode S5E6 of *The Fresh Prince of Bel Air* (NBC, 1990–6), a series that contains numerous instances of direct address,[3] Will Smith's cousin, Carlton Banks (Alfonso Ribeiro), runs across the set into the live audience and into Will Smith's arms [21:00–22:00], a metaleptical conclusion reminiscent of that of *Blazing Saddles*.

The serial format also allows for individual episodes or seasons that can tap into the movie-about-making-movies genre or exploit metaleptical premises. In S5E24 of *Cheers* (NBC, 1982–93), aptly entitled "Cheers: The Motion Picture," the gang decides to make a home movie to convince Woody Boyd's father that Boston is not the cut-throat city he believes it to be. Episodes S2E16, S3E8 and S4E6 of *Community* are documentaries filmed by Abed. Season 6 of the FX anthology series *American Horror Story*, "My Roanoke Nightmare," proposes a true crime docudrama pastiche, before dramatizing the production team's creation of a reality TV follow-up. And episode S6E15 of *Supernatural* has the characters stumble onto the set of an episode of *Supernatural* shot in a parallel universe, before offering a "self-parody"[4] of the cast's personal and professional lives.

The serial format multiplies the opportunities for meta not only because of its length but because of its defining feature: the interval or "gap."[5] The season or episode unit allows for temporary transgressions. The status of the season opener or finale and episode prologue/epilogue is complicated by the fact that neither is a pure beginning or ending: they are both, or more precisely, they are links in the serial chain. The same can be said of the moments preceding and following a commercial break (this is especially true of US-American network television programs whose structure is dictated by commercial breaks). This was already the case in a classical sitcom like *The Goldbergs* (CBS, 1948–57), which blurred the ontological boundary between actress/producer Gertrude Berg and her character, Molly Goldberg; the May 1954 episode "Molly Learns to Rhumba," for instance, concludes with Berg/Goldberg first commenting on the content of the episode before praising the virtues of Rybutol [25:24–26:55].[6] Like opening credits, these moments that bridge the gap between the fiction and the real world flirt with metalepsis. But even the most clear-cut of breaks makes the seams of the serial format apparent. Each interruption is potentially the site where the series can negotiate its seriality: each ending is a potential beginning but each interruption also threatens to be the last. Metamoments located on the brink of these interruptions are thus ideally positioned to recognize the precariousness of the serial form, the ineluctability of an end that must be delayed at all costs.

The functions of these metamoments are varied. Celebrating the season return, for example, constitutes an instance of what J.D. Connor calls "industrial reflexivity," whereby "reflexivity is the tribute art pays to marketing."[7] In such cases, reflexivity can assert a program's space in the mediascape, notably in relation to the competition. This is explicitly the case in the season 5 opener of *Married . . . with Children*, where Peggy Bundy skims through the new fall preview issue of *TV Guide* and asks her husband Al, "Are you so jaded that even the new TV season doesn't get you going?" before reading the description of several shows, including "We Are Fami-Lee" [2:30–3:15]. The ridiculous contents, combined with Al's attitude, invite a degree of complicity not only with the characters but with the actors that portray them. Clearly, the message is: Why watch other—more politically correct—shows when you could be hanging out with the Bundys instead? Favorable references to other programs—for instance, when the characters of a sitcom like *Brooklyn Nine-Nine* (Fox, 2013–18; NBC, 2018–21) talk about the HBO fantasy drama *Game of Thrones* (2011–19) or those of *Community* refer to an older sitcom like *Friends*—similarly create complicity and, in the examples that I have come across, tend to refer to programs that are not competition—basically, you can watch *Brooklyn Nine-Nine* without missing *Game of Thrones*, which the characters wouldn't want to miss either (the sitcom's second season was broadcast on Sunday half-an-hour before season 5 of the HBO series). Even without the blatant humor, episode S3E1 of *Sherlock* ultimately functions along similar lines as S5E1 of *Married . . . with Children*: by thematizing our inclusion within the series's fan community, the season opener suggests that, having waited so long for the series's return, we should all be riveted to our television sets to see what happens next. In all these instances, industrial reflexivity is mediated by a ritual function: the economic survival of the series depends on its ritual power, on its capacity not to lose its audience in the intervals (unlike *Moonlighting*). Hence, such metamoments comment on the precariousness of the series, but they also attempt to make this precariousness engaging by dramatizing it and turning it into a social commitment akin to romance (*Moonlighting*), friendship (*Community*) or family (yes, even, *Married . . . with Children*).

Another common denominator stands out. Given that the serial form is above all a matter of narrative, the focus of meta in series is primarily metanarrative. More specifically, metamoments in series regularly engage with what Jean-Pierre Esquenazi describes as the series's "formula," which is "not so much a script as a story-producing machine, not so much a cast of characters as a reservoir of character types, not so much a mise en scène as a formal framework."[8] Metamoments are instances wherein the series's formula can be (re)negotiated, "deformulated" or "reformulated."[9] Even a minimally metanarrative comment such as Bud Bundy's in S8E1 can serve to problematize the play on repetition and variation that characterizes popular seriality. By disparaging Al's stories, and thus an intrinsic ingredient of the series's formula ("Actually I already know how it ends. He doesn't get the sale or a life."), Peggy sets the stage for a challenge to Al's and the series's talent for variation, which the laugh track and the conclusion of the scene (the story is not just an anecdote but actually the premise of the episode) tend to validate [1:55–4:00]. In so doing, the scene plays for the "second-level reader" who, in Umberto Eco's words, "enjoys the seriality of the series, not so much for the return of the same thing [. . .] but for the strategies of variations," and thus "the way in which the same story is worked over to appear to be different."[10] Meta that is specific to seriality thus explores both the series's own formula (Wolf's "intracomposition metareference") and the serial form and format (Wolf's "extracomposition metareference"), in addition to its genre and sources, its medium, and its production and reception contexts. We shall now see how specific metamoments resort to allegory in order to explore their own formula and theorize a view of the serial form.

ALLEGORIES OF SERIALITY (*THIS IS US*)

Appropriately, the metanarrative allegory of seriality can be produced through the serialization of a motif. We have seen, in Chapter 7, that rewinding is a common motif in contemporary series that are remakes, reboots and/or adaptations (*Bates Motel*, *Hannibal*). The same motif can reflect just as much the series's reliance on pre-existing material as the serial format's repetition with variation. The pilot episode of HBO's *Westworld*, for instance, repeats the awakening of the host Dolores four times [2:38–3:15, 22:46–23:48, 45:03–46:40, 1:06:38–1:06:51], each time with a slight variation: the second is an expanded version of the first; the third opens with a disruption (Dolores's father Peter Abernathy glitches, telling her to escape and citing *The Tempest*); and the fourth ends on a casting change (another host has replaced Peter Abernathy) and another unprogrammed disruption (Dolores swats a fly on her neck). Seriality is thus integrated within one episode. The metanarrative potential of these scenes is later explicated by the dialogue when the hosts' experiences are described as "storylines" [S1E1, 28:05], "loops" and "backstories" [S1E3, 28:13, 28:50]. Such comments are part and parcel of the series's discourse on its formula (in episode S1E3, Ford confesses to Bernard that "[i]t's a tricky thing, weaving the old into the new." [34:19]) and, more generally, on world- and character-building. In effect, the series, as we have seen in Chapter 4, is traversed by an allegory of seriality that is grounded in a spatial paradigm (the maze, to which season 2 adds a library containing the guests' data in S2E10 [35:42–36:54], a sibling motif present in the metafictional writings of Jorge Luis Borges whose libraries were also mazes). The maze, because it bridges the macro (the park) and the micro (the hosts' minds), evokes a storytelling mode that would be simultaneously "centripetal" and "centrifugal," to use Jason Mittell's typology, pushing outwards and inwards[11] and, therefore, expanding in both directions.

The allegory of seriality is just as consubstantial to the premise of Amazon Prime's *Man in the High Castle* (2015–19), an adaptation of Philip K. Dick's 1962 novel. The series makes the clever move of changing the medium of *The Grasshopper Lies Heavy* to one more in tune with its own: Abendsen's novel becomes not just one film, but a series of film reels that the Nazis, the Japanese and the Resistance want to get their hands on. The multiplication of film reels parallels the development of the narrative: it is not just a matter of quantity but of quality, as episode S3E1 reveals that some of the films were "fakes" made by Abendsen while the real ones come from parallel worlds. The change in medium also ensures the series's longevity, of course: there are many reels to discover and they cannot all be burnt (S2E5, S2E10). Finally, it highlights the specificity of the serial form itself: some reels are watched several times (S1E1, S1E2, S1E9, S2E10, S3E3, S3E4, S3E9, S4E1, S4E9) because, like specific episodes, they are more significant than others. If the use of film reels is in keeping with the 1962–3 time-setting, Chang-Min Yu has astutely argued that the series's representation of media comments on the mediascape in which it was produced: "beyond a spectacle of history forking, the filmic replacement serves as a node in the network of discourses of media competition among telephone, film, television and ultimately the digital platform itself."[12] Yu powerfully concludes that

> Without any perceptible interstices, the digital suturing materializes the vision that the films can only dubiously project. The radical continuity becomes an allegory of the digital imaging itself, a seamless picturing process that manifests the perpetual dialectic of media oneupmanship.[13]

What the characters see as proof that the celluloid images are real, we see as evidence of the ease with which such celluloid-looking images can be fabricated in the digital age. On a meta-level, then, the diegetic films both materialize the gaps of seriality (as a dispersed and potentially infinite collection of films) and effect the connection (as digital images that can merge ontologically distinct realms). Here, we encounter an idea put forth in Chapter 7: that the very objects that allegorize the adaptation, remaking and in this case serialization process can simultaneously serve to celebrate what the series identifies as today's technological superiority, in a more discrete instance of Connor's "industrial reflexivity."

Allegories of seriality are not restricted to science fiction and fantasy series. Ariane Hudelet's book-length study of *The Wire* (HBO, 2002–8) insists on the series's reflexive qualities (which Mittell briefly noted), notably by foregrounding the motif of the game.[14] She argues that the scene in episode S1E3 in which D'Angelo Barksdale uses a chess game to explain the power structures of the drug underworld [11:10–14:15] becomes a "two-pronged metaphor" for the diegetic world's economics and the series's network narrative;[15] in so doing, it brings to the fore the game model that structures the series as a whole. Hudelet also cites Detective Lester Freamon explaining to a young colleague, in episode S1E6, the pertinence of the information coming along the wire: "We're building something here, detective. We're building it from scratch. *All* the pieces matter" [23:10]. Freamon's lines establish a parallel between the diegetic detectives' work (collecting fragments of information), the show's "expanding storytelling"[16] (its season-by-season exploration of new neighborhoods and social/professional groups), and the viewers who are meant to piece together a complex narrative.[17] The eponymous wire becomes a metaphor for the gap-link between the series's fragments, indicating that the HBO series involves narrative connections as well as social and political ones. As early as season 1, and long before the series has made apparent its season-based approach, we are invited to *view The Wire* in spatial terms, as a "rhizomatic plot,"[18] echoing recent writings on televisions series and seriality more generally, which tend to emphasize "spatial storytelling" (Mittell), "navigation" rather than "flux" (Claire Cornillon).[19] The epilogue of the series's finale (S5E10) drives in the point [1:26:43–1:31:55] when

Detective James McNulty, who is transporting the homeless person he used as a performer for the serial killer fiction he invented, parks on the side of an expressway to look at the city of Baltimore, effectively pausing the crime narrative and opening up a space for a montage sequence of the city. The series thus thematizes its own end, encouraging us not only to "go home" and bid it farewell, but also "to cast a retrospective gaze on the fictional world we now have a global view of."[20]

Another more recent example of an allegory of seriality in a drama series occurs at the end of episode S1E5 of *This Is Us*, in a scene which functions like a belated statement of intent [36:29–41:09]. To make up for his selfish behavior, Kevin Pearson shares a secret with his nieces, Beth and Tess, and reveals that sometimes, when he receives a script, he paints "the way it makes [him] feel." He then shows them the abstract painting he made after reading the play he is going to star in on Broadway before proposing his interpretation of his own painting (Figure 9.1).

> I felt like the play is about life, you know, and life is full of color, and we each get to come along and we add our own color to the painting, you know. And even though it's not very big, the painting, you sort of have to figure that it goes on forever, you know, in each direction. So, like, to infinity, you know. 'Cause that's kind of like life, right? It's really crazy if you think about it, isn't it? That a hundred years ago some guy that I never met came to this country with a suitcase . . . He has a son, who has a son, who has me. So at first when I was painting, I was thinking, you know, maybe up here that was

Figure 9.1 This Is Us, *episode S1E5: Kevin Pearson shows his nieces the painting he made to make sense of a part in a play.*

that guy's part of the painting, and then, you know, down here that's my part of the painting. And then I start to think, Well, what if we're all in the painting everywhere? And what if we're in the painting before we're born? What if we're in it after we die? And these colors that we keep adding, what if they just keep getting added on top of one another, until eventually we're not even different colors anymore, we're just . . . one thing? One painting. And my dad's not with us anymore. He's not alive. But he's with us. He's with me every day. It all just sort of fits somehow, even if you don't understand how yet. People will die in our lives, people that we love, in the future, maybe tomorrow, maybe years from now. I mean it's kind of beautiful, right, if you think about it, the fact that just because someone dies, just because you can't see them or talk to them anymore, it doesn't mean they're not still in the painting. I think maybe that's the point of the whole thing. There's no dying. There's no you or me or them. It's just us . . . And this sloppy, wild colorful magical thing that has no beginning, that has no end—it's right here. I think it's us.

The painting is presented as the visual expression of Kevin's gut reaction to the play, the means by which he attempts to comprehend a script he is liable to perform, but then becomes an object worthy of analysis in itself. His interpretation of the painting as an allegory of life belies a faith that art has meaning and real-world implications. It falls upon us to realize that the painting might similarly allow us to comprehend the series; in effect, it is our interpretation of Kevin's interpretation of a painting inspired by a play that turns the painting into a mise en abyme of the series and an allegory of the serial form. As a potentially boundless plane, the painting reflects the form of a long series, the disposition of elements on its surface the multiprotagonist narrative (which shifts focalization from one member of the Pearson family to another), the depth created by its texture the series's flashback structure, its manifold colors the potential variations in the formula. The emphasis on three dimensions favors a comprehension of seriality according to a spatial paradigm. The narration furthers the analogy by illustrating Kevin's interpretation: first, by picturing Kevin's great-grandfather, then by introducing more familiar images—flashbacks of his parents, and intercut scenes of Kevin's sister Kate and brother Randall. The "point" is driven home when Kevin's concluding words turn out to be a variation on the series's title. His use of the first-person plural evolves over the course of the monologue from referring to humanity to referring more specifically to the Pearson family, thus confirming the multiple "referents" of "us" in the series's title. Only we, the viewers, however, can interpret the variation. While "it" unproblematically refers to the painting and by extension the series, "this" points both inwards and outwards, to the family and humanity beyond (including the audience, of course), to the fiction and reality. The metamoment thus expounds the three-word statement of intent that is the title. Yet the sequence also reveals the flaws in the analogy and in the series's totalizing ambition. Formally speaking, equating the painting—and thus the series—with wholeness overlooks the singularity of the serial form: the gaps between each episode and commercial break. Another discrepancy concerns the interpretive latitude offered by an abstract painting such as this one and a complex serial narrative whose survival is based on filling in the blanks (and counting on their number). The series's totalizing ambition is thus asserted, its means to achieve it are assumed, but its limitations become apparent because of the inadequacy of the abstract painting/television series analogy.

All these allegories of seriality tend to engage with the terms of both their formula and form, thereby establishing the framework through which we are invited to approach the series. They do so by resorting to motifs that have the potential to become apt metaphors of a series because they materialize spatiality and/or repetition with variation. The allegory of seriality can be furthered through the serialization of the motif, but the metamoment from *This Is Us* proves that an allegory of seriality can be a one-off affair—Sarah Hatchuel analyzes a similar example in episode S1E7 of *Awake* (NBC, 2012), where a book of paintings serves as a metaphor for the series's formula, "its reworking a situation and presenting a new facet each time Michael [its protagonist] goes from one world to the other."[21] Both examples can be added to the long list of instances whereby a work explores its form and medium through another medium (see Chapter 6). While metamoments are quite common in contemporary television (see Chapter 3), less frequent are non-sitcom series that are intensely meta. The last section begins by exploring a paradigmatic example of meta in an early-twenty-first-century series, *LOST*, before analyzing two more exceptional cases, *The Prisoner*, *Twin Peaks* and *Twin Peaks: The Return*.

METASERIES (*LOST*, THE PRISONER, TWIN PEAKS)

One of Mittell's prime examples of reflexivity in "complex television," *LOST* is, no doubt, more paradigmatic of meta in drama series than *The Prisoner* and *Twin Peaks*. The extreme close-up of the eye that opens a third of season 1's episode (S1E1, S1E4, S1E6, S1E10, S1E13, S1E14, S1E16, S1E17, S1E24) and that returns on numerous occasions (S2E1, S3E1, S3E5, S3E12, S3E23, S4E4, S4E8, S4E10, S4E11, S5E6, S5E16, S6E1) becomes an allegory of seriality (as an exemplar of "repetition with variation"[22]) and of the series's formula (the window of the soul puts in relief how the majority of the episodes contain flashbacks, flashforwards and flashsideways focused on one or several characters), while the narrative conceit of the island's energy works as a "metaphor for narrative creation."[23] The series also employs one-shot motifs, such as the record skipping in the season 5 opener[24] [1:48] or the tapestry Jacob is working on in the opening scenes of the season 5 finale [0:05–0:50]. The introduction of surveillance technology in seasons 2 and 3 offers instances of mise en abyme of watching or producing television programs,[25] with one or several characters viewing the very scenes we are watching (Benjamin Linus like a reality TV show producer[26]) and, more generally, becoming increasingly aware that they are being watched (Jack Shephard tells Tom Friendly he knows there's a security camera aimed at the cage in S3E9 [7:52], Kate Austen tells Sawyer Jack saw them making love in S3E17 [9:00], John Locke notices a surveillance camera when he lands in Tunisia in S5E7 [6:54], and Jack and Hugo Reyes realize, in S6E5, that Jacob has "been watching them ... the whole time, all of us," from his lighthouse [34:27]). This awareness likens them to reality TV performers, the series thereby drawing attention to potential similarities (and differences) with one of its main network competitors of the time, *Survivor*[27] (CBS, 2000–); this is reinforced in season 6 when it is revealed that the survivors of flight Oceanic 815 were actually "candidates" for Jacob's succession. It is its debt to reality TV in particular that endows *LOST* with an underpinning game structure typical of diegetic metafiction, which surfaces in some of the dialogue (for instance, in S3E13 when Locke retorts to Ben's query concerning the reason for his anger, "Because you're cheating. You and your people"[28] [28:22]).

The season 2 opener introduces us to the character of Desmond Hume [0:38–3:20], who, inside the hatch (later known as the Swan station), is charged with pressing a button in order to save the world. Sarah Hatchuel has brilliantly analyzed the episode's first shots as a "metaphor for filmic creation: writing a screenplay on a computer (Desmond typing on the keyboard), executive production (Desmond presses the EXECUTE button), action (domestic chores, turning on the equipment), post-production (adding music)."[29] After the implosion of the hatch (from S3E8 on), Desmond, now endowed with limited foresight (most poignantly of Charlie's ineluctable death), becomes a narrative predictor, thus endowed with a metanarrative function as a character with partial access to (if limited control over) the series's script. The discovery of the Dharma initiative films featuring Dr. Chang—another allegory of seriality that is achieved through repetition with variation—has the characters piecing together the mystery, much like the audience watching *LOST*; in episode S2E3, Locke, who has just watched the first reel once, informs Jack, "We're going to need to watch that again"[30] [21:22], right before the commercial break.

LOST is exemplary of how meta operates in contemporary series as the majority of these metamoments occur on the threshold (of a season, an episode or a commercial break) and the stakes are primarily metanarrative and metatextual. Such stakes are more consistently evoked through dialogue, with a line commenting as much on the immediate diegesis as on the show's formula and the serial form. As in *Scream*, the characters regularly mention some of the series's main hypotexts, with Hugo citing pop cultural references (the *Star Wars* franchise in S5E13, *Indiana Jones* in S6E5) and Sawyer, who spends most of season 1 reading, literary ones (*Lord of the Flies* in episode S1E15 where he is tormented by a wild pig, Nabokov's *Laughter in the Dark* in episode S3E8 where Jack, Kate and Locke meet a Russian named Mikhaïl Bakounine, Steinbeck's *Of Mice and Men* in episode S3E4 when he follows Ben Linus onto a cliff).

It is also mainly through the dialogues that the formula's defining features are evoked: that the main characters can die, that they are lost (on an island, in time, and, more generally speaking, spiritually), that they have to "go back" (in space, time and memory), and that they form a cast of characters (and thus that the series is a multiprotagonist narrative). In episode S1E21, Walt, whose father Michael Dawson has just promised him they won't die, retorts, "Boone died" [30:25], drawing attention to the fact that the series's formula authorizes the elimination of main characters. Many lines play on the polysemy of the word "lost"—as a synonym of death ("They were already lost," Danielle Russo says about her shipmates in episode S1E9 [35:14]) or of a mental state ("I'm not lost anymore," Locke says to Sun-Hwa Kwon in S2E5 [23:01])—thus revealing that the series's basic premise is underpinned by moral and spiritual questions. The verbal motif of "going back"—introduced in one of the last lines of the pilot episode when Kate tells Charlie Pace, "We have to go back for [Jack]" [38:30]—foregrounds the essence of the series's formula: that the character arcs are determined by moral choices (saving a person, a dog in S1E3, a relationship in S1E17, the world in S2E3); that each episode will take us back in time through flashbacks; that the characters will have to come to terms with their pasts; and that they will inevitably be drawn back to the island. This culminates in the season 3 finale's final lines when Jack desperately lets out, "We have to go back, Kate. We have to go back!" [40:31], pleading not only for a potential return to the island (and to the main premise), but also underscoring a modification in the series's formula (what we initially believed to be a flashback was actually a flashforward). Going back thus becomes a metaphor for the reinvention of the series's formula, an indication of the repetition at work in the serial format, and an invitation to watch the series anew. The "go back" motif is reinforced by non-verbal motifs: in season 2, the characters press the button of a computer every 108 minutes in order to "save the world," thus ensuring that another cycle/episode will see the day and prevent *LOST* from being terminated in the process; and in

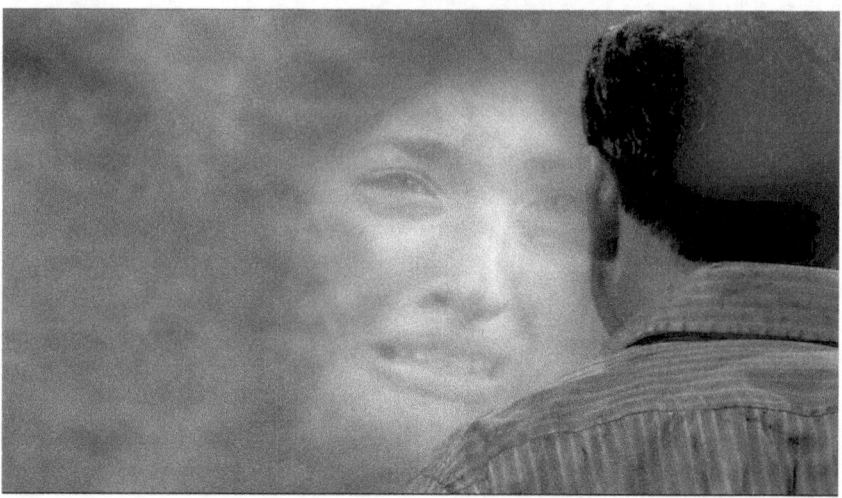

Figure 9.2 LOST, *episode S5E12: Ben Linus is made to watch his daughter's death (a scene from episode S4E9) again.*

episode S5E12, the Smoke Monster forces Ben Linus to watch the images of his adopted daughter Alex's life and death and assume responsibility for it [37:30–38:22] (Figure 9.2).

A metanarrative running joke concerns the status of the secondary characters. In episode S1E10, Hugo draws attention to the fact that many of the passengers are unknown both to the protagonists (and the audience) before proceeding to study the plane's manifest, and Sawyer regularly expresses his annoyance at the presence of the characters occupying the background ("Do you want to keep it down?" he demands in S1E19 [20:53]; "Who the hell are you?" he asks Paulo in S3E11 [6:35]). Episode S1E24 humorously concludes with a secondary character who had managed to graduate to a name (Dr. Leslie Artz) getting blown to pieces by old and highly unstable dynamite [9:28].

This feature of the series's formula is thematized in episode S3E14 and interwoven with the "going back" motif. The episode resorts to a flashback structure to relate the story of two secondary characters, Nikki and Paulo, who, like Sawyer, happen to be con artists. The second scene [0:44–3:49] shows Nikki leaving the set of season 4 of the crime series *Exposé* after her character just got killed by a character portrayed by Billy Dee Williams of *Star Wars* fame, thematizing her disposability as a secondary character. Two scenes later [4:50–8:23], she is shown murdering the executive producer/her lover, with her actual lover and accomplice Paulo, in order to steal some diamonds. The episode then relates Nikki and Paulo's endeavor to find the Russian doll in which they hid their bounty on the island. It proposes a mini-*LOST*: the characters are on their own treasure hunt, and it is for this reason that they have been primarily excluded from the core group's adventures. In effect, the episode has them incorporating important landmarks in the series's overarching narrative (Mr. Eko's brother's plane [18:55], the hatch [19:27]) within their own selfish plot. The episode suggests that these characters have been passed by because they steered away from the main narrative (Paulo was too busy using the hatch to hide the jewels) and, more fundamentally, were impervious to the island's healing/redeeming powers. In so doing, the episode justifies its ignorance of the secondary characters in spite of being a choir series: the other characters don't matter because, presumably, they didn't evolve and are thus deprived of dramatic and moral potential—a rationale that will be justified by the season 6 reveal that the main characters were all potential "candidates." The episode, however, also invites us to cast a different perspective on the series and potentially to watch it anew, much like Nikki when she noted something in the Dharma video the main characters had missed, a scene from episode S3E5 that is replayed in S3E14 (Figure 9.3) [29:58–30:45]. Aptly entitled "Exposé" after the series-within-the-series, the episode thus exposes and justifies the series's formula and limitations—more precisely, the impossibility to show it all in spite of the multiplication of perspectives. Even a lengthy serial like *LOST*, the episode demonstrates, can only provide us with a partial account, substantiating Thomas G. Pavel's claim that "incompleteness constitutes a major distinctive feature of fictional worlds."[31]

Figure 9.3   LOST, *episode S3E14: in The Pearl, Nikki asks Locke, Sayid and Desmond, "Hey guys, what are these other TVs for?"*

Together, these metanarrative comments and metamoments also foreground the ethical questions at the heart of the series—the question of accountability for one's actions. As the island's powers are progressively revealed, the series proposes a discourse on free will that resembles a less political version of *The Prisoner*. Whereas Jacob's prime subordinate Richard Alpert, in S5E12, tells Charles Whitmore, "Jacob wanted it done. The island chooses who the island chooses" [1:25], Jacob will later tell Hugo, in episode S5E17, that, in the end, it is his "choice" to get on the plane and go back to the island [16:55]. Although the characters never voice their realization of their fictional status in metaleptical scenes, *LOST* engages with the question at the heart of metafictional literature on an allegorical mode. Were the crimes committed by the characters scripted and are they consequently excused? Locke's noting that Sayid Jarrah hasn't "lost his touch" as a torturer thematizes the possibility for a person/character to change in S1E21 [19:40]. The characters of Nikki and Paulo did not evolve because the fiction did not allow them to do so. *LOST*'s exploration of its formula and the serial format thus interlocks the epistemological, the ontological and the ethical. In the words of Hatchuel, it "reflects on the mosaic of our lives and on the way in which each element fits in and makes sense, but also on the way in which our lives inscribe themselves within an even larger mosaic, in connection with others, the world, history, beyond our own consciousness."[32]

Almost forty years earlier, *The Prisoner* similarly articulated epistemological, ontological, ethical and political concerns within a serial format that was more strictly episodic. This highly self-conscious series resorts to a myriad of devices frequently associated with reflexivity, including jump-cuts, iris-outs, canted angles, looks to the camera, metalepses and mises en abyme, not to mention the revelation of the Village's whereabouts in the final episode's (S1E17) opening credits [3:35]. It is also a highly intertextual work that builds off its star/producer Patrick McGoohan's previous role as M9 special operative John Drake in the highly successful *Danger Man* (ITC, 1964–7) and includes references to George Orwell's *1984* (the emphasis on surveillance), Anthony Burgess's 1962 novel *A Clockwork Orange* (S1E12), James Bond[33] (S1E15) and *Dark Passage* (in S1E13 when the scientist who masters mind-switching technology turns out to be passing as a barber). For Ziauddin Sardar, the 1967–8 series exemplifies postmodernism before the concept "was hardly a twinkle in the eye of its champions" because it "excels both in dissolving meaning and simulating reality" through word-play and the manipulation of images, and ultimately suggests that "[m]eaning is totally relative."[34]

Centered on a British spy who is imprisoned in the Village on an unknown island after tendering his resignation for reasons unknown to us and the other characters, *The Prisoner* is a mixture of special agent thriller and science fiction,[35] and thus of two of Hutcheon's models of diegetic metafiction, the detective story and fantasy. More fundamentally, the series's formula proposes a game of strategy between the eponymous prisoner Number Six and his jailers led by Number Two: each episode relates a new move—whether Number Two's attempt to make the former spy crack (S1E3, S1E5, S1E12, S1E13, S1E 4, S1E15, S1E16), or Number Six's attempt to escape (S1E1, S1E2, S1E7, S1E8, S1E9, S1E17) or undermine his adversary (S1E4, S1E6, S1E10, S1E11)—followed by an opponent's counter-attack. Their verbal jousts rely on word-play, as Sardar notes, and regularly call on the semantic field of play: observing Number Six's attitude as he fills in a questionnaire at the beginning of the pilot episode, Number Two concludes, "I think we have a challenge" [S1E1, 21:32]; Number Six judges the Village's claim to democracy to be a "farce" [S1E3, 16:20], informs a UK government official that the Village's existence is "not a joking matter" [S1E6, 36:15] and describes his imprisonment in another man's body as a "trick" [S1E12, 37:00]. The underlying game structure is also foregrounded through the presence of actual games: chess at which Number Six excels (S1E9, "Checkmate," has the villagers using human pawns on a giant chess board), cards (in the Western-themed episode S1E14), sports (cricket and boxing in S1E15, and the hilarious Kosho in S1E10 and S1E11), as well as popular forms of entertainment such as carnivals (S1E8) and fairs (S1E15) (the village band even provides some of the diegetic music). In terms of politics, the game of strategies evokes a Cold War context dominated by the armament race, in which binaries of good versus evil are more complex than meets the eye (in episode S1E13, Professor Seltzman says to Number Six, "As both sides want my reversal process, it will be a close race." [39:40]). On a meta-level, however, *The Prisoner* demonstrates that a series is a game with its own set of rules, predominantly based on the conventions of genre and the serial form, which, like a game of chess, can be reset with each episode by facing a new opponent (usually, the New Number Two).

The narrative and generic setup of *The Prisoner* is fertile terrain for metaphenomena: the figure of the spy allows for the thematization of performance; the Village's surveillance system offers numerous instances of mise en abyme;[36] and some of the mind games played on Number Six are ideal material for metalepses. Much of the comments concerning Number Six's talents have an obvious metaperformative quality. As early as episode S1E2, Number Two marvels that Number Six "can make even the *act* of putting on his dressing gown appear as an act of *defiance*" [3:38], and in episode S1E5, "The Schizoid Man," Number Six, dressed as always in black, finds himself competing with a white-clad doppelgänger (the chess motif again),

Figure 9.4 The Prisoner, *episode S1E5: Number Six (in black) meets Number Six (in white), who muses, "When they come to film my life story, you've got the part."*

who jokes, "When they come to film my life story, you've got the part" [15:43] (Figure 9.4). The thematization of performance reaches its climax in the penultimate episode (S1E16) when Number Two recites the famous metatheatrical lines from *As You Like It*, "All the world's a stage, all the men and women merely players" [14:50]. The thematization of acting not only foregrounds the artifice; it asserts that the power of the series's formula lies in the difficulty to break and fathom the enigmatic Number Six because he is a professional performer who is potentially always performing.

The repeated attempts to discipline Number Six and confine him to the boundaries of the Village function like attempts to maintain the series's formula at all costs. Episode S1E12, "A Change of Mind," has the new Number Two's team attempting to neutralize Number Six's "aggressive frontal lobes of the brain," the prisoner having become "unmutual" (i.e., unfit for society). Number Two specifies beforehand that his aim is not to "lose" Number Six [11:29]. The procedure is then transmitted on television within the diegesis [21:10–25:29], an obvious mise en abyme of the actual series. Like Burgess's Alex, Number Six only changes on the surface and manages, in the end, to turn the tables on Number Two, who is declared "unmutual" at the very moment when Two was flaunting his success in front of the Villagers. The episode thus demonstrates that the series is dependent on the mutual unmutuality of Number Six and Number Two, confirming a metanarrative comment made by Number Two while on the red phone (presumably to Number One), early on in episode S1E3: "Yes, sir, I am doing my best. He's very difficult. I know it's important, sir. He's no ordinary person, sir, but if I had a free hand . . . I know, sir, yes. I know I'm not indispensable" [3:20]. Without the basic conflict and mystery, the series ceases to exist, as is made clear in the final episode when the four recurring characters (and actors) are driven back to London and finally let out of a cage [42:46–47:43], a metaphorical mise en abyme of the series itself.

The mises en abyme produced by the diegetic surveillance technology regularly position us alongside Number Six's jailers, observing his reactions on screen and trying to gauge his motives, something which Number Six's looks to the camera draw attention to. In S1E10, "Hammer into Anvil," in particular, Number Two, puzzled by Number Six's circling the word "Security," topped with a question mark, in the Village newspaper, initially utilizes the surveillance system to determine what his prisoner is "up to" [13:00–13:41]. Observing Six from the Control Room, Number Two and his team find themselves in the position of a spectator making hypotheses regarding Number Six's actions on screen when he puts a cuckoo clock outside a house ("What's he up to with that clock? It's a bomb." [33:15]) or wanders into the restricted area ("He could be making for the shores or the hills." [35:30]). The metanarrative quality of such comments is heightened by the mise en abyme, more overtly even than in *Rear Window* (see Chapter 5). Having rendered Number Two completely paranoid by the end of the episode, Number Six visits his adversary and muses, "It's odd, isn't it? All this power at your disposal and yet you're alone" [44:15]. What is initially a mark of the jailor's quasi-omniscience and -omnipotence becomes, on the contrary, proof of his inability to contain and comprehend his prisoner. The mises en abyme insist on the epistemological limitations of audiovisual apparatuses to gain knowledge of what makes a person. But in so doing, they also stress the power of audiovisual fiction to stimulate our imagination, as we, too, formulate hypotheses regarding Number Six's and Number Two's motives.

Similar epistemological limitations and imaginative potentials are foregrounded in the metaleptical sequences. The repeated violations of Number Six's mind provide not only excuses for a Western pastiche (S1E14) or a more traditional (S1E3) or madcap (S1E15) spy thriller; they demonstrate that putting Number Six in another world/genre, including one based on his own memories (S1E3), is not synonymous with unraveling his inner life. This is reinforced by the primacy given to performance: Number Six

Figure 9.5 The Prisoner, *episode S1E3: mise en abyme makes way for metalepsis, as Number Six impossibly addresses Number Two from the contrived dream the latter imposed on him and that is transmitted on a screen.*

regularly demonstrates that he is never just a character or performer in his captors' plot, but regularly becomes a figure of the director/screenwriter, who can rewrite a script, turn his gaze back on his oppressors, and transform a mise en abyme into a metalepsis (Figure 9.5). *The Prisoner* may very well be the most intensely meta English-language series ever created outside of animation and sitcom. If its concern with identity, surface and performance anticipates central themes of postmodernism and poststructuralism, it remains modernist at the core. Although it toys with ontological questions on the narrative level, like postmodernist fiction according to Brian McHale, *The Prisoner* is above all concerned with the epistemological:[37] its formula is grounded in the belief that Number Six is a political and ethical being. For underlying the games of strategy is very much an Orwellian commentary on the essential freedom and agency of human beings, what Chris Gregory describes as "the primal conflict between the Individual and society."[38] In McGoohan's "extended 'morality play',"[39] adhesion to the serial form to the bitter end (in the series finale, the Prisoner returns to London where the Village's hearse is already waiting outside his home) acts as an allegory for the ongoing "struggle of every one of us to maintain our individuality within society."[40] The serial format and the television medium are, in the end, redeemed through the critique of the medium's aesthetic limitations and its complicity in our subjection.

Famous for its "bricolage" aesthetics, based on genre mixing (crime fiction, horror, science fiction, slapstick comedy, soap opera) and numerous intertexts (*Laura* [Preminger, 1944], *Vertigo*, Sherlock Holmes,[41] James Dean, etc.), *Twin Peaks* was, like *The Prisoner* before it, early on described as "epitomiz[ing] the multiple dimensions of televisual postmodernism."[42] It is also an example of how meta a drama series can be (at least in season 1 and *The Return*). Jim Collins recognized this quality as early as 1992 when he foregrounded the series's consciousness vis-à-vis its medium:

> What distinguishes *Twin Peaks* from, say, *Dallas* or *Knots Landing* is not that it encourages this alternation in viewing positions but that it explicitly acknowledges this oscillation and the suspended nature of television viewing. In other words, *Twin Peaks* doesn't just acknowledge the multiple subject positions that television generates; it recognizes that one of the great pleasures of the televisual text is that very suspension and exploits it for its own ends.[43]

Twin Peaks would appear to be very much aware of its form and medium; it remains to be seen how this awareness transpires.

For a start, the series relies on the underlying structures (detective, fantasy, game) Hutcheon identifies in literary metafiction. As it progresses, it increasingly becomes a discovery not just of the town of Twin Peaks, but of the other worlds it is a gateway to. The crime narrative provides an overarching framework with which to apprehend this world, not just for the FBI and police (Cooper is as intrigued by the usual clues as by the symbolism of dreams or the Log Lady's messages), but for the audience for whom watching the series is an exercise in hermeneutics: in *Twin Peaks* the city and the series, potentially every sign begs to be examined, and some even provoke crises of signification. Underpinning the detective model, the game structure, as in *Sunset Blvd.*, momentarily comes to the surface in episode S1E3 when Special Agent Dale Cooper attempts to solve the case by tapping into Tibetan spirituality and the intuition he derived from a dream (i.e., throwing a rock each time Sheriff Truman reads a suspect's name aloud) [20:17–26:22]. Guy Astic's analysis of this scene as a "half-serious, half-comic commentary on how to engage with the story and the unfolding of *Twin Peaks*"[44] makes a case for its being meta.

In the early stages, the show's meta quality seems to expand with every episode. The teenage characters perform roles; like Nancy Drew, amateur detectives Audrey Horne (S1E6–S2E2) and Donna Hayward (S2E1–S2E6) go undercover to find out more about Laura's death and get in over their heads in the process. Introduced in episode S1E3, the soap opera *Invitation for*

Love seems to be playing on every TV at any hour of the day, thus connecting distinct time-spaces and foregrounding the seams of the series's narrative structure. The series-within-the-series regularly operates as a mise en abyme, fulfilling a metanarrative function by ironically redoubling certain situations in the diegesis's real world. In episode S1E5, for instance, the voices coming from the television set mention two sisters that, like Laura and Maddie, are difficult to tell apart [3:40], while in episode S2E13, the soap's voiceover ("Each day brings a new beginning") associates the serial format with Shelly and Bobby's new—and depressing—job: taking care of Leo [9:05].

More fundamentally, perhaps, many metamoments engage with the fact that the series's basic premise and formula are founded, in Astic's words, on Laura Palmer's "paradoxical existence" as "an absent figure who is nonetheless very much alive for those who watch *Twin Peaks*."[45] Her spectral quality both haunts her friends and neighbors, and profoundly sutures the serial narrative (in this respect, she fulfills the same function as her 1944 namesake[46]). This is staged through the portrait shot at Laura's funeral, in which the majority of the series's characters are united around her grave [S1E4, 25:26]. It is dramatized through the performances of those who seek to imitate her (Donna and Audrey) or look like her (in episode S2E6, Maddie admits that, "for a while, [she] got to be somebody different." [21:30]). It is more systematically conjured up through the various recording devices that endow her with ubiquity,[47] whether photographs, or sound and audiovisual recordings (James's home video in S1E2, Laura's tape in S1E8). Like the heroine from the classical noir film, Laura is present as an image, as her prom queen photograph reminds us during the end credits of each season 1 episode. Unlike her 1944 namesake whose painting overlooks her apartment, however, Laura Palmer's presence is disseminated across a range of reproducible media. In spite of the use of such technology, which Walter Benjamin argued deprived the work of art of its aura, Astic speaks of "l'aura de Laura" (Laura's aura), borrowing the phrase from a 1988 article by Serge Daney on the 1944 film.[48] The series thus offers a neat counter-argument to Benjamin's famous "loss of the aura" thesis by dramatizing how a haunting audiovisual image can breathe life into a work of fiction: the series is founded on an absent presence that is mirrored within the diegesis by the characters' interest in, and sometimes even obsession with, Laura Palmer.

The viewing of James's video in the pilot episode is, in this respect, a key metamoment [49:04–58:21]. The power of Laura's presence is expressed visually when Agent Dale Cooper pauses the image and a horizontal line cuts across her nose, materializing the fallibility of the machine and, metonymically, the precariousness of the video image and human life (Figures 9.6.1 and 9.6.2). If the look to the camera is authorized diegetically

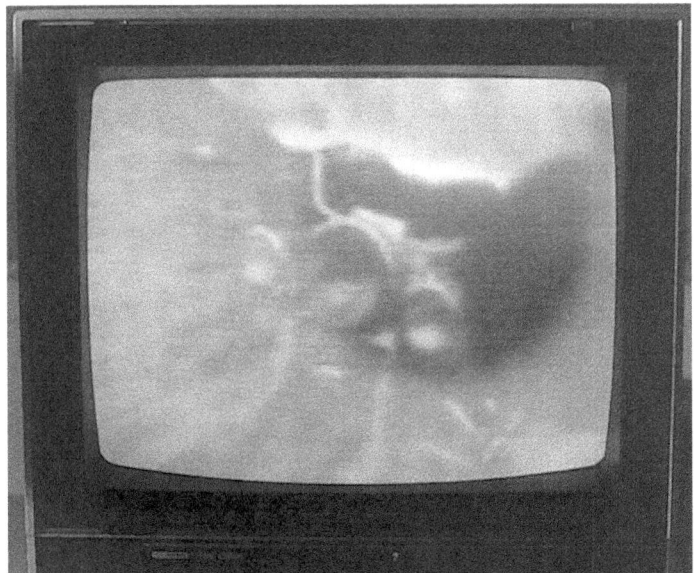

Figures 9.6.1 and 9.6.2 Twin Peaks, *episode S1E1: the video image of Laura Palmer reveals the presence of the cameraman's (James Hurley's) motorcycle, reflected in her eye.*

by the video-within-the-film (Laura is looking at James the cameraman), it nonetheless destabilizes ontological boundaries: in effect, her eye is not just an image; it is also a screen-within-the-screen, revealing the presence of James's motorcycle offscreen, and thus an eye that recorded the identity of the invisible cameraman. In other words, Laura, in spite of the diegetic apparatus (James's camera) and of the narrative setup (her death), is a subject looking back at us, one that can tap into the power of the apparatus that contains her; her structuring absence is not that of a corpse but of a subjectivity radiating outwards and giving birth to a fiction in which every sign (such as the motorcycle) potentially matters. This metamoment, therefore, comments both on the series's formula that is centered on Laura's structuring absence, but also celebrates—contra Benjamin but pro-Bazin (photography and cinema as fulfilling the memorial function of the visual arts that preceded them) and pro-Sontag and Barthes ("the photograph of the missing being, as Sontag says, will touch me like the delayed rays of a star."[49])—the power of the recorded image and/or voice as a trace of a subjectivity that lives on through it, an idea which, as we have seen, is taken up in *Mulholland Dr.*'s Silencio scene.

Some of the features that contribute to the series's meta quality (Laura's aura, *Invitation to Love*) tend to recede into the background in season 2. However, the second arc introduced in season 2 renders covert the series's game structure, which merges with the detective structure when Windom Earl, the series's Moriarty, invites Cooper to play chess with real people. Many comments in season 2 constitute playful winks at elements from the series's formula that have become cult among the series's fanbase. In episode S2E19, broadcast on 11 April 1991, for instance, Gordon Cole, played by David Lynch himself, comments on two of the show's notorious features—"This world of *Twin Peaks* seems to be *filled* with beautiful women. [. . .] Join us for pie."—possibly a wink to the 4 October 1990 issue of *Rolling Stone* magazine, which featured "The Women of *Twin Peaks*" on its cover. Cole, like a director, then proceeds to describe the very shot he appears in while kissing Shelly: "You are witnessing," he tells Bobby Briggs, "a front three-quarter view of two adults sharing a tender moment" [34:50–36:48].

The meta intensifies in the feature film *Twin Peaks: Fire Walk with Me* (Lynch, 1992) and *Twin Peaks: The Return*. The prequel's opening credits feature a track-in that ends with a television set being destroyed, suggesting that the film will simultaneously return to its television origins and distance itself from its source material.[50] The sequel opens with a prologue that replays the scene from the season 2 finale, in which Laura Palmer said to Agent Dale Cooper: "I'll see you again in twenty-five years. Meanwhile . . ." [0:55]. The dangling link word draws attention to the specificity of the serial format:

the interval. *Twin Peaks: The Return* proposes not so much to fill in the twenty-five-year gap as to gauge the result of the events that occurred therein—some things have changed, others hardly. But it also proposes to express the interval through an aesthetics of delay.[51] The opening double episode thematizes this project by making the act of waiting a central motif: Dale Cooper is still in the Red Room where we left him [0:32]; a young man, Sam Colby, is paid to wait for something to appear in a glass box [9:03–12:47]. The mysterious glass box stands as a metonym for the both the show and the medium (Figure 9.7): "I'm supposed to watch the box and see if anything appears inside," Sam explains to a young woman named Tracey [28:40]. The irony is that Cooper's "return," and thus, metafictionally, the beginning of the show, is going to kill the diegetic audience [33:00–34:33]. Like the rock-throwing scene in S1E3, the glass box scene provides us with a framework to approach *Twin Peaks: The Return*: it is going to be a long, quiet experience, in which the audience is going to end up waiting another fifteen episodes for Cooper aka Dougie to "wake up," as Phillip Gerard puts it in Part 6 [14:05]; meanwhile, we should remain attentive to the slightest event on screen. For Dougie's awakening and the ensuing climax, will, significantly, be triggered by an intertext on his own television—the scene from *Sunset Blvd.* in which Cecil B. DeMille orders, "Get Gordon Cole" [40:00]—one director pointing the way to another.

More so even than in season 2, and characteristic in this respect of many contemporary series, the metanarrative discourse on seriality and *Twin Peaks* itself transpires through dialogue. When, in Part 7, Benjamin Horne's assistant Beverly Paige asks him about Laura Palmer, he answers, "That, my

Figure 9.7 Twin Peaks: The Return *Part 1: Sam Colby watching the glass box, and waiting.*

dear, is a *long* story" [45:19]; and, in Part 9, Agent Albert Rosenfield sarcastically inquires about the improbable story of William Hastings's affair with the local librarian, "What happens in season two?" [29:40]. More frequently and consistently than in the 1990–1 series, Lynch the showrunner/director regularly seems to be speaking through the character of Gordon Cole; Part 4, for instance, concludes with Cole saying to Rosenfield, "I hate to admit this, but I don't understand this situation at all" [53:38], a nod to audiences who find Lynch's work meaningless as well as to Lynch's own reluctance to elucidate the meaning of his work in interviews. Dale Cooper's avatars are also endowed with a metanarrative function. In Part 5, Mr. C's supernatural powers allow him to predict events (in his jail cell, he says, "And now, food is coming." [4:57]), and he even seems to display metanarrative control over the narration when he addresses his jailers via the surveillance system [53:24–55:23].

But it is ultimately Dougie/Cooper who metonymically stands for the series itself. For Dougie, waking up means learning how to be Agent Dale Cooper again, the character from the original series. Like a series, Dougie's behavior is based on repetition with variation (for instance, when he tries out several slot machines toward the end of Part 3 [45:23–51:24]). Dazed and confused (like many *Twin Peaks* viewers!), he repeats snippets of the other characters' lines and regularly produces unsuspected meaning in the process, sometimes with metafictional implications. In Part 6, for instance, when his employer Bushnell Mullins expresses his confusion at Dougie's scribbles, the latter repeats, "Make ... sense of it" [42:12], an injunction that is also an invitation for us viewers to do the same. His wife Janey-E Jones and colleagues' comments metafictionally associate Dougie with seriality and the world of *Twin Peaks*—in Part 5, Janey-E worries that Dougie is "having one of [his] episodes" [14:22], and one of his colleagues jokes a moment later, "Off in dreamland again, huh, Dougie?" [16:25]. These comments also inform us that the Dougie Jones created by Bad Cooper similarly behaved on a serial mode and, thus, ironically, that the real Dale Cooper will keep on behaving like his double's creation until he is fully awake; even after he has regained his senses and destroyed his doppelgänger in Part 17, Cooper continues to fulfill this metanarrative function, Cooper/MacLachlan's farewell to Cole/Lynch, "See you at the curtain call" [37:10], taking on ironic meaning with hindsight, as the season ends on a cliffhanger.

Parts 1 and 2 and the prologue in particular are programmatic in that the "return" will include not just the return to the wonderful world of *Twin Peaks*, but also the recycling of actual footage. In so doing, the sequel develops the original series's (and especially season 1's) discourse on Laura's aura and the power of recorded sounds and images to memorialize the dead. In Part 2, Laura asserts her status as paradox when she says to Cooper: "I am dead ... yet I live" [18:48]. In *The Return*, however, the auratic potential of audiovisual material is extended to characters (BOB and Phillip Jeffries) whose actors (Frank Silva and David Bowie) passed away in the twenty-five-year interval. In Part 14, Jeffries/Bowie (to whom the episode is dedicated) is resurrected through images from *Fire Walk with Me* that are reproduced in black and white [13:16–14:11]. And in Part 8, the genesis of BOB is depicted as the birth of an icon—the menacing image of BOB's face contained in a drop of gelatinous material [24:35]—which the giant Fireman watches shortly thereafter on a screen in an instance of mise en abyme (Figure 9.8) [33:35–34.30]. Contrary to the 1990–1 series, however, these images are not systematically presented as recordings within the diegesis, and the reflexive device that is favored is not so much the mise en abyme as the metalepsis. Another such instance occurs in Part 10, when Gordon Cole opens his hotel room door and finds himself face to face with an image of Laura Palmer from *Fire Walk With Me* in place of Albert Rosenfield [40:47]. Like *Inland Empire*, *Twin Peaks: The Return* is haunted by images from previous audiovisual works, but these images also happen to originate from the same creators—on a meta-level, Cole seeing Laura Palmer is the showrunner/director haunted by his character. Accordingly, the resolution of the sequel's premise in Part 17 is followed by the possibility of its own undoing—that is, by the rebooting of *Fire Walk With Me*, whose images appear yet again in modified form in black and white [43:21–52:35]. Can *Twin Peaks* survive if Dale Cooper saves Laura Palmer? Part 18 seems to demonstrate that, in a

Figure 9.8 Twin Peaks: The Return *Part 8: the Fireman watches the birth of BOB, which we witnessed moments before.*

world inhabited by not one but many doubles, it is always possible to explore another tangent; fictional worlds are incomplete indeed.

The Showtime series's use of digital pursues the exploration of the ontology of audiovisual images initiated in the ABC series and present in much of Lynch's work.[52] In effect, it adopts an anti-illusionist stance by emphasizing how fake—that is, how digital—its CGI are. The plasticity of the digital image is emphasized through motifs evoking a liquid or gaseous ontology (the bubble, the drop), thus implying that the digital image is closer to water and oil painting than analog photography. The keyed, superimposed and monochromatic images draw attention to the fact that every diegetic element is an image subject to manipulation, even when it has a referent in reality such as an actor or actress. The iconic Dale Cooper's body is particularly subjected to a myriad of digital effects in a scene that revisits Lynch's 1976 *Eraserhead* as well as other pre-existing images (one image of Cooper falling through cosmic space resembles both Scottie's nightmares in Vertigo and the opening credits of AMC's *Mad Men*, as Julien Achemchame has noted[53]). During Cooper's release from, and Dougie Jones's return to, the Black Lodge in Part 3 [16:33–26:24], the transition from one world to another is described as the violent alteration of an image, one that leads the characters to spew their guts. Thus expressed as a material deformation, interdimensional travel makes way for metalepsis: it is as if the characters were living in a digital world (where the Red Room could just be superimposed over a desert landscape or a living room floor and wall), and as if digital post-production could affect the diegesis (the fake vomit). The 2017 series asks whether the digital image retains the auratic quality of the analog image (which Benjamin contested in the first place) in spite of its potential lack of indexicality. *L(')aura* endures because it is the mark of the absence of something or someone that wasn't there in the first place—it is the absence of an absence, not of a person or a thing. If this is true of an image without a referent, then it is potentially true of any image. The reflection on the digital image ends up strengthening the case for the aura of the recorded image by going one step further than the original series and *Mulholland Dr.* The vitality of the aura stems not from the vitality of the actual referent but from that of the figure or fiction.

Conclusion

These case studies have confirmed our preliminary conclusions: that meta specific to seriality is metanarrative; that the borders of intervals are privileged sites for metamoments; that the latter rely heavily on dialogue[54] and/or the serialization of motifs that are apt metaphors of seriality; and that the exploration of a series's formula and/or the serial format by no means preclude engagement with other concerns, as the studies of *The Prisoner*, *Twin Peaks* and the series analyzed in the rest of the book clearly demonstrate. *Twin Peaks* and *LOST* constitute more typical examples of how meta can vary in intensity within the same series and/or be gradually built up through serialization. Although this is equally true of *The Prisoner* and *Twin Peaks: The Return*, these series remain exceptional given the high degree of concentration of meta-phenomena throughout, with virtually every scene engaging with seriality, the hypotexts and/or architexts, the boundary between creation and reception, the television medium and the materiality of the image. These case studies have also made apparent that the concern for the serial form, like that for genre, has economic, political and ethical implications that devolve from the very precariousness of any series—as a program striving to build up loyalty in order to survive within an ecosystem, as a formula that restricts its cast of characters' movements. These conclusions can easily be transposed to other modes of seriality, including film or transmedia franchises. In the case of the latest James Bond, *No Time to Die* (Joji Fukunaga, 2021), the negotiation of this precariousness is also an instance of "industrial reflexivity," the film's promotion emphasizing its thematization of its star's (Daniel Craig's) departure and the franchise's future (including the possibility of a female Bond).[55]

CHAPTER 10

History and Historiography

HISTORIOGRAPHIC METAFICTION (*CULLODEN*)

History provides much of the material for many films and series, whether in the form of the historical film, the biopic, the war movie, the empire film or the Western. In a chapter entitled "Based on a True Story," Thomas Leitch goes so far as to identify such works as adaptations, suggesting that historical events are akin to source texts that can be tailored to fit the needs of a work of fiction.[1] Historical fiction is thus founded on a dialogical relationship between fiction and reality; it is also based on a dialogical relationship between past and present. Robert A. Rosenstone says historical films are meant to "make the past meaningful for us in the present,"[2] and Pierre Sorlin reminds us that "we have a chance of finding a view of the present embedded in a picture of the past."[3] These two foundational relations (fiction–history, past–present) come together in the historiographic question: How is the past understood, fashioned and fictionalized at a specific moment in time? To pursue the comparison with adaptation, history is a source that is ceaselessly being rewritten because of new discoveries and perspectives. History would thus seem to be a prime concern for meta, since it is understood as simultaneously real (the event really happened) and constructed (it has been understood in a certain way, is sometimes the subject of competing narratives, and can be revised). Metamoments that address the work's exploitation and portrayal of history interrogate the relationship between fiction and reality more obviously, perhaps, than those that explore their reliance on genre and pre-existing fictions.

In literary scholarship, metafiction's concern with history was not detected at the outset, perhaps because it did not seem to tie in with metafiction's apparent narcissism. In 1984, Waugh, citing novels such as Fowles's 1969 *French Lieutenant's Woman*, Doctorow's 1971 *The Book of Daniel*, Malcolm Bradbury's 1975 *The History Man* and Robert Coover's 1977 *The Public Burning*, observed that history could be presented as "an alternative world" and revealed to be "a provisional construct" or "personal reconstruction."[4] What wasn't evident in 1980 when Hutcheon published *Narcissistic Narrative* had become so eight years later when she published *A Poetics of Postmodernism*, which includes a chapter on "historiographic metafiction." In it, she discusses novels like *The Public Burning*, Doctorow's 1975 *Ragtime*, Salman Rushdie's 1981 *Midnight's Children* and 1983 *Shame*, Graham Swift's 1983 *Waterland* and Fowles's 1985 *A Maggot*. So by 1988, historiographic metafiction had become an identifiable trend in postmodernist fiction, and a novel like *The French Lieutenant's Woman*, which Hutcheon had studied in 1980 without emphasizing its historiographic dimension, was no longer an exception.

Historiographic metafiction, Hutcheon explains, interrogates "the epistemological and ontological relations between history and fiction": "[t]he epistemological question of how we know the past joins the ontological question of the traces of that past."[5] It does so by underlining what fiction and history have in common—their ordering of events in narrative form, the distinction they make between facts and events,[6] their constructedness as "cultural sign systems" and "ideological constructions,"[7] the fact that "their definitions and interrelations are historically determined and vary with time"[8]—and what distinguishes them: "[t]he problematizing of the nature of historical knowledge, in novels like this, points both to the need to separate and to the danger of separating fiction and history as narrative genres."[9] Comparing historiographic metafiction to definitions of the historical novel, Hutcheon identifies both the issues historiographic metafiction broaches—"subjectivity, intertextuality, reference, ideology"[10]—and the strategies it deploys: it "espouses a postmodern ideology of plurality and recognition of difference"; it "plays upon the truth and lies of the historical record"; it "incorporates but rarely assimilates such data"; it emphasizes "its enunciative situation" and "reinstalls a kind of (very problematic) communal project";[11] it privileges "two modes of narration, both of which problematize the entire notion of subjectivity: multiple points of view [. . .] or an overly controlling narrator";[12] it resorts to intertextuality in order to "confront the past of literature – and of historiography,"[13] and uses "the paratextual conventions of historiography (especially footnotes) to both inscribe and undermine the authority and objectivity of historical sources and explanation."[14] Hutcheon concludes that "[h]istoriographic metafiction acknowledges the paradox of the *reality* of the past but its *textualized accessibility* to us today";[15] "the lesson here is that the past once existed, but that our historical knowledge of it is semiotically transmitted."[16] Historiographic metafiction does more than address fiction's use of history as raw material; it draws attention to the material's problematic link to reality, that is, to its textuality and narrative qualities, and to the rift between the real events and its presentation of such events. Historiographic metafiction thus explores the fictionalization of material that had, to varying degrees, already been subjected to a fictionalizing process.

We have already seen that much of the meta is lost and/or displaced in the film adaptations of famous literary metafictions of the 1970s (certainly, neither *The French Lieutenant's Woman* [1981] nor *Ragtime* [1981] qualify as historiographic metafiction, at least not to the same extent as their source texts). But a British artist whose work in television and film largely qualifies as historiographic metafiction did emerge in the 1960s: Peter Watkins. His work has been described as both historiographic[17] and metaphorical,[18] and parallels have been drawn between his work and the main tenets of New Historicism, notably because of their reflexivity and polyphony.[19] Like many of his contemporaries, Watkins wears the Brechtian influence on his sleeves,[20] and the abundance of reflexive devices in his work has been duly noted: looks and addresses to the camera[21]; mises en abyme[22] (*La Commune*, 2000); anachronisms (*Culloden*, 1964; *La Commune*); fake-looking backdrops that are introduced as "constructions"[23] and, more generally, the laying bare of the filmmaking process[24] (*La Commune*); actors who speak alternately as their characters or as themselves (*The Freethinker*, 1994; *La Commune*[25]); voiceovers that are at once objective and subjective[26] (*Culloden*; *La Commune*); "impossible" setups comprised of "unacceptable elements"[27] (*Culloden*, *La Commune*); narrative fragmentation[28] (*Edvard Munch*, 1974; *The Freethinker*). Although indebted to documentary (location shooting, non-professional actors, etc.), Watkins's work is, like Hutcheon's covert diegetic metafiction, grounded in fantasy and game-show[29] (*The War Game*, 1966; *Punishment Park*, 1971) structures. Watkins's early interest in the relationship between history and the media, eventually put forth in the "History and Media" seminar he headed in 1977,[30] increasingly evolved into a "questioning of the problematic power of representation itself,"[31] including that of his own work. Commenting on *La Commune*, Antoine Coppola suggests that "the disturbing feeling caused by a polyphony in which nobody speaks from the same place, nor even presents themselves on the same ontological level, may be the film's resigned view of its own ideal setup."[32]

Broadcast on the BBC in December 1964, five years before the publication of *The French Lieutenant's Woman*, *Culloden* is an exemplar of "historiographic metafiction" in an audiovisual medium. It relates the story of the 1746 battle between the Highland army, enlisted in the cause of the Jacobite pretender Charles Edward Stuart, and the English army, headed by General George Wade and Prince William Cumberland, protecting the reign of Cumberland's father, George II. Apt material for a historical film indeed, it is based on historian John Prebble's book published three years before. But it is the radical form Watkins chooses that makes it historiographic metafiction: that of a news report, replete with handheld footage, narrative voiceover, interviews and even an on-location consultant, Whig historian Andrew Henderson, author of *The Life of William Augustus, Duke of Cumberland*, published in 1766. The film proposes an allohistory of a different kind than will be observed in *The Man in the High Castle* (the novel and the series) or *Inglourious Basterds*: the main facts pertaining to the historical event are not altered; it is the mode of narration itself that is anachronistic. As a news report that cannot be, *Culloden* is a playful fabrication, an implausible hoax.

The film combines the two modes of narration common to historiographic metafiction in literature according to Hutcheon. The main voiceover represents an obvious "controlling narrator," identifying the people we see, shedding light on their backgrounds and motives, providing facts and figures, and detailing the mechanics of war machinery. Its authority, however, is tempered by other voices—there are other interviewers, performed by Tony Cosgrove and Watkins himself, and the interviewees are diverse—and, of course, by the images themselves. Indeed, close-ups single out both historical figures and common soldiers, comprised of enlisted men, as well as farmers, fishermen and convicts. Furthermore, if the noblemen are shown and mentioned on a regular basis, Cumberland is never interviewed and Stuart is interviewed on three occasions before the battle but never during or after—grimacing, he even tries to cover the camera in the humiliation of defeat [59:42]. In the second half of the film, Cumberland's and Stuart's voices are systematically drowned out by the voiceover's interventions [39:26–40:03, 59:23–59:44, 1:04:56–1:05:57, 1:07:36–1:08:44]; instead, the mike is directed at their officers (Lord George Murray, John William O'Sullivan, Captain Caroline Frederick Scott, Major Lain Lockhart, Lord George Sackville), and more so even to the common soldiers and victims of the battle and its aftermath. The film's frame structure drives home the point, presenting the historical figures (Sir Thomas Sheridan, Sir John MacDonald, then John O'Sullivan and Prince Charles) in the prologue [0:00–1:53], and concluding on a series of shots [1:08:45–1:10:53] that dwell on the faces of "the people who [Stuart] has led to so much suffering," and whom the English will drive into the grave or a life in exile after the historical figures have quit the stage. One shot epitomizes this approach: the final medium shot of Charles Stuart, which zooms in to an extreme close-up of the Highlander standing behind him. In so doing, *Culloden* decenters the perspective on history in revisionist fashion, reminding us that the events we read in the pages of history books affected the lives of ordinary people at least as much, if not more so, than those of the men who instigated them and whose social status enabled them to escape the consequences of their actions.

Fifteen minutes into the film, *Culloden*'s status as diegetic metafiction is made explicit by the introduction of a character whom the voiceover

Figure 10.1 Culloden: *Andrew Henderson, "Whig historian, biographer of Cumberland, eyewitness of the battle of Culloden," addresses the camera like a news reporter without recognizing his own biased position.*

presents as "Andrew Henderson, Whig historian, biographer of Cumberland, eyewitness of the battle of Culloden" [15:28–16:02]. In a matter-of-fact tone, Henderson cuts himself out as a rigorous person, stating the time and his position on "a rough sketch map" of his making (Figure 10.1). Protected by a wall and aided by a telescope, he observes and comments on the events from a safe distance—a distance that is also an obstruction since, ironically, he cannot see as much of the battle as we can.[33] His descriptions reinforce the film's underlying game structure not only by anachronistically turning the eighteenth-century historian into a twentieth-century news reporter, but because some of his lines could just as well have been spoken by a sports presenter ("There are large gaps in the center. The entire line is completely askew" [19:40–19:45]). The fourth time we see Henderson, one of Cumberland's battalions is taking position directly behind the wall that is sheltering him and his assistant [29:07–29:26]. The maneuver confirms that the apparently neutral historian was all along siding with Cumberland. In the first scene already, the close-up of his map had revealed his position, marked by a cross, to be not only "at approximately right angles to the rebel lines," as he phrases it, but very close to those of the Duke of Cumberland whom he had distinguished himself from ("We are here. And the Duke of Cumberland's army is here."). The series of scenes thus draws attention to the historian's omission concerning his political allegiances, which the voiceover had already alerted us to when presenting him as the Duke's biographer. They thematize the film's more general, and perhaps more overt, reflection on the writing of history. The traces of events we base our knowledge of history on are, Michèle Lagny argues, shown to be partial.[34] If the film is largely based on "the history book of the same name by John Prebble, who was credited as historical adviser,"[35] it foregrounds its awareness that history is written by men who have allegiances and whose knowledge of events is limited, and that history is never neutral and is most often written from the perspective of the victors. The writing of history is always political.

Culloden does not propose to be neutral, and the "biased" historian actually "parallel[s]" the filmmaker's "view," as Dave Rolinson suggests. The purpose of this impossible documentary is not merely playful, but profoundly moral and political. It is stated quite explicitly in the sentences that follow the title [2:05–2:28]. The "account" that is mentioned four times in four sentences, each separated by line returns, must not be understood solely as the narrative of a famous battle; it is also to be a moral accounting. In effect, the word's polysemy is evoked by its combined repetition and association with the adjectives "mishandled," "brutal," "tragic" and "responsible" (a synonym of "accountable") and only one verb, tellingly not an action verb in spite of the forthcoming event but an emotion verb ("suffered"), which is associated with the victims. The titles are thus programmatic not only regarding the film's narrative and moral perspective on the event; they also give us an idea of the rhetorical strategies that will be deployed: repetition, juxtaposition and blanks (the line returns).

Indeed, the moral bent transpires largely in the main voiceover's presentation of the events, and in the juxtapositions of words and images. Instances where the narrator lists numbers constitute examples of what Hutcheon describes as the "incorporation" of data as opposed to their "assimilation." For instance, spoken over a close-up of a weary Highlander eyeing the approach of the English army, the voiceover's enumeration of deadpan facts ("9,000 men. 15 battalions of infantry. 12 squadrons of cavalry. 8 companies of militia. 220,000 rounds of musket ammunition. Ten 3-pounder battalion canons, 800 3-pound cannon balls, 500 bags of cannon grapeshot.") emphasizes the technological gap between the two armies and thus heralds the damage that will be inflicted on the Highlanders' bodies [10:23–10:44]. During the battle and its aftermath, the omnipresent voiceover will occasionally leave us to face the brutality of the sounds and images on our own, for instance when the Highland army's lack of know-how and weaponry leads them to "cease fire" [25:45–27:12] or following the voiceover's declaring, "Casualties: 850" [30:36–33:28]. The silences—and, I would argue, the professional deadpan tone—open spaces wherein our own sensibility and judgment are engulfed, as in Iser's theory of blanks (see Chapter 5). The third rhetorical device that makes manifest the voiceover's moral function involves the repetition of phrases starting with the deictic "this," which are occasionally repeated often enough to produce an anaphora. From the beginning, the pronoun is used to present people ("To this man, who is rent, today's battle is a matter of honor." [4:20]), the functioning of a social system ("This is the system of the Highland clan: human rent." [4:03]) or a machine ("This is round shot. This is what it does." [24:14]), and later the wounded ("This is Lachlan MacDonald of Lochaber. Right leg severed below the knee joint, he has been lying on the moor unattended for fifteen hours. For most of the time, it has been raining." [50:28]) and the horrific genocide following the battle ("This is one of them [the fugitive rebel families]. [. . .] This is what happens." [1:02:29–1:03:33]). In so doing, "this" establishes a sense of closeness between the voice we are listening to and the images we are seeing, one that the use of "that" in the more disturbing instances could have somewhat dispelled. In so doing, the voiceover of *Culloden* demands that we confront the images, including the most horrible. This rhetorical device is, accordingly, sometimes combined with another—silence—in which the images are meant to speak for themselves: the traumatized faces; the freeze frame of a hollering man in pain; the upheld hands which the camera struggles to focus on (Figure 10.2).

Polyphony, enunciative self-consciousness, the *mise en scène* of history-making and the foregrounding of its limitations—*Culloden* has all the characteristics of historiographic metafiction noted by Hutcheon (certainly more so than Kinji Fukasaku's *Battles Without Honor and Humanity* films [1973–4], which merely "equate historiographic fiction and historiographic and journalistic discourses by evincing that, in the end, they all rely on the textual and aesthetic resources"[36]). History, *Culloden* tells us, is not only partial and incomplete, but the documentary setup Watkins resorts to in much of his work mirrors the fundamental problems involved in the writing of history; the crew is limited by the people and information it has access to (the traces of history), and their narrative is also affected by their own decisions (the subjectivity of any narrative). The TV movie thus "refuses to fashion a comprehensive history of the battle"[37] and invites audiences to involve themselves critically and emotionally in its construction. Underlying Watkins's playful narrative setups are thus profound political and ethical considerations: our connection to history and memory is, in effect, a connection to humanity, and attention to the facts should not supersede acknowledgement of human suffering. The work of Peter Watkins remains exceptional—as exceptional as the novels discussed by Hutcheon. The rest of this chapter will explore audiovisual fictions

Figure 10.2 Culloden: *the chatty informative voiceover is silenced, leaving us alone with the images of the massacre.*

that manipulate their historical material in a more obvious way (as in the case of the allohistory, for instance) before analyzing examples of more typical historical films that nonetheless interrogate their use of their historical material.

ARE ALLOHISTORIES ALWAYS META? (*INGLOURIOUS BASTERDS*, *THE MAN IN THE HIGH CASTLE*)

An allohistory (short for alternate history) is a fiction that reinvents the course of history. Famous instances include Philip K. Dick's *The Man in the High Castle* and the Amazon Prime series based on it, David Gibbons and Alan Moore's 1986–7 graphic novel *Watchmen* as well as the 2009 film and the 2019 HBO series based on it, Philip Roth's 2004 novel *The Plot Against America* and the 2020 HBO mini-series, and Tarantino's *Inglourious Basterds* and *Once Upon a Time . . . in Hollywood*; other notable examples are the British movie *It Happened Here* (Kevin Brownlow and Andrew Mollo, 1964), and Robert Harris's 1992 novel *Fatherland* and its television adaptation (HBO, Christopher Menaul, 1994). Such works have much in common with dystopian fiction, as is suggested by the 1964 British film's nod to Sinclair Lewis's 1935 novel *It Can't Happen Here*, the story of the rise of fascism in the

1930s US. The dystopian quality is immanent to the historical material these works are based on. The majority imagine what would have happened if Nazi Germany had conquered Great Britain (*It Happened Here*), Europe (*Fatherland*) or split up the world with the Japanese empire (*The Man in the High Castle*), or if the USSR had landed on the moon first (*For All Mankind*, Apple TV+, 2019–).[38] *The Plot Against America* and *Watchmen* portray totalitarian regimes with a US origin (fascist sympathizers in the 1930s, a Nixon dictatorship in the 1980s), *C.S.A: The Confederate States of America* (Willmott, 2004) a nation in which the Confederacy won the Civil War. Tarantino's allohistories thus go against the grain by tapping into the subgenre's utopian potential by envisioning a brighter outcome (World War II ends sooner and Sharon Tate survives the Manson family attack).

Based on a "what if" premise, the allohistory also has much in common with the parallel dimension story and intradiegetic metalepsis. At the end of Dick's *Man in the High Castle*, Trade Minister Nobusuke Tagomi glimpses the "real" San Francisco, with its Embarcadero Freeway and white people who refuse to give up their seats in a lunch counter to a Japanese man, and the oracle informs Juliana and author Hawthorne Abendsen that the book he wrote (*The Grasshopper Lies Heavy*) is "true," and thus that Germany and Japan lost the war.[39] The Amazon Prime series expands the parallel-dimension premise, with characters visiting Kennedy's US (Tagomi in season 2, Juliana Crain and John Smith in season 4), and the Reich plotting to conquer the other worlds (in seasons 3–4). Dick's seminal novel has also been analyzed as metafiction.[40] What it proves is that, even without a final reveal of the sort, an allohistory is based on a fantasy or science fiction structure (the back cover of Dick's novel describes it as "a seminal work in science fiction," and imdb.com categorizes *The Man in the High Castle*, *It Happened Here* and *Fatherland* under Science Fiction, not History). Yet while Hutcheon identified fantasy as one of the predominant models of covert diegetic metafiction, there is nothing covert about an allohistory; the fantasy may be structural, but no effort is made to conceal it—on the contrary, its visibility ensures its narrative and economic viability (it is clearly marketed as such). What the overtness of such works dramatizes is the possibility of entirely reimagining history. This is where the allohistory rejoins historiographic metafiction: it effectively performs—and thus proves—the thesis that history is not a stable objective set of facts; that it is a question of perspective; that it is textual, raw material that can be fashioned and refashioned. Does it necessarily follow that an allohistory is per se meta? Indeed, the allohistory, as a creative approach, raises a similar question as parody. For if all allohistories reimagine history, the question remains as to whether or not a given work delves into the implications of its own and/or its medium's relationship to history.

This is the case of *Inglourious Basterds*, which was analyzed as both allohistory and metacinema as early as 2012 in the collected volume edited by Robert von Dassanowsky, and later in my own research on the films of Tarantino (2018, 2019). With two chapters centered on a Parisian movie theater named Le Gamaar and many characters working in the film industry (producer Joseph Goebbels, confirmed star Bridget von Hammersmark and rising star Frederick Zoller, film critic Archie Hicox, movie theater proprietor Shosanna Dreyfuss, and projectionist Marcel), cinema is veritably at the heart of the narrative: Goebbels's propaganda film *Stolz der Nation* (*Nation's Pride*) is meant to assert Nazi power and boost morale, and is thus central to the war effort; Archie Hicox is recruited for Operation Kino because of his civilian occupation; and Shosanna and Marcel use celluloid to burn the Nazi High Command. The film thus dramatizes the importance of propaganda films during World War II, a point that is made explicit by Hicox when tested on his knowledge of German cinema in a meeting with General Ed Fenech and Winston Churchill:

> Goebbels considers the films he's making to be the beginning of a new era in German cinema. An alternative to what he considers the Jewish German intellectual cinema of the twenties. And the Jewish controlled dogma of Hollywood. [. . .] Since Goebbels has taken over, film attendance has steadily risen in Germany over the last eight years. But Louis B. Mayer wouldn't be Goebbels's proper opposite number. I believe Goebbels sees himself closer to David O. Selznick. [1:06:27–1:07:13]

The context Hicox provides establishes a framework that is at once historical, narrative and aesthetic; it also implies that an understanding of film history is central to the understanding of both *Inglourious Basterds* and history. Finally, it invites us to act as critics and (re)view *Inglourious Basterds* and the films screened or mentioned within the diegesis in the light of his statement.

Knowledge of the history of the film screened at Le Gamaar at the beginning of Chapter 3—*The White Hell of Piz Palu* (1929), directed by Arnold Frank and G.W. Pabst, and produced by two Jews, Paul Kohner and Harry R. Sokal [38:20–40:18]—confirms Hicox's lesson, as Jewish actor Kurt Gerron was edited out of the film's 1935 rerelease.[41] The screening of *Stolz der Nation* in Chapter 5 reveals that, if the film succeeds as a Nazi crowd-pleaser, it fails, however, to fulfill Goebbels's aesthetic project, largely indebted as it is to German Expressionism (Dutch angles), Soviet cinema (the Eisensteinian montage) and Hollywood cinema (*Sergeant York* [Hawks, 1941] and, though anachronistic, *To Hell and Back* [Hibbs, 1955], starring US soldier and actor Audie Murphy whom Zoller is based on) [2:10:38–2:23:17].[42] The failure of Goebbels's project is confirmed when Marcel and Shosanna's home movie replaces *Stolz der Nation* on the screen: the graphic match Marcel and Shosanna created, which cuts from a frontal close-up of Zoller addressing their foes to one of Shosanna doing the same, demonstrates that a Jewish face can be spliced into Goebbels's propaganda film as effortlessly as it was edited out of *The White Hell of Piz Palu* (and as effortlessly as Shosanna took apart the title on the billboard), at least in part because their influences are the same (Expressionism again, and possibly Carl Theodor Dreyer's 1928 *The Passion of Joan of Arc*[43]) [2:23:18–2:25:46]. The film's fate—that Shosanna should become a disembodied voice as her spectre dances among the smoke and flames—similarly taps into our cinematic memories, from the cinema of attractions (George Méliès's 1901 *The Man with the Rubber Head*) to German Expressionism (Fritz Lang's 1933 *The Testament of Dr. Mabuse*) to classical Hollywood (the 1939 *The Wizard of Oz*, also directed by a Jew, Victor Fleming). Marcel and Shosanna's project not only literalizes the historical fact that films can be used as weapons (during World War II but, more generally, throughout the twentieth and twenty-first centuries); it proves that film's impurity is a matter of circulation (of artists, films, motifs) in (film) history and evokes one of the most famous examples—the influence of German Expressionism on classical Hollywood cinema.

Inglourious Basterds boldly asserts that film history is history; it also abides by the credo that films reflect (on) history. This is made abundantly clear during the Who's Who card game in Chapter 4, involving Major Hellstrom, two of the Basterds and two film people, von Hammersmark and Hicox [1:24:57–1:27:02].[44] Moments before identifying the name on his forehead as King Kong, Hellstrom asks in German: "Am I the history of the Negro in America?" By so jesting, the SS officer proposes a subtextual analysis of the 1933 Hollywood film that has become common currency today,[45] and shows himself to be the equal of Archie Hicox, author of a "subtextual criticism study of the work of German director G.W. Pabst" [1:05:40], moments before outing the Englishman as a failed spy/actor. The SS officer also fulfills—less obviously perhaps—the same function as Hicox in the opening scene of Chapter 4: he provides us with a framework through which to analyze *Inglourious Basterds*. First, by reminding us that films can have subtexts and function as allegories; that there is a history of racism in the US, and thus that Nazi Germany and the US have something in common (*King Kong* was released the year Hitler took full control of Germany, and *Stolz der Nation* brings to mind D.W. Griffith's 1915 *Birth of a Nation*[46]); and finally, that intertextuality can be simultaneously playful and meaningful.

In effect, it turns out that many of the film's intertexts draw attention to the colonialism, imperialism and racism that characterizes the Allied forces' recent histories. When introducing himself to his men at the beginning of

Chapter 2 [22:45], Aldo Raine states that he has Apache blood and invites them to scalp their foes, thus drawing a parallel between the nineteenth-century American Indian wars and World War II. This had already been suggested by the visual allusion to *The Searchers* in Chapter 1[47] [20:28], with Landa the Jew Hunter in the role of the violent racist Ethan Edwards who comes close to murdering his own niece for having been kidnapped and soiled by the Comanche. The musical intertexts map out a global history of Western imperialism: the theme from *The Alamo* (Wayne, 1960) evokes the myth of the "liberation" of Texas from Mexico; that from *Eastern Condors* (Kam-Bo Hung, 1987) the US presence in Vietnam; the music from *Battle of Algiers* (Pontecorvo, 1966) and *The Mercenaries* (Cardiff, 1968) Europe's colonization of Africa and its violent aftermath.[48] *Inglourious Basterds* is intensely meta, and it is not just so as an allohistory but because it poses the relationship between film history and history—and between fiction and reality—as a fundamental means of comprehension of world history and unashamedly takes this relationship as its bedrock. The allohistorical fantasy offers a narrative premise that participates in the film's historiographic project of examining history through the lens of film history, but is also associated with other devices, notably intertexts, that would signify without it. In a sense, the explosive climax, which reprises that of *Gremlins* (Dante, 1984), serves to drive in the point in case we missed out on all the subtextual fun.

A work which alternates between the dramatic and metafictional potential of allohistory—and thus between a conspiracy narrative à la *Fatherland* (in which Hitler has successfully concealed the Holocaust and is attempting to initiate an era of détente with US President John F. Kennedy) and the historiographic ambition of *Inglourious Basterds*—is Amazon Prime's *Man in the High Castle*. The adaptation's change of medium, discussed in Chapter 9, also introduces a change in perspective, the black-and-white films reinforcing the historical distance between a diegesis that remains firmly entrenched in 1962 (the novel's publication date) and our own twenty-first-century position as streaming platform consumers. The series's meta potential is announced at the beginning of each episode, whose opening credits start on the image and sound of a projector revving, as if the fiction were coming to life before our very eyes. It is firmly established in the pilot episode, which likewise opens with a shot of a movie projector set in a movie palace where one of the main characters, Joe Blake, is then shown watching US-Nazi propaganda on screen before the screening of a Rock Hudson movie entitled *The Punch Party* [1:09–2:30]. Nine scenes later, the heroine, Juliana Crain, is shown viewing a mysterious film and is soon joined by her boyfriend Frank Frink [18:35–22:24]. A discussion ensues.

> *Juliana*: It's newsreel film. It shows us winning the war.
> *Frank*: But we didn't win the war.
> *Juliana*: That's what they told us.
> *Frank*: Jesus, I know what this is. [. . .] The Man in the High Castle. [. . .] Some guy Ed told me about. He makes these anti-fascist movies.
> *Juliana*: "Makes them?" GIs in Times Square?
> *Frank*: No, I know, they look real.
> *Juliana*: They look real 'cause they are real.
> *Frank*: But they can't be real, can they?

As in Dick's novel, *The Grasshopper Lies Heavy* is potentially metaleptic and calls into question the very fabric of reality—if the reel is "real," then reality cannot be. But by changing the medium, the series, like *Inglourious Basterds*, also dramatizes the essential role of film during World War II to construct a certain version of history, promote an ideology and/or boost morale (season 3 centers on the battle between pro- and anti-Nazi propaganda, headed by none other than Goebbels's niece, Nicole Dörmer, and Juliana); films can become weapons and have military, economic, ideological and moral value. Unlike *Fatherland*, in which photos constitute irrefutable proof of the Holocaust, the series also questions the medium's ontology and counts on its audience's knowledge that images can be tampered with, and that it has become increasingly easy to do so in the digital age; in this respect, it is closer to Baudrillard than to Sontag and Barthes. Fernando Gabriel Pagnoni Berns and Emiliano Aguilar even suggest that the series brings together several of Walter Benjamin's key arguments concerning the power of images—that "fascism turned political life into spectacle as a way to narcotize people"—and malleability—that "the isolated image" can be "blasted out of the continuum of history" and that "the past is constructed by the present."[49]

Yet once the narrative/aesthetic/political/philosophical premise has been set up, the series tends to keep its meta potential in check. The reels fulfill, first and foremost, a narrative function: combined with the death of her sister Trudy, they trigger Juliana's involvement in the Resistance and are the objects of her quest; and they are cloaked in a mystery whose resolution must be delayed for the series to last (in S3E7, the characters watching the film are still asking the same questions). Thus, the question of the fabrication of history and historicity is mostly tangential to the imperatives of both genre and seriality. In season 1, the issue is occasionally broached in the scenes featuring an Americana art dealer named Robert Childan, which rather faithfully adapt the source material. For instance, in episode S1E8 [32:43–34:41], when Robert attempts to demonstrate the "historicity" of Sitting Bull's necklace by comparing the fake one designed by Frank to the real one on the photograph of the Hunkpapa Lakota leader, his customer, a Japanese lawyer named Paul, initially protests that a photograph does not constitute evidence as such, but Paul's wife Betty protests that she can feel "wu" (personal sorrow) emanating from the necklace. The scene thus dramatizes two famous paradigms concerning the theory of the photographic image: the idea that photographic images provide proof that the referent really exists (Bazin, Sontag and Barthes again) and the loss of the aura inherent in technological reproducibility (Benjamin again).

Such metamoments are, by comparison, much more frequent in Dick's novel. Most of the characters are familiar with Abendsen's novel whose contents are summed up early on,[50] and excerpts are even cited halfway through the novel.[51] These scenes operate as mises en abyme, the diegetic novel mirroring Dick's allohistory (it turns out that Abendsen's novel does not tell the "real" story of World War II but an alternative one in which the UK and the US went to war after the Allies' victory). Characters end up questioning their own existence; shortly after his vision of the real San Francisco, Mr. Tagomi thinks, "I am a mask, concealing the real. Behind me, hidden, actuality goes on, safe from prying eyes."[52] And the novel ends on ontological uncertainty; Tagomi, taken by a heart attack, is still wondering about the "Inner Truth," while Juliana sees its meaning validated by the fact that Abendsen's novel was written entirely by the oracle.[53]

Such metamoments are by necessity interspersed in the Amazon Prime series. Season 1 reserves the viewing of a new reel to the conclusion of episode S1E9: footage of hydrogen bombs exploding is followed by a shot of a demolished Golden Gate Bridge and scenes of Joe shooting Frank in the head [44:42–47:10]. The series, like the novel, thus makes clear that, in spite of its use of archive footage, *The Grasshopper Lies Heavy* is not presenting our world; even Juliana realizes that "this isn't like the other film" (from episode S1E1), which was made up entirely of World War II footage. The metalepsis's ontological menace on the characters' existence is visualized by Frank's shadow which is cast against the screen where his "movie self" is about to die (Figure 10.3), thereby suggesting that, like Norma Desmond (Chapter 4) or Coppola's *Dracula* (Chapter 7) standing in the light of the projector, he is a creature of light and shadow. The back shot suggests we are in a similar position as the characters, wondering, how can such an impossible film have been made? What is the story behind this metalepsis? And how can we trust diegetic reality after watching it? But the difference is: we know that both these worlds are distinct from our own in spite of similarities. Thus positioned, the metalepsis serves primarily to build up the stakes of the season finale and, above all, to justify the series's continuation; the premise's meta potential is thereby reduced to a narrative conceit.

Figure 10.3 The Man in the High Castle, *episode S1E9: Juliana and Frank watch the second* Grasshopper Lies Heavy *reel, which shows Joe executing Frank in the ruins of San Francisco, Frank's shadow cast against the movie screen foreshadowing his fate and/or expressing the metaleptical variant.*

This is confirmed in subsequent seasons. Much like season 1, season 2 starts with a metamoment: Juliana, like her namesake at the end of Dick's novel, meets the Man in the High Castle, Hawthorne Abendsen, and tells him about the film she watched, while Hitler—thanks to intercutting—is shown watching the same film [35:37–36:35]. Abendsen confirms the films' importance without elucidating their origin—it turns out that specific films may foresee a potential future (a nuclear threat in San Francisco) that is, fortunately, avoided at the end of the season. The metamoment effectively launches season 2; the metalepsis's value is above all narrative and dissipates as the series progresses: ontological stability is introduced as we learn that some films are fake, created by Abendsen who spliced images together, and that the real ones originate from parallel dimensions (S3E1).

Because the allohistory posits a relationship between fiction (allo) and reality (history), at the very least, it performs a historiographic function by reimagining history. It can be combined with other reflexive devices such as intertextuality (*Inglourious Basterds*), but it can also avoid questioning its own implication in the fabrication of history or its medium (*Fatherland*) or downplay it to meet narrative and economic requirements (*The Man in the High Castle*). Like metalepsis, then, allohistory is potentially meta; it is less potent than parody, whose referent is formal or textual, because the relationship it establishes between fiction and history is primarily a diegetic concern: the allohistory acknowledges history as story, not necessarily as text. To fulfill its meta potential, the formal/textual qualities of the story need to be put into relief.

SELF-CONSCIOUS HISTORICAL FILM (*SCHINDLER'S LIST*, *JFK*, *NO*)

This is equally true of the historical film. A historical film—or one of its scenes—becomes meta when it self-consciously interrogates its own construction of history and/or the historiography of such constructions in its medium and related media. Although the historical film does not resort to an outrageous premise (as in the case of the allohistory) or setup (as in the case of Watkins), its modes of engagement with its material can call on diegetic and formal devices that are similar to those we have just observed; they are, however, less abundant and/or salient in order to avoid compromising the historical verisimilitude the genre aims at upholding.

One example of a film that insists less on the mediatization of history as on the power of historical fiction is *Schindler's List* (Spielberg, 1993). Spielberg scholars have identified reflexivity as a common feature of the US-American director's work but have mainly associated it with intertextual phenomena. Some have argued that, in *Schindler's List*, the visual allusions to earlier Holocaust films—*Night and Fog* (Resnais, 1956), *Shoah* (Lanzmann, 1985), ... *and the Fifth Horseman Is Fear* (Brynych, 1965), etc.—serve to "subsume"[54] earlier efforts and present the 1993 film as "a master narrative for the murder of the Jews of Europe";[55] Sara Horowitz in particular deplores Spielberg's "unproblematized transparency" and lack of self-consciousness.[56] I would argue, to the contrary, that the film is very much aware of its status as fiction. The famous scene in which Oskar Schindler and Ingrid, on horseback from a hilltop, look on in horror at the Kraków ghetto below, as Jews are brutally herded out into the streets, mishandled and even executed [1:08:06–1:10:34], is a particularly salient metamoment that asserts the moral power of historical fiction in general and of the film specifically; in this respect, it proposes not a "deliberate embellishment"[57] but functions much like "Caparzo's suicidal attempt to save a little girl," a "mise en abyme" of the main plot of *Saving Private Ryan* (Spielberg, 1998).[58]

Amidst the brutality, a tiny figure emerges in an establishing shot—a girl wearing a red coat whose color breaks the film's black-and-white scheme. Although Schindler remains speechless throughout, the direction of his gaze, the shot/reverse shot technique and the use of red indicate that his attention is also focused on the little girl making her way through the streets and the horror (Figures 10.4.1 and 10.4.2). The narration thus suggests that the scene is not only viewed from Schindler's eyes, but, more importantly,

Figures 10.4.1 and 10.4.2 Schindler's *List*: while Oskar Schindler watches, from a hilltop, the exactions in the Kraków ghetto, a little girl in red appears, wandering through the horror.

that it is filtered through his subjectivity, so much so that when the Nazi businessman and his companion quit the scene, the status of the images of the little girl that follow is quite uncertain: are they picturing Schindler's mental images as he rides off or "real" events that are occurring in his absence? This fantastic hesitation is heightened by the spectral quality of the girl as she moves up a staircase (the focus is on the railings, while she is but a blur passing by in the background), but also by her reintegrating the black-and-white world when she hides under the bed and hears the Nazi soldiers outside (implying that she may actually be a full-fledged focalizer/subject). The Little Red Riding Hood may or may not be a figment of Schindler's imagination. The color red thus stands for the confusion between history—it is the color of the flag the Jews waved at the Allied forces—and fairy tale, and thus of fiction, within the black-and-white (or gray) documentary world of history.

The scene therefore qualifies its director's stated "goal" to achieve "authenticity"[59] (Spielberg did, after all, choose to adapt a novel). And it dramatizes that the diegetic spectator's moral consciousness is awoken to the horror once he has experienced it imaginatively through the eyes of an other who may, in fact, not even exist. We are not only witnessing Schindler's moral awakening, but the film's justification of its own approach to its historical material: like the protagonist, we are similarly meant to be touched by fictional or fictionalized characters evolving in the pages of history. *Schindler's List* is asserting the validity of historical fiction to move its audiences by articulating story (a singular and often fictitious individual's experience) and history (the actual events) as a means to preserve memory. If the scene is tragic in its depiction of real-life horror, as a metamoment it is a celebration of the power of fiction to provoke moral awakening through perception and emotion. And it is integral to Spielberg's moral project: that if a Nazi who wasn't a good man to start with can end up saving Jews, then "viewers with little prior interest" can similarly "emerge from the theater convinced that the Holocaust 'really happened.'"[60] Such an achievement can be put down to the power of fiction.

A film that addresses its own approach to its material more consistently is *JFK* (Stone, 1991). While some commentators accused the film's director of propaganda[61] and unfounded "speculation,"[62] others noted its "self-reflexive edge" (i.e., that its "investigation of the past [. . .] suggests much about the difficulty of any historical undertaking and the near impossibility of arriving at definitive historical truths"[63]). Others yet argued that the real question is whether the film's challenge of categorical distinctions such as documentary and fiction "succeeds in prompting viewers to consider how central to the writing of history are questions about access to and the organizing of images."[64] In *The Archive Effect*, Jaimie Baron notes that the concern around films like *JFK* and *Underground* (Kusturica, 1995) had at least as much to do with how the footage was "recontextualized so as to imply particular historical and ideological meanings," as with viewers' ability to decipher the "seams" between authentic and fabricated footage.[65]

Close analysis of *JFK*, however, reveals that it actually thematizes its own construction of a historical plot, and thus somewhat distances itself from its source material, District Attorney Jim Garrison's 1988 *On the Trail of the Assassins*. Both versions of the assassination (the official and Garrison's) are compared to fiction on several occasions: prime suspect Clay Shaw protests that the District Attorney has him "consorting with a sordid cast of characters" [1:27:25]; the Chief of Special Ops says he "knew the Warren Commission was fiction" [1:52:20]; and at the trial, during his concluding statements, Garrison wonders "[w]ho was impersonating" the intelligence personnel in the crowd, and possibly even the homeless people who were arrested [2:52:38]. Fiction is wielded by all parties as a means to discredit the presentation of historical facts. The artificiality of Garrison's own account is materialized by the miniature of the Dallas crime scene, which the DA, standing over it like an omniscient god, uses to demonstrate his point in court [2:41:39–2:42:43]. By cutting back and forth between close-ups of the miniature, excerpts from the Zapruder film, and black-and-white and color images of witnesses, the film draws attention to the artificiality of its prime strategy—the juxtaposition and deliberate confusion of actual archive footage and mock-archive footage.

The film had early on drawn attention to the centrality of editing [56:36–1:03:11]. Indeed, the scene where Garrison and his team attempt to piece together Oswald's suspicious past is punctuated by brief close-ups of anonymous hands creating the photograph of Lee Harvey Oswald that would appear on the 21 February 1964 cover of *Life* magazine (Figure 10.5). This scene not only fuels the paranoid thesis that historical documents can be fabricated; in laying bare the film's two main strategies—editing (through the close-up of the knife cutting a photo) and the fabrication of mock-archive images starring the actors—it reveals that both Stone and Garrison are resorting to the exact same strategies as those accused by the D.A. Garrison's question "Who was impersonating them?" can thus be seen as a commentary on the stars' own impersonation of historical persons, all the more so as Tommy Lee Jones and Joe Pesci's reliance on kitsch-looking wigs and make-up to portray Clay Shaw and David Ferrie undermines all pretense of verisimilitude. While Garrison ceaselessly proclaims he is looking for the

Figure 10.5 JFK: *the falsification of the photograph of Lee Harvey Oswald that would appear on the cover of* Life *magazine thematizes how words and images can be used to fabricate history by possible conspirators as well as by Garrison and Stone.*

"truth," *JFK* suggests that he is blinded by the fact that his plot is potentially as fictitious as the one he is trying to unravel, as is suggested by the many extreme close-ups of his face with light and images playing over his glasses. Regardless of the director's statements about his own beliefs concerning the conspiracy,[66] the film is anything but naive. A "deconstructionist's heaven,"[67] the film also deconstructs itself; it self-consciously recognizes its own participation in the fabrication of images and history, of a Baudrillardian hyperreality founded on simulation and simulacrum, thus anticipating the more overt meta of *Natural Born Killers* (Stone, 1994).[68] Its interrogation of official history leads it to propose a narrative verging on allohistory, or rather, to suggest that all histories are potential allohistories. The question remains, however, as to whether viewers are sufficiently equipped to distinguish between archive and mock-archive footage, and "alert" to these metamoments to call into question the conspiracy narrative.

One contemporary director who has repeatedly embraced history as his prime material is the Chilean Pablo Larraín, notably in recent biopics like *Neruda* and *Jackie* (both 2016) and *Spencer* (2021). His Dictatorship Trilogy—*Tony Manero* (2008), *Post Mortem* (2010) and *No* (2012)—is of particular interest in a study of meta because its focus on different periods of the Pinochet regime is mapped over media history (live performance in 1973 in *Post Mortem*; late 1970s cinema in *Tony Manero*; television in 1988 in *No*). Though each story is standalone, the trilogy has a certain thematic and aesthetic homogeneity, each film exploring the relationship between fantasy and history, and employing vintage cameras and handheld cinematography. The first follows Raúl Peralta, a man who is obsessed with, and basically wants to be, Tony Manero, the hero of *Saturday Night Fever* (Badham, 1977). Raúl, with the help of three other amateur dancers, is putting together a show that reprises the US-American movie's choreographies, but his worship of the movie character largely exceeds the bounds of the movie theater or stage, and he regularly practices Tony's moves and lines alone in his room. He also wants to win a Tony Manero lookalike contest broadcast on TV and is ready to do so by any means necessary: he murders people for money, a television set or, as the final scene hints, to basically get rid of the competition [1:31:40–1:32:52].

The three movie-theater scenes [6:33–7:38; 33:37–34:26; 51:28–51:58] that dramatize Raúl's adoration of the 1977 blockbuster (and his indifference to Travolta's 1978 follow-up *Grease*) differ from those of *The Purple Rose of Cairo* and *Cinema Paradiso*, and are somewhat closer in this respect to the pornographic movie scenes of *Taxi Driver* (Scorsese, 1976): the shot/reverse shots highlight not so much pleasure as incongruity—that is, the radical gap between the US-American movie character and his Chilean lookalike. The

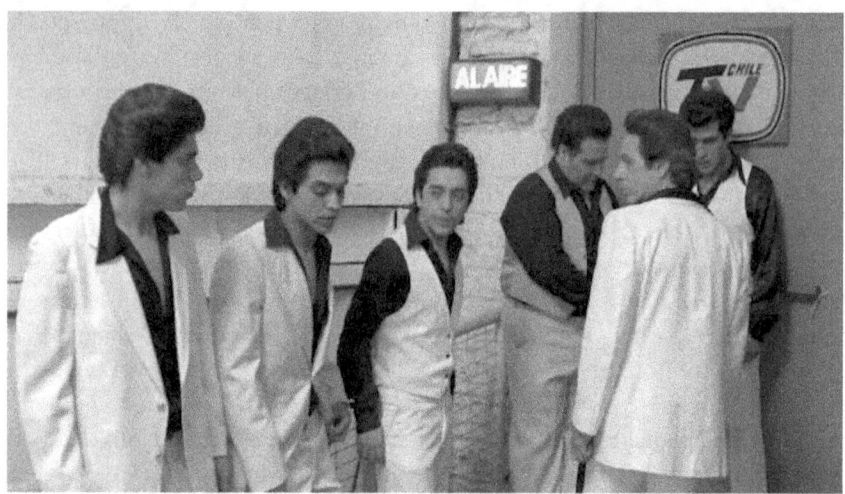

Figure 10.6 Tony Manero: *Raúl Peralta assesses the much younger competition prior to the Tony Manero lookalike contest.*

linguistic difference is blatant (Raúl's English is heavily accented), as is the age difference (actor Alfredo Castro was 53 when he played the part of Raúl, Travolta 23 for Tony Manero). Raúl's ineptitude is evinced when he has a hard time executing moves that exert too much pressure on his knees [17:20]; it is driven in at the end of the movie when his young co-dancer, Goyo, who effects these moves with ease, is selected for the lookalike contest [1:17:05], and confirmed when Raúl ends up being the eldest contestant by far in the final competition (Figure 10.6) [1:24:20].

Raúl's blindness to the incongruity of his obsession mirrors his blindness to the social and political reality of Pinochet's Chile. His denial is expressed in the opposition between interior and exterior spaces; movie theaters, the group's rehearsal room and Raúl's bedroom provide havens from streets inhabited by the physical and sonic presence of the men who enforce the regime. Raúl even benefits from the political situation on at least two occasions, when he robs a man murdered by the police [41:10] and later takes his partner Goyo's place after two men turned up to interrogate the young man [1:20:24]; it is as if the regime were rewarding the protagonist for turning a blind eye on social reality. Scholars have thus argued that Raúl's movie-based fantasy is a "ready-made projection"[69] and an "allegory" of 1970s Chile. As a fan and serial killer, Raúl embodies both "the logical culmination of the system" and a "nation striving [...] to emulate the glittery appearance of another,"[70] a US-style "consumer-based capitalist society."[71] Vania Barraza Toledo argues, however, that Raúl also holds up a mirror to the citizens of Chile at the time of the film's release who would rather "ignore or forget"[72] the nation's troubled history. The representation of spectatorship thus serves as a historiographic allegory of a specific moment in the nation's history and its present relation to it.

While *Post Mortem* functions along similar lines, with the protagonist's (Mario Cornejo's) obsession for a dancer both reinforcing and metaphorizing his denial of reality/history,[73] *No* proposes a departure and an expansion in terms of both its narrative and its approach to its historical material. The film is centered on an actual historical event—the 1988 referendum that was designed to confirm Pinochet's place at the head of Chile but surprisingly put an end to his regime—features historical figures (Lucho Guzman, René Saavedra), and its protagonist, René, is not a madman but an adman, who seems to take good care of his son Simon and to be very much at ease with social interactions. *No* pursues the allegorical approach of the previous films: the adman is an incarnation of the "neoliberal model" marketing an "empty dream,"[74] a subtext that has as much resonance in 2012 as in 1988. Both Alexis Howe and Nike Jung point out that René's main argument for using the same tagline to sell a soft drink [1:30], the NO campaign [34:50] and a TV series [1:46:45] is that it "fits with the current social context."[75] Certain of the historical alterations that were criticized upon the film's release (notably the fact that the NO+ logo was not invented by the campaign but by militant artists[76]) clearly serve to reinforce the political subtext—that in spite of the defeat announced in the film's title, the social model promoted by Pinochet was proved "victorious" since it provided the tools that would enable the NO campaign to "sell democracy as if it were a commodity."[77] The point is driven in during the end credits when archive footage shows Pinochet congratulating his successor President Aylwin [1:48:10–1:48:55].

No is more meta than the first two installments in the Dictatorship trilogy because its premise—a battle between two televised campaigns—allows it, even more so perhaps than *JFK*, to interrogate the power of images in the creation of history as well as its own use of images. The parallel is evident in the title, which collapses the film and the historical campaign it is based on. For while the title immediately situates the film on the "right" (or in this case "left") side of history, it also aligns itself with an advertisement campaign and thus with propaganda—in other words, it cautions us against its own representation of history. The semantic and visual impact of the two-letter word inscribes the film within a regime of negativity, drawing attention to the ambivalence of the NO campaign's victory. This is thematized more overtly when a militant (Ricardo) speaks out against René's pragmatic "advertising semiology" for the campaign by stating that there are "ethical limits": "This is legitimization. This is a campaign to silence what really happened. [. . .] I see here what you really are. Those images are what you are. [. . .] I will not be party to something for which history will never forgive us" [36:40–38:15].

No is also the first of Larraín's films to mix archive footage and mock-archive footage, something which he would repeat in *Jackie*. This strategy was criticized upon the film's release because it was viewed as yet another device to "camouflage" and "simplify" history.[78] Francesco Zucconi argues, on the contrary, that the mixture of archive and fiction produces a discourse on the writing of history: "[t]he impression is that by making a comparison between the archival images and their cinematic reproduction Larraín is attempting to thematise the inner anachronism encrusted in every historical narration."[79] The assumed imperative to camouflage is effectively undermined by the casting of real people playing their own roles over twenty years later (including former President Patricio Aylwin, NO campaign leader Eugenio Tironi, and campaign members Juan Forch and Carmen María Pascal). In Nike Jung's words, "[t]he result is an authenticity which has an artificiality that is acknowledged, both evoking and deconstructing the concept of the real"; by showcasing the medium "as a material body," he suggests, "*No* encourages reflections on how our access to historical knowledge is configured by technology, on the capacity of the medium 'objectively' to record and convey historical truth."[80]

I agree with Jung and Zucconi and would add that the film is also warning us of its own antics, again more deliberately than *JFK*. The film reflexively flaunts its own manipulation of images and history even as it exposes both campaigns' manipulation of images and history. We are witnesses not only to the construction of the past and thus history, but also of the present and even the future. We are also witness to how quickly each campaign reacts to its adversary's latest commercial. In a binary configuration where the goal is to convince people to vote yes or no, any discourse, whether based on words, images or music, can be resignified into its opposite. The YES campaign, for instance, spoofs one of their opponents' commercials featuring a married husband who wants to coerce his wife into having sex: the YES wife's enthusiastic "Yes!" replaces the NO wife's depressing "No" (Figures 10.7 and 10.8) [1:25:02; 1:34:07]. The act of plagiarism illustrates Veronica's earlier complaint that René's advertisement is "a copy of the copy of the copy" [1:04:21], which René himself used against Lucho: "It's a copy of the copy of the copy of the copy of the copy. It's all mixed together there" [1:18:49]. Such comments hark back to the lookalike motif of *Tony Manero* and bring to mind the writings of Baudrillard. Both campaigns are responsible for creating national narratives that are founded in simulacra, so that the battle for the referendum becomes an exemplar of how history and reality can be emptied of meaning in a hyperreal society. Any word/plot/fiction/concept can be

Figures 10.7 and 10.8 No: *the YES campaign parodies the NO campaign, turning a depressed and sexually inactive couple into its opposite.*

turned into its opposite, and Pinochet has no problem whatsoever speaking in the name of "democracy" because it is just another word, not a system of government [27:40].

Yet, in spite of the warnings voiced within the diegesis, the narration is increasingly taken over by the advertisements, as if to confirm the victory of propaganda and of Pinochet's market-led ideology over Chile and the film.

Figures 10.9.1 and 10.9.2 No: *René's presentation of a teaser for the soap opera* Bellas y audaces *(thanks to an ellipsis) gives way to the production of the teaser itself, the narration enacting the power of capitalist ideology to produce images.*

When Lucho and René are presenting the teaser for the soap opera *Bellas y audaces* (TVN, 1988), René's words are shown to be quasi-performative: the James Bond-themed concept he is selling magically makes way (through an ellipsis) for the advertisement itself, with René's pitch continuing in voiceover (Figures 10.9.1 and 10.9.2) [1:19:29–1:21:06]. For a moment, the narration blurs three moments in the production process (the concept, the shooting, the finished product), and thus three ontological levels.

Beyond the intermedial devices derived from television, the film's naturalist aesthetics allows room for more discrete reflexive devices: frame-within-the-frame composition is used to reinforce René's status as a witness of history and its mediation when he watches TV [14:15]; lens flares draw attention to the surface of the image and come to symbolize René and his team's blindness (to their own validation of Pinochet's vision for Chile) but potentially our own as well (to the film's own manipulation of history) [26:10]. The *cinéma vérité* style is regularly undermined by the editing which multiplies cuts; some are justified diegetically (for instance, in the more violent sequences), while others are purely expressive (for instance, when the narration alternates between shots of René and his son from inside and outside their car after a riot [1:30:48–1:31:10] or when they're walking the streets in its aftermath [1:37:29–1:37:52]). *No* is thus grounded in a dialectic between opposition (as its title indicates) and similarity (as the campaign demonstrates): it contrasts the violence of the street, which René is a passive witness to, with the media images he creates and consumes; it also highlights the commonality of the formal and narrative devices used in television and documentary, propaganda and realism. In so doing, *No* evinces the paradox and impasse of historiographic metafiction: that in spite of their constructedness, a distinction between history and fiction remains morally and politically necessary, for fear that all historical truth collapses into allohistory.

Conclusion

Meta-works that engage with historical material are, no doubt, less likely to be charged with narcissism than those which focus on the apparatus, their genre or form. Significantly, the themes, motifs and devices explored in Chapters 4, 5 and 6—the production of propaganda, the witnessing of history and its mediation, or the exploration of archive footage—are more obviously connected to real-world concerns in these works. And yet, historical fiction remains suspect because of its joining of polar opposites and the imperative to adapt history, and it is this suspicion that these meta-works address. Like the novels of historiographic metafiction discussed by Hutcheon, these works adhere to the contemporary view that history is a matter of narrative and subjective reconstruction, and foreground the constructedness of history by insisting on textuality, artifice and polyphony (the work of Peter Watkins is exemplary in this respect). They also evince an awareness that the circulation of sounds and images plays a central part in our shaping and understanding of history, a process they inevitably participate in (*JFK*, *No*). This awareness is both dramatized in their plots and explored formally. The layers of time can be materialized by intertextual layers, a historiographic approach whereby art and film history becomes the grid through which history can be apprehended (*Inglourious Basterds*). The mediation of history through art and mass media is celebrated as a potential—the power to memorialize (*Schindler's List*) and provide catharsis (*Inglourious Basterds*)—but its more troubling dimensions are equally observed, notably the power to fictionalize history and weaponize its traces (*The Man in the High Castle*, *JFK*, *No*). All these works approach their historical material with a consciousness that it is morally and politically charged, and thus that their own engagement with history is eminently political and necessarily questionable. It is to the political potential of meta that we now turn.

CHAPTER 11

Politics

THE POLITICAL POTENTIAL OF META (*TOUT VA BIEN*)

Meta is narcissistic, solipsistic, has no real-world implications, and is too clever for its own good. These were the chief accusations leveled at literary metafiction in the 1970s and 1980s.[1] Today they are regularly directed at more popular fare. (An online article entitled "*Rick and Morty* Almost Swallows Itself Whole in a Too Meta Midseason Premiere" states that episode S4E6, in which Rick is endowed with a second butt crack, "disappears so far and deep into its own ass that it needed extra space to make it possible."[2]) Yet, at this stage of the book, it has become clear that, in connecting fiction, art and media to the real world, meta allows for varied ethical and political implications. Movies about movie-making and -going can expose the capitalist and/or repressive ideology underpinning the industry that stifles artistic impulses (*Contempt, Cinema Paradiso, Escape from the "Liberty" Cinema, The Player, Mulholland Dr.*) and/or the audience's status as subjects of consumer society (*Gremlins, Cult, Westworld*). Films and series can broach the political ambiguities of exploiting historical material (*JFK, No*) and/or interrogate their own historiographic role (*Culloden, Inglourious Basterds*). Generally speaking, meta can examine the political and ideological implications of a variety of conventions, whether pertaining to genre, narration and representation. Of the latter categories, representation is, no doubt, the most obviously connected to the real world, since most works aim to re-present, if not the world, at least some of its characteristics (starting perhaps with the commonality and diversity of human experiences). But representation and formal conventions are often—perhaps always—intertwined, if only because representation is mediated by form.

The subtext of *Pulp Fiction*[3], for instance, reveals that the series of misfortunes that drive each one of the three stories are systematically targeted at the film's African American crime lord, Marsellus Wallace, and organized in a gradation: his money, his wife, his body. These assaults materialize the white characters' more or less visible racial hatred: the rapists, of course; Lance, a drug dealer who brags Vincent Vega cannot purchase heroine this good from black dealers; the white students who mistook Marsellus Wallace for a "bitch"; and even Vincent Vega who shoots a young black man by "accident" and comes close to sleeping with his boss's wife. In the mid-1990s US, *Pulp Fiction* suggests, a powerful black man may govern the diegesis of a Hollywood gangster movie, but remains an intolerable figure nonetheless. The film's narrative structure seeks to disavow these tensions by framing them within the trajectory of the film's second powerful black man, Jules Winnfield, whose redemption is effected by his renouncing the stereotypical and problematic role of blaxploitation gangster (with its black buck legacy) and appropriating another role, that of Kwai Chang Caine from the TV show *Kung Fu* (ABC, 1972–5), modeled on East Asian philosophy, and already appropriated by a white man (actor David Carradine). *Pulp Fiction* demonstrates that representations stick (and are thus signs of subjection) but can also be resignified (thus constituting acts of agency). If the 1994 film, like all Tarantino's films, illustrates the political potential of meta in popular cinema, this chapter will focus more exclusively on works whose subject matter is more evidently political, and that explore the relation between political fiction and social-political reality.

Waugh's and especially Hutcheon's books sought to respond to the criticism that metafiction discounted the political. Both scholars insist on the political concerns of various avant-gardes, whose "novels supposedly expose the way in which these social practices are constructed through the language of oppressive ideologies, by refusing to allow the reader the role of passive consumer or any means of arriving at a 'total' interpretation of the text."[4] If Waugh ends up leaving the question as to "the politically 'radical' status of aesthetically 'radical' texts" dangling,[5] Hutcheon, on the other hand, discusses several cases of political metafiction. What the works of the French and Italian avant-gardes (Tel Quel and Gruppo 63 which was responding to what its members perceived as the failure of neorealism) and of Quebec writers Hubert Aquin and Leonard Cohen had in common,[6] in addition to a Marxist-inspired ideological framework, was a belief that "it was through the consciousness of its own fictiveness" that fiction "could and did achieve a genuine political function, as a challenge, a contesting"[7]; with a novel like *Trou de mémoire* (1968), centered on the manuscript of a fictional Quebec revolutionary who also turns out to be its editor, "it is, in fact, through metafictional form that Aquin hopes to liberate his country and his literature."[8] These considerations lead Hutcheon to open the final paragraph of *Narcissistic Narrative* with these powerful words: "To read is to act; to act is both to interpret and to create anew—to be revolutionary, perhaps in political as well as literary terms."[9] Metafiction's political potential would reside in the role and responsibility it invites the reader to take up: that of active interpreter and potential deconstructionist. In today's parlance, we would say that metafiction, in so doing, empowers the audience, recognizes and calls on their agency.

Fredericksen notes that reflexivity, in *Man with a Movie Camera* and *Wind from the East*, is, likewise, a "political strategy" that aims to upset "[t]he partial aphasia of the spectator,"[10] but apart from this brief comment, Stam's *Reflexivity in Film and Literature* stands practically alone among early writings on metacinema and reflexivity in dealing extensively with politics, given that Judith Mayne's 1975 PhD dissertation on the ideologies of metacinema is difficult to come by. Like Hutcheon, Stam takes the avant-gardes and their predecessors as a starting point to explore the politics of reflexivity in the book's last two chapters, each of which focuses on a given tradition: the carnivalesque (as theorized by Mikhaïl Bakhtin) and Brechtian aesthetics. These traditions are shown to mix politics with formal play; non-exclusive, they are typically combined in modernist works (notably in the films of Godard). They differ, however, in the sense that Brechtian aesthetics are rooted in an ideological and philosophical framework (Marxism), whereas the carnivalesque originates in a cultural practice whose politics is certainly not as structured and is not necessarily articulated. Stam's analysis of "the carnival of modernism" shows how reflexive devices—in Alfred Jarry's 1896 play *Ubu King*, *Un Chien andalou*, *The Exterminating Angel* (Buñuel, 1962), Godard's *The Riflemen* and *Week-end* (1967), and Joaquim Pedro de Andrade's 1969 film adaptation of Mário de Andrade's 1928 novel *Macunaíma*—are quite deliberately utilized to assault bourgeois propriety. Stam describes this approach as a modernist version of the "carnivalesque strategies" analyzed by Bakhtin, a practice that allows "brief entry into a sphere of utopian freedom by turning the world upside down."[11] He concludes that

> The notion of the carnivalesque relativizes the overvaluation—often shared by bourgeois and Marxist critic alike—of the serious mimetic mode, suggesting the possibility of a realism which is not an illusionism, just as it suggests the possibility of a Left cultural critique which precludes neither laughter nor the pleasure principle.[12]

This leads to a chapter entitled "The Pleasures of Subversion," which discusses a more obvious influence on modernist cinema: Bertolt Brecht. The German playwright, Stam explains, rejected the "facile reductionism" operated by some Marxist critics for whom art was synonymous with "false consciousness"[13] and pure consumerism. For him, as for the later French and Italian avant-gardes discussed by Hutcheon, "distancing" devices have a political function: that of "shock[ing] the audience into an awareness that both social life and art are *human* creations and therefore can be changed."[14] By drawing attention to its own artifice, self-conscious art foregrounds (in Marxist terms) the materialism of our experiences and (in more contemporary terms, perhaps) the constructedness of identity (the idea that identities, whether personal or collective, are social constructs).

It is not only the arsenal of Brechtian strategies but the above precept that is reprised in *Tout va bien* (Godard and Gorin, 1972). Described by Stam as "a film whose form says everything about itself,"[15] *Tout va bien* is, like other films analyzed in his book, not just reflexive but profoundly meta. It tells the story of a couple, Susan and Jacques, who become interested in a strike at a meat-processing plant, and of how their involvement resonates with their experience of May 1968 and provokes a change in their political and romantic lives, which are intimately connected. Susan is a US-American radio announcer, Jacques a French New Wave director who now directs commercials, and "together [they] figure forth the *cinéaste* himself,"[16] frustrated with his early work. They also incarnate, because of their professions, the audiovisual medium and allegorize possible (dis)connections between sounds and images. *Tout va bien* resorts to distancing devices inherited from theater (the set is revealed in lateral tracking shots [12:16, 18:06, 25:51, 30:11, 41:20], several characters deliver monologues to the camera in static shots [14:17, 18:37, 27:36, 54:31, 1:16:57]) and to more specifically audiovisual ones (discontinuities in the soundtrack, voices muffled by sounds). It notably puts into practice Godard's reformulation of Luc Moullet's famous statement: "travelling shots are a question of morality." Not only do the tracking shots "call attention to themselves," and thus to the artifice, as Stam notes, "they impose a political pattern on [the event]."[17] This is also true of the staging.

> The schematic decor, consisting of a double-deckered cutaway set, "signifies" the political and economic structure of society and shows the divisions between classes as well as their interdependence. Everything in the film—the posed portraits of social classes, the tripartite division of the soundtrack, the position statements—highlights the conflict of three political forces: capital, the Communist party, and the Leftists.[18]

The social and cinematic allegories are thus eminently intertwined: "[t]echnique in *Tout va bien* is not something that exists in the service of the political message—it *is* the political message"; and it leads to the realization "that one cannot separate the politics of the story from the politics of the telling."[19]

The film opens with two voiceovers discussing the economics of filmmaking and how it can compromise one's political ambitions: movies require money, which requires stars, which requires a love story, and so forth [2:05–3:26]. This is followed by a discussion of plot, characterization and setting, and a hilarious parody of the famous second scene from *Contempt*, with the couple fully dressed walking alongside a river in a bleak urban environment (instead of Bardot naked in bed bathing in a pink light in sunny Italy) [3:27–6:57]. The voiceovers return at the end to comment on the silent fictional couple sitting at a table in a café [1:32:39–1:33:43]. As in many metafictional stories and novels of the time[20] (John Barth's 1968 "Night Sea Journey") and even *Tristram Shandy* (whose narrator invites the reader to "paint" the widow Wadman "to your own mind" in Chapter XXXVIII), "[t]he story and the characters are not shown as pre-existing; rather, they are shown in the process of their invention."[21] Yet the concluding voiceovers also insist on the characters' relationship to social and political reality in spite of their fictionality: "(*male voice*) Yes, some films make the audience think that He and She solve one problem only to go on to the next, and that's how life is. But in this film, we leave Him and Her looking at each other wordlessly. (*female voice*) We'll just say that He and She have started to think of themselves in a historical context." The rejection of narrative resolution opens up a space for an existential and political epiphany that remains one possible interpretation formulated by the female voiceover.

Another such space is created when Susan, in the latter third of the film, momentarily takes control of the narration during an argument [1:08:18–1:14:09], in spite of being identified as a character portrayed by a famous actress in the prologue. She speaks of "images in her head," which are inserted between her close-ups, and ends up looking to the camera. In this

Figure 11.1   Tout va bien: *after deploring their own complicity with consumer society, Susan/Jane Fonda looks to the camera and says that she needs a picture of Jacques at work and of "this image," paradoxically asserting her agency by performing her subjection to patriarchy's most prized symbol.*

metalepsis, at least two ontological boundaries are blurred in turn: between her imagination and reality, and between the diegesis and the narration. Jacques recognizes the political implications of her metanarrative takeover by asking her to "end this happening." The scene thus expresses not only the female character's resentment against the couple's complicity in capitalist society, but also her retaliation against the privileges of men both within and without the diegesis, signified with violence by the frontal medium close-up of her blotting her face out with the photograph of "a woman's hand on a man's dick" (Figure 11.1). It is by leaving a space for Susan to speak out that the male directors draw attention to the political contradictions of their project in terms of both feminist and Marxist politics. The casting of Jane Fonda and Yves Montand, actors famous for their leftist sensibilities, invites us to consider the doubts expressed by their characters as valid for themselves as much as for Godard: their jobs and politics are a constant tightrope act.

In many ways, Carter's *Metafilm* pursues the questions raised in Stam's final chapters by examining a contemporary corpus in the light of a post-Marxist framework. With the exception of *Medium Cool* (Wexler, 1969) discussed in the introduction, the works he analyzes—*Funny Games, Ararat, Magnolia* (P.T. Anderson, 1999), *Even the Rain* (Bollaín, 2010), *Fruitvale Station* (Coogler, 2013) and, albeit to a lesser extent, *Hugo* (Scorsese, 2011)—are art films that were released between 1997 and 2013. Writing in the mid-2010s, Carter takes it for granted that meta does not preclude politics and doesn't beat about the bush to say his corpus is comprised of "political metafilms."[22] Five of the seven films are explicitly political, engaging with our moral responsibility in the creation and reception of violence, overtly in four cases (the plots of *Medium Cool, Ararat, Fruitvale Station* and *Even the Rain* deal with antiwar protest, genocide, racial violence and the destruction of the environment) and allegorically in one case (the violence of visual culture in *Funny Games*, see Chapter 8); even *Hugo*'s "demystification" of filmmaking "involves a rhetorical merger between self-regard and illustration of social structures," a recognition that film is "a designed thing, the result of living labor that holds potential both to sustain its makers and undergo expropriation."[23] These works, in Carter's analysis, "challenge the affective states that they associate with lethargy, intractability, escapism, and despair"[24] by resorting to a variety of reflexive strategies; in so doing, they abide by the avant-garde credo that distancing and deconstruction posit an active spectatorship liable to inspire political awakening or commitment.

More specific to Carter's argument is how the issues they raise tie in to some of the concerns addressed by two trends in contemporary materialist theory: the "critical materialism" of Tony Scott and Nancy Welch (2014) and the "new materialism" of Laurie Gries (2015). Both perspectives attend to the circulation of objects, but whereas Gries emphasizes the "vitality" of the "pulse of things" and how these bodies coevolve, Scott and Welch, influenced by Marxism, insist on the economics and history of circulation, "and more specifically," on the human agents "who benefit in financial and political terms."[25] Carter coins the term "reflexive materialism" to describe the films' discourses, which, he argues, resonates to varying degrees with these two theoretical perspectives, "demonstrating their productive coexistence in some cases and sharp antagonism in others."[26] But Carter goes much further than identifying an underlying ideological framework to these films; he contends that the "reflexive materialism" they evince aims to "cooperate with [human agency]" and, in so doing, "works to frame a political collective."[27] Carter, here, follows the post-Marxist thinker Bruno Latour's understanding of the term "collective," which goes beyond "direct action politics" and can be "distinguishe[d] [...] from sheer human solidarity by linking it to varied forms of material interactivity (*We*)."[28] For Carter, self-aware films can "at once invoke and participate in the Latourian 'collective.'"[29] *Magnolia*, for instance, "fashion[s] collectives" thanks to music-video sequences that envelop the characters,[30] while *Fruitvale Station* supports "collective grieving by incorporating documentary images at the film's end."[31] Carter thus defends a view of self-conscious films as active agents in our interactions, ones that engage (with) us politically and ethically. Implicit in his argument is that it is their self-awareness that is constitutive of agency (theirs and our own).

The argument that metafiction, reflexivity and metafilm may have political potential should not, however, lead us to defend the reverse claim. Carter clearly assumes that his conclusions are an effect of his corpus and does not claim that they hold true for the variety of meta-phenomena that circulate in film and television. Moreover, he agrees with Stam that reflexivity is not "progressive" nor even political per se.[32] The same is obviously true for the intense form of reflexivity that is meta. While reflexivity can be content to merely destabilize conventions that are connected ideologically to patriarchal capitalism, for instance, meta has the potential to vigorously interrogate the political implications of its material. What follows is, therefore, a study of the politics of meta in *Colossal Youth* (Costa, 2006), S1E1 of *Black Mirror* (2011) and *I, Daniel Blake* (Loach, 2016), works that differ in many respects but have in common that they are resolutely political and worry about the political impact they may or may not have.

QUESTIONING THE EFFICACY OF POLITICAL FILMS AND SERIES (*COLOSSAL YOUTH*, *BLACK MIRROR*, *I, DANIEL BLAKE*)

In Chapter 3 of the French edition of *Le Spectateur émancipé* (2008), "Les paradoxes de l'art politique," Jacques Rancière examines one of his chief concerns: the political efficacy of art. For the French philosopher, "the efficacy of art does not consist in delivering messages, offering behavioral models or counter-models or teaching how to decipher representation."[33] It lies not so much in a given work's subject matter, nor in its mode of representation (political art need not be mimetic), and definitely not in the message it seeks to convey. Rather, it devolves from the politics of art as such—from art's capacity to "create a novel landscape of the visible, new forms of individualities and connections, different rhythms of apprehension of the given, new scales."[34] This harks back to the Marxist philosopher's famous thesis regarding "le partage du sensible," in which "partage" refers to both "distribution" (as per the official English translation) and "sharing."[35] The paradox of political art is that it derives its power from what is simultaneously a strength ("the distribution of the sensible") and a weakness ("aesthetic efficacy signifies the efficacy of the suspension of any direct relation between the production of artistic forms and that of a specific effect on a specific audience"[36]). This efficacy can only be the that "of a dissensus"[37]—a rift that both allows for the eruption of a variety of regimes of the sensible, and recognizes the fundamental gap between art and the world, a relation, Rancière implies, that can only be indirect. In the concluding lines of the previous chapter, he argues that this dissensus participates in "a process of political subjectivation" because its questioning of the visible and its foregrounding of a multitude of capacities of perception "sketch out a new topography of the possible."[38] After theorizing the political potential of aesthetics in general, Rancière adds another condition for a fiction to qualify as political or, in his words, "critical":

> I would call critical fictions that call into question the lines of separation between various expressive regimes, as well as the performances that "invert the cycle of degradation produced by victimization" by displaying the capacity to speak and play of those society relegates to its "passive" margins. But critical work, the work of separating, is also that which examines its own limitations as a practice, one that refuses to anticipate its effects and takes into account the aesthetic separation through which this effect is produced.[39]

In order to be critical and thus actively political, art must not only play its role of making experience shareable; it must also question its own limitations. Political efficacy, for Rancière, lies in the recognition that the "distribution of the sensible" is attempted both in spite of and through a fundamental disconnection—hence the paradox announced in the chapter's title.

In *Le Spectateur émancipé*, Rancière briefly illustrates his thesis with the films of Pedro Costa,[40] but he provides a more detailed analysis of Costa's fifth feature film, *Colossal Youth* (2006), in the final chapter of his 2011 *The Intervals of Cinema*. The film follows Ventura, an immigrant from Cape Verde, as he wanders around a Lisbon shantytown called Fontaínhas, visiting people (who might or might not be family) suffering from poverty, drug abuse and other ailments; scattered flashbacks, which are mainly marked by the presence of a bandage round Ventura's head, depict his shared life with a friend named Lento, in a run-down shack, and his repeatedly inviting his friend to learn the love letter he composed by heart. Rancière's interest in the Portuguese filmmaker's work has to do with its singularity. Although it focuses on the "exploited," it neither highlights economic causality, nor favors the didactic and militant approach of much political cinema, but attempts, rather, to emphasize the aesthetic potential of the experience of poverty, which has led some to criticize Costa for "aestheticizing" poverty.[41] Rancière focuses in particular on the artforms depicted in the film (a love letter, a museum, a song).

> The relationship between the paintings and the preceding still-life, between the dilapidated shack and the art gallery, but also perhaps between the love letter and the hanging of the paintings in the gallery thus compose a highly specific poetic displacement – a *figure* [that] in the middle of the film [comments on] the filmmaker's art, [on] his relationship with [museum art, and on the relationship that both have with the protagonist's] body, and consequently on [Costa's film's and the museum art's] respective politics.[42]

In brief, these artforms are the central motifs in a series of metamoments that occur throughout the film; together, they construct a theory of political art, with the museum standing for the institutionalization of art on the one hand, and the love letter and music for the aesthetic forms of the people on the other.

In Rancière's analysis, there is more at stake in the museum scene and the ensuing discussion between Ventura and the museum guard [40:16–47:23] than the message according to which "the pleasures of art are not for proletarians, nor museums for the workers who built them";[43] as a space where "art is shut inside a frame without transparency or reciprocity,"[44] the museum precludes the distribution of the sensible. However, the film demonstrates that it is not enough just to open the museum to the workers; the crux of the matter "is how to make an art that is adequate to these travellers, an art from inside them and one they could share in exchange."[45] This is where the love letter and the song come in; by allowing interactions between several characters, they insist on the "the proximity of art to all forms asserting a capacity for sharing or a shareable capacity"[46]—more precisely in the case of this film, sharing the characters' experience of "facing the unshareable."[47] Instead, Rancière argues, *Colossal Youth* acknowledges that it "cannot be the equivalent of the poet's love letter or the music of the poor," and it must be content of its status as a "surface on which the experience[s] of those relegated to the margins of economic circuits and social pathways"[48] are played out.

The metamoments of *Colossal Youth* avoid the radical reflexivity of the avant-gardes and are in many ways closer to the serialization of motifs observed in mainstream films and series. In addition to such motifs, much of the meta of *Colossal Youth* surfaces in the dialogue, especially in the final quarter of the film. *Colossal Youth* thematizes its awareness of its own limitations when Lento castigates Ventura for his obsession with his letter in the face of real-life horrors:

> Just when things are working for us, this *coup d'état* breaks out. Soldiers all over... in their armored cars, ready for a fight, checking IDs. They're bound to come here. Don't go out for anything. I went to confession. The priest asked me if I ever ate human flesh. [. . .] Yesterday at dawn they passed by in a jeep. They took Yaya up into the hills. They beat him up and tied him to a pine tree. Poor guy was the first, but not the last. [. . .] It's no use now. The letter will never reach Cape Verde. [. . .] There's no more mail, Ventura." [1:47:14–1:49:18]

And yet, Lenton will reveal to Ventura that, in the end, he did memorize the letter (or at least its opening lines) [2:20:02–2:20:20]. Indeed, the film depicts the narrative and imaginative power of all its characters. Paulo, a master schemer who faked his own death to obtain money for his own funeral [1:39:45–1:43:41], takes on a metanarrative function by concocting a script Ventura would perform for Paulo's mother [2:02:49–2:05:51]. Unlike Vanda's bedroom in which the television is kept on, provoking apathy in her daughter and Ventura alike, Xana can see animals on the wall of her dilapidated home and invites Ventura to play along (Figure 11.2) [1:51:15–1:54:29]; the diegetic screen is relegated offscreen in order to stimulate our own imaginative capacities and visualize images based on the characters' words. The power of language to make the invisible visible is evoked in what is, perhaps, the love letter's most poignant line: "I learn beautiful new words just for you and me, tailor-made for us both like fine silk pajamas." The letter's fate contradicts its intention and the line's underlying ideology (of keeping beauty for oneself) by being distributed among many. Art is shareable, and the power to perform and create art is shared. Far from naively upholding the efficacy of political art, *Colossal Youth* offers a celebration of the essential vitality and universal capacity for art, a point on which Costa, interestingly enough, rejoins Hutcheon's defense of metafiction (see Chapter 1) as well as the optimism of Spielberg (see Chapter 4).

For Rancière, it is not just that political cinema (or art) can be meta; it must be meta to some degree, as in it must engage with the paradox inherent in

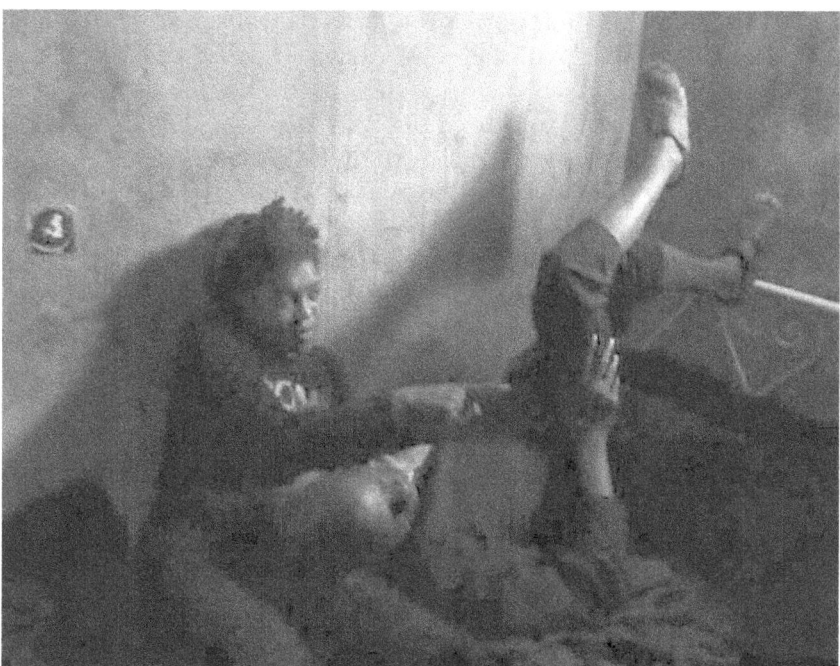

Figure 11.2 Colossal Youth: *Xana and Ventura imagine they can see turtles, a hen, a cop, a lion and the devil on the dilapidated wall offscreen.*

its project—to change a world it is fundamentally disconnected from. Such doubt is also evident in the films studied by Stam and Carter. Stam's analysis of *Tout va bien* concludes with a discussion of how the film's "modernist self-consciousness is accompanied by Marxist self-criticism"; it "asks how one communicates the process of class struggle," and both essays and criticizes a variety of "approaches."[49] Although Carter never cites Rancière, his analyses of *Ararat*, *Even the Rain* and *Fruitvale Station* provide fodder for the French philosopher's argument, as they more or less overtly "convey their inadequacy to the problems they pose."[50] Carter says of *Ararat* that, "rather than just proving vulnerable to analysis that exposes those contradictions [forgetting the Armenian genocide on the one hand or 'ced[ing] rhetorical advantage to the heirs of those who engineered it' by 'attempt[ing] to prove it' on the other], the movie expresses its own troubled awareness of them."[51] *Even the Rain*'s exploration of the damages filmmaking causes on the environment is "not merely an expression of mea culpa"; the movie "suggests that those problems will not be resolved by cinematic narrative, and that they require dedicated attention rather than one-time address. [. . .] [Bollaín] intimates that film may be better at posing problems than solving them."[52] As for the docudrama *Fruitvale Station*, it "makes a forceful argument for the right to document police behavior,"[53] and thus a claim for political efficacy, all the while admitting that it "cannot give us that view [of what really happened], and announces its inadequacy to the task,"[54] thus suggesting, like *Colossal Youth*, that a "portion of grief" remains "unshareable."[55] These three movies about making movies or capturing live footage acknowledge their limitations as films to resolve the political problems they pose. In fact, Carter contends that such "doubt" is part and parcel of the discourse of "reflexive materialism," and that it envelops the transformative potential of the collective[56]—an idea that resonates with Rancière's "distribution of the sensible."

Black Mirror and *I, Daniel Blake* are obviously more mainstream than the work of Pedro Costa, and the Ken Loach film is less obviously meta than the films discussed by Carter. Both have a political subject matter. Echoing a rumor that UK Prime Minister David Cameron had sex with a dead pig's head when he was a student (showrunner Charlie Brooker claims the similarity was fortuitous[57]), episode S1E1 of *Black Mirror*, "The National Anthem," relates the lengths to which British Prime Minister Michael Callow is forced to go to, to save beloved Princess Susannah, held hostage by an unidentified terrorist, and his career, of course. *I, Daniel Blake* recounts how a fifty-nine-year-old carpenter, who has recently suffered a heart attack, struggles, and is not alone in doing so, against a rigid, absurd, dehumanized and dehumanizing system that fails to take into account the reality of his medical and economic situation. Both political tales are very much grounded in our contemporary mediascape: the PM's ordeal is relayed by the media (primarily Internet and television), with the public weighing heavily on his decision, while the fifty-nine-year-old, more at ease fixing and building things with his hands, battles with technology (phones, computers) to try and solve his problem, and ultimately gets his fifteen minutes of fame when young people takes pics of, and selfies with, him, that will presumably be posted on Facebook, Twitter, Instagram, and the like.

"The National Anthem" is, like the anthology series as a whole, highly reflexive[58] and resorts to many of the devices identified by Fredericksen, Metz and Stam: mise en abyme, frame-within-the-frame composition, self-referentiality, citation. At the end of Part One,[59] when the PM has been briefed about the full extent of the situation, notably that the video is already circulating on the Internet, one of his advisers admits: "This is virgin territory, Prime Minister. There is no playbook" [7:46], a metanarrative comment that refers just as much to Brooker's screenplay, celebrating its brilliance or, given the David Cameron affair, pointing to its lack of originality, and thus asserting the series's formula of proposing premises based on existing situations. Scenes with diegetic screens abound, and both the Princess and the PM are presented as media figures performing partly against their will [1:30, 35:45]. The depiction of diegetic audiences at regular intervals (every five scenes or so) plays a structural role that is bound to the episode format, and one member even compares the terrorist's instructions to Dogme 95's guidelines for making a naturalistic fiction film [16:25]. The fictitious news footage that opens Part Four and the end credits [31:12–31:20, 41:39–42:20] mediates the transition from actual commercials to the series, simultaneously establishing a connection between fiction and reality and foregrounding the fundamental dissensus between the two. The episode is highly self-conscious of its format, medium, cinephile audience and the mediascape to which it belongs.

It represents this mediascape as being part of the problem (the image had already been downloaded and duplicated before the government got it off YouTube, and had already been viewed 50,000 times before the PM found out about it) and offering few solutions (the authorities' countermoves are systematically thwarted by the terrorist's own command of digital media). This impasse is dramatized through a series of events in Part Three [18:38–31:05] that the narration relates to each other through intercutting. CGI-ing a porn star's body in place of the PM's turns out to be quasi-impossible technically speaking, and no longer an option when one of porn star Rod Senseless's fans breaks the news on the Internet; this leads the terrorist to counter with an archaic special effect, a fake finger, which the media ludicrously fails to detect and immediately presents as real. When special forces finally track down the terrorist's upload signal and identify the location with satellite technology, all the armed men equipped with mini-cameras manage to find is a decoy dummy. Last but not least, a nosy journalist, Malaika, who surveils netsurfers' reactions to UKN coverage and has taken kinky selfies of herself to pry information out of a 10 Downing Street employee, ends up getting wounded during the operation. Clearly, the new media has made it possible for an individual or a small group to destabilize a G7 nation. And yet, to what purpose?

The triviality of the terrorist's demand, aimed exclusively at making a mockery of a politician, is initially a mystery, eliciting such hypotheses as personal revenge, after the Irish and Islamic leads have been invalidated. The final twist reveals, however, that the triviality of the political lies elsewhere. The whole terrorist setup was, in effect, a performance staged by a Turner-prize-winning artist named Carlton Bloom, who released the Princess thirty minutes before the transmission and committed suicide. Alex Cairns, one of the Prime Minister's advisers, concludes, "So it's a statement" [40:19], but she does not spell out its content, and it is left to us viewers to do so. The statement seems to be a simple critique of our contemporary mediascape, of the extent to which our uses of new media have trivialized our relationship to others and the world, and thus our sense of ethics and politics. After a brief discussion on the ethics of their profession as TV news reporters, in which the program head concludes that they're "not a chatroom" [9:08], the old media (here, television) are forced to subject themselves to the temporality of the Internet and publish the story as early as Part One. Not only has the news become "infotainment," a term that was widespread in the 1980s and 1990s to refer to talk shows as much as to the tendency of "newscasts or newsmagazines" to "reach mainly for visceral appeal,"[60] but politics have become entertainment: in this case, a reality TV show in which the PM's decisions are exclusively based on real-time polling, and a life-or-death matter is reduced to the question of whether or not he should fuck a pig.

The statement is precisely that the power of the new media turns our eyes away from what lies right before us. As Sébastien Lefait has noted, the kidnapping would have ended if all eyes had not been riveted to their screens.[61] No one, not one tech-savvy millennial, nor even a CCTV employee, spotted the dazed Princess stumbling along the aptly named Millennium Bridge [35:30–39:27] (Figures 11.3.1–11.3.3). The kidnapping of Princess Susannah has proven that it is not because of its intrinsic qualities that technology fails but because of our uses. And the end credits show that the diegetic audiences never really got the point in spite of the fact that the whole sham was revealed. If the bulk of the episode demonstrates the subjection of politics to media,[62] and if the end credits prove that the PM's advisers' attempt to keep a lid on the truth about "last year's event" has failed, the event has ultimately been recuperated by the PM and his team to reinforce his image and power. The PM's whimpering, "I love my wife, God forgive me," may have been heartfelt and struck a chord in audiences, yet the fact remains that, from the start, he chose to play for the ratings rather than for his family. "The National Anthem" is thus not just castigating audiences on their behavior; it is also sounding an Orwellian alarm because of the dangerous collusion between politics and the media, whereby news, entertainment and perhaps even propaganda are confused.

Whereas Henry Jenkins lauds the possibilities of convergence culture,[63] "The National Anthem" demonstrates how little faith it has in that culture's politics: the shared experience is calculatedly trivial and immediate. The digital age has offered new channels of expression to the troubled masses, but it has also sped up the trivializing of the political, producing a hyperreal version of Guy Debord's society of the spectacle.[64] And yet, like Jenkins, the episode demonstrates that the potential lies in a medium's uses:[65] an individual can momentarily destabilize governments, but meaning is likely to be lost in the flux of information, circulating so as to become just another piece of fake news. Carlton Bloom's statement is programmatic of the series whose showrunner has the same initials. By opening with this episode, *Black*

Figures 11.3.1–11.3.3 Black Mirror, *episode S1E1: Great Britain watches Prime Minister Michael Callow have sexual intercourse with a pig, oblivious that Princess Susannah has already been released on the Millennium Bridge.*

Mirror asserts its awareness of its own limitations as political fiction: it reveals how little faith it has in its medium of then (it was screened on television in 2010) and of its future medium (it was purchased by Netflix in 2016), and how much it doubts its own efficacy as political fiction. But by addressing these concerns on a meta-level, the mise en abyme of spectatorship alerts us to the fact that there is nonetheless something to get. More overtly satirical and less emotional than episodes S1E2 and S1E3, "The National Anthem" serves as a statement of intent for the anthology series as a whole: its thematic concern with the politics and ethics of the digital age, and its concern with the potential of political fiction in that era.

By contrast, *I, Daniel Blake* is sparse on reflexive devices, and its two metamoments are confined to the final act. Including a Ken Loach film in a discussion on meta might seem far-fetched, yet self-consciousness was actually central to the director's early work for the BBC. The 1964 BBC series *Diary of a Young Man* and the 1965 *Wednesday Play* episode *Up the Junction* bear the influence of Brecht and Godard,[66] as does his first feature-length film, *Poor Cow* (1967), which ends with a series of jump-cuts. Even *Kes* (1969), the movie which was to become the model of Loachian social realism,[67] features a metamoment. John Hill's analysis of the classroom scene [1:08:50–1:15:08] brings to mind Stam's analysis of the Balzac reading in *400 Blows*, in which a class discussion also provides a framework through which to view the film as a whole (see Chapter 1).

> Billy is shown to galvanise the class with his impassioned account of how he has trained his hawk. The subject of the class is, in fact, the distinction between 'fact and fiction' (words seen written on the blackboard); however, it has also been the project of the film to break down this distinction and minimise the gap between character and 'performer' with the result that the actor appears to be describing what he himself, and not just the character has learnt.[68]

The scene, in effect, operates as a mise en abyme of the film itself, with the rapt audience reflecting our own interest in Billy's relationship with the kestrel, Billy's "fact"-based narrative the film's realist approach, and Billy/actor David Bradley's words, tone and gestures the power of performance to make the invisible—here, the kestrel—visible (as in the baseball scene in Keaton's *Cameraman*, see Chapter 3).

The final scenes of *I, Daniel Blake* function much in the same way, but are given far more prominence than in Loach's second feature film because of their length, position and the fact that both refer to the film's title. The two metamoments are mises en abyme that establish parallels between Dan's productions and the Loach film on the one hand, and the diegetic and actual audiences on the other. After admitting to Ann, the most/only understanding social worker he's met, that he's lost the self-respect he took pride in, Dan dons a black cap and goes outside to spray-paint his demand for a speedy appeal on the wall of the local Department of Work and Pensions centre (Figures 11.4.1–11.4.3) [83:09–87:22]. The metamoment starts when the title of the film, which had been omitted from the opening and end credits, appears on the wall; it is confirmed when Dan describes his singular revolt as "me new art installation." The very long back shot of Dan painting shows him dwarfed by his own words; the sequence then alternates between medium shots of Dan the suffering individual we have followed throughout the film, and the very long shot of Dan the newbie performer. The event is presented as a performance wherein the individual is part of his art but the work itself is bigger than the individual. Meta, here, makes a case against the narcissism of (meta)fiction/performance by demonstrating that it has real-world connections (Daniel's act retrospectively reconfigures the Department of Work and Pensions centre into his own backstage, endowing him with the agency he feels deprived of) and is open to the world (the audience).

Yet the validation of art's real-world potential is shortly undercut by the diegetic audience's reactions, which immediately trivialize Dan's act: two young passers-by take a selfie with the fifty-nine-year-old tagger; a group of bachelorettes with bunny ears, framed by what appears to be the entrance of a night club aptly named BUZ,[69] cheer him on; and a possibly drunk Scotsman praises Dan's courage and holds his hand up like a champ. The camera espouses the diegetic audience's point of view from the opposite sidewalk, inviting us to watch Dan's act from their perspective. Though all eyes are momentarily on Dan, potentially including those of many unseen netsurfers (the name of the nightclub, which recalls the contemporary practice of creating an online buzz, would seem to allude to the possibility), the political revolt expressed by his act is largely lost on them, and the figure of the political artist is turned into a clown, with the grotesque Scotsman ultimately taking over Dan's role when he gets arrested. The significance of Dan's act is not, however, lost on us, the film's actual viewers, because we benefit from the two perspectives—Dan the individual and Dan the tagger—hence the significance of the positioning of this scene in the final act and of the alternation between very long and medium shots. It is not lost on us either because the Scotsman is very much the equivalent of the fool of Renaissance drama, a modern-day Falstaff, a debt the film seems to acknowledge when the character salutes "Sir Daniel Blake." After all, the minor character is responsible both for turning the solemn moment into farce and uttering the film's most explicit political accusation, one Daniel's pride and self-reliance have made him incapable of expressing:

276 *Meta in Film and Television Series*

Figures 11.4.1–11.4.3 I, Daniel Blake: *Daniel Blake's "new art installation" and its immediate and networked audience.*

> Hey, a miscarriage of justice, eh. [...] You should be arresting the wankers who came up with sanctions. Eh? That preachy baldy cunt. What's his name? Ian Duncan fucking what-his-face. Aye, and the posh dicks in their mansions who came up with the fucking bedroom tax for disabled—Listen, youse are all gonna be out of a fucking job anyway. Privatizing you, eh? All the fucking Tories, man. Aye, members of the fucking big club, eh. Fucking posh Eton twats. Sir Daniel fucking Blake, pal! Hey, should be a statue made for you, pal. Fucking Sir Daniel Blake! Yer a fucking beauty!

The politics of both Dan's art installation and the film are thus made explicit.

Dan is allowed a second chance to make a statement: the letter he has prepared to be read at his appeal is meant to be his very own *j'accuse* based on a firsthand experience Zola didn't have. But a fatal heart attack—a touch of Loachian melodrama—prevents him from accomplishing this second performance, and thus from effectively reaching a broader audience and, more importantly, the representatives of the system. It also prevents the film from becoming a courtroom drama, a mainstream genre that is well suited for pointing the finger at systemic injustices (*Kramer vs. Kramer* [Benton, 1979], *Amistad* [Spielberg, 1997], *Small Axe: Mangrove* [Amazon Prime, McQueen, 2020]). Instead, the film remains firmly entrenched in the kind of social realism the Loach team is famous for. It ends on a small victory. Katie's reading Dan's letter at his funeral for an audience of friends partly breaks what threatened to be a cyclical structure [97:07–98:10]; if the film opens on the disembodied voice of the member of the institution who mistakenly assesses his medical condition [0:34–2:53], Dan, even in death, is entitled to the last word, which would not have been the case had a lawyer been pleading his case. This final scene, which gives its name to the film via the last line of Dan's letter, is the film's second metamoment. It casts a retrospective look on the rest of the film and on Loach's work as a whole. It is hard not to see Daniel (who calls himself Dan) as the double of Kenneth (who calls himself Ken). *I, Daniel Blake*, is, in fact, I, Ken Loach. Not just the man, but the "auteur" that the European art cinema circuit has constructed[70]—which, in reality, is the collective[71] behind the label "a Ken Loach film," including long-time members producer Rebecca O'Brien, screenwriter Paul Laverty, editor Jonathan Morris and composer George Fenton. Together, the two mises en abyme reveal an awareness of some of the stakes involved in making political art, which very much resonate with Rancière's theoretical propositions: a belief that sharing the sensible is a political act; a recognition of the fundamental dissensus between art and politics; and a concern for the efficacy of political art.

The correlation between creating and sharing is established through the film's portrait of the craftsman as an old man. Dan builds things with his own hands, stands up to institutions and their representatives, and steps in to help others in similar or worse predicaments; Katie says of the letter's author that "he wasn't a pauper to [them]" and "gave [them] things that money can't buy." Dan is an exemplar of class solidarity, and his generosity is manifested through his craft (he fixes Katie's house and builds a wooden wind chime for her daughter Daisy). Through its eponymous hero, *I, Daniel Blake* merges two trends Loach's films of the 1990s and 2000s had, according to Hill, adopted: stories of the losers of post-Thatcher Great Britain, and stories of those who fought against oppression in other contexts.[72] Although its plot seems more in line with the films that "explore the consequences for those left with no job at all,"[73] such as *Riff-Raff* (1991), *Raining Stones* (1993) and *My Name Is Joe* (1993), *I, Daniel Blake* also depicts the solidarity between Daniel and his friends and neighbors, recalling the collectives of bygone eras portrayed in *Land and Freedom* (1995) and *The Wind That Shakes the Barley* (2006). This can, perhaps, be put down to Daniel's age; compared to his young friends, the fifty-nine-year-old is a man from another time, one in which work still has meaning, a rarity in Loach's films from the 1990s on.[74] The dystopian state of institutions is thus counterbalanced by the utopian potential of a community[75] whose members strive to help each other regardless of age, gender and racial differences—yet another aspect that is simultaneously celebrated and mocked by the Scotsman when he gives Dan his coat.

The final act of the film thus derives its emotional power from the combination of the drama it depicts and its awareness of its own limitations as a political film. If critics have discussed the ambiguities of the politics of Loach's films,[76] Loach and his team's prime concern has always been how best to reach the audience. "[T]his urge to provoke audiences to 'step back' from the drama, and reflect on the film's relationships to the social world it addresses,"[77] is, according to Hill, what led Loach and Tony Garnett to work with television in the 1960s, and is what prompted Loach's return to cinema in the late 1990s.[78] Loach and his collaborators have had their fair share of success—the 1964 *Wednesday Play* episode movie *Cathy Come Home* and the 1996 *Modern Times* documentary series episode *The Flickering Flame* provoked changes in attitudes and laws.[79] *I, Daniel Blake*'s final scenes seem to suggest that the efficacy of Loach's twenty-first-century films is limited by the fact that they merely succeed to reach those who would attend a Daniel Blake/Kenneth Loach event anyway—and who are thus already sympathetic to the utopian ideal they defend; for the general public, these performances are at best curiosities lost in the flux of media images circulating online. The film's view of the digital age's convergence culture—its capacity to seek and share knowledge—recalls Tony Garnett's worries concerning television; "[f]or Garnett, the weakness of television was its relative ubiquity which meant that films risked getting lost amid the constant flow of material being broadcast."[80] The precariousness of a twenty-first-century Ken Loach film is of a different nature than that of TV programs of the 1960s: like the buzz created by Daniel Blake's art installation, it is doomed to be lost in an ocean of data.

The movie's self-awareness is particularly poignant because it comes so late in the film and in the eighty-year-old director's career—after twenty-two fiction films (not including a variety of TV programs, shorts and documentaries). And yet, Dan's strength of character also echoes Loach's team's determination to keep on making these films in spite of their limited effect, and to keep on making them based on the same generic and political terms—a mixture of objective realism with a hint of melodrama and comedy.[81] The hero thus embodies the ideal Loach's team strives for. Hence the utopian, perhaps even unrealistic, depiction of the working class in this and other films. Dan's group should be interpreted as a fiction of what society could be, and not necessarily what it actually is;[82] it can also be interpreted as a model for what fiction should be: a sharing of the sensible. The representation of technology is treated along equally ambivalent lines. Although it represents an obstacle for the fifty-nine-year-old, the film nonetheless acknowledges the possibility of working-class youths of the world coming together thanks to convergence culture, through the subplot of Dan's young neighbors making a profit selling shoes by collaborating with a Chinese soccer fan named Stan Li (like the famous Marvel comics writer who appears in reflexive cameos in various transmedia adaptations of his work). This potential receives further attention in the 2019 follow-up film *Sorry We Missed You*, in which the son Seb combines Daniel Blake's talent for graffiti and Blake's neighbors' ease with digital media. If Dan's graffiti and letter produce a fairly overt metafictional discourse via mise en abyme, the utopian/dystopian model that structures the film produces a more covert one that recalls Hutcheon's "fantasy model." Though these two discourses work in tandem, it is interesting to note that the most hopeful is ultimately the most covert. It is also that which, instead of admitting a weakness like the overt discourse, seeks to take advantage of what is essentially a handicap—the dissensus between political art and reality—and thus reaffirm the political power of fiction as fiction, and recover the energy to keep on creating such works.

Conclusion

Meta can be political and very much so, a fact that audiences and scholars have become increasingly aware of over time. Rancière's writings indirectly suggest that it is a condition for art to qualify as political. An intense form of reflexivity, meta can inscribe itself within various traditions of subversive anti-illusionism, from Brechtian aesthetics to more popular forms such as the carnivalesque. But while the politics of reflexivity can be limited to the improprieties of formal play and the destabilization of bourgeois tastes, the politics of meta are founded in its aboutness: its awareness of how highly sensitive its material can be calls for a foregrounding and an exploration of the relation between the fiction/art/medium and the world. Meta that is political tends to lean toward the latter term (and thus toward what Wolf calls "extracompositional" metareference). This explains why it can inhabit the unlikeliest of places, such as the naturalist cinema of a Pedro Costa or Ken Loach. Political metamoments address this relation from opposite perspectives: how the work approaches its political material, and thus represents the world, and/or how it means to weigh in politically, and thus change the world. Both perspectives are founded on a contradiction: they express doubt and faith in the work itself and in the power of art and fiction. Doubt emerges from the fact that the relation between the work and the world established by meta is, like that between signifier and signified, founded on a disconnection. Political metamoments can cast doubt on the filmmakers' right to adopt ideological frameworks that are in contradiction with their professional practices as filmmakers. They can cast doubt on the work's ability to reach an audience both physically, imaginatively and politically—that is, to be seen, felt and understood—and thus on the Brechtian and avant-garde credo that distanciation is conducive to active spectatorship and political commitment. They can also cast doubt on the medium's ability to reach the audience, particularly in a contemporary world characterized by hypermediality and the constant renewal of data. With these doubts, the familiar questions of authorship, medium and reception, explored in Chapters 4, 5 and 6, are approached from a political and ethical angle rather than from an aesthetic one. And yet, these doubts coexist alongside faith. A faith that art can express these doubts, can engage with political discourses such as feminism (*The Portrait of a Lady*), Marxism (*Tout va bien*) and its contemporary variants, and convergence culture (*Black Mirror*, *I, Daniel Blake*), as much as it can with aesthetic ones and historiography. It expresses a faith in the politics of aesthetics, in the function of art to distribute the sensible, to allow for a degree of mediation, a tenuous but powerful connection (*Colossal Youth*, *I, Daniel Blake*). Even when in doubt, meta remains a celebration of the potential for even the most pessimistic work of art or fiction to engage simultaneously with its potentials and limitations.

Conclusion

Meta is intense reflexivity; it is a matter of quality; it is an interpretation. Meta is also very messy, and it is this intuition that the reduction of meta-phenomena to just plain "meta" in the popular usage expresses.

Meta is not about the reflexive devices but it certainly mobilizes them. The analyses in this book have demonstrated that many of the devices commonly associated with meta (mise en abyme, metalepsis, direct address and, to a lesser extent, allohistory) are only potentially meta or, rather, have meta potential, that is, can be mobilized in an interpretation that qualifies as meta; parody alone is essentially meta because it supposes a target and is thus interpreted as a critique. While typological approaches have tended to separate the variety of meta-phenomena, with entire books devoted to the movie about making movies, the mise en abyme and metalepsis in particular, the analyses of Part II prove that they are regularly associated and can sometimes even morph into one another. Mises en abyme are standard fare in movies (or series) about making movies (or series) (*Contempt*, *Cult*); the repeated use of a mise en abyme or a motif can produce an allegory of cinema (*Rear Window*) or seriality (*LOST*, *Westworld*); and the sibling devices that are the mise en abyme and the metalepsis can be combined (*WandaVision*) or mutate into the other (S1E3 of *The Prisoner*). If such phenomena would tend to justify the conflation of such terms in the popular usage of "meta," the analyses have also proven that analysis and interpretation beg us to consider and untangle such phenomena together—the mutation of a mise en abyme into a metalepsis, for instance, is also the precise moment when ontological boundaries between fiction and reality collapse within the diegesis. Analyzing meta-phenomena thus requires the use of specific terms such as the movie about making movies and mise en abyme, metalepsis and metanarrative, to make sense of them. From the perspective of film analysis, then, the entanglement of such devices may offset the typological approach since they are meant to be analyzed together, but it nonetheless justifies the definition of such terms as a critical framework. Typologies of reflexivity and meta-phenomena remain relevant enterprises; it is just that with meta such terms are the means, not the end.

The conflation of meta-phenomena in the popular usage of "meta" can also be explained by the frequency with which some of them are used. We have seen that metanarrative comments voiced by characters or voiceovers already existed in classical cinema (*The Big Sleep*, *Sunset Blvd.*), but have become particularly salient in mainstream productions since the 1990s, with specific characters taking on the role of metanarrative commentator or predictor (*Scream*, *Community*), no doubt a symptom of a more popular form of cinephilia whose encyclopedic knowledge was enabled not just by the movies but by television and Internet. The multiplication of screens in the digital age (computers, smartphones, surveillance systems, animated posters) is another important factor; it has enhanced, even in more naturalist works (*The Wire*, *I, Daniel Blake*), the possibility of situations that could accommodate mises en abyme and intermedia reflexivity, which were previously limited to representations of diegetic performances or movie- and television-watching. These two evolutions may further account for the 1990s turn of the meta screw discussed in Chapter 3.

The aboutness of meta is just as deeply entangled as its forms. While, in appearance, my one- or sibling-term title chapters seemed primed to propose a typology of the aboutness of meta, each chapter has repeatedly proven how works or moments that seem to focus primarily on one angle end up engaging with others. Some connections are to be expected, notably between creation, reception and the medium (*Blow-up*), since the three represent the central components of apparatus theory and, more generally, of a communication system. Other connections are perhaps less obvious: between media and history (*Culloden*); creation, spectatorship, medium and genre (*Mulholland Dr.*); medium, seriality and politics (*The Prisoner*); creation, materiality and history (*Fellini Roma*, *No*); adaptation, genre, medium and history (*Bram Stoker's Dracula*); creation, spectatorship, medium and politics (*Colossal Youth*); medium, adaptation, genre and seriality (*Twin Peaks: The Return*); creation, reception, medium, genre, history and politics (*Inglourious Basterds*). If meta is a matter of quality, then it is these works, which I have described as intensely meta, that qualify most as metafilms/metaseries or instances of metacinema/metatelevision, more so even than hypermeta works in which meta-phenomena are more apparent and numerous (*Scream*, *Community*). This intensity can be also be limited to a metamoment, as in the *Queen Kelly* screening in *Sunset Blvd.* (a mise en abyme that foregrounds both cinema's and the star's historicity and materiality) or the eponymous hero's art installation scene in *I, Daniel Blake* (a mise en abyme that explores the creation of political art and its potential reception).

The focus of meta is just as entangled as its concerns. The fact that many metamoments provide a statement of intent with which to approach the work itself lends some credence to the charge of narcissism made against all things meta. Yet the analyses have repeatedly demonstrated that even an interpretation that seems focused primarily on the functioning of the work itself engages more broadly with its form or medium (*Dead Man* with the history of the Western genre, *The Portrait of a Lady* with the history and theory of representations of women) and can even open onto the world (the painting in *This Is Us* is not just a blueprint for the series, it also invites us to consider our own relationship to the series as a means to make sense of our own lives). Such examples destabilize distinctions between meta that is concerned with the creation, reception and materiality of the work itself or in general (Wolf's intra- vs. extra-composition metareference, LaRocca's "reflexive" vs. "referential" awareness) on the one hand, or with the medium or truth (Wolf's fictio- and fictum-centered metareference) on the other. There are no doubt degrees of focus—and of narcissism—but in practice meta as theory in practice potentially englobes more than the work itself. Meta's entanglement is thus a question of form (the devices common to reflexivity), content and focus (the aboutness specific to meta).

Meta-phenomena are not only entangled formally and thematically; they are brought together by the interpretive act that creates the framework we call meta. Meta emerges from our ability to identify these devices or stakes and formulate an interpretive framework that is about the work, its medium and its role in the world. Meta is interpretation because it requires us to "actualize" it (Hutcheon), to "make sense of it" (Dougie in *Twin Peaks: The Return*), to create it (hence the frequent collapsing of creation and reception). It invites us to disentangle the strands and formulate its theoretical propositions about creation and reception, its forms and its medium, its aesthetic and political potential, and, more profoundly, about its relation to the world. Even in the case of hypermeta where meta is spelled out within the diegesis, we are invited to look beyond the playful profusion of surface meta in search of a framework that engages more profoundly with the work's "meta-ness" (*Scream*, *Community*).

This is where the question of explicitness comes in. The degree of explicitness can concern just as much form and content: a movie about making movies is obviously about cinema and a metanarrative comment uttered by a character is arguably easier to pick up on (*Scream*, *Community*) than non-verbal modes of reflexivity (*Blow-up*, *Blow Out*). They may, however, be easier to overlook in works whose genres are not expected to be fertile terrain for reflexivity (*Colossal Youth*, *I, Daniel Blake*). But the analyses herein have also demonstrated that the question of explicitness and implicitness is not only a matter of degree but of location, simultaneity and/or accumulation. Works are rarely meta through and through, and metamoments regularly occupy key positions such as beginnings, endings and intervals, moments that typically mark the transition from the real world or other programs to the work. Often, a metanarrative comment will draw attention to the more general phenomenon at work and explicate the theory underlying the practice (the magician's words in *Mulholland Dr.*'s Silencio scene). Similarly, a string of metanarrative comments or the serialization of a motif will repeatedly draw attention to the meta potential and encourage us to make sense of it. Explicitness is not just a matter of genre or formal devices. An allegory can be more or less obvious, and the underlying structures of diegetic metafiction, which Hutcheon labeled covert, can operate overtly while retaining their meta potential: they are relevant because they are structuring, not quasi-invisible. The fact that these structures are regularly combined, though one in particular may be favored, is another characteristic of meta's entanglement; it supposes a multifarious view of our engagement with art and fiction as hermeneutics *and* immersion *and* sensuality *and* play, points to how these modes of engagement can interact, and ultimately seems to suggest that play is, in effect, the common denominator.

Meta regularly inscribes itself within the history of the medium, invites us "to consider the full expanse of cinematic history,"[1] as well as the history of that medium's theory, a practice inherited from the avant-gardes via art cinema. Metatextuality—which establishes a critical dialogue with other works through frequent recourse to intertexts, direct engagement with hypotexts, investigation of architexts—can be historicized, notably by exploring a film's or series's position in a genre's history *(My Name Is Nobody, Dead Man, Mulholland Dr., Community)* or even in art history *(Contempt)*. Works can also grapple with the theoretical debates that have informed film and audiovisual media at least since the invention of cinema. The tension between formalist and realist ontologies of cinema is explored in *Blow-up*, *Blow Out* and *Bram Stoker's Dracula*, while works like *Fellini Roma*, *Family Viewing*, *Twin Peaks* and *Mulholland Dr.* make a case for the auratic quality of reproducible audiovisual media (thus contra Benjamin), sometimes by demonstrating the memorializing power of the photographic image (thus siding with Sontag and Barthes). Through the practice of meta, film and media theory is illustrated, resolved and/or cast in doubt (convergence culture in S1E1 of *Black Mirror*). Meta's potential to theorize is by no means limited to its own medium, and thus to engagement with film and media theory. It can also dialogue with feminism *(The Portrait of a Lady)*, Marxism *(Tout va bien)* and postmodernist philosophy *(JFK, Scream, Funny Games, No)*, and can fulfill a historiographic function, exploring how the representation of history in a given medium or genre mirrors and participates in the writing of history *(Culloden, Bram Stoker's Dracula, Dead Man, Inglourious Basterds)*, or foregrounding the fact that each new representation of history is participating in this enterprise (*No*). The messiness of meta allows it to accommodate multiple, even contradictory interpretations (and I am here anticipating interpretations that will contradict my own), and it is this openness that ensures its continued relevance. A film like *Rear Window* will presumably always remain of interest because its take on spectatorship (and on creation and the medium) is so much more than its director's and its period's conception of spectatorship. Similarly, a film like *Fellini Roma*, an ideal illustration of cinema as a synchretic art, can invite us to consider the theoretical legacy of the early-twentieth-century writings to more recent theories of intermediality and remediation. Though the overbearing presence of meta in today's mediascape may partly be a symptom of the zeitgeist, the very fact that meta does not make sense on its own, that it is not (unlike theory) a text but a subtext we interpret, ensures its continued relevance, for new audiences will necessarily activate it in new ways (although, granted, a theoretical text can also be reinterpreted in novel ways).

Meta is theory in practice. It invites us to be analytical. It also leads us to realize not only that fiction and art are vital human activities that offer a variety of pleasures and teachings, but also that the relationship between fiction/art and the world is founded in the human. Regardless of the entry point that had been announced in each chapter title, many of the analyses have led us through a variety of concerns involving art, fiction and media to ethical questions involving sharing (*Community*, *Colossal Youth*), care (*Scream*), freedom (*The Prisoner*), responsibility (*Culloden*) and commitment (*I, Daniel Blake*). Meta is predicated on the idea that our relationship to fiction mirrors our relationship to the world. As such, meta, and this has to my knowledge never been fully recognized, is underpinned by ethical considerations. Potentially, all narratives have ethical value—Paul Ricœur famously described narrative as *"the first laboratory of moral judgment."*[2] But with meta, this ethical value is what emerges from our engagement with the work's layeredness, an entanglement that is latent in the Greek etymology: through meta, we are made to engage "with" the work and its relation to the world, and potentially "beyond" that relation. The ethics of meta is thus that which interrogates the ethics of the work, that is, the work's relation to the world. This was implicit in Waugh's definition of metafiction as "pos[ing] questions about the relationship between fiction and reality"; it has recently been reasserted by LaRocca when he posits that metacinema "give[s] us back to our own reality anew, differently."[3] But the specificity of this relation is that it is mediated by meta, and thus by those who interpret the work as meta: us. The ethics of meta thus concerns our own work in the "*laboratory of moral judgement*," our elaboration of an interpretation of the work's relation to the world. As we are implicated in this interpretation, we are implicated in this relation: the work's relation to the world is potentially our own mediation of our own relation to the world, starting with our own realization that art, fiction and the world are human constructs. Meta thus proves our own profound entanglement with meta.

If one judges meta by its cover, meta can be an entangled affair politically speaking as well, and, like reflexivity, is by no means subversive per se. Meta can serve to aggressively mark one's territory in a crowded competitive mediascape (*Married with . . . Children*); it might serve to assert the artist's brilliance and place in cultural history (*My Name Is Nobody*) or condemn the audience and mediascape (*Funny Games*, S1E1 of *Black Mirror*). But it can also be the last line of defense of an essential human activity, a desperate plea for the necessity and vitality of art and fiction (*Colossal Youth, I, Daniel Blake*). Through meta, art and fiction are made relevant because meta taps into their potential as critical entertainment, as theory in practice, as sensual, immersive hermeneutic play. Even at its most critical and even in the bleakest (*Colossal Youth*) or most pessimistic (*Black Mirror*) of works, meta is, in the end, always a celebration of art and fiction, of aesthetics overcoming economics, of its capacity to touch and be shared, and, at the very least, to express an awareness of its own limitations and precariousness, starting with art and fiction's disconnection from the world. As an invitation to interpretation, meta is an invitation to defend the value of art and fiction and actively establish a connection anyway. As a process, then, meta empowers us by asking us to surmount the disconnection; it trusts our capacity to do so—yet another legacy of a part of the avant-gardes. The responsibility, then, falls on us, as scholars, teachers and fans, to avoid enforcing power relations by imposing monolithic views and rejecting the diverse modes of engagement and the variety of interpretations meta may allow.

This leads us to the most obvious blind spot in *Meta in Film and Television Series*—documentary—which is due as much to lack of space as to my own limitations as a scholar. Reflexivity and meta-phenomena have long been a concern of documentary film theory. As early as 1989, Carl Plantinga described the "metadocumentary" as having "the epistemic function of explicitly examining the documentary and representation," and cited *Man with a Movie Camera* and Chris Marker's 1958 *Letter from Siberia* and 1983 *Sans Soleil* as paradigmatic examples.[4] Bill Nichols, in his 2001 typology of the six modes of documentary, identified a "reflexive mode," which "calls attention to the assumptions and conventions that govern documentary filmmaking" and "[i]ncreases our awareness of the constructedness of the film's representation of reality"[5]; Nichols also cites *Man with a Movie Camera*, as well as Peter Watkins's 1966 pseudo-documentary *The War Game* and Jill Godmilow's re-enacted documentary *Far from Poland* (1984). Fernando Andacht enlists

Peircian semiotics in his critique of self-reflexivity in documentary, which he sees as driven by a "self-conscious ordeal" grounded in a "doctrine of dualism" that does little to help elucidate the genre: "documentaries do reveal aspects of the real in a way still little understood but which should not be obscured by a reflexive analysis which accounts for everything which is shown by these kinds of representation as a fiction or a mere fabrication."[6] We recognize, here, the familiar charges of solipsism and elitism. What follows is an attempt to associate the findings of *Meta in Film and Television Series* with the literature on the reflexive- or meta-documentary in order to formulate a few working hypotheses regarding meta in documentaries.

The distinction between reflexivity and meta as an intense mode of reflexivity remains operable for documentary and is actually spelled out in the combination of Plantinga's and Nichols's definitions: reflexivity "calls attention," whereas meta "examines." *Man with a Movie Camera* alone proves that documentaries can be through and through meta and that many reflexive devices (mises en abyme, metaphors for the camera eye, attention to the film's materiality and the screen's surface, etc.[7]) operate similarly in documentary and fiction. Documentaries can also be punctuated by singular metamoments that provide frameworks to comprehend the work's relationship to its material. The 1961 *Chronicle of a Summer* famously opens with Edgar Morin and Jean Rouch defining *cinéma vérité* and musing on its possibilities, and closes on the pair discussing a test audience's reaction to their film; the opening scenes of *Waltz with Bashir* [Folman, 2008], Yotam Shibolet argues, foreground the differences between Ari Folman's "reflexive and meta" approach to documentary filmmaking and his diegetic namesake's more "traditional" approach[8]). The inclusion of incongruous elements (Bollywood musical scenes in *The Act of Killing*[9] [Oppenheimer and Cynn, 2012]) can become highly reflexive by creating a disruption within the reality-based fabric of the documentary, much like the opposite phenomenon of documentary erupting in fiction (as in *No* and *Fruitvale Station*, or Godard's *The Riflemen* which mixes fairy tale and documentary elements[10]). Thomas E. Wartenberg describes how, in *The Act of Killing*, the re-enactment of torture scenes by the actual perpetrators produces an "ontological collapse," "where occupying the position of a victim of torture [in a 'fictional' re-enactment] results in an emotional experience that undermines his [Congo's] ability to separate his playacting from the reality of his situation"[11]—a situation that sounds eerily like metalepsis.

Meta in documentary can very much engage with all of the concerns explored in this book: industry, fandom, and authorship (in *Exit through the Gift Shop* [Banksy, 2010], the graffiti artist ends up making a documentary about the fan who was making a documentary about him); the use of historical material and its historiographic potential (Godard's documentary series *Histoire(s) du cinéma* [Canal+, 1989–9], whose thesis is that "film history is the story of a missed opportunity to engage with its century's history"[12]); its political efficacy (Godard's segment in the 1967 collective documentary *Loin du Vietnam*, in which the voiceover expresses doubt as to how to approach the war and notes that the French working class doesn't watch Godard's films even though they both adhere to anticapitalist ideas). Meta specific to documentary addresses the paradox at the heart of documentary practice and of contemporary documentary theory—that documentary mediates and thus constructs the reality it seeks to document. In 1983 already, Bill Nichols stated that "documentaries were forms of representation, never clear windows onto 'reality'; the film-maker was always a participant-witness and active fabricator of meaning."[13] The "anti-positivist critique of conventional documentary filmmaking with its alleged objectivity and neutrality"[14] emerged, like metafiction, in the 1970s and is apparent, according to Dagmar Brunow, in the Black British cinema of the 1980s (Brunow discusses *Handsworth Songs* [Akomfrah, 1986] in particular). Shibolet suggests that the digital age has, no doubt, intensified the manipulation of images, but it has also revealed that the "era of video evidence was just a temporary fluke."[15] By emphasizing the transformative power of film, a majority of documentary theory has, therefore, sided with Vertov against John Grierson (for "betraying documentary's radical potential"[16]), and, beyond documentary, with the formalists against the realists. Putting theory into practice, the "reflexive mode" similarly "emphasizes epistemological doubt" and "stresses the deformative intervention of the cinematic apparatus in the process of representation."[17]

Meta is likely to be just as entangled in documentary as in fiction, if not more so. While reflexivity in fiction tends to flaunt the construction of a fictional world, in documentary it flaunts the construction of the real world as a quasi-fictionalization. With fiction, the transformation of reality is a given and even an asset, the conditions for immersion and play; with documentary, it is a problem, one that may impede the kind of immersion in reality a documentary could otherwise provide. In both cases, reflexivity works to break immersion (in the fiction or recreated reality), while meta works to negotiate the relation between the fictional or recreated world and the actual world. Indeed, the thin line that separates the documentary from its material (the mediation by an interviewer, a camera, a microphone, the footage in the editing room) makes the relationship between a documentary film or series and the world at once more obvious and more problematic than the relationship between fiction and the world. Self-consciousness regarding the constructedness of reality can lead the documentary to be perpetually walking the razor's edge, on the verge of transgressing its ontological boundaries, and thus of metalepsis in a genre that is paradoxically founded on continuity between the documentary and the world. This tightrope act is not only aesthetic but ethical and political. Indeed, another prime concern of both documentarians and documentary theory involves the "burden of responsibility" the documentarian has vis-à-vis her/his material"—to report on it fairly and accurately" and to consider "the effect of their acts on the lives of those filmed."[18] Documentaries are peopled with real people, not characters; the question of the filmed subject's freedom is thus even more problematic in documentary than in fiction.

Theorizing through practice, meta in documentary interrogates the genre's potential to document reality as well as its politics, ethics and limitations. Shibolet, for instance, analyzes the eruption of "archival footage of inconceivable violence" at the end of the animated documentary *Waltz with Bashir* not as a paradoxical assertion of the power of indexical images which the film has striven to deconstruct, but, rather, as a confirmation that they fail to provide access to the actual experience of the other: "rather than downplaying Israeli responsibility, I view the ending as authentically portraying the difficulty in meaningfully perceiving it when focalized through an Israeli perspective."[19] For Shibolet, "[i]ndexical proof is not presented as inherently deceitful, but rather as inherently partial and dependent on the context of its creation and interpretation."[20] Meta in documentary has in common with meta in fiction that it interrogates the dis-connection between the work and the world, and like fiction, documentary is saved by its capacity to do so. If it is still our interpretive acts that do the connecting, in the case of documentary, emphasis is put, however slightly, on disconnection. In our poststructuralist, postmodernist, hypermedia day and age, the difference between meta in documentary and fiction, I would venture, is but one of degree.

Notes

CHAPTER 1

1. https://www.dailyxtra.com/pedro-almodovar-gets-personal-with-pain-and-glory-162835, accessed 12 May 2021.
2. https://variety.com/2019/film/reviews/cannes-film-review-pedro-almodovars-pain-and-glory-1203218880/#!, accessed 12 May 2021.
3. https://uproxx.com/sepinwall/for-community-how-much-meta-is-too-much, accessed 12 May 2021.
4. https://tv.avclub.com/scream-queens-gets-meta-as-hell-with-a-few-ghost-stori-1798185699, accessed 12 May 2021.
5. https://mondaymorningmoviequarterback.wordpress.com/2017/10/17/the-cabin-in-the-woods-meta-horror, accessed 12 May 2021.
6. https://www.reddit.com/r/rickandmorty/comments/750j98/is_the_show_getting_too_meta, accessed 12 May 2021.
7. https://www.comingsoon.net/tv/features/1158542-the-13-best-meta-episodes-of-supernatural, accessed 12 May 2021.
8. https://www.looper.com/316835/the-most-meta-episodes-in-tv-history, accessed 27 December 2021.
9. https://www.mad-movies.com/fr/module/99999735/2382/meta-slasher, accessed 12 May 2021.
10. https://lecinemaavecungranda.com/2018/11/09/apres-seance-the-house-that-jack-built, accessed 12 May 2021. My translation.
11. https://www.espinof.com/listas/todas-peliculas-quentin-tarantino-ordenadas-peor-a-mejor, accessed 12 May 2021.
12. https://www.merriam-webster.com/dictionary/meta, accessed 12 May 2021.
13. https://www.dictionary.com/browse/meta?s=t, accessed 12 May 2021.
14. https://www.merriam-webster.com/words-at-play/meta-adjective-self-referential, accessed 11 May 2021.
15. https://www.today.com/popculture/seinfeld-stars-reunite-yada-yada-yada-wbna32693291, accessed 11 May 2021.
16. Abel 59.
17. Angus, *Metadrama and the Informer in Shakespeare and Jonson* 4.
18. Gass 24–5; Wolf, "Metareference across Media" 3.
19. White x.

20. Genette, *Palimpsests* 11.
21. Stam, *Reflexivity* xx.
22. Metz, *Impersonal Enunciation* 58–94.
23. Metz, *Impersonal Enunciation* 94.
24. Fredericksen 300.
25. Fredericksen 312.
26. Fredericksen 305.
27. Siska 287.
28. Metz, *Impersonal Enunciation* 72, 74.
29. Stam, *Reflexivity* xiv.
30. Von Dassanowsky vii–ix.
31. Carter 11.
32. Stuckey 3.
33. Cerisuelo, *Hollywood* 92–3, my translation.
34. Chinita, "Metacinema as Authorial Enunciation."
35. Chinita, "The Tricks of the Trade" 7.
36. Chinita, "The Tricks of the Trade" 7–8; Stam, *Reflexivity* 43–55, 102–4.
37. See Rebekah Brammer's 2019 article "Peeling Back the Layers: Exploring Metafiction in *Birdman or (The Unexpected Virtue of Ignorance)*."
38. Wolf, "Metareference across Media" 5, 11.
39. LaRocca 8.
40. LaRocca 2.
41. Sitney 118.
42. Ames 21, 25, 31, 33.
43. Ames 13.
44. Wolf, "Metareference across Media" 3.
45. Hutcheon, *Narcissistic Narrative* 18.
46. Waugh 1.
47. Hutcheon, *Narcissistic Narrative* 47.
48. McHale 52, 196, 198, 205, 229.
49. Hutcheon, *Narcissistic Narrative* 7–8.
50. Stam, *Reflexivity* iv.
51. Withalm 128.
52. Metz, *Impersonal Enunciation* 74; *Énonciation impersonelle* 21.
53. This is confirmed in one parenthesis in particular ("which is metafilmic and more fully reflexive" *Impersonal Enunciation* 222).
54. Cerisuelo, *Hollywood* 85.
55. Metz, *Impersonal Enunciation* 379.
56. Metz, *Impersonal Enunciation* 158.
57. Wolf, "Metareference across Media" 22.
58. https://www.etymonline.com/word/meta-, accessed 22 March 2022.
59. https://www.etymonline.com/word/meta-, accessed 22 March 2022.
60. The first entry in fourth edition of *The American Heritage Dictionary*.
61. Cohan also uses the word when introducing the Hollywood backstudio picture (4).

62. Wolf, "Metareference across Media" 12.
63. Nöth 8.
64. Wolf, "Metareference across Media" 44–5.
65. Wolf, "Metareference across Media" 3, 9–10.
66. Wolf, "Metareference across Media" 7, 37–8.
67. Wolf, "Metareference across Media" 15.
68. Wolf, "Metareference across Media" 15.
69. Wolf, "Metareference across Media" 18.
70. Wolf, "Metareference across Media" 12.
71. Wolf, "Metareference across Media" 17.
72. Wolf, "Metareference across Media" 22.
73. Wolf, "Metareference across Media" 43–4.
74. Roche, *Quentin Tarantino* 9.
75. Yacavone, "Cognitive and Affective Dimensions"; LaRocca 11.
76. Jörg Metelmann and Scott Loren, in their book *Irritation of Life*, use the term when discussing the flashback structure of *Usual Suspects* (Synger, 1995) and *Titanic* (Cameron, 1997) (50) or the way *Mulholland Drive* (Lynch, 2001) comments "on the immersive spaces of melodramatic cinema" (127), Rui Gonçalves Miranda when analyzing the spectator's "comprehension of the diverse layers [. . .] at play" in *Our Beloved Month of August* (Gomes, 2008) (46).
77. Siska 285.
78. Fredericksen 301.
79. Stam, *Reflexivity* 29–70.
80. Hutcheon, *Narcissistic Narrative* 23, 28, 48–56.
81. Stam, *Reflexivity* 19.
82. Wolf, "Metareference across Media" 31.
83. Roche, *Making and Remaking Horror* 147–52.
84. Wolf, "Metareference across Media" 31.

CHAPTER 2

1. Févry, *La Mise en abyme filmique*; Boillat, "*Stranger than Fiction*"; Limoges, "La métalepse au cinéma"; Limoges, "Réflexivité métaphorique."
2. Hutcheon, *Narcissistic Narrative* 6.
3. Hutcheon, *Narcissistic Narrative* 23.
4. Hutcheon, *Narcissistic Narrative* 7.
5. Hutcheon, *Narcissistic Narrative* 28–9.
6. Hutcheon, *Narcissistic Narrative* 31–3.
7. Hutcheon, *Narcissistic Narrative* 88.
8. Hutcheon, *Narcissistic Narrative* 136.
9. Hutcheon, *Narcissistic Narrative* 120.
10. Hutcheon, *Narcissistic Narrative* 154.
11. Waugh 19.
12. Ryan 270–2.

13. Wolf, "Metareference across Media" 36–43.
14. Wolf, "Metareference across Media" 37.
15. Ryan 270.
16. Wolf, "Metareference across Media" 37.
17. Wolf, "Metareference across Media" 38.
18. Wolf, "Metareference across Media" 38.
19. Wolf, "Metareference across Media" 43.
20. Withalm 125–9.
21. Stuckey 3.
22. Sibony, *Entre-deux*.
23. Yacavone, "Cognitive and Affective Dimensions."
24. Wolf, "Metareference across Media" 63.
25. Wolf, "Metareference across Media" 63.
26. Sirvent 69; Tore 249.
27. Metz, *Impersonal Enunciation* 42.
28. Hutcheon, *Narcissistic Narrative* 54–6.
29. Wolf, "Metareference across Media" 48.
30. Wolf, "Metareference across Media" 59.
31. Wolf, "Metareference across Media" 55.
32. Hutcheon, *Narcissistic Narrative* 6.
33. Wolf, "Metareference across Media" 25.
34. Wolf, "Metareference across Media" 47.
35. Tore 250, 257.
36. Fish 14.
37. Gelly and Roche 17.
38. Wolf, "Metareference across Media" 26.
39. Hutcheon, *Narcissistic Narrative* 7.
40. Wolf, "Metareference across Media" 26.
41. Eco, *Limits of Interpretation* 50–4.
42. Lacan 179.
43. Hutcheon, *Narcissistic Narrative* 145.
44. Waugh 2.
45. Hutcheon, *Narcissistic Narrative* 27.
46. Wolf, "Metareference across Media" 17.
47. Waugh 34–49.
48. Waugh 43.
49. Waugh 12.
50. Waugh 9.
51. Waugh 49.
52. Waugh 18.
53. Schaeffer 32–50, 120–6.

CHAPTER 3

1. Gunning 64.
2. Stam, *Reflexivity* 77–8.
3. Fredericksen 302.
4. James 4.
5. James 81.
6. James 270; Limoges, "La métalepse" 132–5.
7. Feuer 102–10; Stam, *Reflexivity* 90–4, 129; James 21.
8. Clover 168.
9. Bordwell, *Narration in the Fiction Film* 209–10.
10. Fredericksen 302.
11. Stam, *Reflexivity* 177–84.
12. Thompson and Bordwell 419, 478.
13. McHale 3–25; Hutcheon, *A Poetics of Postmodernism* 3–8.
14. Stam, *Reflexivity* 8–10.
15. Wolf, "Is There a Metareferential Turn?" 9.
16. Wolf, "Is There a Metareferential Turn?" 6–7.
17. Wolf, "Is There a Metareferential Turn?" 7.
18. Wolf, "Is There a Metareferential Turn?" 16–17.
19. Wolf, "Is There a Metareferential Turn?" 13.
20. Wolf, "Is There a Metareferential Turn?" 16.
21. Wolf, "Is There a Metareferential Turn?" 25–9.
22. Nöth 3; Colapietro 31.
23. Wolf, "Is There a Metareferential Turn?" 29–32.
24. Wolf, "Is There a Metareferential Turn?" 32–6.
25. Böhn 152.
26. Wolf, "Is There a Metareferential Turn?" 28, 31.
27. Collins 249.
28. Behlil 111–14.
29. Hagener and de Valck 25.
30. Jenkins 146.
31. See Erika Fülop.
32. Mittell 16.
33. Yacavone, "Cognitive and Affective Dimensions."
34. Wolfe, *The Metareferential Turn in Contemporary Arts and Media* vi.
35. Wolfe, *The Metareferential Turn in Contemporary Arts and Media* vii.
36. Hutcheon, *Narcissistic Narrative* 2.
37. Hutcheon, *Narcissistic Narrative* 30.
38. Hutcheon, *Narcissistic Narrative* 2; Waugh 38.
39. Hutcheon, *Narcissistic Narrative* 42, 72, 76, 78, 98, 100, 142; Waugh 84, 91, 134.
40. Balogun 261.
41. Ohmovère 61.

42. McHale discusses Rushdie's *Midnight Children* on several occasions, Hutcheon Coetzee and Rushie's *Shame* in her chapter on historiographic metafiction.
43. See, for instance, Luebering (ed.), *The Literature of Spain and Latin America* 130; Kong, *The Raiders and Writers of Cervantes' Archive: Borges, Puig and Márquez*.
44. Mwangi 27.
45. Mwangi x–xi.
46. See Katarzyna Lipińska.
47. See A.P. Anupama's 2018 article "Deconstructiong the Spectator through Meta-Cinema: Bharathiraja's 'Bommalattam'."
48. Napier 24, 35.
49. Stuckey 2.
50. Stuckey 19.
51. Ragel, *Le Film en suspens* 63, my translation.
52. See Ragel, "L'Olivier du Gilan."
53. Limoges, "Réflexivité métaphorique" 52–4.
54. Jakobson 186.
55. Genette, *Narrative Discourse* 228–9, 231–4.
56. Genette, *Palimpsests* 4.
57. Barbara Pfeifer and Henry Keazor are, in fact, the only contributors on film and television in Wolf's two volumes to cite Hutcheon and McHale.
58. Unlike Leonard and Barbara Quart who deplore *Ragtime*'s (1981) "traditional narrative" (72) and betrayal of its politics (72–3), Joanna E. Rapf notes that "it is about volatile forms and the function of cinema to order those forms and create 'history'" (19). The film does incorporate some reflexive devices (intertextuality through the casting of James Cagney and Norman Mailer, abrupt cutting), but fails to propose a discourse on "the importance of creating history, of giving form to the disjunctive, chaotic experiences of life" (20). The exception, according to Rapf, is the newsreel sequence that "reflects Doctorow's vision about the recording of history," but it "passes so fast it is almost unnoticeable" (21). Rapf's analysis would suggest this specific scene qualifies as a metamoment.
59. Southern 4–5.
60. Nile Southern's 2012 presentation of the film insists on the experimental and political dimensions of the film, and on how it "captured [. . .] the tumultuous Zeitgeist of its times" (4), but there is no mention of its reflexive or metafictional qualities.
61. Neupert 300–30.
62. Neupert 19–20.
63. Waugh 1.
64. Hutcheon and Waugh mainly discuss the works of Robbe-Grillet and Sarraute and do not mention Duras.
65. Neupert 62.
66. Neupert 276.
67. Neupert 329.

68. Neupert 236.
69. In his preface to Douchet's *La Nouvelle Vague*, Dominique Païni only notes that the Nouvelle Vague was contemporary to abstract art and the Nouveau Roman and "reflected an era of conquest, transition and growth" (9, my translation); Yannick Rolandeau merely inscribes the Nouvelle Vague within 1950s youth culture in France (Dadism, Nouveau Roman) and around the world (rock music) (25–6).
70. Douchet, *Nouvelle Vague* 13, my translation.
71. See Jovanovic, *Brechtian Cinemas*.
72. Takayuki 72–4.
73. Waugh 10.
74. Hutcheon, *Narcissistic Narrative* 110–11.
75. Albera, *L'Avant-garde* 144.
76. Albera, *L'Avant-garde* 25.
77. Huyssen vii–ix; see also Friedberg 163–4.
78. Bordwell, *Narration in the Fiction Film* 210–11, 233.
79. Stam, *Reflexivity* xvii, 8, 90, 169, 182, 254.
80. Albera, *L'Avant-garde* 144.
81. Hicks 46.
82. James 86–8.
83. James 89, 399.
84. Albera, *L'Avant-garde* 146, 152.
85. Thompson and Bordwell 155; Biesen 188–9.
86. Eimert 159.
87. Albera, *L'Avant-garde* 153.
88. Sitney 206.
89. Sitney 28.
90. Sitney 225, 391.
91. Stam, *Reflexivity* 159.
92. Bordwell, *Narration in the Fiction Film* 66, 160.
93. Deleyto, "Self-consciousness and the Classical Text" 25.
94. Humphries 119, 121–2.
95. James 45–6.
96. Sitney 30, 90.
97. Brenez, *Cinémas d'avant-garde* 3; see also James 400.
98. Albera, *L'Avant-garde* 144.
99. Albera, *L'Avant-garde* 147–8.
100. James 54; Sitney 331–8.
101. Brenez, *Manifestations* 182.
102. Albera, *L'Avant-garde* 147–8.
103. Casetti 41.
104. Spies, *La Télévision dans le miroir*.
105. Morreale 40–1.
106. Denis 167, 183.

107. Jones, *Honey I'm Home!* 169.
108. Biltereyst 107; Couldry 41.
109. Hill, *Reality TV* 76.
110. Edwards 79–80.
111. Metz 30–2.
112. Edwards 79.
113. Wilkie 15–16.
114. *Rethinking the Children's Television Act for a Digital Media Age*, 22 July 2009, p. 25.
115. Mittell 19, 46, 60–1, 99, 208.
116. See Noël Carroll's reading of Stanley Cavell's *The World Viewed* (349).
117. Michelson, "The Man with the Movie"; Metz, *Impersonal Enunciation* 87, 102; Stam, *Reflexivity* 82.
118. Michelson, *Kinetic Icon* 115.
119. Fredericksen 309–10.
120. Stam, *Reflexivity* 80–1.
121. Stam, *Reflexivity* 98.
122. Stam, *Reflexivity* 78.
123. James 21.
124. Goudet 51.
125. Kràl 207.
126. Goudet 74.
127. Goudet 78, my translation.
128. Smith, *Buster Keaton* 177.
129. James 21.
130. Gabriele 28.
131. Elsaesser and Hagener 81.
132. Metz 86.
133. Tore 256.

CHAPTER 4

1. Ames 9; Withalm 131–4; Cohan 11; Belloï, "Des images."
2. Cerisuelo, *Hollywood* 81, 97.
3. Ames 7–8.
4. Cerisuelo, *Hollywood* 73; Achemchame, "La naissance."
5. Cohan 19–48.
6. Ames 12, 14.
7. Ames 10; Cohan 12–15.
8. Ames 4.
9. Cohan 12.
10. Cohan 15.
11. Stam, *Reflexivity* 109–10.
12. Cerisuelo, *Hollywood* 250.
13. Cullen 9.

14. Cerisuelo, *Hollywood* 129.
15. Ames 1; Cohan 49–84.
16. Ames 29.
17. Stam, *Reflexivity* 86; Cerisuelo, *Hollywood* 267.
18. Ames 57.
19. Cohan 14.
20. Cerisuelo, *Hollywood* 142–6; Achemchame, "La naissance."
21. Menegaldo 146.
22. Cohan 1.
23. Stam, *Reflexivity* 85.
24. Phillips 123.
25. Stam, *Reflexivity* 86.
26. Cerisuelo, *Hollywood* 267.
27. Ames 198.
28. Stam, *Reflexivity* 86.
29. Cerisuelo, *Hollywood* 236.
30. Cerisuelo, *Hollywood* 264–5.
31. Phillips 115.
32. Phillips 110.
33. Phillips 115.
34. Phillips 118.
35. Cerisuelo, *Hollywood* 241.
36. Cerisuelo, *Hollywood* 243–5, 253.
37. Cerisuelo, *Hollywood* 243.
38. Phillips 115; Ames 205.
39. Limoges, "Réflexivité métaphorique" 52–4.
40. Stam, *Reflexivity* 89.
41. The motif of doors and gates (the Paramount gate, of course, but also the front door where Joe parts with Betty) delimits the boundaries between worlds.
42. Albera, *Les Formalistes* 9.
43. Ames 200.
44. Ames 199.
45. Ames 221.
46. Cerisuelo, *Le Mépris* 53.
47. Cerisuelo, *Le Mépris* 10; Marie 159.
48. Bondanella 161.
49. Marie 264, my translation.
50. Marie 229.
51. Marie 229, 251–3.
52. Stam, *Reflexivity* 102.
53. Cerisuelo, *Le Mépris* 85, my translation.
54. Stam, *Reflexivity* 99.
55. Cerisuelo, *Le Mépris* 51; Marie 203–4.
56. Jacques Aumont quoted in Marie 251.

57. Marie 207.
58. Marie 198.
59. Cerisuelo, *Le Mépris* 22, 26.
60. Marie 208.
61. Marie 221.
62. Marie 170.
63. Quoted in Cerisuelo, *Le Mépris* 19, my translation.
64. Cerisuelo, *Le Mépris* 59.
65. Cerisuelo, *Le Mépris* 46–7, my translation.
66. Cerisuelo, *Le Mépris* 17.
67. Cerisuelo, *Le Mépris* 34–44; Marie 230.
68. Writing in 1992, Stam was certainly not aware of the falsity of the Bazin quote (*Reflexivity* 59).
69. Cerisuelo, *Le Mépris* 56, 74; Marie 206–7.
70. Esquenazi, *Godard* 16, my translation.
71. Cerisuelo, *Le Mépris* 53.
72. Cerisuelo, *Le Mépris* 75, my translation.
73. Stam, *Reflexivity* 159.
74. Cerisuelo, *Le Mépris* 22.
75. Cerisuelo, *Le Mépris* 28; Marie 172–3.
76. Cerisuelo, *Le Mépris* 57–8.
77. Stam, *Reflexivity* 22.
78. Cerisuelo, *Le Mépris* 11; Marie 161.
79. Cerisuelo, *Le Mépris* 68, my translation.
80. Bordwell, *Narration in the Fiction Film* 151–3, 213.
81. Stam, *Reflexivity* 59.
82. Marie 188–9.
83. Stam, *Reflexivity* 22.
84. Roche, "Comment Hollywood."
85. Roche, "The Death."
86. Sarnelli, "Ghostly Femininities."
87. Roche, "The Death."
88. Roche, "The Blues" 455.
89. Roche, "The Blues" 457.
90. Limoges, "Réflexivité métaphorique" 47–8.
91. Deleuze 78, 82.
92. Benjamin, "The Work of Art."
93. Deleyto, *From Tinseltown* 141–2.
94. Cugier and Louguet 14.
95. Albera, *Les Formalistes* 11.
96. See Achemchame, "La naissance."
97. Boillat, *Cinéma* 51–2.
98. Boillat, *Cinéma* 51, my translation.
99. Morris 637.

100. Taurino and Casoli 62.
101. The *My Darling Clementine* shot is repeated with James Delos in S2E2 [32:40].
102. Hatchuel, "What a piece of work."
103. Ivănescu 92.
104. Taurino and Casoli 70.
105. Hatchuel, "What a piece of work."
106. Mittell 300; Cornillon 117.
107. Taurino and Casoli 71.
108. Ivanescu 87.
109. Waugh 119–20.

CHAPTER 5

1. Ames 15–16.
2. Altman 44–8.
3. Staiger, *Perverse Spectators* 24–41.
4. Stokes and Maltby 1–3.
5. Hall 102.
6. Mayne 66.
7. Bacon-Smith, *Enterprising Women*; Jenkins, *Textual Poachers*.
8. Hutcheon, *Narcissistic Narrative* 27; Waugh 4–5, 13, 106.
9. Cornillon 94.
10. Stuckey 48.
11. Radstone 34.
12. Vahdani, "*Nuovo Cinema Paradiso*."
13. Radstone 34.
14. Radstone 43.
15. Ames 108–36.
16. Chinita, "Meta-cinema as Authorial Enunciation."
17. Genette 58–77.
18. Boillat, "*Stranger than Fiction*" 29; Limoges, "La métalepse" 132.
19. Limoges, "La métalepse" 132–9.
20. Limoges, "La métalepse" 128.
21. Boillat, "*Stranger than Fiction*" 29, my translation.
22. Boillat, "*Stranger than Fiction*" 26, my translation.
23. Limoges, "La métalepse" 140.
24. Boillat, "*Stranger than Fiction*" 29.
25. Limoges, "La métalepse" 139.
26. Menegaldo 151.
27. Sklar 188–9; Thompson and Bordwell 211–12.
28. Menegaldo 139–41.
29. Doane 1; Ames 117.
30. Ames 128.
31. Ames 125.

32. Ames 111; Menegaldo 152.
33. Thompson and Bordwell 203.
34. Cavell 81.
35. Thompson and Bordwell 203.
36. Ames 119.
37. Menegaldo 154.
38. Ames 132.
39. Lipińska, "*L'Évasion du cinéma.*"
40. Waugh 92.
41. See Eric S. Mallin's brilliant article, "'You Kilt My Foddah': Or Arnold, Prince of Denmark."
42. Ames 125.
43. Doane 163–6.
44. Trumpener, "Fragments of the Mirror"; Van Eynde, *Vertiges de l'image*.
45. Douchet, "Hitch and His Public."
46. Hitchcock/Truffaut 178.
47. Douchet, "Hitch and His Public" 8.
48. Stam, *Reflexivity* 43.
49. Douchet, "Hitch and His Public" 8.
50. Douchet, "Hitch and His Public" 10.
51. Stam, *Reflexivity* 44.
52. Stam, *Reflexivity* 44.
53. Berton, "*Fenêtre sur cour.*"
54. Stam, *Reflexivity* 46.
55. Limoges, "Réflexivité métaphorique" 47–8, my translation.
56. Yacavone, "Cognitive and Affective Dimensions."
57. Stam, *Reflexivity* 49, 52–3.
58. Metz, *Imaginary Signifier* 56.
59. Stam, *Reflexivity* 50.
60. Paul Gordon 15–16.
61. Stam 49.
62. Douchet, "Hitch and His Public" 9.
63. Stam 49.
64. Metz, *Imaginary Signifier* 13.
65. Metz, *Imaginary Signifier* 40.
66. Mulvey 23–4.
67. Stam 54.
68. Modleski 76.
69. Modleski 76.
70. Modleski 72.
71. Modleski 77.
72. Modleski 79.
73. Harris 1987; Prédal 1991, 120; Tomasulo 2006. José Moure compares *Blow-up* to *Vertigo* (68).

74. Moure 66, 95, my translation.
75. Moure 9, 107–8, my translation.
76. Moure 96, my translation.
77. Thierry Roche 83.
78. Hare, "*Blow-up*—Between Form and Formlessness."
79. Thierry Roche also insists that Thomas is not just an artist but a spectator (58, 140).
80. Thierry Roche 112. Iser argued that the reader "is made to fill" in the blanks in the text with his/her "own (text-guided) mental images in order to constitute the meaning of the work" (172).
81. Thierry Roche 54–5.
82. Thierry Roche 141.
83. Bernardi, *Antonioni* 128, my translation.
84. Ropars-Wuilleumier 215; Moure 127–8.
85. Thierry Roche 117.
86. Limoges, "Réflexivité métaphorique" 44–5.
87. Thierry Roche 84.
88. Bazin 9–16; Barthes 76–7; Sontag 154.
89. Albera, *Les Formalistes* 8–9; Arnheim 57.
90. Moure 55.
91. Thierry Roche 144.
92. Librach 166; Dumas 78, 116.
93. Dumas 184–5.
94. Thierry Roche 11, my translation.
95. Dumas 182, 185, 189.
96. Dumas 191.
97. Ramaeker 191–6.
98. Librach, "Sex, Lies and Audiotape."
99. Librach, "Sex, Lies and Audiotape."
100. Librach, "Sex, Lies and Audiotape."
101. Dumas 184.
102. Chion, *Audio-vision* 68.
103. Metz, *Film Language* 93–4.

CHAPTER 6

1. Metz, *Impersonal Enunciation* 108; Raus 11.
2. Albera, *Les Formalistes* 9.
3. Kazanski in Albera, *Les Formalistes* 105.
4. Hutcheon, *Narcissistic Narrative* 117.
5. Hutcheon, *Narcissistic Narrative* 35, 100.
6. Waugh 137.
7. Siska 286.
8. Stam, *Reflexivity* 126.

9. Stam, *Reflexivity* 265.
10. Stam, *Reflexivity* 234.
11. Wolf, "Is There a Metareferential Turn?" 5.
12. Wolf, "Metareference Across Media" 13, 50.
13. Wolf, "Is There a Metareferential Turn?" 16.
14. Nöth 21.
15. Yacavone, "Recursive Reflections."
16. Szczepanik 29.
17. Szczepanik 30.
18. Szczepanik 33.
19. Szczepanik 29.
20. Yacavone, "Cognitive and Affective Dimensions."
21. Szczepanik 30.
22. Chinita, "Metacinema as Authorial Enunciation."
23. Kazanski quoted in Albera 119, my translation.
24. Bolter and Grusin 6.
25. Bolter and Grusin 45.
26. Bolter and Grusin 14–15.
27. Bolter and Grusin 46, 48, 153–4.
28. Arrivé, "Introduction: Remedying Remediation."
29. Bolter and Grusin 15.
30. Wolf, "Metareference across Media" 13.
31. Aldouby 5–6.
32. Bondanella, *The Films of Federico Fellini* 141; Burke, "The Cinema of Federico Fellini" 31; West 487.
33. Aldouby 4.
34. Aldouby 15.
35. Aldouby 13.
36. McHale 9–11.
37. Vanelli 213.
38. O'Healy 210.
39. Metz, *Impersonal Enunciation* 243.
40. Past 355.
41. West 487.
42. Burke, "Preface" viii.
43. Bondanella, *The Cinema* 197–8; Past 357.
44. Bazin, "The Ontology of the Photographic Image."
45. Stam, *Reflexivity* 227.
46. Stam, *Reflexivity* 16.
47. Bolter and Grusin 59.
48. Arrivé, "Introduction: Remedying Remediation."
49. Del Río, "Fetish and Aura" 41.
50. Del Río, "Fetish and Aura" 43.

51. See, for instance, Bill Angus's *Metadrama and the Informer in Shakespeare and Jonson*, and "Metadrama, Authority, and the Roots of Incredulity."
52. Del Río, "Fetish and Aura" 29.
53. Del Río, "Fetish and Aura" 47.
54. Del Río, "Fetish and Aura" 48.
55. Del Río, "Fetish and Aura" 47.
56. Boillat, "The Comic Book Effect" 139–40, 147–54.
57. Boillat, "The Comic Book Effect" 140.
58. Boillat, "The Comic Book Effect" 153.
59. Boillat, "The Comic Book Effect" 153.
60. From "How I Quit Collecting Records" and "An Argument at Work" in *American Splendor* #4 (1979) and "Read This" in *American Splendor* #6 (1981). Thanks to Jean-Paul Gabilliet for identifying the original material.
61. Sperb 124.
62. Peeters 48–9.
63. Round 101.
64. Mickwitz 37.
65. Round 95.
66. Dyer 60.
67. Hatfield 109.
68. Sperb 128.
69. Sperb 129–31, 133.
70. Landesman 173.
71. Roche, "*Rabbits*."
72. Kampmann 232.
73. Ryan 287.
74. Waugh 119–20.

Chapter 7

1. Hutcheon 170.
2. Stam 28.
3. Stam 29.
4. Leitch, *Film Adaptation* 111.
5. Leitch, *Film Adaptation* 111.
6. Leitch, *Film Adaptation* 111–13.
7. Leitch *Film Adaptation* 124.
8. See Letort and Wells-Lassagne, *Premières pages, premiers plans* 13–15; Geraghty and Wells-Lassagne 234–5.
9. De Mourgues 12; Gray 75–6.
10. Iser 137.
11. Peeters 48–9.
12. Boillat, "The Comic Book Effect" 143.
13. Roche, "Books and Letters."

14. Rothwell 54; Hatchuel, *Shakespeare* 96.
15. Sarah Hatchuel argues that metatheatricality tends to be lost in film adaptations of Shakespeare, in which "enunciation generally dissolves into narration" (*Shakespeare* 95). Judit Pieldner, in her discussion of film adaptations of *Hamlet*, follows Hatchuel, stating that the "meta-cinematic effects," which are meant "to comply with the meta-theatrical devices of the Elizabethan stage," are likely to lose their "anti-illusionistic character" (46).
16. Bentley 127.
17. Bentley 137–8.
18. De Lauretis 2.
19. Cooper, "'I am Isabel'."
20. Bentley 138.
21. Bentley 131.
22. Bentley 140.
23. Roche, *Making and Remaking Horror* 133–5; Roche, "The Remake as (Dis) avowal."
24. Leitch, "Twice-Told Tales" 44.
25. Hatchuel, *Rêves* 77, my translation.
26. Stam, *Reflexivity* 159.
27. Stam, *Reflexivity* 160.
28. Stam, *Reflexivity* 160.
29. Waugh 125.
30. Waugh 69.
31. Palmer 189–90.
32. Palmer 198.
33. Hutcheon describes Charles as upholding a view of creation as possession, while Sarah stands for creation as freedom (*Narcissistic Narrative*, 66–8, 85).
34. Palmer 196.
35. Eckart Voigts-Virchow describes it as *A Cock & Bull Story* "pastiche" of *Day for Night* (146).
36. Friant-Kessler and Hudelet describe *A Cock & Bull Story* as an "anti-*French Lieutenant's Woman* of sorts" (165).
37. See Friant-Kessler and Hudelet's analysis of the "subtle elements that denounce the genuine authenticity of this making of" (163).
38. Lefait, "Du *Making of*" 507.
39. Hudelet, "Austen and Sterne" 266–9.
40. Voigts-Virchow 146; Friant-Kessler and Hudelet 166.
41. Voigts-Virchow 145.
42. Hudelet, "Austen and Sterne" 259.
43. Note that the script of *Inherent Vice* does not account for this break in time-space.
44. Deleuze 69, 82.
45. Hudelet, "Austen and Sterne" 256–7.
46. Tomasulo, "*Adaptation* as Adaptation" 164.

47. Leitch, *Film Adaptation* 112.
48. Tomasulo, "*Adaptation* as Adaptation" 169.
49. Wells-Lassagne, "Adaptation, or Falsifying Memory" 508.
50. Tomasulo, "*Adaptation* as Adaptation" 168.
51. Hutcheon, *Narcissistic Narrative* 1–2; Waugh 18–19, 99.
52. Tomasulo, "*Adaptation* as Adaptation" 167.
53. Leitch, *Film Adaptation* 96, 201.
54. Francis, Jr. 23.
55. Francis, Jr. 26.
56. Roger 324, my translation.
57. Roger 317.
58. Santas, "The Remake of *Psycho*"; Roger 321.
59. Roger 318.
60. Roger 318, my translation.
61. Roger 322, my translation.
62. Francis, Jr. 30–1.
63. Whalen 100.
64. Stam, *Literature and Film* 16.
65. Jonathan's final letter is quite simply juxtaposed to Castle Dracula [35:35–35:55].
66. Ortoli, "*Bram Stoker's Dracula*" 239–40.
67. Leitch, *Film Adaptation* 108.
68. Whalen 100.
69. Ortoli, "*Bram Stoker's Dracula*" 237.
70. Ortoli, "*Bram Stoker's Dracula*" 239, my translation.
71. Leitch, *Film Adaptation* 107; Wells-Lassagne, "Filming Theory."
72. Roche, *Making and Remaking* 138–9, 149–52.

CHAPTER 8

1. See Stuckey 38–60.
2. Metz, *Impersonal Enunciation* 87–8.
3. Genette, *Palimpsests* 1.
4. Hutcheon, *Narcissistic Narrative* 29.
5. Waugh 5.
6. Waugh 69.
7. Waugh 83.
8. Waugh 84.
9. Waugh 86.
10. Waugh 42.
11. See Iché, *L'Esthétique du jeu dans les Alice de Lewis Carroll*.
12. Hutcheon, *Narcissistic Narrative* 83–4.
13. See Hardin, "Non-Cooperative Game Theory"; and Rodríguez, "A Theoretical View of Games in Literature."

14. Frayling 162, 492.
15. Murillo 103–4.
16. Suárez 105.
17. "Twilight Western" is the translation of the French "Western crépusculaire," which designates works centered on ageing heroes. Jean-Louis Leutrat argues that this trend has existed since the silent era and can even be traced back to the figure of the "vanishing Indian" (61–4).
18. Murillo 24–9.
19. Suárez 106–11.
20. Thanks to my colleague Vincent Deville for pointing this reference out to me.
21. Murillo 206–7.
22. Frayling 266–7.
23. See the distinction Slotkin makes between Theodore Roosevelt's and Frederick Jackson Turner's view of the Frontier Myth (29–62).
24. Stam, *Reflexivity* 132.
25. Stam, *Reflexivity* 191–3.
26. See Roche, *Quentin Tarantino*.
27. Hutcheon, *Theory of Parody* xii.
28. Hutcheon, *Theory of Parody* 2.
29. Sorin 211, my translation.
30. Stam, *Reflexivity* 6, 26, 131, 134–5, 160, 162, 180, 186–8, 195.
31. Hutcheon, *Theory of Parody* 20.
32. Hutcheon, *Narcissistic Narrative* 34.
33. Hutcheon, *Narcissistic Narrative* 10.
34. Hutcheon, *Narcissistic Narrative* 25.
35. Hutcheon, *Narcissistic Narrative* 100.
36. Waugh 73.
37. Hutcheon, *Narcissistic Narrative* 83.
38. Waugh 53.
39. Waugh 31.
40. Waugh 82.
41. Hutcheon, *Narcissistic Narrative* 51–4.
42. Waugh 66.
43. Altman 21.
44. Altman 22.
45. Stam, *Reflexivity* 135.
46. Hutcheon, *Narcissistic Narrative* 50.
47. Waugh 10.
48. Waugh 64.
49. Mléčková 49–50.
50. Frayling 348–9, 356.
51. Frayling 353, 358.
52. Frayling 348, 362.
53. Leone the producer ended up directing several scenes (Frayling 353, 362).

54. Frayling 360.
55. Frayling 354.
56. Frayling 356.
57. Frayling 355.
58. Hutcheon, *Theory of Parody* 20.
59. Aquila 231.
60. Roche, David, *Quentin Tarantino*, in particular Chapters 2 and 3.
61. Carter 21.
62. Carter 24.
63. Carter 23.
64. Carter 23.
65. Chion, *Audio-vision* 8–9, 222.
66. Carter 30–1.
67. See Limoges, "La métalepse" 134–6.
68. Clover 182–205.
69. Carter 39.
70. Carter 24.
71. Carter 32.
72. Carter 37.
73. Wood 112–14.
74. Carter 47.
75. Church 239.
76. Wee 47.
77. Craig and Fradley 84.
78. Wells 97.
79. Dufour 180.
80. Craig and Fradley 84.
81. Worland 270.
82. Chion, *Voice* 21.
83. Pheasant-Kelly 159.
84. Dufour 182.
85. Baudrillard, *Simulacra and Simulation*.
86. Freud, *Beyond the Pleasure Principle* 19.
87. Williams, "Film Bodies."
88. Austerlitz 370.
89. Austerlitz 372.
90. Wells-Lassagne, "Transforming the traditional sitcom."
91. Wells-Lassagne, "Transforming the traditional sitcom."
92. Wells-Lassagne, "Transforming the traditional sitcom."
93. Austerlitz 375.
94. Wells-Lassagne, "Transforming the traditional sitcom."
95. Wells-Lassagne, "Transforming the traditional sitcom."
96. Anders 9.
97. Waugh 82.

Chapter 9

1. See Hélène Machinal 50–61; Christophe Gelly, "The Abominable Bride."
2. See Esther Zuckerman's article "The Obsessive's Guide to 'Sherlock' Opener 'The Empty Hearse'" in *The Atlantic*, 20 January 2014, https://www.theatlantic.com/culture/archive/2014/01/obsessives-guide-sherlock-empty-hearse/357169, accessed 25 November 2021.
3. See https://freshprince.fandom.com/wiki/Fourth_Wall_Breaks, accessed 25 November 2021.
4. Cornillon 94.
5. Mittell 27, 51.
6. This episode is available on line: https://www.youtube.com/watch?v=jvvGild9acw&list=PLIwO5hInBPuylOW10_w2ieR06uI6-Fkw8, accessed 25 November 2021.
7. Connor 521.
8. Esquenazi, *Séries télévisées* 91, my translation.
9. Lifschutz 275, 297.
10. Eco, "Innovation" 174.
11. Mittell 222–3.
12. Yu, "Digital Dreams."
13. Yu, "Digital Dreams."
14. Hudelet, The Wire 145; Mittell 148.
15. Hudelet, The Wire 26–7, my translation.
16. Mittell 222.
17. Hudelet, The Wire 51–2.
18. Hudelet, The Wire 56, my translation.
19. Mittell 300; Cornillon 117.
20. Hudelet, The Wire 189, my translation.
21. Hatchuel, *Rêves* 211, my translation.
22. Hatchuel, *LOST* 39.
23. Hatchuel, *LOST* 56.
24. Hatchuel, *LOST* 43.
25. Lefait, *Surveillance* 119; Hatchuel, *LOST* 29.
26. Lefait, *Surveillance* 124–7.
27. Lefait, *Surveillance* 117–40.
28. Lefait, *Surveillance* 136–8.
29. Hatchuel, *LOST* 37.
30. Mittell 46.
31. Pavel 107.
32. Hatchuel, *LOST* 130–1, my translation.
33. Gregory 16.
34. Sardar 1–5.
35. Gregory 7.
36. Gregory 33, 48; Lefait, *Surveillance* 106–8.

37. McHale 9–11.
38. Gregory 102.
39. Gregory 137.
40. Gregory 177.
41. Astic 91, 105, 140–1.
42. Collins 256. See also O'Day 119; Storey 155–6.
43. Collins 262.
44. Astic 68, my translation.
45. Astic 6, my translation.
46. Dick Tomasovic quoted in Astic 109.
47. Astic 118.
48. Astic 140.
49. Barthes 80–1.
50. Roche, "*Twin Peaks: Fire Walk With Me.*"
51. See Roche, "L'esthétique du temps" 26–9, 32–4.
52. See Roche, "*Rabbits.*"
53. Achemchame, "*Twin Peaks*" 75.
54. Hatchuel also shows how, in S1E11 of *Awake*, the psychiatrist's lines comment on the narrative (Hatchuel, *Rêves* 215–16).
55. See Eliana Dockterman's astute piece, "How *No Time to Die*'s Unpredected Ending Sets Up the Future of the Bond Franchise," time.com, 8 October 2021, https://time.com/6103054/no-time-to-die-ending-james-bond-future, accessed 14 March 2022.

CHAPTER 10

1. Leitch, *Film Adaptation* 280–2.
2. Rosenstone, *History on Film* 424.
3. Sorlin 19.
4. Waugh 104–5, 108.
5. Hutcheon, *Poetics* 122.
6. Hutcheon, *Poetics* 122.
7. Hutcheon, *Poetics* 112.
8. Hutcheon, *Poetics* 105.
9. Hutcheon, *Poetics* 111.
10. Hutcheon, *Poetics* 121.
11. Hutcheon, *Poetics* 114–15.
12. Hutcheon, *Poetics* 117.
13. Hutcheon, *Poetics* 118.
14. Hutcheon, *Poetics* 123.
15. Hutcheon, *Poetics* 114.
16. Hutcheon, *Poetics* 122.
17. Lagny, "Entre documentaire et fiction" 143.
18. Gomez 106.

19. Lagny, "Entre documentaire et fiction" 144.
20. Dubois 25; Lagny, "Entre documentaire et fiction" 141.
21. Dubois 27.
22. Lagny, "Entre documentaire et fiction" 141.
23. Dubois 26; Nolley 99.
24. Coppola 151.
25. Gomez 111; Nolley 98.
26. Denis, "La subversion des genres" 160.
27. Denis, "La subversion des genres" 156, 158.
28. Gomez 109.
29. Denis, "Médias et politique" 68–9.
30. Gomez 108–9.
31. Nolley 100, my translation.
32. Coppola 152, translation.
33. Lagny 38–9.
34. Lagny 38–9.
35. Dave Rolinson, "*Culloden* (1964)," http://www.screenonline.org.uk/tv/id/520802/index.html, accessed 19 March 2021.
36. Escobar 110.
37. Nolley 94, my translation.
38. See Gavriel Rosenfield's *The World Hitler Never Made: Alternate History and the Memory of Nazism*.
39. Dick, Philip K. *The Man in the High Castle*. Berkley Publishing Corporation, 1962, pp. 221–4.
40. See Canaan, "Metafiction and the Gnostic Quest in *The Man in the High Castle*."
41. Roche, *Quentin Tarantino* 71.
42. Coates, "Hyperreality"; Kligerman 154; Roche, *Quentin Tarantino* 17, 215.
43. Roche, *Quentin Tarantino* 39.
44. Roche, *Quentin Tarantino* 23–4.
45. Haber 135; Roche, *Quentin Tarantino* 23–4.
46. Nama 101–2; Semenza 74–5; Roche, *Quentin Tarantino* 24–5; Roche, *Inglourious Basterds* 20.
47. Schlipphacke 118; Roche, *Quentin Tarantino* 185–7.
48. Ortoli, *Musée imaginaire* 449; Roche, *Quentin Tarantino* 238.
49. Pagnoni Berns and Aguilar 35, 40.
50. Dick, *The Man in the High Castle* 62, 77.
51. Dick, *The Man in the High Castle* 150–3.
52. Dick, *The Man in the High Castle* 226.
53. Dick, *The Man in the High Castle* 231, 245–7.
54. Hansen 82.
55. Horowitz 123.
56. Horowitz 122.
57. Cheyette 230.
58. Morris 951.

59. Zelizer 27.
60. Horowitz 119.
61. Leo, "Oliver Stone's paranoid propaganda."
62. Steel 30.
63. Rosenstone, "*JFK*: Historical Fact/Historical Film" 510.
64. Simon 15.
65. Baron 86–7.
66. See for instance Jennifer Vineyard's "Oliver Stone: There's nothing in 'JFK' I would go back on," cnn.com, 22 November 2013, https://edition.cnn.com/2013/11/22/showbiz/oliver-stone-jfk-50th-anniversary/index.html, accessed 1 January 2022.
67. Steel 30.
68. See Fraser, "Road Sickness."
69. Toledo 166.
70. Jung 121–2.
71. Howe 421.
72. Toledo 168.
73. Toledo 166–7.
74. Toledo 168.
75. Howe 428; Jung 127.
76. Howe 425.
77. Howe 421.
78. Zucconi 140.
79. Zucconi 137.
80. Jung 126.

Chapter 11

1. Hutcheon, *Narcissistic Narrative* 1–2, 37; Waugh 7–10, 35.
2. Garrett Martin, "*Rick and Morty* Almost Swallows Itself Whole in a Too Meta Midseason Premiere," pastemagazine.com, 27 April 2020, https://www.pastemagazine.com/comedy/rick-and-morty/rick-and-morty-season-4-midseason-premiere-review, accessed 4 January 2022.
3. Roche, *Quentin Tarantino* 42–4, 64.
4. Waugh 13.
5. Waugh 149.
6. Hutcheon, *Narcissistic Narrative* 111–5, 130–6, 155–62.
7. Hutcheon, *Narcissistic Narrative* 135.
8. Hutcheon, *Narcissistic Narrative* 155.
9. Hutcheon, *Narcissistic Narrative* 161–2.
10. Fredericksen 315–16.
11. Stam, *Reflexivity* 167.
12. Stam, *Reflexivity* 208.
13. Stam, *Reflexivity* 209.

14. Stam, *Reflexivity* 211.
15. Stam, *Reflexivity* 219.
16. Stam, *Reflexivity* 216.
17. Stam, *Reflexivity* 219.
18. Stam, *Reflexivity* 218.
19. Stam, *Reflexivity* 219–22.
20. Waugh 90–4.
21. Stam, *Reflexivity* 220.
22. Carter 5, 158.
23. Carter 142–3.
24. Carter 11.
25. Carter 3–4.
26. Carter 8.
27. Carter 11.
28. Carter 11–12.
29. Carter 22.
30. Carter 109.
31. Carter 127.
32. Stam, *Reflexivity* 16; Carter 141.
33. Rancière, *Le Spectateur émancipé* 61, my translation.
34. Rancière, *Le Spectateur émancipé* 72–3, my translation.
35. Rancière, *The Politics of Aesthetics* 12–19.
36. Rancière, *Le Spectateur émancipé* 64, my translation.
37. Rancière, *Le Spectateur émancipé* 66, my translation.
38. Rancière, *Le Spectateur émancipé* 54–5.
39. Rancière, *Le Spectateur émancipé*, p. 85, my translation.
40. Rancière, *Le Spectateur émancipé* 87–90.
41. Rancière, *Intervals of Cinema* 127–9.
42. Rancière, *Intervals of Cinema* 141. In brackets, my modifications to the original translation which is flawed.
43. Rancière, *Intervals of Cinema* 131.
44. Rancière, *Intervals of Cinema* 132–3.
45. Rancière, *Intervals of Cinema* 134.
46. Rancière, *Intervals of Cinema* 137.
47. Rancière, *Intervals of Cinema* 139.
48. Rancière, *Intervals of Cinema* 142.
49. Stam, *Reflexivity* 220.
50. Carter 11.
51. Carter 64.
52. Carter 89.
53. Carter 113.
54. Carter 131.
55. Carter 129.
56. Carter 12.

57. Leo Benedictus, "Charlie Brooker on Cameron and #piggate: 'I'd have been screaming it into traffic if I'd known'," theguardian.com, 21 September 2015, accessed 3 January 2022.
58. See David Roche, "'You know, when you suspect something, it's always better when it turns out to be true.'" See also Machinal, *Posthumains en série* 233–9.
59. The division into four parts has been eliminated on Netflix.
60. Murray, *Encyclopedia of Television News* 103–5.
61. Lefait, "It's not a technological problem" 128.
62. Lefait, "It's not a technological problem" 141.
63. Jenkins, *Convergence Culture: Where Old and New Media Collide*.
64. Guy Debord, *Society of the Spectacle*.
65. Jenkins contends that "the skills we acquire through play may have implications for how we learn, work, participate in the political process, and connect with other people around the world" (22–3).
66. Hill, *Ken Loach* 106.
67. Hill, *Ken Loach* 123.
68. Hill, *Ken Loach* 122.
69. The night club existed but was not on the same street as the Department of Work and Pensions.
70. Hill, *Ken Loach* 4, 171.
71. Hill, *Ken Loach* 4.
72. Hill, *Ken Loach* 174.
73. Hill, *Ken Loach* 179.
74. Hill, *Ken Loach* 175.
75. Hill describes *Looking for Eric* (2009) as "a fantasy of collectivism" (199).
76. Hill, *Ken Loach* 219.
77. Hill, *Ken Loach* 132.
78. Hill, *Ken Loach* 221.
79. Hill, *Ken Loach* 61–2; Pilard 224–5.
80. Hill, *Ken Loach* 132.
81. Hill, *Ken Loach* 182.
82. This echoes historical adviser Donal Ó Drisceoil's statement that *The Wind That Shakes the Barley* depicts what might have been rather than what happened (quoted in Hill, *Ken Loach* 220).

Conclusion

1. LaRocca 5.
2. Ricœur 140.
3. LaRocca 10.
4. Plantinga 319.
5. Nichols, *Introduction* 34.
6. Andacht 166, 176, 178.
7. Stam, *Reflexivity* 82.

8. Shibolet 276.
9. Wartenberg 255.
10. Stam, *Reflexivity* 193.
11. Wartenberg 262, 267.
12. Rancière, *Film Fables* 237.
13. Nichols, "The Voice" 18.
14. Brunow 343.
15. Shibolet 272.
16. Winston 6, 26.
17. Nichols, *Representing Reality* 61.
18. Nichols, *Introduction* 6, 48.
19. Shibolet 286.
20. Shibolet 287.

Glossary of Meta-phenomena

hypermeta   works whose meta-ness is evident and overt (*Scream*, *Community*).
meta   a popular term to designate works that refer to themselves, their genre or their medium explicitly and/or implicitly; sometimes synonymous with **mise en abyme**, **metalepsis** or **reflexivity**; in this book, an intense form of reflexivity that invites an interpretation on the work and/or its medium.
metacinema   cinema that is explicitly and/or implicitly about cinema.
metacinematic, metafilmic   when reflexive devices point to the apparatus or film (Metz).
metadiegesis   a narrative within the narrative (Genette).
metafiction   fiction that is explicitly and/or implicitly about fiction; mostly used for the novel and short story.
metafilm   an instance of **metacinema**; for Cerisuelo, a synonym of movies about making movies.
metalepsis   the transgression of an ontological boundary between worlds that are not connected either within the diegesis or between the diegesis and the real world (Limoges's "intradiegetic" or "extradiegetic" metalepsis).
meta-level   a secondary layer of meaning where the work comments on itself and/or its medium.
metamoment   a scene that can be interpreted as meta.
metanarrative   a narrative that is explicitly and/or implicitly about narrative.
metatextuality   when a work comments on its intertext without necessarily citing it (Genette).
metatheater (also metadrama)   theater that is explicitly and/or implicitly about theater.
metaperformance   performance that is explicitly and/or implicitly about performance.
metareference   a special kind of reflexivity that implies a metacommunicative statement (Wolf).
mise en abyme   the reflection within the work of a story (*Hamlet*), its content (*Mulholland Dr.*) or its medium (any diegetic screen); I find that it is pertinent to distinguish between the mise en abyme and the film-within-the-film to avoid turning the mise en abyme into a synonym of intradiegetic narrative.
movie about making movies   a film genre which represents the production of films.
reflexivity   the laying bare of the fiction/artifice/illusion to various degrees.
self-reference   a sign referring to itself (Nöth); a synonym of **self-reflexivity**.
self-reflexivity   when the works points specifically to itself; like Yacavone, I argue that the term is redundant because reflexivity always entails a degree of self-reflexivity.

Filmography

FILMS

Adaptation. Directed by Spike Jonze, written by Charlie Kaufman, based on *The Orchid Thief* by Susan Orlean, with performances by Nicholas Cage (Charlie Kaufman), Meryl Streep (Susan Orlean), Chris Cooper (John Laroche) and Tilda Swinton (Valerie Thomas), 2002.

American Splendor. Directed by Shari Springer Berman and Robert Pulcini, written by Shari Springer Berman, based on the comic series by Harvey Pekar and Joyce Brabner, with performances by Paul Giamatti (Harvey Pekar), Hope Davis (Joyce Brabner), Judah Friedlander (Toby Radloff) and Harvey Pekar (as himself), 2003.

Blazing Saddles. Directed by Mel Brooks, written by Mel Brooks, Norman Steinberg and Andrew Bergman, with performances by Cleavon Little (Bart), Gene Wilder (Jim) and Madeline Kahn (Lili Von Shtüpp), 1974.

Blow Out. Written and directed by Brian De Palma (and Bill Mesce Jr.), with performances by John Travolta (Jack), Nancy Allen (Sally) and John Lithgow (Burke), 1981.

Blow-up. Directed by Michelangelo Antonioni, written by Michelangelo Antonioni and Tonino Guerra, based on a short story by Julio Cortázar, with performances by David Hemmings (Thomas), Vanessa Redgrave (Jane) and John Castle (Bill), 1966.

Bram Stoker's Dracula. Directed by Francis Ford Coppola, written by James V. Hart, based on the novel by Bram Stoker, with performances by Gary Oldman (Dracula), Winona Ryder (Mina Murray), Anthony Hopkins (Professor Abraham Van Helsing) and Keanu Reeves (Jonathan Harker), 1992.

The Cameraman. Directed by Edward Sedgwick and Buster Keaton, written by Clyde Bruckman, Lew Lipton and Joseph Farnham, with performances by Buster Keaton (Buster), Marceline Day (Sally) and Harold Goodwin (Stagg), 1928.

A Cock & Bull Story. Directed by Michael Winterbottom, written by Frank Cottrell-Boyce, based on the novel *The Life and Opinions of Tristram Shandy, Gentleman* by Laurence Sterne, with performances by Steve Coogan (Tristram Sandy, Walter Shandy, Steve Coogan), Rob Brydon (Capt. Toby Shandy, Rob Brydon), Naomie Harris (Jennie) and Gillian Anderson (Widow Wadman, Gillian Anderson), 2005.

Colossal Youth. Written and directed by Pedro Costa, with performances by Ventura (Ventura), Vanda Duarte (Vanda), Beatriz Duarte (Beatriz), Alberto "Lento" Barros (Lento) and Paulo Nunes (Paulo), 2006.

Contempt. Written and directed by Jean-Luc Godard, based on the novel by Alberto Moravia, with performances by Brigitte Bardot (Camille Javal), Jack Palance (Jeremy Prokosch), Michel Piccoli (Paul Javal), Fritz Lang (as himself) and Giorgia Moll (Francesca Vanini), 1963.

Dead Man. Written and directed by Jim Jarmusch, with performances by Johnny Depp (William Blake) and Gary Farmer (Nobody), 1995.

Family Viewing. Written and directed by Atom Egoyan, with performances by David Hemblen (Stan), Aidan Tierney (Van), Gabrielle Rose (Sandra) and Arsinée Khanjian (Aline), 1987.

Fellini Roma. Directed by Federico Fellini, written by Federico Fellini and Bernardino Zapponi, with performances by Peter Gonzales (Fellini, Age 18), Fiona Florence (Dolores/ Young Prostitute), Pia De Doses (Princess Domitilla), Marne Maitland (Guide in the Catacombs), Renato Giovannoli (Cardinal Ottavinia), Elisa Mainardi (Pharmacist's wife/ Cinema Spectator), Federico Fellini (as himself), Anna Magnani (as herself) and Gore Vidal (as himself), 1972.

The French Lieutenant's Woman. Directed by Karel Reisz, written by Harold Pinter, based on the novel by John Fowles, with performances by Meryl Steep (Sarah, Anna) and Jeremy Irons (Charles, Mike), 1981.

The Funhouse. Directed by Tobe Hooper, written by Lawrence J. Block, with performances by Elizabeth Berridge (Amy Harper), Shawn Carson (Joey Harper) and Wayne Doba (The Monster), 1981.

Funny Games. Written and directed by Michael Haneke, with performances by Susanne Lothar (Anna), Ulrich Mühe (Georg), Arno Frisch (Paul), Frank Giering (Peter) and Stefan Clapczynski (Schorschi), 1997.

I, Daniel Blake. Directed by Ken Loach, written by Paul Laverty, with performances by Dave Johns (Daniel Blake) and Hayley Squires (Katie), 2016.

Inglourious Basterds. Written and directed by Quentin Tarantino, with performances by Brad Pitt (Lt. Aldo Raine), Mélanie Laurent (Shosanna Dreyfus), Christoph Waltz (Col. Hans Landa), Diane Kruger (Bridget von Hammersmark), Michael Fassbender (Lt. Archie Hicox) and Daniel Brühl (Frederick Zoller), 2009.

Inherent Vice. Written and directed by Paul Thomas Anderson, based on the novel by Thomas Pynchon, with performances by Joaquin Phoenix (Larry "Doc" Sportello), Josh Brolin (Lt. Det. Christian F. "Bigfoot" Bjornsen), Owen Wilson (Coy Harlingen), Katherine Waterston (Shasta Fay Hepworth) and Joanna Newsom (Sortilège), 2014.

JFK. Written and directed by Oliver Stone, based on books by Jim Garrison and Jim Marrs, with Kevin Costner (Jim Garrison), Gary Oldman (Lee Harvey Oswald), Joe Pesci (David Ferrie) and Tommy Lee Jones (Clay Shaw), 1991.

Jurassic Park. Directed by Steven Spielberg, written by David Koepp, based on the novel by Michael Crichton, with performances by Sam Neill (Grant), Laura Dern (Ellie), Jeff Goldblum (Malcolm), Richard Attenborough (Hammond), Joseph Mazzello (Tim) and Ariana Richards (Lex), 1993.

Lemonade Joe, or the Horse Opera. Directed by Oldřich Lipský, written by Oldřich Lipský and Jiří Brdečka, with Karel Fiala (Lemonade Joe), Rudolf Deyl (Doug Badman alias Hogofogo), Miloš Kopecký (Horace Badman alias Hogofogo), Květa Fialová (Tornado Lou), Olga Schoberová (Winnifred Goodman), 1964.

Man with a Movie Camera, written and directed by Dziga Vertov, performances with Mikhail Kaufman (*The Cameraman*) and Yelizaveta Svilova (Woman editing film), 1929.

Mulholland Dr. Written and directed by David Lynch, with performances by Naomi Watts (Betty/Diane Selwyn), Laura Harring (Rita/Camilla Rhodes) and Justin Theroux (Adam Kesher), 2001.

My Name Is Nobody. Directed by Tonino Valerii, written by Fulvio Morsella and Ernesto Gastaldi, based on an idea by Sergio Leone, with performances by Terence Hill (Nessuno) and Henry Fonda (Jack Beauregard), 1973.

No. Directed by Pablo Larraín, written by Pedro Peirano, based on the play by Antonio Skármeta, with Gael Garcia Bernal (René Saavedra), Alfredo Castro (Lucho Guzman) and Antonia Zegers (Veronica Carvajal), 2012.

The Player. Directed by Robert Altman, written by Michael Tolkin, with performances by Tim Robbins (Griffin Mill), Greta Scacchi (June Gudmunsdottir), Peter Gallagher (Larry Levy) and Vincent D'Onofrio (David Kahane), 1992.

The Portrait of a Lady. Directed by Jane Campion, written by Laura Jones, based on the novel by Henry James, with performances by Nicole Kidman (Isabel Archer), John Malkovich (Gilbert Osmond), Barbara Hershey (Madame Serena Merle) and Martin Donovan (Ralph Touchett), 1996.

Psycho. Directed by Gus Van Sant, written by Joseph Stefano, based on the novel by Robert Bloch, with performances by Vince Vaughn (Norman Bates), Anne Heche (Marion Crane), Julianne Moore (Lila Crane), Viggo Mortensen (Sam Loomis) and William H. Macy (Milton Arbogast), 1998.

The Purple Rose of Cairo. Written and directed by Woody Allen, with performances by Mia Farrow (Cecilia), Jeff Daniels (Tom Baxter/Gil Shepherd) and Danny Aiello (Monk), 1985.

Tom Jones. Directed by Tony Richardson, written by John Osborne, based on the novel by Henry Fielding, with performances by Albert Finney (Tom Jones), Susannah York (Sophie Western), George Devine (Squire Allworthy) and Joyce Redman (Jenny Jones), 1963.

Rear Window. Directed by Alfred Hitchcock, written by John Michael Hayes, based on the short story by Cornell Woolrich, with performances by James Stewart (L.B. Jefferies), Grace Kelly (Lisa Fremont), Wendell Corey (Tom Doyle), Thelma Ritter (Stella) and Raymond Burr (Lars Thorwald), 1954.

Schindler's List. Directed by Steven Spielberg, written by Steven Zaillian, based on the book by Thomas Keneally, with performances by Liam Neeson (Oskar Schindler), Ralph Fiennes (Amon Goeth) and Ben Kingsley (Itzhak Stern), 1993.

Scream. Directed by Wes Craven, written by Kevin Williamson, with performances by Neve Campbell (Sidney Prescott), Courteney Cox (Gale Weathers), David Arquette (Deputy Dewey), Skeet Ulrich (Billy), Drew Barrymore (Casey), Rose McGowan (Tatum), Matthew Lillard (Stuart) and Jamie Kennedy (Randy), 1996.

Sherlock Jr. Directed by Buster Keaton, written by Jean C. Havez, Joseph A. Mitchell and Clyde Bruckman, with performances by Buster Keaton (Projectionist/Sherlock Jr.), Kathryn McGuire (The Girl) and Ward Crane (The Local Sheik/The Villain), 1924.

Sunset Blvd. Directed by Billy Wilder, written by Charles Brackett, Billy Wilder and D.M. Marshman Jr., with performances by William Holden (Joe Gillis), Gloria Swanson (Norma Desmond), Erich von Stroheim (Max von Mayerling), Nancy Olson (Betty) and Cecil B. DeMille (himself), 1950.

The Texas Chainsaw Massacre. Directed by Marcus Nispel, written by Scott Kosar, based on the 1974 screenplay by Kim Henkel and Tobe Hooper, with performances by Jessica Biel (Erin) and Andrew Bryniarski (Thomas Hewitt/Leatherface), 2003.

Through the Olive Trees. Written and directed by Abbas Kiarostami, with performances by Mohamad Ali Keshavarz (Film Director), Farhad Kheradmand (Farhad), Hossein Rezai (Hossein) and Tahereh Ladanian (Tahereh), 1994.

Tony Manero. Directed by Pablo Larraín, written by Alfredo Castro, Mateo Iribarren and Pablo Larraín, with performances by Alfredo Castro (Raúl Peralta), Amparo Noguera (Cony) and Héctor Morales (Goyo), 2008.

Tout va bien. Written and directed by Jean-Luc Godard and Jean-Pierre Gorin, with performances by Yves Montand (Him, Jacques) and Jane Fonda (Her, Suzanne), 1972.

SERIES

Black Mirror. Created by Charlie Brooker, with performances by Rory Kinnear (Michael Callow, episode S1E1) and Lindsay Duncan (Alex Cairns, episode S1E1). Channel 4, 2011–14. Netflix, 2016–. 5 seasons, 22 episodes.

Community. Created by Dan Harmon, with performances by Joel McHale (Jeff Winger), Danny Pudi (Abed Nadir), Gillian Jacobs (Britta Perry), Allison Brie (Annie Edison), Donald Glover (Troy Barnes), Chevy Chase (Pierce Hawthorne), Ken Jeong (Ben Chang), Yvette Nicole Brown (Shirley Bennett) and Jim Rash (Dean Pelton). NBC, 2009–15. 6 seasons, 110 episodes.

LOST. Created by J.J. Abrams, Jeffrey Lieber and Damon Lindelof, with performances by Jorge Garcia (Hugo "Hurley" Reyes), Josh Holloway (James "Sawyer" Ford), Yunjin Kim (Sun-Hwa Kwon), Evangeline Lilly (Kate Austen), Terry O'Quinn (John Locke), Naveen Andrews (Sayid Jarrah), Matthew Fox (Dr. Jack Shepard), Daniel Dae Kim (Jin-Soo Kwon), Emilie de Ravin (Claire Littleton), Michal Emerson (Ben Linus), Dominic Monaghan (Charlie Pace), Henry Ian Cusick (Desmond Hume), Kiele Sanchez (Nikki Fernandez) and Rodrigo Santoro (Paulo). ABC, 2004–10. 6 seasons, 119 episodes.

The Magic School Bus. Created by Joanna Cole, Bruce Degen and Kristin Laskas Martin, with performances by Lily Tomlin (Ms. Valerie Frizzle), Daniel DeSanto (Carlos Ramon), Erica Luttrell (Keesha Franklin), Tara Meyer (Dorothy Ann), Maia Filar (Phoebe Terese), Lisa Jai (Wandi Li), Stuart Stone (Ralphine Tennelli) and Malcolm-Jamal Warner (The Producer). PBS, 1994–7. 4 seasons, 52 episodes.

The Man in the High Castle. Created by Frank Spotnitz, based on the novel by Philip K. Dick, with performances by Alex Davalos (Juliana Crain), Rufus Sewell (John Smith), Joel de la Fuente (Inspector Kido), Luke Kleintack (Joe Blake), Rupert Evans (Frank Frink) Brennan Brown (Robert Childan), D.J. Qualls (Ed McCarthy) and Cary-Hiroyuki Tagawa (Nobusuke Tagomi). Amazon Prime, 2015–19. 4 seasons, 40 episodes.

Married . . . with Children. Created by Ron Leavitt and Michael G. Moye, with performances by Ed O'Neill (Al Bundy), Katey Sagal (Peggy Bundy), Christina Applegate (Kelly Bundy) and David Faustino (Bud Bundy). Fox, 1987–97. 11 seasons, 262 episodes.

The Prisoner. Created by Patrick McGoohan, with performances by Patrick McGoohan (Number Six), Angelo Muscat (The Butler), Peter Swanwick (Supervisor), Leo McKern (Number Two), Bill Cummings (Henchman). ITV, 1967–8. 1 season, 17 episodes.

This Is Us. Created by Dan Fogelman, with performances by Milo Ventimiglia (Jack Pearson), Mandy Moore (Rebecca Pearson), Sterling K. Brown (Randall Pearson), Chrissy Metz (Kate Pearson) and Justin Hartley (Kevin Pearson). NBC, 2016–22. 6 seasons, 93 episodes.

Twin Peaks. Created by Mark Frost and David Lynch, with performances by Kyle MacLachlan (Special Agent Dale Cooper), Michael Ontkean (Sheriff Harry S. Truman), Mädchen Amick (Shelly Johnson), Dana Ashbrook (Bobby Briggs), Richard Reymer (Benjamin Horne), Lara Flynn Boyle (Donna Howard), Sherilyn Fenn (Audrey Horne), Warren Frost (Dr. Will Hayward), James Marshall (James Hurley), Michael Horse (Deputy Tommy "Hawk" Hill), Ray Wise (Leland Palmer), Sheryl Lee (Maddy Ferguson/Laura Palmer) and David Lynch (Gordon Cole). ABC, 1990–1. 2 seasons, 30 episodes.

Twin Peaks: The Return. Created by Mark Frost and David Lynch, with performances by Kyle MacLachlan (Dale Cooper/Dougie/Mr. C), Sheryll Lee (Laura Palmer), Michael Horse (Deputy Chief Tommy "Hawk" Hill), Miguel Ferrer (FBI Agent Albert Rosenfield), David Lynch (FBI Deputy Director Gordon Cole), Robert Forster (Sheriff Frank Truman),

Naomi Watts (Janey-E. Jones), Laura Dern (Diane Evans) and Harry Goaz (Deputy Andy Brennan). Showtime, 2017. 1 season, 18 episodes.

Westworld. Created by Lisa Joy and Jonathan Nolan, based on the movie by Michael Crichton, with performances by Evan Rachel Wood (Dolores Abernathy), Jeffrey Wright (Bernard Lowe), Ed Harris (Man in Black), Thandiwe Newton (Maeve Millay), Tessa Thompson (Charlotte Hale), James Marsden (Teddy Flood), Luke Hemsworth (Ashley Stubbs), Angela Sarafyan (Clementine Pennyfeather) and Anthony Hopkins (Dr. Robert Ford). HBO, 2016–. 4 seasons, 36 episodes.

The Wire. Created by David Simon, with performances by Dominic West (Det. James McNulty), Lance Reddick (Lt. Cedric Daniels), Sonja Sohn (Det. Shakima Greggs), Wendell Pierce (Det. William "Bunk" Moreland), Clarke Peters (Det. Lester Freamon) and Lawrence Gilliard Jr. (D'Angelo Barksdale). HBO, 2002–8. 5 seasons, 60 episodes.

TV MOVIES

Black Mirror: Bandersnatch. Directed by David Slade, written by Charlie Brooker, with performances by Fionn Whitehead (Stefan Butler), Craig Parkinson (Peter Butler), Alice Lowe (Dr. Haynes), Asim Chaudhry (Mohan Thakur) and Will Poulter (Colin Ritman). Netflix, 2018.

Culloden. Written and directed by Peter Watkins, with performances by Tony Cosgrove (Lt. Ward), Olivier Espitalier-Noel (Prince Charles Edward). BBC, 1964.

Bibliography

BOOKS AND ARTICLES ON THE CORPUS

Achemchame, Julien. "*Twin Peaks* ou les vertiges de l'intertextualité." In Twin Peaks: *Mark Frost et David Lynch*, edited by Sarah Hatchuel, Le Bord de l'eau, 2019, pp. 59–83.

—. "La naissance toujours renouvelée de l'industrie hollywoodienne: *A Star Is Born* (1937) et ses remakes." *La Furia Umana*, vol. 41, 2021, http://www.lafuriaumana.it/index.php/75-archive/lfu-41/1033-julien-achemchame-la-naissance-toujours-renouvelee-de-l-industrie-hollywoodienne-a-star-is-born-1937-et-ses-remakes, accessed 13 March 2022.

Aldouby, Hava. *Federico Fellini: Painting in Film, Painting on Film*. University of Toronto Press, 2013.

Anders, Lisann. "Diversity and Unity in the TV Show *Community*." *PopMeC*, 2020, pp. 1–16, https://popmec.hypotheses.org/3274, accessed 19 October 2021.

Anupama, A.P. "Deconstructing the Spectator through Meta-Cinema: Bharathiraja's 'Bommalattam'." *Sahapedia*, 30 November 2018, https://www.sahapedia.org/deconstructing-the-spectator-through-meta-cinema-bharathirajas-bommalattam, accessed 25 March 2021.

Aquila, Richard. *The Sagebrush Trail: Western Movies and Twentieth-Century America*. The University of Arizona Press, 2015.

Astic, Guy. Twin Peaks: *les laboratoires de David Lynch*. Rouge Profond, 2005.

Austerlitz, Saul. *Sitcom: A History in 24 Episodes: from* I Love Lucy *to* Community. Chicago Review Press, 2014.

Belloï, Livio. "Des images seconds dans le cinema premier: Réflexivité et integration narrative dans *Erreur tragique* (L. Feuillade, 1912) et *The Evidence of the Film* (L. Marston, E. Thanhouser, 1913)." *La Furia Umana*, vol. 41, 2021, http://www.lafuriaumana.it/index.php/75-archive/lfu-41/1037-livio-belloi, accessed 13 March 2022.

Bentley, Nancy. "Conscious Observation: Jane Campion's *Portrait of a Lady*." In *Henry James Goes to the Movies*, edited by Susan M. Griffin, University Press of Kentucky, 2002, pp. 127–46.

Bernardi, Sandro. *Antonioni: Personnage paysage*. 2002. Presses Universitaires de Vincennes, 2006.

Berton, Mireille. "*Fenêtre sur cour*, la petite lucarne et l'Amérique des années 50, notes sur la construction du (de la) téléspectateur(trice)." *Décadrages, cinéma à travers champs*, no. 3, 2004, https://journals.openedition.org/decadrages/556, accessed 9 January 2021.

Biesen, Sheri Chinen. "Hitchcock from UK to US: *Jamaica Inn, Rebecca, Suspicion*." In *Film and Literature Modernism*, edited by Robert P. McParland, Cambridge Scholars Publishing, 2013, pp. 188–95.

Boillat, Alain. *Cinéma, machine à mondes*. Georg, 2014.

—. "The Comic Book Effect in the Age of CGI: When Film Adaptations of Comic Books Evoke the Fixity of Their Model." In *Comics and Adaptation*, 2015, edited by Benoît Mitaine, David Roche and Isabelle Schmitt-Pitiot, University Press of Mississippi, 2018, pp. 135–58.
Bondanella, Peter. *The Cinema of Federico Fellini*. Princeton University Press, 1992.
—. *The Films of Federico Fellini*. Cambridge University Press, 2002.
Brammer, Rebekah. "Peeling Back the Layers: Exploring Metafiction in *Birdman or (The Unexpected Virtue of Ignorance)*." *Screen Education*, vol. 93, 2019, pp. 122–8.
Brunow, Dagmar. "Deconstructing Essentialism and Revising Historiography: The Function of Metareference in Black British Filmmaking." In *The Metareferential Turn in Contemporary Arts and Media: Forms, Functions, Attempts at Explanation*, edited by Werner Wolf in collaboration with Katharina Bantleon and Jeff Thoss, Rodopi, 2011, pp. 341–55.
Burke, Frank. "Preface." In *Federico Fellini: Contemporary Perspectives*, edited by Frank Burke and Marguerite R. Waller, University of Toronto Press, 2002, pp. vii–ix.
—. "Federico Fellini: Realism/Representation/Signification." In *Federico Fellini: Contemporary Perspectives*, edited by Frank Burke and Marguerite R. Waller, University of Toronto Press, 2002, pp. 26–46.
Canaan, Howard. "Metafiction and the Gnostic Quest in *The Man in the High Castle*." *Journal of the Fantastic in the Arts*, vol. 12, no. 4, 2002, pp. 382–405.
Cerisuelo, Marc. *Le Mépris*. Les Éditions de la Transparence, 2006.
Cheyette, Bryan. "The Uncertainty of *Schindler's List*." In *Spielberg's Holocaust: Critical Perspectives on* Schindler's List, edited by Yosefa Loshitzky, Indiana University Press, 1997, pp. 226–38.
Church, David. "Afterword: Memory, Genre, and Self-Narrativization; Or, Why I Should Be a More Content Horror Fan." In *American Horror Film: The Genre at the Turn of the Millenium*, edited by Steffen Hantke, University Press of Mississippi, 2010, pp. 235–41.
Coates, Kristen. "Hyperreality in *Inglourious Basterds*: Tarantino's Interwoven Cinematic World in 1940s France." *The Film Stage*, 26 June 2010, https://thefilmstage.com/the-classroom-hyperreality-in-inglourious-basterds-tarantinos-interwoven-cinematic-world-in-1940s-france, accessed 11 September 2017.
Collins, Jim. "Postmodernism and Television." In *Channels of Discourse Reassembled: Television and Contemporary Criticism*, 1982, edited by Robert C. Allen, Routledge, 1992, pp. 246–75.
Cooper, Annabel. "'I Am Isabel, You Know?' The Antipodean Framing of Jane Campion's *Portrait of a Lady*." *M/C Journal*, vol. 11, no. 5, 2008, https://journal.media-culture.org.au/index.php/mcjournal/article/view/99, accessed 30 December 2021.
Coppola, Antoine. "Documentaire et mémoire historique chez Peter Watkins et Imamura Shohei." In *L'Insurrection médiatique: médias, histoire et documentaire dans le cinéma de Peter Watkins*, edited by Sébastien Denis and Jean-Pierre Bertin-Maghit, Presses Universitaires de Bordeaux, 2010, pp. 147–54.
Craig, Pamela and Martin Fradley. "Teenage Traumata: Youth, Affective Politics, and the Contemporary American Horror Film." In *American Horror Film: The Genre at the Turn of the Millennium*, edited by Steffen Hantke, University Press of Mississippi, 2010, pp. 77–102.
Dassanowsky, Robert von (ed.). *Quentin Tarantino's* Inglourious Basterds*: A Manipulation of Metacinema*. Continuum, 2012.
Del Río, Elena. "Fetish and Aura: Modes of Technological Engagement in *Family Viewing*." In *Image and Territory: Essays on Atom Egoyan*, edited by Monique Tschofen and Jennifer Burwell, Wilfrid Laurier University Press, 2007, pp. 29–52.
Deleyto, Celestino. "Self-Consciousness and the Classical Text: An Analysis of *Swing Time*." *Film Criticism*, vol. 16, no. 3, 1992, pp. 17–33.
—. *From Tinseltown to Bordertown: Los Angeles on Film*. Wayne State University Press, 2016.

Denis, Sébastien. "Médias et politique chez Peter Watkins. Des jeux du cirque médiatiques aux médias alternatifs." In *L'Insurrection médiatique: médias, histoire et documentaire dans le cinéma de Peter Watkins*, edited by Sébastien Denis and Jean-Pierre Bertin-Maghit, Presses Universitaires de Bordeaux, 2010, pp. 63–74.

—. "La subversion des genres et des techniques chez Peter Watkins." In *L'Insurrection médiatique: médias, histoire et documentaire dans le cinéma de Peter Watkins*, edited by Sébastien Denis and Jean-Pierre Bertin-Maghit, Presses Universitaires de Bordeaux, 2010, pp. 155–65.

Douchet, Jean. "Hitch and His Public." 1960. In *A Hitchcock Reader*, edited by Marshall Deutelbaum and Leland Poague, Wiley-Blackwell, 2009, pp. 19–24.

Dubois, Régis. "Quelle alternative à la monoforme? Perspective historique." In *L'Insurrection médiatique: médias, histoire et documentaire dans le cinéma de Peter Watkins*, edited by Sébastien Denis and Jean-Pierre Bertin-Maghit, Presses Universitaires de Bordeaux, 2010, pp. 19–30.

Dufour, Éric. *Le Cinéma d'horreur et ses figures*. Presses Universitaires de France, 2006.

Dumas, Chris. *Un-American Psycho: Brian De Palma and the Political Invisible*. Intellect, 2013.

Escobar, Patrick Maurer. "Fukasaku' Kinji's *Battles Without Honor and Humanity*: A Historiographic Metafiction of Post-War Japan." *Journal of Japanese & Korean Cinema*, vol. 5, no. 1–2, pp. 99–112.

Esquenazi, Jean-Pierre. *Godard et la société française des années 60*. Armand Colin, 2004.

Francis, Jr., James. *Remaking Horror: Hollywood's New Reliance on Scares of Old*. McFarland, 2013.

Fraser, Ryan. "Road Sickness: The Case of Oliver Stone's *Natural Born Killers*." *Cinémas: Revue d'études cinématographiques*, vol. 18, no. 2–3, 2008, https://id.erudit.org/iderudit/018554ar, accessed 9 January 2021.

Frayling, Christopher. *Sergio Leone: Something to Do with Death*. Faber and Faber, 2000.

Friant-Kessler, Brigitte and Ariane Hudelet. "Bastardy Spiralling down the Gutter: Sterne and Winterbottom's Games of Pleasures." In *In Praise of Cinematic Bastardy*, edited by Sébastien Lefait and Philippe Ortoli, Cambridge Scholars, 2012, pp. 158–69.

Gelly, Christophe. "'The Abominable Bride': Sherlock and Seriality." *Exploring Seriality on Screen: Audiovisual Narratives in Film and Television*, edited by Ariane Hudelet and Anne Crémieux, Routledge, 2021, pp. 213–32.

Gordon, Paul. *Dial "M" for Mother: A Freudian Hitchcock*. Fairleigh Dickinson University Press, 2008.

Gomez, Joseph A. "« Nous faisons tous partie de l'Histoire »: temps, Histoire et subversion de la monoforme." In *L'Insurrection médiatique: médias, histoire et documentaire dans le cinéma de Peter Watkin*s, edited by Sébastien Denis and Jean-Pierre Bertin-Maghit, Presses Universitaires de Bordeaux, 2010, pp. 101–12.

Gonçalves Miranda, Rui. "*Our Beloved Month of August*: Between Filming of the Real and the Reality of Filming." In *Portugal's Global Cinema: Industry, History and Culture*, edited by Mariana Liza, I.B. Tauris, 2018, pp. 33–46.

Goudet, Stéphane. *Buster Keaton*. Cahiers du cinéma/Le Mone, 2007.

Gregory, Chris. *Be Seeing You: Decoding* The Prisoner. University of Luton Press, 1997.

Haber, Karen. *Kong Unbound: The Cultural Impact, Pop Mythos, and Scientific Plausibility of a Cinematic Legend*. Gallery Books, 2005.

Hansen, Miriam Bratu. "*Schindler's List* is Not *Shoah*: Second Commandment, Popular Modernism, and Public Memory." In *Spielberg's Holocaust: Critical Perspectives on* Schindler's List, edited by Yosefa Loshitzky, Indiana University Press, 1997, pp. 77–103.

Hare, Bill. "*Blow-up*—Between Form and Formlessness." *MAP*, vol. 8, 2006, https://mapmagazine.co.uk/blow-up-between-form-and-for, accessed 24 December 2021.

Harris, Thomas. "*Rear Window* and *Blow-Up*: Hitchcock's Straighforwardness vs. Antonioni's Ambiguity." *Literature/Film Quarterly*, vol. 15, 1983, pp. 60–3.
Hatchuel, Sarah. *Shakespeare: From Stage to Screen*. Cambridge University Press, 2004.
—. LOST: *Fiction vitale*. Presses Universitaires de France, 2013.
—. *Rêves et séries américaines: La fabrication d'autres mondes*. Rouge Profond, 2015.
—. "« What a piece of work is your machine, Harold »: Shakespeare et la réinvention de l'humanité dans les séries américaines d'anticipation." *TV/Series* vol. 14, 2018, https://journals.openedition.org/tvseries/3068, accessed 15 November 2021.
Hatfield, Charles. *Alternative Comics: An Emerging Literature*. University Press of Mississippi, 2005.
Hicks, Jeremy. *Dziga Vertov: Defining Documentary Film*. I.B. Tauris, 2007.
Hill, John, *Ken Loach: The Politics of Film and Television*. BFI/Palgrave Macmillan, 2011.
Horowitz, Sara R. "But Is It Good for the Jews? Spielberg's Schindler and the Aesthetics of Atrocity." In *Spielberg's Holocaust: Critical Perspectives on* Schindler's List, edited by Yosefa Loshitzky, Indiana University Press, 1997, pp. 119–39.
Howe, Alexis. "Ye, No, or Maybe? Transitions in Chilean Society in Pablo Larrain's *No*." *Hispania*, vol. 98, no. 3, 2015, pp. 421–30.
Hudelet, Ariane. "Austen and Sterne: Beyond Heritage." In *A Companion to Literature, Film, and Adaptation*, edited by Deborah Cartmell, Wiley-Blackwell, 2012, pp. 256–71.
—. The Wire: *Les règles du jeu*. Presses Universitaires de France, 2016.
Humphries, Reynold. *Fritz Lang: Genre and Representation in his American Films*. The Johns Hopkins University Press, 1989.
Ivănescu, Andra. "*Westworld* and the Pursuit of Meaningful Play." In *Reading Westworld*, edited by Alex Goody and Antonio Mackay, Palgrave Macmillan, 2019, pp. 79–96.
Jung, Nike. "History, Fiction and the Politics of Corporeality in Pablo Larrain's Dictatorship Trilogy." In *Film, History and Memory*, edited by Jenni M. Carlsten and Fearghal McGarry, Palgrave Macmillan, 2015, pp. 118–33.
Kligerman, Eric. "Reels of Justice: *Inglourious Basterds*, *The Sorrow and the Pity*, and Jewish revenge fantasies." In *Quentin Tarantino's* Inglourious Basterds: *A Manipulation of Metacinema*, edited by Robert von Dassanowsky, Continuum, 2012, pp. 135–62.
Kràl, Petr. *Les Burlesques ou parade des somnanbules*. Stock cinéma, 1986.
Lagny, Michèle. "Imiter pour dénoncer: le paradoxe du cinéaste confronté aux médias." In *L'Insurrection médiatique: médias, histoire et documentaire dans le cinéma de Peter Watkin*s, edited by Sébastien Denis and Jean-Pierre Bertin-Maghit, Presses Universitaires de Bordeaux, 2010, pp. 31–9.
—. "Entre documentaire et fiction, la mémoire-histoire chez Peter Watkins." In *L'Insurrection médiatique: médias, histoire et documentaire dans le cinéma de Peter Watkins*, edited by Sébastien Denis and Jean-Pierre Bertin-Maghit, Presses Universitaires de Bordeaux, 2010, pp. 139–46.
Landesman, Ohad. "*Holy Motors*: Metamediation on Digital Cinema's Present and Future." In *Metacinema: The Form and Content of Filmic Reference and Reflexivity*, edited by David LaRocca, Oxford University Press, 2021.
Lefait, Sébastien. *Surveillance on Screen: Monitoring Contemporary Films and Television Programs*. Scarecrow Press, 2013.
—. "Du *Making of* comme forme mémorielle: *Tristram Shandy: A Cock & Bull Story* (Winterbottom, 2005)." In *Memory in/of English-speaking Cinema*, edited by Zeenat Saleh and Melvyn Stokes, Michel Houdiard, 2014, pp. 505–18.
—. "'It's not a technological problem we have, it's a human one': *Black Mirror*, ou la dystopie intégrée." *Otrante*, vol. 42, 2017, pp. 127–44.

Leo, John. "Oliver Stone's paranoid propaganda." *US News & World Report*, 13 January 1992.
Librach, Ronald S. "Sex, Lies and Audiotape: Politics and Heuristics in *Dressed to Kill* and *Blow Out*." *Literature/Film Quarterly*, vol. 26, no. 3, 1998, pp. 166–7.
Lipińska, Katarzyna. "*L'Évasion du cinema Liberté* (1990) de Wojciech Marczewski, un métafilm sur la fin du communism polonaise." *La Fura Umana*, vol. 41, 2021, http://www.lafuriaumana.it/index.php/75-archive/lfu-41/1036-katarzyna-lipinska-l-evasion-du-cinema-liberte-1990-de-wojciech-marczew-un-metafilm-sur-la-fin-du-communisme-polonais, accessed 13 March 2022.
Loren, Scott and Jörg Metelmann. *Irritation of Life: The Subversive Melodrama of Michael Haneke, David Lynch and Lars von Trier*. Schüren, 2013.
Machinal, Hélène. *Posthumains en série: Les détectives du futur*. Presses Universitaires François Rabelais, 2020.
Mallin, Eric S. "'You Kilt My Foddah': Or Arnold, Prince of Denmark." *Shakespeare Quarterly*, vol. 50, no. 2, 1999, pp. 127–51.
Marie, Michel. *Comprendre Godard: Travelling avant sur* À bout de souffle *et* Le Mépris. Armand Colin, 2006.
Menegaldo, Gilles. "Where the Spectator Stands: Projection and Reception in the Cinema of Woody Allen (*Play It Again, Sam, Stardust Memories, The Purple Rose of Cairo*)." In *Approaches to Film and Reception Theories*, edited by Christophe Gelly and David Roche, Presses Universitaires Blaise Pascal, 2012, pp. 137–57.
Michelson, Annette. "'The Man with the Movie Camera': From Magician to Epistemologist." *Artforum*, vol. 10, no. 7, 1972, pp. 60–72.
—. "The Kinetic Iconic and the Work of Mourning: Prolegoma to the Analysis of a Textual System." In *The Red Screen: Politics, Society, Art in Soviet Cinema*, edited by Anna Lawton, Routledge, 1992, pp. 113–30.
Mickwitz, Nina. *Documentary Comics: Graphic Truth-Telling in a Skeptical Age*. Palgrave Macmillan, 2016.
Mléčková, Kateřina. "Western Goes East: *Limonádový Joe* and its possible interpretations." Thesis, Masarykovy Univerzity, 2006.
Modleski, Tania. *The Women Who Knew Too Much: Hitchcock and Feminist Theory*. Routledge, 1988.
Morreale, Joanne. *The Donna Reed Show*. Wayne State University Press, 2012.
Morris, Nigel. *Empire of Light: The Cinema of Steven Spielberg*. Wallflower Press, 2007. Ebook.
Moure, José. *Michangelo Antonioni, cinéaste de l'évidemment*. L'Harmattan, 2001.
Murillo, Céline. *Le Cinéma de Jim Jarmusch: un monde plus loin*. L'Harmattan, 2016.
Nama, Adilifu. *Race on the QT: Blackness and the Films of Quentin Tarantino*. University of Texas Press, 2015.
Napier, Susan. "'Excuse Me, Who Are You?' Performance, the Gaze, and the Female in the Works of Kon Satoshi." In *Cinema Anime*, edited by Steven T. Brown, Palgrave Macmillan, 2006, pp. 23–42.
Nolley, Ken. "Peter Watkins et l'Histoire. Du discours sur l'Histoire à la déconstruction de la violence du discours." In *L'Insurrection médiatique: Médias, histoire et documentaire dans le cinéma de Peter Watkins*, edited by Sébastien Denis and Jean-Pierre Bertin-Maghit, Presses Universitaires de Bordeaux, 2010, pp. 91–100.
O'Healy, Áine. "Interview with the Vamp: Deconstructing Femininity in Fellini's Final Films (*Intervista, La voce della luna*)." In *Federico Fellini: Contemporary Perspectives*, edited by Frank Burke and Marguerite R. Waller, University of Toronto Press, 2002, pp. 26–46.
Ortoli, Philippe. "*Bram Stoker's Dracula* de Coppola: du mythe de cinéma au mythe du cinéma."

In Dracula, *l'œuvre de Bram Stoker et le film de Francis Ford Coppola*, edited by Gilles Menegaldo and Dominique Sipière, Ellipses, 2005, pp. 235–42.

—. *Le Musée imaginaire de Quentin Tarantino*. Cerf-Corlet, 2012.

Pagnoni, Berns, Fernando Gabriel and Emiliano Aguilar. "Say Heil! To Architecture." In *The Man in the High Castle and Philosophy: Subversive Reports from Another Reality*, edited by Bruce Krajewski and Joshua Heter, Open Court, 2017, pp. 31–44. Ebook.

Palmer, R. Barton. "From Obstrusive Narration to Crosscutting: Adapting the Doubleness of John Fowles's *The French Lieutenant's Woman*." In *Authorship in Film Adaptation*, edited by Jack Boozer, University of Texas Press, 2008, pp. 179–202.

Past, Elena M. "Environmental Fellini: Petroculture, the Anthropocene, and the Cinematic Road." In *A Companion to Federico Fellini*, edited by Frank Burke, Marguerite Waller and Marita Gubareva, Wiley Blackwell, 2020, pp. 347–60.

Pheasant-Kelly, Fran. "Reframing Parody and Intertexuality in *Scream*: Formal and Theoretical Approaches to the 'Postmodern' Slasher." In *Style and Form in the Hollywood Slasher*, edited by Wickham Clayton, Palgrave Macmillan, 2015, pp. 149–60.

Phillips, Gene D. *Some Like It Wilder: The Life and Controversial Films of Billy Wilder*. The University Press of Kentucky, 2010.

Pieldner, Judit. "Space Constructions in Adaptations of *Hamlet*." *Acta Universitatis Sapientiae, Philogica*, vol. 4., no. 1, 2012, pp. 43–58, http://www.acta.sapientia.ro/acta-philo/C4-1/Philo41-4.pdf, accessed 2 June 2021.

Prédal, René. *Michelangelo Antonioni ou la vigilance du désir*. Les Éditions du Cerf, 1991.

Quart, Leonard and Barbara Quart. "Ragtime without a Melody." *Literature/Film Quarterly*, vol. 10, no. 2, 1982, pp. 71–4.

Radstone, Susannah. "Cinema/memory/history." *Screen*, vol. 36, no. 1, 1995, pp. 34–47.

Ragel, Philippe. "L'Olivier du Gilan: résurgences." *Entrelacs*, no. 6, 2007, pp. 103–18.

—. *Le Film en suspens: La cinéstase, un essai de définition*. Presses Universitaires de Rennes, 2015.

Ramaeker, Paul. "Notes on the split-field diopter." *Film History*, vol. 19, 2007, pp. 179–98.

Rapf, Joanna E. "Volatile Forms: The Transgressive Energy of *Ragtime* as Novel and Film." *Literature/Film Quarterly*, vol. 26, no. 1, 1998, pp. 16–22.

Roche, David. "The Death of the Subject in David Lynch's *Lost Highway* and *Mulholland Drive*." *E- rea*, vol. 2, no. 2, 2004, https://erea.revues.org/432, accessed 9 January 2022.

—. "Books and Letters in Joe Wright's *Pride & Prejudice* (2005): Anticipating the Spectator's Response through the Thematization of Film Adaptation." *Persuasions On-Line*, vol. 27, no. 2, 2007, http://www.jasna.org/persuasions/on-line/vol27no2/roche.htm, accessed 9 January 2022.

—. "The Blues of David Lynch." *Film and Colour*, edited by Raphaëlle Costa de Beauregard, Michel Houdiard, 2009, pp. 447–59.

—. "*Twin Peaks: Fire Walk With Me* (1992) and David Lynch's Aesthetics of Frustration." *Textes & Contextes*, vol. 5, 2010, https://revuesshs.u-bourgogne.fr/textes&contextes/document.php?id=1103, accessed 9 January 2021.

—. "Comment Hollywood figure l'intériorité dans les films « hollywoodiens » de David Lynch: *Lost Highway* (1997), *Mulholland Drive* (2001) et *Inland Empire* (2006)." *E-rea*, vol. 9, no. 1, 2011, https://erea.revues.org/1872, accessed 9 January 2022.

—. *Making and Remaking Horror in the 1970s and 2000s: Why Don't They Do It Like They Used To?* University Press of Mississippi, 2014.

—. "The Remake as (Dis)avowal: The Ambivalent Stances of the Hollywood Blockbuster Remakes of the 2000s." *Représentations*, 2015, https://representations.univ-grenoble-alpes.fr/IMG/pdf/2-roche_remakes1_def.pdf, accessed 9 January 2022.

—. "L'esthétique du temps dans *Twin Peaks*. In *Twin Peaks: A l'intérieur du rêve*, edited by Sarah Hatchuel, Le Bord de l'eau, 2018, pp. 17–35.

—. "Spielberg's Poetics of Horror." *Steven Spielberg, Hollywood Wunderkind & Humanist*, edited by David Roche, Presses Universitaires de la Méditerranée, 2018.

—. "*Rabbits* (2002) et *INLAND EMPIRE* (2008): Réflexion sur la création audiovisuelle à l'ère du numérique." *LIGEIA: dossiers sur l'art*, vol. 165–8, 2018, pp. 149–59.

—. "'You know, when you suspect something, it's always better when it turns out to be true.': Memory and Media in "The Entire History of You," episode S1E3 of *Black Mirror* (Channel 4/Netflix, 2011–)." *TV/Series*, vol. 14, 2018, https://journals.openedition.org/tvseries/3094, accessed 3 January 2021.

—. *Inglourious Basterds de Quentin Tarantino*. Vendémiaire, 2019.

Roche, Thierry. *Blow up, un regard anthropologique*. Yellow Now, 2010.

Roger, Philippe. "La Couleur du 'remake'." In *Film and Colour*, edited by Raphaëlle Costa de Beauregard, Michel Houdiard, 2009, pp. 314–25.

Ropars-Wuilleumier, Marie-Claire. "L'espace et le temps dans la narration des années 60: *Blow up* ou le négatif du récit." In *L'Œuvre de Michelangelo Antonioni* (volume 2), edited by Lorenzo Cuccu, Cinecitta International, 1966/1984.

Rosenstone, Robert A. "*JFK*: Historical Fact/Historical Film." *American Historical Review*, vol. 97, no. 2, 1992, pp. 506–11.

Rothwell, Kenneth Sprague. *A History of Shakespeare on Screen: A Century of Film and Television*. Cambridge University Press, 1999.

Round, Julia. "The Transformations of Harvey Pekar's *American Splendor*: 'Ordinary Life is Pretty Complex Stuff.'" In *Real Lives, Celebrity Stories: Narratives of Ordinary and Extraordinary People Across Media*, edited by Bronwen Thomas and Julia Round, Bloomsbury, 2014, pp. 95–110.

Santas, Constantine. "The Remake of *Psycho* (Gus Van Sant, 1998): Creativity or Cinematic Blasphemy?" *Senses of Cinema*, vol. 10, 2000, https://www.sensesofcinema.com/2000/feature-articles/psycho-2, accessed 15 November 2021.

Sarnelli, Laura. "Ghostly Femininities: *Christabel*, *Carmilla*, and *Mulholland Drive*." *Anglistica*, vol. 12, no. 1, 2008, pp. 83–100.

Schlipphacke, Heidi. "*Inglourious Basterds* and the gender of revenge." In *Quentin Tarantino's Inglourious Basterds: A Manipulation of Metacinema*, edited by Robert von Dassanowsky, Continuum, 2012, pp. 113–34.

Semenza, Greg M. Colón. "The Ethics of Appropriation: *Samson Agonistes*, *Inglourious Basterds*, and the Biblical Samson Tale." *Adaptation*, vol. 7, no. 1, 2004, pp. 62–81.

Shibolet, Yotam. "*Waltz with Bashir*'s Animated Traces: Troubled Indexicality in Contemporary Documentary Rhetorics." In *Metacinema: The Form and Content of Filmic Reference and Reflexivity*, edited by David LaRocca, Oxford University Press, 2021, pp. 271–90.

Simon, Art. "The Making of Alert Viewers: The Mixing of Fact and Fiction in *JFK*." *Cineaste*, vol. 19, no. 1, 1992, pp. 14–15.

Smith, Imogen Sara. *Buster Keaton: The Persistence of Comedy*. CreateSpace Independent Publishing Platform, 2013.

Southern, Nile. "*End of the Road* Rides Again: Revival of a Sixties Anti-Establishment Classic." *Cineaste*, vol. 37, no. 4, 2012, pp. 4–9.

Speck, Oliver C. (ed.). *Quentin Tarantino's Django Unchained: The Continuation of Metacinema*. Bloomsbury, 2014.

Sperb, Jason. "Removing the Experience: Simulacrum as an Autobiographical Act in *American Splendor*." *Biography*, vol. 29, no. 1, 2006, pp. 123–39.

Steel, Ronald. "Oliver Stone's riveting offense against history: Mr. Smith Goes to the Twilight Zone." *The New Republic*, vol. 206, 3 February 1992, pp. 30–2.

Suárez, Juan A. *Jim Jarmusch*. University of Illinois Press, 2007.

Takayuki, Tatsumi. "The Advent of Meguro Empress: Decoding the Avant-Pop Anime *TAMALA 2010*." In *Cinema Anime*, edited by Steven T. Brown, Palgrave Macmillan, 2006, pp. 65–77.

Taurino, Giulia and Sara Casoli. "Factitive Maps: Manipulating Spaces and Characters in Vast Narratives." *Reading Westworld*, edited by Alex Goody and Antonio Mackay, Palgrave Macmillan, 2019, pp. 61–78.

Toledo, Vania Barraza. "Reviewing the Present in Pablo Larraín's 'Historical Cinema'." *Iberoamericana*, vol. 151, 2013, pp. 159–72.

Tomasulo, Frank P. "'You're tellin' me you didn't see': Hitchcock's *Rear Window* and Antonioni's *Blow-Up*." In *Alfred Hitchcock: Influence, Imitation, and Intertexuality*, edited by David Boyd and R. Barton Palmer, University of Texas Press, 2006, pp. 145–72.

—. "*Adaptation* as Adaptation: From Susan Orlean's *The Orchid Thief* to Charlie (and 'Donald') Kaufman's Screenplay to Spike Jonze's Film." In *Authorship in Film Adaptation*, edited by Jack Boozer, University of Texas Press, 2008, pp. 161–78.

Truffaut, François. *Hitchcock*. 1966. A Touchstone Book, 1985.

Trumpener, Katie. "Fragments of the Mirror: Self-Reference, Mise-en-Abyme, *Vertigo*." In *Hitchcock's Rereleased Films: From* Rope *to* Vertigo, edited by Walter Raubicheck and Walter Srebnik, Wayne State University Press, 1991, pp. 175–88.

Vahdani, Alizera "*Nuovo Cinema Paradiso*: A Reflection of Italian Society." *Offscreen*, vol. 15, no. 8, 2011, https://offscreen.com/view/nuovo_cinema_paradiso, accessed 9 January 2022.

Van Eynde, Laurent. *Vertige de l'image: L'esthétique réflexive d'Alfred Hitchcock*. Presses Universitaires de France, 2015.

Vanelli, Marco. "'Io non me ne intendo': Fellini's Relationship to Film Language." In *A Companion to Federico Fellini*, edited by Frank Burke, Marguerite Waller and Marita Gubareva, Wiley Blackwell, 2020, pp. 207–21.

Voigts-Virchow, Eckart. "*Metadaptation*: Adaptation and Intermediality – Cock and Bull." *Journal of Adaptation in Film & Performance*, vol. 2, no. 2, 2009, pp. 137–52.

Wartenberg, Thomas E. "*The Act of Killing*: Empathy, Morality, and Re-Enactment." In *Metacinema: The Form and Content of Filmic Reference and Reflexivity*, edited by David LaRocca, Oxford University Press, 2021, pp. 255–70.

Wee, Valerie. "The *Scream* Trilogy: 'Hyperpostmodernism,' and the Late-Nineties Slasher Film." *Journal of Film and Video*, vol. 57, no. 3, 2006, pp. 50–61.

Wells, Paul. *The Horror Genre: From Beezlebub to Blair Witch*. Wallflower, 2000.

Wells-Lassagne, Shannon. "Filming Theory in Patricia Rozema's *Mansfield Park* (1999)." In *Approaches to Film and Reception Theories*, edited by Christophe Gelly and David Roche, Presses Universitaires Blaise Pascal, 2012, pp. 191–205.

—. "Transforming the Traditional Sitcom: Abed in *Community*." *TV/Series*, vol. 1, 2012, https://journals.openedition.org/tvseries/1560, accessed 15 November 2021.

—. "Adaptation, or Falsifying Memory." In *Memory in/of English-speaking Cinema*, edited by Zeenat Saleh and Melvyn Stokes, Michel Houdiard, 2014, pp. 501–15.

West, Rebecca. "*Roma*: Amor Through the Looking-Glass." In *A Companion to Federico Fellini*, edited by Frank Burke, Marguerite Waller and Marita Gubareva, Wiley Blackwell, 2020, pp. 487–9.

Whalen, Tom. "Romancing Film: Images of *Dracula*." *Literature/Film Quarterly*, vol. 23, no. 2, 1995, pp. 99–101.

Worland, Rick. *The Horror Film: An Introduction*. Blackwell, 2007.
Yu, Chang-Min. "The Digital Dreams Its Rivals: *The Man in the High Castle* (Amazon Prime, 2015)." *Film Criticism*, vol. 40, no. 3, 2016, https://quod.lib.umich.edu/f/fc/13761232.0040. 305?view=text;rgn=main, accessed 15 November 2021.
Zelizer, Barbie. "Every Once in a While: *Schindler's List* and the Shaping of History." In *Spielberg's Holocaust: Critical Perspectives on* Schindler's List, edited by Yosefa Loshitzky, Indiana University Press, 1997, pp. 18–40.
Zucconi, Francesco. "When the Copywriter is the Protagonist: History and Intermediality in Pabloa Larrain's *No* (2012)." *Film and Media Studies*, vol. 12, 2016, pp. 129–47.

METACINEMA, METAFICTION, REFLEXIVITY AND OTHER META-PHENOMENA

Abel, Lionel. *Metatheatre: A New View of Dramatic Form*. Jill & Wang, 1963.
Ames, Christopher. *Movies about the Movies: Hollywood Reflected*. The University of Kentucky Press, 1997.
Andacht, Fernando. "On the use of self-disclosure as a mode of audiovisual reflexivity." *Self-Reference in the Media*, edited by Winfried Nöth and Nina Bishara, Mouton de Gruyter, 2007, pp. 165–81.
Angus, Bill. *Metadrama and the Informer in Shakespeare and Jonson*. Edinburgh University Press, 2016.
—. "Metadrama, Authority, and the Roots of Incredulity." In *Drama and the Postmodern: Assessing the Limits of Metatheatre*, edited by Daniel K. Jernigan, Cambria Press, 2008, pp. 45–58.
—. *Intelligence and Metadrama in the Early Modern Theatre*. Edinburgh University Press, 2019.
Arrivé, Mathilde. "Introduction: Remedying Remediation?" *Leaves*, vol. 7, 2019, https://climas.u-bordeaux-montaigne.fr/numeros-parus/59-leaves-n-07-textes/409-introduction-remedying-remediation-mathilde-arrive, accessed 13 December 2021.
Böhn, Andreas. "Nostalgia of the Media / in the Media." In *Self-Reference in the Media*, edited by Winfried Nöth and Nina Bishara, Mouton de Gruyter, 2007, pp. 143–54.
Boillat, Alain. "*Stranger than Fiction*: Métalepse de Genette et quelques univers filmiques contemporains." *Cinéma & Cie*, vol. 12, no. 18, 2012, pp. 21–31.
Carter, Christopher. *Metafilm: Materialist Rhetoric and Reflexive Cinema*. Ohio State University Press, 2018.
Casetti, Francesco. *Inside the Gaze: The Fiction Film and Its Spectator*. 1983. Indiana University Press, 1999.
Cerisuelo, Marc. *Hollywood à l'écran, essai de poétique historique des films: l'exemple des métafilms américains*. Presses de la Sorbonne Nouvelle, 2000.
Chinita, Fátima. "The Tricks of the Trade (Un)exposed." *Networking Knowledge*, vol. 7, no. 4, 2014, https://ojs.meccsa.org.uk/index.php/netknow/article/view/353/183, accessed 5 May 2017.
—. "Metacinema as Authorial Enunciation: A Taxonomy of Hybrid Films." *La Furia Umana*, vol. 41, 2021, http://www.lafuriaumana.it/index.php/75-lfu-41/1030-fatima-chinita-metacinema-as-authorial-enunciation-a-taxonomy-of-hybrid-films, accessed 10 September 2021.
Cohan, Steven. *Hollywood by Hollywood: The Backstudio Picture and the Mystique of Making Movies*. Oxford University Press, 2018.
Colapietro, Vincent. "Distortion, Fabrication, and Disclosure in a Self-Referential Culture: the Irresistible Force of Reality." In *Self-Reference in the Media*, edited by Winfried Nöth and Nina Bishara, Mouton de Gruyter, 2007, pp. 31–43.
Connor, J.D. "The Biggest Independent Pictures Ever Made: Industrial Reflexivity Today." In *The Wiley-Blackwell History of American Film Volume IV*, edited by Cynthia Lucia, Roy Grundmann and Art Simon, Wiley-Blackwell, 2012, pp. 517–41.

Currie, Mark (ed.). *Metafiction*. Longman/Routledge, 1995.
Dällenbach, Lucien. *La Récit spéculaire: Essai sur la mise en abyme*. Seuil, 1977.
Févry, Sébastien. *La Mise en abyme filmique: Essai de typologie*. Éditions du Céfal, 2000.
Fredericksen, Don. "Modes of Reflexive Film." *Quarterly Review of Film & Video*, vol. 4, no. 3, 1979, pp. 299–320.
Fülop, Erika. "La Logique de l'abyme: Ambiguïté et paradoxe, nouvelles perspectives sur l'auto-enchâssement." In *Comprendre la mise en abyme*, edited by Tonia Raus and Gian Maria Tore, Presses Universitaires de Rennes, 2019, pp. 103–19.
Gass, William. *Fiction and the Figures of Life*. Knopf, 1970.
Genette, Gérard. *Métalepse: De la figure à la fiction*. Seuil, 2004.
Hutcheon, Linda. *Narcissistic Narrative: The Metafictional Paradox*. Wilfrid Laurier University Press, 1980.
—. *A Theory of Parody: The Teachings of Twentieth-Century Art Forms*. 1985. Routledge, 1991.
—. *A Poetics of Postmodernism: History, Theory, Fiction*. Routledge, 1988.
Kampmann, Walther Bo. "Self-reference in computer games: A formalistic approach." In *Self-Reference in the Media*, edited by Winfried Nöth and Nina Bishara, Mouton de Gruyter, 2007, pp. 219–36.
LaRocca, David. "Introduction: An Invitation to the Varieties and Virtues of 'Meta-ness' in the Art and Culture of Film." In *Metacinema: The Form and Content of Filmic Reference and Reflexivity*, edited by David LaRocca, Oxford University Press, 2021, pp. 1–28.
Limoges, Jean-Marc. "La métalepse au cinéma: Aux frontières de la transgression." *Cinergie*, vol. 1, 2012, pp. 126–44.
—. "Réflexivité métaphorique, mise en abyme (méta)textuelle et métaphore cinématographique." In *Comprendre la mise en abyme*, edited by Tonia Raus and Gian Maria Tore, Presses Universitaires de Rennes, 2019, pp. 43–59.
Madsen, Rune Bruun. "When Fiction Points the Finger – Metafiction in Films and TV Series." *Kosmorama.org*, 2015, http://www.kosmorama.org/ServiceMenu/05-English/Articles/When-fiction-points-the-finger.aspx, accessed 25 November 2019.
Mayne, Judith. *The Ideologies of Metacinema*. PhD, State University of New York at Buffalo, 1975.
Metz, Christian. *L'Énonciation impersonelle ou le site du film*. Méridiens Klincksiek, 1991.
—. *Impersonal Enunciation, or the Place of Film*. 1991. Oxford University Press, 2016.
Mwangi, Evan Maina. *Africa Writes Back to Self: Metafiction, Gender, Sexuality*. State University of New York Press, 2009.
Nöth, Winfried. "Self-reference in the media: The semiotic framework." In *Self-Reference in the Media*, edited by Winfried Nöth and Nina Bishara, Mouton de Gruyter, 2007, pp. 3–30.
Raus, Tonia. "Présentation: Cette impression que l'on n'en finira jamais." In *Comprendre la mise en abyme: Arts et médias au second degré*, edited by Tonia Raus and Gian Maria Tore, Presses Universitaires de Rennes, 2019, pp. 7–19.
Ricardou, Jean. *Problèmes du nouveau roman*. Seuil, 1967.
Roche, David. *Quentin Tarantino: Poetics and Politics of Cinematic Metafiction*. University Press of Mississippi, 2018.
Rose, Margaret. *Parody//Meta-fiction: An Analysis of Parody as a Critical Mirror to the Writing and Reception of Fiction*. Croom Helm, 1979.
Ryan, Marie-Laure. "Looking through the computer screen: Self-reflexivity in net.art." In *Self-Reference in the Media*, edited by Winfried Nöth and Nina Bishara, Mouton de Gruyter, 2007, pp. 269–89.
Schmidt, Nicolas. "Les usages du procédé du film dans le film." *CinémAction*, vol. 118, 2007, pp. 102–12.

Scholes, Robert. "Metafiction." *Iowa Review*, vol. 1, 1970, pp. 100–15.
Sirvent, Michel. "Réflexions sur la mise en abyme. Entre récit écrit et récit filmique." In *Comprendre la mise en abyme*, edited by Tonia Raus and Gian Maria Tore, Presses Universitaires de Rennes, 2019, pp. 61–72.
Siska, William C. "Metacinema: A Modern Necessity." *Literature/Film Quarterly*, vol. 7, no. 4, 1979, pp. 285–9.
Sorin, Cécile. *Pratiques de la parodie et du pastiche au cinéma*. L'Harmattan, 2010.
Spies, Virginie. *La Télévision dans le miroir: théorie, histoire et analyse des émissions réflexives*. L'Harmattan, 2004.
Stam, Robert. *Reflexivity in Film and Literature: From* Don Quixote *to Jean-Luc Godard*. Columbia University Press, 1992.
Stuckey, G. Andrew. *Metacinema in Contemporary Chinese Film*. Hong Kong University Press, 2018.
Szczepanik, Petr. "Intermediality and (Inter)media Reflexivity in Contemporary Cinema." *Convergence*, vol. 8, no.4, 2002, pp. 29–36.
Tore, Gian Maria. « Post-scriptum – Puissances et limites de la mise en abyme. Ou quand il y a fait de langage ». In *Comprendre la mise en abyme: Arts et médias au second degré*, edited by Tonia Raus and Gian Maria Tore, Presses Universitaires de Rennes, 2019, pp. 247–62.
Toth, Josh. *Truth and Metafiction: Plasticity and Renewal in American Narrative*. Bloomsbury, 2020.
Waugh, Patricia. *Metafiction: The Theory and Practice of Self-Conscious Fiction*. Routledge, 1984.
White, Hayden. *Metahistory: The Historical Imagination in Nineteenth-Century Europe*. The Johns Hopkins University Press, 1973.
Withalm, Gloria. "The self-reflexive screen: Outlines of a comprehensive model." In *Self-Reference in the Media*, edited by Winfried Nöth and Nina Bishara, Mouton de Gruyter, 2007, pp. 125–42.
Wolf, Werner. *Ästhetische Illusion und Illusionsdurchbrechung in der Erzählkunst: Theorie und Geschichte mit Schwerpunkt auf englischem illusionsstörenden Erzählen*. Niemeyer, 1993.
—. "Metareference across Media: The Concept, its Transmedial Potentials and Problems, Main Forms and Functions." *Metareference across Media: Theory and Case Studies*, edited by Werner Wolf in collaboration with Katharina Bantleon and Jeff Thoss, Rodopi, 2009, pp. 1–85.
—. "Is There a Metareferential Turn, and If So, How Can It Be Explained?" *The Metareferential Turn in Contemporary Arts and Media: Forms, Functions, Attempts at Explanation*, edited by Werner Wolf in collaboration with Katharina Bantleon and Jeff Thoss, Rodopi, 2011, pp. 1–47.
Yacavone, Daniel. "The Cognitive and Affective Dimensions of Cinematic Reflexivity." *La Furia Umana*, vol. 41, 2021, http://www.lafuriaumana.it/index.php/75-lfu-41/1029-daniel-yacavone-reconceiving-cinematic-reflexivity, accessed 15 August 2021.
—. "Recursive Reflections: Types, Modes and Forms of Cinematic Reflexivity." In *Metacinema: The Form and Content of Filmic Reference and Reflexivity*, edited by David LaRocca, Oxford University Press, 2021, pp. 85–115.

GENERAL FILM AND MEDIA THEORY AND CRITICISM

Albera, François (ed.). *Les Formalistes russes et le cinéma: poétique du film*. Nathan, 1996.
Albera, François. *L'Avant-garde au cinéma*. Armand Colin, 2005.
Altman, Rick. *Film/Genre*. BFI, 1999.
Arnheim, Rudolf. *Film as Art*. 1933. University of California Press, 1957.
Bacon-Smith, Camille. *Enterprising Women: Television Fandom and the Creation of Popular Myth*. University of Pennsylvania Press, 1992.

Baron, Jaimie. *The Archive Effect: Found Footage and the Audiovisual Experience of History*. Routledge, 2014.

Baudry, Jean-Louis. "Ideological Effects of the Basic Cinematographic Apparatus." 1970. *Film Quarterly*, vol. 28, no. 2, 1974–5, pp. 39–47.

—. "The Apparatus." 1975. *Camera Obscura*, vol.1, no. 1, 1976, pp. 104–26.

Bazin, André. "The Ontology of the Photographic Image." 1945. In *What Is Cinema? Volume 1*, University of California Press, 2005, pp. 9–16.

Behlil, Melis. "Ravenous Cinephiles." *Cinephilia: Movies, Love and Memory*, edited by Marijke de Valck and Malte Hagener, Amsterdam University Press, 2005, pp. 111–24.

Bellour, Raymond. *Le Corps du cinéma: hypnoses, émotions, animalités*. P.O.L., 2009.

Benjamin, Walter. "The Work of Art in the Age of Mechanical Reproducibility." Third version. *Walter Benjamin: Selected Writings, Volume 4. 1938–1940*, edited by Howard Eiland and Michael W. Jennings, Harvard University Press, 2003, pp. 251–83.

Biltereyst, Daniel. "Reality TV, Troublesome Pictures and Panics: Reappraising the Public Controversy around Reality TV in Europe." *Understanding Reality Television*, edited by Su Holmes and Deborah Jermyn, Routledge, 2004, pp. 91–110.

Bobo, Jacqueline. "Black Women's Responses to *The Color Purple*." *Jump Cut*, vol. 33, 1988, pp. 43–51.

Bolter, Jay David and Richard Grusin. *Remediation: Understanding New Media*. MIT Press, 1999.

Bordwell, David. *Narration in the Fiction Film*. University of Wisconsin Press, 1985.

Brenez, Nicole. *Manifestations: écrits politiques sur le cinéma et autres arts filmiques*. De l'incidence éditeur, 2019.

Carroll, Noël. *Philosophy and the Moving Image*. Oxford University Press, 2021.

Cavell, Stanley. *The World Viewed: Reflections on the Ontology of Film*. The Viking Press, 1971.

Chion, Michel. *The Voice in Cinema*. 1982. Columbia University Press, 1999.

—. *Audio-vision: Sound on Screen*. 1990. Columbia University Press, 1994.

Clover, Carol. *Men, Women, and Chain Saws: Gender in the Modern Horror Film*. Princeton University Press, 1992.

Cornillon, Claire. *Sérialité et transmédialité*. Honoré Champion, 2018.

Couldry, Nick. "My Media Studies: Thoughts from Nick Couldry." *Television & New Media*, vol. 10, no. 1, 2009, pp. 40–2.

Cugier, Alphonse and Patrick Louguet (ed.). *Impureté(s) cinématographique(s)*. L'Harmattan, 2007.

De Lauretis, Teresa. *Technologies of Gender: Essays on Theory, Film, and Fiction*. Indiana University Press, 1987.

De Mourgues, Nicole. *Le Générique de film*. Méridiens Klincksieck, 1994.

Deleuze, Gilles. *Cinema 2: The Time-Image*. 1985. University of Minnesota Press, 1989.

Denis, Sébastien. *Le Cinéma d'animation: techniques, esthétiques et imaginaires*. 2007. Armand Colin, 2017.

Doane, Mary Ann. *The Desire to Desire: The Woman's Film of the 1940s*. Indiana University Press, 1987.

Douchet, Jean. *Nouvelle Vague*. Preface by Dominique Païni. Cinémathèque française/Hazan, 1998.

Dyer, Richard. *Stars*. 1979. BFI, 1998.

Edwards, Leigh H. *The Triumph of Reality TV: The Revolution in American Television*. Praeger, 2013.

Elsaesser, Thomas, and Malte Hagener. *Film Theory: An Introduction Through the Senses*. Routledge, 2010.

Esquenazi, Jean-Pierre. *Les Séries télévisées: l'avenir du cinéma?* Armand Colin, 2010.

Feuer, Jane. *The Hollywood Musical*. Indiana University Press, 1982.
Friedberg, Anne. *Window Shopping: Cinema and the Postmodern*. University of California Press, 1993, pp. 163–4.
Gabriele, Alberto. *The Emergence of Pre-Cinema: Print Culture and the Optical Toy of the Literary Imagination*. Palgrave Macmillan, 2016.
Gelly, Christophe and David Roche (eds). *Approaches to Film and Reception Theories*. Presses Universitaires Blaise Pascal, 2012.
Geraghty, Christine and Shannon Wells-Lassagne. "Introduction: the incipit in screen adaptation." *Screen*, vol. 56, no. 2, 2015, pp. 234–7.
Gray, Jonathan. *Show Sold Separately: Promos, Spoilers, and Other Media Paratexts*. New York University Press, 2010.
Gunning, Tom. "The Cinema of Attraction: Early Film, its Spectator and the Avant-garde." *Wide-Angle*, vol. 8, no. 3–4, 1986, pp. 63–70.
Hagener, Malte and Marijke de Valck. "Cinephilia in Transition." *Mind the Screen: Media Concepts According to Thomas Elsaesser*, edited by Jaap Kooijman, Patricia Pisters and Wanda Strauven, Amsterdam University Press, 2008, pp. 19–31.
Hall, Stuart. "Encoding, Decoding." In *The Cultural Studies Reader*, edited by Simon During, Routledge, 1993, pp. 90–103.
Hill, Annette. *Reality TV: Audiences and Popular Factual Television*. Routledge, 2004.
James, David E. *The Most Typical Avant-Garde: History and Geography of Minor Cinemas in Los Angeles*. University of California Press, 2005.
Jenkins, Henry. *Textual Poachers: Television Fans and Participatory Culture*. Routledge, 1992.
—. *Convergence Culture: Where Old and New Media Collide*. 2006. New York University Press, 2008.
Jones, Gerard. *Honey I'm Home! Sitcoms: Selling the American Dream*. St Martin's Press, 1992.
Jovanovic, Nenad. *Brechtian Cinemas: Montage and Theatricality in Jean-Marie Straub and Danièle Huillet, Peter Watkins, and Lars von Trier*. State University of New York Press, 2018.
Leitch, Thomas. "Twice-Told Tales: Disavowal and the Rhetoric of the Remake." In *Dead Ringers: The Remake in Theory and Practice*, edited by Jennifer Forrest and Leonard R. Koos, State University of New York Press, 2002, pp. 37–62.
—. *Film Adaptation and Its Discontents: From* Gone with the Wind *to* The Passion of Christ. The Johns Hopkins University Press, 2007.
Letort, Delphine and Shannon Wells-Lassagne (eds). *L'Adaptation cinématographique: premières pages, premiers plans*. Éditions Mare & Martin, 2014.
Leutrat, Jean-Louis and Suzanne Liandrat-Guigues. *Splendeur du western*. Rouge Profond, 2007.
Lifschutz, Vladimir. *This is the end: Finir une série télé*. Presses Universitaires François Rabelais, 2018.
Mayne, Judith. *Cinema and Spectatorship*. Routledge, 1993.
Metz, Christian. *The Imaginary Signifier: Psychoanalysis and Cinema*. 1977. Indiana University Press, 1986.
Mittell, Jason. *Complex TV: The Poetics of Contemporary Television Storytelling*. New York University Press, 2015.
Mulvey, Laura. "Visual Pleasure and Narrative Cinema." *Screen*, vol. 16, no. 3, 1975, pp. 6–18.
Murray, Michael D. (ed.). *Encyclopedia of Television News*. Oryx Press, 1999.
Neupert, Richard. *A History of the French New Wave Cinema*. 2002. The University of Wisconsin Press, 2007.

Nichols, Bill. "The Voice of Documentary." *Film Quarterly*, vol. 36, no. 3, 1983, pp. 17–30.
—. *Representing Reality: Issues and Concepts in Documentary*. Indiana University Press, 1991.
—. *Introduction to Documentary*. Indiana University Press, 2001.
O'Day, Marc. "Postmodernism and Television." In *The Routledge Companion to Postmodernism*, edited by Stuart Sim, Routledge, 1998, pp. 112–20.
Pilard, Philippe. *Histoire du cinéma britannique*. Nouveau Monde Éditions, 2010.
Plantinga, Carl. *A Theory of Representation in the Documentary Film Vol. 1*. PhD, University of Wisconsin–Madison, 1989.
Rancière, Jacques. *The Aesthetics of Politics: The Distribution of the Sensible*. 2000. Continuum, 2004.
—. *Film Fables*. 2001. Bloomsbury, 2016.
—. *Le Spectateur émancipé*. La Fabrique, 2008.
—. *The Intervals of Cinema*. 2011. Verso, 2014.
Rolandeau, Yannick. *Nouvelle Vague: Essai critique d'un mythe cinématographique*. L'Harmattan, 2018.
Rosenstone, Robert A. *History on Film/Film on History*. Routledge, 2012.
Silverman, Kaja. *The Acoustic Mirror: The Female Voice in Psychoanalysis and Cinema*. Indiana University Press, 1988.
Sitney, P. Adams. *The American Avant-garde, 1943–2000*. 1974. Oxford University Press, 2002.
Sklar, Robert. *Movie-Made America: A Cultural History of American Movies*. 1975. Vintage Books, 1994.
Sorlin, Pierre. *The Film in History: Restaging the Past*. Barnes & Noble, 1980.
Staiger, Janet. *Interpreting Films: Studies in the Historical Reception of American Cinema*. Princeton University Press, 1992.
—. *Perverse Spectators: The Practices of Film Reception*. New York University Press, 2000.
Stam, Robert and Alessandra Raengo (eds). *Literature and Film: A Guide to the Theory and Practice of Film Adaptation*. Blackwell, 2005.
Stokes, Melvyn and Richard Maltby (eds). *Identifying Hollywood's Audiences: Cultural Identity and the Movies*. BFI, 1999.
Storey, John. "Postmodernism and Popular Culture." In *The Routledge Companion to Postmodernism*, edited by Stuart Sim, Routledge, 1998, pp. 147–57.
Tan, Ed S., *Emotion and the Structure of Narrative Film: Film as an Emotion Machine*. 1996. Routledge, 2011.
Thompson, Kristin, and David Bordwell. *Film History: An Introduction*. 1994. McGraw Hill International Edition, 2010.
Wilkie, Ian. "'Through wall's chink': or, Audience Interplay in Comic Acting." *Acting Comedy*, edited by Chistopher Olsen, Routledge, 2016, pp. 5–24.
Williams, Linda. "Film Bodies: Gender, Genre, and Excess." *Film Quarterly*, vol. 44, no. 4, 1991, pp. 2–13.
Winston, Brian. *The Documentary Film Book*. BFI, 2019.
Wood, Robin. *Hollywood from Vietnam to Reagan . . . and Beyond*. 1986. Columbia University Press, 2003.

General Theory and Criticism

Balogun, Fidelis Odun. *Ngugi and African Post-Colonial Narrative: The Novel as Oral Narrative in Multi-Genre Performance*. World Heritage Press, 1997.

Bibliography

Barthes, Roland. *Camera Lucida: Reflections on Photography*. 1980. Hill and Wang, 1981.
Baudrillard, Jean. *Simulacra and Simulation*. 1981. University of Michigan Press, 1995.
Cullen, Jim. *The American Dream: A Short History of an Idea that Shaped a Nation*. Oxford University Press, 2003.
Debord, Guy. *Society of the Spectacle*. 1967. Zone Books, 1995.
Eco, Umberto. "Innovation and Repetition: Between Modern and Post-Modern Aesthetics." *Daedalus*, vol. 114, no. 4, 1985, pp. 161–84.
—. *The Limits of Interpretation*. 1990. Indiana University Press, 1994.
Eimert, Dorothea. *Art and Architecture of the 20th Century*. 2010. Parkstone International, 2016.
Fish, Stanley. *Is There a Text In this Class? The Authority of Interpretive Communities*. Harvard University Press, 1980.
Freud, Sigmund. 1920. *Beyond the Pleasure Principle*. Norton, 1959.
Genette, Gérard. "Métonymie chez Proust." In *Figures III*. Seuil, 1972, pp. 41–63.
—. *Narrative Discourse: An Essay in Method*. 1972. Cornell University Press, 1980.
—. *Palimpsests: Literature in the Second Degree*. 1982. University of Nebraska Press, 1997.
Gries, Laurie. *Still Life with Rhetoric: A New Materialist Approach for Visual Rhetorics*. Utah State University Press, 2015.
Hardin, Michael. "Non-Cooperative Game Theory and Female-Readers: How to Win the Game of Hopscotch." *Hispanófila*, vol. 111, 1994, pp. 57–72.
Huyssen, Andreas. *After the Great Divide: Modernism, Mass Culture, Postmodernism*. Indiana University Press, 1986.
Iché, Virginie. *L'Esthétique du jeu dans les Alice de Lewis Carroll*. L'Harmattan, 2015.
Iser, Wolfgang. *The Act of Reading: A Theory of Aesthetic Response*. Routledge and Kegan Paul, 1978.
Jakobson, Roman. *Selected Writings VII: Contributions to Comparative Mythology. Studies in Linguistics and Philology, 1972–1982*, edited by Stephen Rudy, with a preface by Linda R. Waugh. Mouton Publishers, 1985.
Lacan, Jacques. *Écrits: A Selection*. 1966. Routledge, 1989.
Lasch, Christopher. *The Culture of Narcissism: American Life in an Age of Diminishing Expectations*. Warner Books, 1979.
Lyotard, Jean-François. *The Postmodern Condition: A Report on Knowledge*. 1979. Manchester University Press, 1984.
McHale, Brian. *Postmodernist Fiction*. 1987. Routledge 1989.
Ohmovère, Claire. "Inconclusiveness in Ben Okri's *The Famished Road*." In *The Famished Road: Ben Okri's Imaginary Homelands*, edited by Vanessa Guignery, Cambridge Scholars Publishing, 2013, pp. 59–76.
Pavel, Thomas G. *Fictional Worlds*. Harvard University Press, 1986.
Peeters, Benoît. *Lire la bande dessinée*. Flammarion, 2003.
Ricœur, Paul. *Oneself as Another*. 1990. The University of Chicago Press, 1992.
Rodríguez, Lydia H. "A Theoretical View of Games in Literature: Julio Cortázar and Cristina Peri Rossi." *Hipertexto*, vol. 10, 2009, pp. 82–9.
Rosenfield, Gavriel. *The World Hitler Never Made: Alternate History and the Memory of Nazism*. Cambridge University Press, 2005.
Sardar, Ziauddin. *Postmodernism and the Other: The New Imperialism of Western Culture*. Pluto Press, 1998.
Schaeffer, Jean-Marie. *Pourquoi la fiction ?* Seuil, 1999.
Scott, Tony and Nancy Welch. "One Train Can Hide Another: Critical Materialism for Public Composition." *College English*, vol. 76, no. 6, 2014, pp. 562–79.

Sibony, Daniel. *Entre-deux: l'origine en partage*. Seuil, 1991.
Slotkin, Richard. *Gunfighter Nation: The Myth of the Frontier in Twentieth-Century America*. 1992. University of Oklahoma Press, 1998.
Sontag, Susan. *On Photography*. Penguin, 1977.

Index

Abel, Lionel, 6, 38
Achemchame, Julien, 9, 61, 65, 67, 230
acousmêtre, 196
Act of Killing, The (Oppenheimer and Cynn, 2012), 287
Adam-12 (NBC, 1968–75), 168
"Adventure of the Empty House, The" (story, Conan Doyle, 1903), 205
Alamo, The (Wayne, 1960), 243
Albera, François, 45–8, 72, 83, 116, 122
Aldouby, Hava, 126–7
Alexandra's Project (De Heer, 2003), 133
Alias (ABC, 2001–6), 51
All in the Family (CBS, 1971–9), 93
Allen, Woody, 97
  Annie Hall (1997), 95
  Purple Rose of Cairo, The (1985), 53, 92, 100–6, 108, 251
  Stardust Memories (1980), 46, 62, 67
allegory, 10, 16, 20, 22, 28, 30–1, 84, 90–1, 106–7
allohistory, 239–40
Altman, Rick, 92, 186, 204
American Horror Story (FX, 2011–), 51, 63, 206
American Splendor (Berman and Pulcini, 2003), 44, 140–5
Ames, Christopher, 10, 61, 63–5, 68–9, 72–3, 83, 92, 99, 101–3, 106
Amis, Martin, 11
Amorous History of the Silver Screen, An / Yinmu yanshi (Cheng Bugao, 1931), 39
. . . and the Fifth Horseman Is Fear / . . . a pátý jezdec je Strach (Brynych, 1965), 247
Andacht, Fernando, 286–7
Anders, Lisaan, 203
Anderson, Patrick Donald, 61, 63

Anderson, Paul Thomas
  Boogie Nights (1997), 66–7
  Inherent Vice (2014), 44, 166–8, 306n43
  Magnolia (1999), 264, 265
Andrei Rublev (Tarkovsky, 1966), 125, 130
Anger, Kenneth, 47–8
Angus, Bill, 6, 305n51
Antonioni, Michaelangelo, 43, 75, 77
  Avventura, L' (1960), 75
  Blow-up (1966), 55, 107, 112–18, 120, 122, 139–40, 178, 282–4, 302n73
  Identificazione di una donna (1982), 61–2
  Passenger, The (1975), 87
Anupama, A. P., 39
Appaloosa (Harris, 2008), 86
apparatus theory, 94–5
Appel, Jr., Alfred, 7
Aquila, Richard, 191
Aquin, Hubert, 260
  Trou de mémoire (1968), 260
Arnheim, Rudolf, 71
Arrivé, Mathilde, 125, 132
Artist, The (Hazanavicius, 2011), 62, 64–7
Astic, Guy, 223–4
Au-delà de Gibraltar (Barman and Boucif, 2001), 93
Augustin, roi du kung-fu (Fontaine, 1999), 93, 95
Aumont, Jacques, 74
Auster, Paul, 17
Austerlitz, Saul, 200
avant-gardes, 37, 44–7, 57, 122, 184, 187, 260–1, 284, 286
Avery, Tex, 35
Awake (NBC, 2012), 212, 311n54

Bacon-Smith, Camille, 94

Bad and the Beautiful, The (Minnelli, 1952), 62
Bad Influence (Hanson, 1990), 302
Badham, John
  Dracula (1979), 176
  Saturday Night Fever (1977), 93, 251
Bakhtin, Mikhaïl, 261
Baldessari, John, 48
Balogun, Fidelis Odun, 39
Balzac, Honoré de, 16, 274
Barnes, Julian, 11
Baron, Jaimie, 249
Barrage contre le Pacifique, Un (Panh, 2008), 44
Barth, John, 11, 17, 32
  End of the Road (1958), 42
  LETTERS (1979), 181
  Lost in the Funhouse (1968), 186, 263
Barthelme, Donald, 11, 17
Barthes, Roland, 116, 138, 226, 244–5, 284
Barton Fink (Coen, 1991), 62, 65–7, 92
Bates Motel (A+E, 2013–17), 158, 205, 208
Batman (ABC, 1966–8), 139
Battle of Algiers, The / La battaglia di Algeri (Pontecorvo, 1966), 243
Battlestar Galactica (Sci-Fi, 2004–9), 158
Baxters, The (WCVB, syndication, 1979–81), 146
Bazin, André, 75, 85, 116, 122, 130, 138, 150, 226, 245, 300n68
Baudrillard, Jean, 109, 198, 244, 251, 254, 272
Baudry, Jean-Louis, 94, 101, 109, 120
Be Kind Rewind (Gondry, 2008), 67, 159
Becky Sharp (Mamoulian, 1935), 103
Beavis and Butthead (MTV, 1993–2001), 192
Bega's Battle (Data East, 1983), 147
Behlil, Melis, 37
Bellas y audaces (TVN, 1988), 256
Belloï, Livio, 61
Bellour, Raymond, 94
Benjamin, Walter, 82, 132, 138, 150, 224, 226, 230, 244–5, 284
Bentley, Nancy, 155–6
Berberian Sound Studio (Strickland, 2012), 62
Bergman, Ingmar, 35
  Persona (1966), 122–3, 177
Berton, Mireille, 107
Beyond the Rocks (Wood, 1922), 69

Bicycle Thieves / Ladri di biciclette (De Sica, 1948), 92
Biesen, Sheri Chinen, 46
Big Sleep, The (novel, Chandler, 1939), 182
Big Swallow, The (Williamson, 1901), 51–2, 56
Biltereyst, Daniel, 49
Birdman or (The Unexpected Virtue of Ignorance) (Iñárritu, 2014), 10, 42, 83
Birth of a Nation, The (Griffith, 1915), 242
Black Christmas (Clark, 1974), 194
Black Mirror (Channel 4, 2011–14; Netflix, 2016–19), 286
  Bandersnatch (2018), 145–50
  "Metalhead" (S4E5), 147
  "National Anthem, The" (S1E1), 265, 270–4, 280, 284
  "Nosedive" (S3E1), 147
  "San Junipero" (S3E4), 146
Blonde (Dominik, 2022), 62
Bobo, Jacqueline, 94
Böhn, Andreas
Boillat, Alain, 19, 84, 99–100, 139, 153
Bolter, Jay David, and Richard Grusin, 124–5, 132
Bommalattam (Bharathiraja, 2008), 39
Bondanella, Peter, 74, 126, 130
Bordwell, David, 35–6, 45, 47, 77, 94
Borges, Jorge Luis, 12, 39, 42, 209
Brakhage, Stan, 46
Brammer, Rebekah, 8, 10, 42
Braveheart (Gibson, 1995), 165
Breakfast Club, The (Hughes, 1985), 200
Brecht, Bertolt, Brechtian, 7, 26, 44–5, 118, 234, 261–2, 274, 280
Brenez, Nicole, 47–8
Brooklyn Nine-Nine (Fox, 2013–18; NBC, 2018–21), 207
Brooks, Mel
  Blazing Saddles (1973), 66, 185, 187–8, 191, 206
  Spaceballs (1987), 200
Brunow, Dagmar, 288
Budgett, Greg, and Gary Dumm, 140
Buñuel, Luis, 35, 43
  Chien andalou, Un (Buñuel and Dalí, 1929), 48, 261
  Exterminating Angel, The / El ángel exterminador (1962), 261

Burch, Noël, 7
Burke, Frank, 126, 129
Burton, Tim
   Ed Wood (1994), 62 66, 93, 95, 159
   Planet of the Apes (2001), 156–7

C.S.A: The Confederate States of America (Willmott, 2004), 240
Cabin in the Woods, The / Das Cabinet des Dr. Caligari (Goddard, 2011), 3, 83, 180
Cabinet of Dr. Caligari, The (Wiene, 1920), 45
Calvacanti, Alberto, 46
   Dead of Night (1945), 46
   Rien que les heures (1926), 46
Calvino, Italo 11, 181
   Cosmicomics (1965), 25
Cameron, James
   Terminator 2: Judgment Day (1991), 123
   Titanic (1997), 293n76
Canaan, Howard, 240
Canterville Ghost, The (Dassin and McLeod, 1944), 153
Caravaggio (Jarman, 1986), 126
Carmilla (novel, LeFanu, 1872), 80
Carpenter, John
   Halloween (1978), 17, 93, 96, 181–2, 194–7
   In the Mouth of Madness (1995), 93, 100
Carroll, Lewis, 41, the *Alice* books, 181
Carroll, Noël, 298n116
Carter, Chistopher, 8–10, 52, 191–4, 264–5, 269–70
Casablanca (Curtiz, 1942), 93, 95–6
Casetti, Francesco, 7, 41, 48
Cassavetes, John, 46
   Shadows (1958), 46
   Woman under the Influence, A (1974), 46
Castle, William, 82
Cavell, Stanley, 103, 122, 298n116
Cerisuelo, Marc, 8–10, 13, 22, 61, 64–9, 74–7, 317
Cervantes, Miguel de, 7, 39, 42, 57, 185
Cheers (NBC, 1982–93), 206
Cheyette, Bryan, 247
Chaplin, Charles, Sir, 69–70
   Knockout, The (Sennett, 1914), 97
   Modern Times (1936), 184
Chaplin (Attenborough, 1992), 62

Chinita, Fátima, 8, 10, 22, 24–5, 99, 123–4
Chion, Michel, 120, 191, 196
Chronicle of a Summer / Chronique d'un été (Paris 1960) (Morin and Rouch, 1961), 287
Church, David, 194
Cinema is a Miracle / Sinema bir mucizedir (Başaran, 2005), 93
Cinema Paradiso / Nuovo Cinema Paradiso (Tornatore, 1988), 92, 96–9, 251, 259
Clockwork Orange, A (novel, Burgess, 1962), 218, 220
Clover, Carol, 193–4
Coates, Kristen, 241
Cock & Bull Story, A (Winterbottom, 2005), 44, 92–3, 152, 160, 162–6, 169, 171, 306n35–6
Cocteau, Jean, 45–6
   Beauty and the Beast / La Belle et la Bête (1946), 45, 177
Coetzee, J. M., 296n42
Cohan, Steven, 10, 61, 63–5, 67, 79, 292n61
Cohen, Leonard, 260
Cohen, Noam, 5
Colapietro, Vincent, 36
Colbert Report, The (Comedy Central, 2005–14), 49
Cold Mountain (Minghella, 2003), 165
Collins, Jim, 37, 223
Comicalamities (Messmer, 1928), 35
Community (NBC, 2009–15), 2–4, 28–30, 93–4, 96, 180, 185–6, 191, 200–8, 282–5, 317
Connor, J. D., 6, 145, 203, 207, 210
Cooper, Annabel, 155
Coover, Robert, 11, 17
   Public Burning, The (1977), 232–3
Coppola, Antoine, 234
Coppola, Francis Ford
   Apocalypse Now (1979), 174
   Bram Stoker's Dracula (1992), 156, 168–9, 173–8, 245, 284, 307n65
   Conversation, The (1974), 118
   Godfather, The (1972), 174
   Godfather Part II, The (1974), 95
Cornell, Joseph, 48
Cornillon, Claire, 90, 96, 206, 210
Cortázar, Julio, 39, 112, 116, 181
Cosmopolis (novel, DeLillo, 2003), 44

Costa, Pedro, 280
　Colossal Youth / Juventude em marcha (2006), 265–70, 280, 282–3, 285–6
Couldry, Nick, 49
Coup de torchon (Tavernier, 1980), 93
Craig, Pamela, and Martin Fradley, 194
Craven, Wes
　Last House on the Left, The (1972), 191, 194
　Scream (1996), 93, 96, 158, 171, 180–1, 185–6, 191, 193–200, 204, 215, 282–5, 317
　Scream 2 (1997), 96, 197
　Scream 3 (2000), 62, 66, 107
　Scream 4 (2011), 4, 197, 199–200
　Wes Craven's New Nightmare (1994), 62, 66, 100
Cronenberg, David
　Cosmopolis (2012), 44
　eXistenZ (1999), 100
　Maps to the Stars (2014), 61–2, 64
　Videodrome (1982), 138
Crumb, Robert, 140
Cugier, Alphone, and Patrick Louguet, 82
Cullen, Jim, 65
Cult (The CW, 2013), 63, 95, 259, 281
Curb Your Enthusiasm (HBO, 2000–), 5, 62–3
Currie, Mark, 11, 38

Dada, 45, 297n69
Dalí, Salvador, 46
Dallas (CBS, 1978–91), 223
Dällenbach, Lucien, 8
Dances with Wolves (Costner, 1990), 184
Daney, Serge, 224
Danger Man (ITC, 1964–7), 218
Dante, Joe
　Gremlins (1984), 93, 96, 243, 259
　Hollywood Boulevard (1976), 62
　Inner Space (1987), 50
　Matinée (1993), 62
Dardenne, Jean-Pierre et Luc, 65
Dark Passage (Daves, 1947), 69, 218
Dassanowsky, Robert von, 8–9, 241
Davie, Alan, 113
De Lauretis, Teresa, 155
Dead Poets Society (Weir, 1989), 200

Dead Set (E4, 2008), 63
Deadpool (Miller, 2016), 44, 180
Dean, James, 223
Debord, Guy, 138, 272
Deleuze, Gilles, 82, 168
Deleyto, Celestino, 47, 82
Denis, Sébastien, 48, 234
DePalma, Brian
　Blow Out (1981), 62, 92–3, 107, 118–20, 122, 283–4
　Body Double (1984), 62, 93
　Dressed to Kill (1980), 118, 120
Deren, Maya, 47
Derrida, Jacques, 24
Destry Rides Again (Marshall, 1939), 187
Dick Tracy (Beatty, 1990), 139
Dick Van Dyke Show, The (CBS, 1961–6), 62
Dirty Dozen, The (Aldrich, 1967), 46
Django (Corbucci, 1966), 86
Django! Prepare your coffin! / Preparati la bara! (Baldi, 1968), 190
Doane, Mary Ann, 101, 107
Doctor Who (BBC, 2005–), 4, 51, 180
Doctorow, E. L., 11
　Book of Daniel, The (1971), 232
　Ragtime (1975), 11, 42, 233, 296n58
The Donna Reed Show (ABC, 1958–66), 48
Douchet, Jean, 43–4, 107–9
Dracula (novel, Stoker, 1897), 173–4
Dracula (Browning, 1931), 176
Dracula movies (Hammer Films, 1958–74), 176
Dreyer, Carl Theodor
　Passion of Joan of Arc, The / La passion de Jeanne d'Arc (1928), 242
　Vampyr (1932), 176
Dubois, Régis, 234
Dufour, Éric, 194, 197
Dulac, Germaine, 47, 109
Dumas, Chris, 118, 120
Duras, Marguerite, 43–4, 296n64
　India Song (1975), 43, 155
　Lover, The / L'Amant (1984) 44
　Barrage contre le Pacifique, Un (1950) 44
Dyer, Richard, 143

Eastern Condors / Dung fong tuk ying (Kam-Bo Hung, 1987), 243

Eco, Umberto, 31, 208
Edison, Thomas, 176
Edwards, Leigh H., 49
Egoyan, Atom, 46
   Ararat (2002), 9, 61–2, 139, 264, 269–70
   Calendar (1993), 139
   Family Viewing (1987), 133–9, 150, 284
   Where the Truth Lies (2005), 61–2, 64, 66
Eimert, Dorothea, 46
Eisenstein, Sergei, Eisensteinian, 45, 47, 241
Eliot, T. S., 44
Elsaesser, Thomas, and Malte Hagener, 56
End of the Road (Avakian, 1970), 42–3, 296n60
Epstein, Jean, 47, 109
   Cœur fidèle (1923), 45
Escape from the "Liberty" Cinema / Ucieczka z kina 'Wolność' (Marczewski, 1990), 39, 95, 100, 105, 259
Escobar, Patrick Maurer, 42, 238
Esquenazi, Jean-Pierre, 76, 208
Even the Rain / También la lluvia (Bollaín, 2010), 264, 269–70
Evidence of the Film, The (Marson and Thanhouser, 1913), 61
Exit through the Gift Shop (Banksy, 2010), 287
Extra Girl, The (Jones, 1923), 47

Far from Poland (Godmilow, 1984), 286
Fassbinder, Rainer Werner
   Beware of the Holy Whore / Warnung vor einer heiligen Nutte (1971), 62, 64
   Despair (1978), 42
Fatherland (novel, Harris, 1992; TV movie, HBO, Menaul, 1994), 239–40, 243–4, 247
Faulkner, William, 44
Feuer, Jane, 35, 186
Févry, Sébastien, 6, 19
Fellini, Federico, 35, 64, 81, 95
   Amarcord (1973), 93, 96–7
   Casanova di Federico Fellini, Il (1976), 126
   8½ (1963), 10, 16, 46, 62, 67, 126, 129, 165
   Fellini Roma (1972), 126–32, 140, 150, 282, 284–5

Intervista (1987), 62, 126
Juliet of the Spirits / Giulietta degli spiriti (1965), 126
Toby Dammit (1968), 126
I Vitelloni (1953), 99
Fielding, Henry, 159–60
   Joseph Andrews (1742), 42
   Tom Jones (1749), 42, 159
Film Johnnie, A (Nichols, 1914), 61
Firemen of Viggiù, The / I pompieri di Viggiù (Mattoli, 1949), 98
Fish, Stanley 30–1
Flash, The (The CW, 2014–), 96
Flintstones, The (ABC, 1960–6), 48
For All Mankind (Apple TV+, 2019–), 240
Ford, John, 87, 183, 190
   Grapes of Wrath, The (1940), 69
   Iron Horse, The (1924) 184, 187
   Man Who Shot Liberty Valance, The (1962), 86–7
   My Darling Clementine (1946), 86, 187, 301n101
   Searchers, The (1956), 86, 243
   Stagecoach (1939), 97, 187
formalist (view of cinema), 72, 83, 116–17, 122, 124, 178, 284, 288
Forrest Gump (Zemeckis, 1994), 166
Fowles, John, 186
   French Lieutenant's Woman, The (1969), 11, 42, 159–61, 163, 181, 232–3, 306n33
   Maggot, A (1985), 233
Francis, Jr., James, 171–2
Fraser, Ryan, 251
Frayling, Christopher, 182, 184, 187–90, 308n53
Fredericksen, Don, 6–8, 16, 26, 35, 41, 52, 261, 270
Friends (NBC, 1994–2004), 200, 207
Fresh Prince of Bel Air, The (NBC, 1990–6), 206
Freud, Sigmund, Freudian, 109, 198
Friant-Kessler, Brigitte, and Ariane Hudelet, 163, 165, 306n36
Friday the 13th (Cunningham, 1980), 194
Friedberg, Anne, 45
Fruitvale Station (Coogler, 2013), 264–5, 269–70, 287

Fukasaku, Kinji
   Battle Royale I and *II* / *Batoru rowaiaru* (2000, 2003), 83
   Battles Without Honor and Humanity / *Jingi naki tatakai* (1973–4), 42, 238
Fülop, Erika, 37

G.I. Joe (First Run Syndication, 1983–6), 200
Gabriele, Alberto, 56
Game of Thrones (HBO, 2011–19), 207
García Márquez, Gabriel, 11
Garnett, Tony, 278–9
Gass, William, 6, 38
Gelly, Christophe, 31, 205
Gemzøe, Anker, 23
Genet, Jean, 45
Genette, Gérard, 6–7, 19, 25, 38, 41–2, 44, 53, 99, 152, 180, 317
George Burns and Gracie Allen Show, The (CBS, 1950–8), 35, 48
Gilliam, Terry, 42
   Man Who Killed Don Quixote, The (2018), 44
Global Groove (Paik, 1973), 82
Godard, Jean-Luc, 12, 32, 35, 43, 45, 57, 82, 118, 132–3, 185, 261, 274
   Breathless / *À bout de souffle* (1960), 46
   Contempt / *Le Mépris* (1963), 28, 46, 52, 62, 64–5, 67, 73–82, 92–3, 122, 259, 262–3, 281, 284
   Histoire(s) du cinéma (Canal+, 1989–9), 288
   Loin du Vietnam (1967), 288
   Numéro deux (with Miéville, 1975), 132
   Pierrot le fou (1965), 184
   Riflemen, The / *Les Carabiniers* (1963), 184–5, 261, 287
   Sauve qui peut (la vie) (with Miéville, 1980), 123
   Tout va bien (with Gorin, 1972), 262–3, 269, 280, 284
   Week-end (1967), 261
   Wind from the East / *Le Vent d'est* (with Vertov and Gorin, 1970), 261
Goldbergs, The (CBS, 1948–57), 207
Good Place, The (NBC, 2016–20), 180
Gordon, Paul, 109
Gomez, Joseph A., 234
Gonçalves Miranda, Rui, 293n76
Gone Girl (novel, Flynn, 2012), 5

Goodbye, Dragon Inn / *Bu san* (Tsai, 2003), 93, 97, 180
Goudet, Stéphanie, 54
Grapes of Wrath, The (novel, Steinbeck, 1939), 69
Gray, Jonathan, 153
Grease (Kleiser, 1978), 251
Great Expectations (Lean, 1946), 153
Great Train Robbery, The (Edison, Porter, 1903), 51
Greenaway, Peter, 46
   Draughtman's Contract, The (1982), 125, 165
   Prospero's Books (1991), 123
Gregory, Chris, 218–19, 222
Grierson, John, 46, 288
Gries, Laurie, 264–5
Gruppo 63, 260
Gunning, Tom, 35

Haber, Karen, 242
Hagener, Malte, and Marijke de Valck, 37
Hall, Stuart, 94
Halloween (Zombie, 2007), 17, 179
Handsworth Songs (Akomfrah, 1986), 288
Haneke, Michael
   Benny's Video (1992), 133
   Funny Games (1997), 9, 96, 133–4, 185, 191–5, 198–9, 204, 264, 284, 286
Hannibal (NBC, 2013–15), 158, 205, 208
Hansen, Miriam Bratu, 247
Hardin, Michael, 181
Hare, Bill, 113
Harris, Thomas, 112
Hatchuel, Sarah, 87–8, 155, 158, 213–14, 218, 306n15, 311n54
Hatfield, Charles, 143
Hawks, Howard
   Big Sleep, The (1948), 47, 182, 282
   Hatari! (1962), 75
   Rio Bravo (1959), 74, 96, 187
   Sergeant York (1941), 241
Heaven's Gate (Cimino, 1980), 183–4
Hellraiser (Barker, 1987), 80
Hellzapoppin' (Potter, 1941), 35, 62
Henderson, Andrew, 234–6
Herman, Pee-wee, 50
Hicks, Jeremy, 45
High Noon (Zinnemann, 1952), 182

Hill, Annette, 49
Hill, John, 274, 277–9, 315n82
Hill, Terrence, 188–9
historiographic metafiction, 233
History Man, The (novel, Bradbury, 1975), 232
Hitchcock, Alfred, 57, 172
   North by Northwest (1959), 95
   Psycho (1960), 75, 107, 109, 171–3, 181, 197
   Rear Window (1954), 10, 16, 28, 107–12, 114, 118, 120, 195, 221, 281, 285
   Rebecca (1940), 107
   Spellbound (1945), 46
   Vertigo (1958), 107, 109–10, 156, 223, 230, 302n73
Hollywood (Cruze, 1923), 47
Hollywood (Netflix, 2020), 63
Hollywood or Bust (Tashlin, 1956), 55
Holy Motors (Carax, 2012), 145
Honeymooners, The (CBS, 1955–6), 48
Hooper, Tobe
   Funhouse, The (1981), 181–2, 195, 197
   Texas Chain Saw Massacre, The (1974), 17, 157
Horowitz, Sara R., 247, 249
House That Jack Built, The (von Trier, 2018), 4, 126
Howe, Alexis, 252–3
Hudelet, Ariane, 165, 169, 210–11, 306n37
Huillet, Danièle, and Jean-Marie Straub, 44
Hulk (Lee, 2003), 139
Humphries, Reynold, 47
Hunger Games (2012–15), 83
Hutcheon, Linda, 8, 11–12, 14, 16, 19–22, 24, 26–9, 31–4, 36, 38–9, 41–2, 44, 54, 61, 71, 80, 88, 95, 100, 106, 117, 121–2, 138, 142, 146, 148, 152, 170, 180–1, 185–6, 190, 195, 214, 219, 223, 231–5, 237–8, 240, 257, 259–61, 268, 279, 283–4, 296n42, 296n57, 296n64, 306n33
Huyssen, Andeas, 45
hypermediacy, 124
hypermeta, 13, 283, 317

I Walked with a Zombie (Tourneur, 1943), 186
Iché, Virginie, 181

Indiana Jones (1981–2008), 215
industrial reflexivity, 207
Inhumaine, L' (L'Herbier, 1924), 48
Inside Daisy Clover (Mulligan, 1965), 65
intermedia, 123–5
intermedia reflexivity, 123
Intimate Exchanges (play, Ayckbourne, 1982), 44
Iser, Wolfgang, 114, 153, 174, 238, 303n80
It Can't Happen Here (novel, Lewis, 1935), 239–40
It Happened Here (Brownlow and Mollo, 1964), 239–40
Ivănescu, Andra, 88, 90
Ivory, James, 165
   Jane Austen in Manhattan (1980), 152, 169
   Room with a View, A (1985), 166

Jakobson, Roman, 7, 41
James, David E., 35, 45, 47–8, 52–3, 56
James Bond (1962–), 218, 256
   No Time to Die (Fukunaga, 2021), 231
Jameson, Frederick, 126
Jane Eyre (Stevenson, 1943), 153
Jarmusch, Jim
   Dead Man (1995), 182–4, 203, 283–4
   Mystery Train (1989), 184
   Stranger than Paradise (1984), 184
Jarry, Alfred, 7, 44–5, 185
   Ubu King / Ubu roi (1896), 261
Jenkins, Henry, 37, 94, 272, 315n65
Jones, Gerard, 48
Jonson, Ben, 137
Jonze, Spike
   Adaptation (Jonze, 2002), 14, 29, 62, 152, 169–71
   Being John Malkovich (Jonze, 1999), 170
Jovanovic, Nenad, 44
Joyce, James, 44
Jung, Nike, 252–4
Jurassic Park (1993–2001), *Jurassic World* (2015–22) franchises, 83

Kampmann Walther, Bo, 145
Kaufman, Charlie, 16, 171, 201
Kawin, Bruce, 7
Kazanski, Boris, 122, 124

Keaton, Buster, 52, 68–9
  Cameraman, The (1928), 52–5, 117, 274
  Sherlock Jr. (1924), 52–5, 93, 95, 100, 102, 105, 108, 156
Keazor, Henry, 42, 296n57
Kiarostami, Abbas, 64
  Life and Nothing More / Zendegi va digar hich (1992), 39, 62
  Taste of Cherry / Ta'm e guilass (1997), 66
  Through the Olive Trees / Zire darakhatan zeyton (1994), 39–41, 52, 61–2, 66
King Kong (Cooper and Schoedsack, 1933), 242
Kitano, Takeshi, 46
  Hana-bi (1997), 39
  Takeshis' (2005), 39
Kligerman, Eric, 241
Knots Landing (CBS, 1979–93), 223
Král, Petr, 54
Kramer vs. Kramer (Benton, 1979), 277
Kubrick, Stanley, 185
  Barry Lyndon (1975), 165
  Full Metal Jacket (1987), 157
  Lolita (1962), 42
Kung Fu (ABC, 1972–5), 260
Kurosawa, Akira
  Rashômon (1950), 45
  Yojimbo / Yôjinbô (1961), 39
Kusturica, Emir
  Arizona Dream (1993), 93, 95–6
  Black Cat, White Cat / Crna macka, beli macor (1998), 96
  Underground (1995), 249

La La Land (Chazelle, 2016), 83
Lacan, Jacques, Lacanian, 32
Lagny, Michèle, 234, 236–7
Landesman, Ohad, 145
Lang, Friz, 74, 76
  Fury (1936) 96
  House by the River (1950), 47
  M (1931), 74
  Metropolis (1927), 46, 184
  Rancho Notorious (1952), 74, 187
  Testament of Dr. Mabuse, The (1933), 242
  Woman in the Window, The (1944), 47, 69
LaRocca, David, 10, 15 188, 283–5
Larraín, Pablo

  Jackie (2016), 251, 254
  Neruda (2016), 251
  No (2012), 251, 253–9, 282, 284–5, 287
  Post Mortem (2010), 251, 253
  Spencer (2021), 251
  Tony Manero (2008), 93, 251–4
Lasch, Christopher, 38
Last Action Hero (McTiernan, 1993), 53, 100, 105–6
Last Movie, The (Hopper, 1971), 45
Last Tycoon, The (Kazan, 1976), 62
Latour, Bruno, 265
Laughter in the Dark (Papas, 1986), 42
Laura (Preminger, 1944), 223–4
Lefait, Sébastien, 164, 214, 219, 272, 290
Leitch, Thomas, 152, 157, 169, 171, 176, 179, 232
Lemonade Joe / Limonádový Joe aneb Konská opera (Lipský, 1964), 185, 187–8
Leo, John, 249
Leone, Sergio, 184–5, 188–91, 308n53
  For a Few Dollars More / Per qualche dollaro in più (1965), 187–8
  Good, the Bad, and the Ugly, The / Il buono, il brutto, il cattivo (1966), 182, 189
  Once Upon a Time in the West / C'era una volta il West (1968), 86, 182, 184, 187, 190, 194–5
Letort, Delphine, and Shannon Wells-Lassagne, 153
Letterman, David, 142–3
Leutrat, Jean-Louis, and Suzanne Liandrat-Guigues, 308n17
Levinson, Paul, 132
Librach, Ronald S., 118–20
Life and Death of Peter Sellers, The (Hopkins, 2004), 62
Lifschutz, Vladimir, 208
Limoges, Jean-Marc, 19, 35, 41, 70, 81, 99, 100, 107, 115, 193, 317
Lipińska, Katarzyna, 39, 105
Living in Oblivion (DiCillo, 1995), 62, 64, 67, 93
Liyong, Taban Lo, 39
Loach, Ken, 65, 280
  Cathy Come Home (BBC, 1964), 278
  Diary of a Young Man (BBC, 1964), 274
  Flickering Flame, The (1996), 278

I, Daniel Blake (2016), 33, 265, 270, 274–80, 282–3, 285–6, 315n69
Kes (1969), 274
Land and Freedom (1995), 278
Looking for Eric (2009), 315n75
My Name Is Joe (1993), 278
Poor Cow (1967), 274
Raining Stones (1993), 278
Riff-Raff (1991), 278
Sorry We Missed You (2019), 279
Up the Junction (BBC, 1965), 274
Wind That Shakes the Barley, The (2006), 278, 315n82
Logan's Run (Anderson, 1976), 87
Lolita (Lynne, 1997), 42
Long Day Closes, The (Davies, 1992), 93
Looking for Richard (Pacino, 1996), 152, 163
Lord of the Flies (novel, Golding), 215
Loren, Scott and Jörg Metelmann, 293n76
LOST (ABC, 2004–10), 51, 133, 213–18, 230–1, 281
Lost in Austen (ITC, 2008), 169
Lost in La Mancha (Fulton and Pepe, 2002), 152
Lover, The / L'Amant (Annaud, 1992), 44
Lumière, Auguste and Louis, 76
  L'Arrivée d'un train en gare à La Ciotat (1896), 52, 176
Lynch, David
  Eraserhead (1976), 230
  Inland Empire (2006), 62, 65–6, 82, 93, 100, 145, 229
  Mulholland Dr. (2001), 9, 62, 65–6, 79–82, 93, 122, 226, 230, 259, 282–4, 293n76, 317
  Rabbits (2002), 145
  Twin Peaks: Fire Walk with Me (1992), 226, 229
Lyotard, Jean-François, 6, 41

Mabel's Dramatic Career (Sennett, 1913), 61
Machinal, Hélène, 205
Mad Men (AMC, 2007–15), 200, 230
Madsen, Rune Bruun, 23, 26
Magic School Bus, The (PBS, 1994–8), 50–1
Magnani, Anna, 129
Mallin, Eric S., 105

Maltese Falcon, The (novel, Hammett, 1930; film, Huston, 1941), 182
Man in the High Castle, The (novel, Dick 1962), 209, 235, 239–40, 243–5
Man in the High Castle, The (series, Amazon Prime, 2015–19), 100, 209–10, 235, 239–40, 243–6, 258
Man of a Thousand Faces (Pevney, 1957), 62
Manhandled (Dwan, 1924), 69
Manhunter (Mann, 1986), 158
Mankiewicz, Joseph
  All About Eve (1950), 80, 83, 189
  Barefoot Contessa, The (Mankiewicz, 1954), 75
  Cleopatra (1963), 74
Mansfield Park (Rozema, 1999), 154, 179
Macunaíma (novel, Mário de Andrade, 1928; film, Joaquim Pedro de Andrade, 1969), 261
Marie, Michel, 74–7
Marker, Chris
  La Jetée (1962), 114, 141
  Letter from Siberia (1958), 286
  Sans Soleil (1983), 286
Married . . . with Children (Fox, 1987–97), 93–4, 205, 207–8, 286
Marvel comics, Marvel Cinematic Universe, 153, 279
Marx Brothers, 56
Marxism, Marxist, 260–3, 265–6, 269, 280
Matrix, The (Wachowskis, 1999), 100
Matter of Life and Death, A (Powell and Pressburger, 1946), 103
Mayne, Judith, 42, 94, 261
McHale, Brian, 12, 36, 39, 126, 150, 222, 296n42
McQueen, Steve, 46
  Small Axe: Mangrove (Amazon Prime, 2020), 177
medium, 125
Medium Cool (Wexler, 1969), 264
Méliès, Georges, 52
  Man with the Rubber Head, The / L'Homme à la tête en caoutchouc (1901), 242
  Vanishing Lady, The / La Femme qui disparaît (1897), 176
Menegaldo, Gilles, 101–3
Mendelsohn, Erich, 46

Mercenaries, The (Cardiff, 1968), 243
metacinema, 8–10, 15
metacinematographic, metacinematic, 12–13, 292n53, 317
metadaptation, 169
metadiegesis, metadiegetic, 41, 317
metadiscourse, 12
metadrama, 6, 317
metafiction, 11–12, 19–20, 317
   diegetic/linguistic, overt/covert 20
metafilm, 8–10, 15, 317
metafilmic, 12–13, 292n53, 317
metahistory, 6, 13
metaization, 14
metalanguage, 4, 13, 41
metalepsis, 6, 99–100, 317
   extradiegetic and intradiegetic, 100, 317
meta-level, 4, 13–14, 29
metalinguistics, 13
metamoment, 17–18, 317
metaperformance, 49, 317
metaphysics, 13–14
metanarrative, 12, 317
metareference, 14, 20–2, 317
   intracomposition/extracomposition, explicit/implicit, fictio/fictum, critical/non-critical, 21–2
metatextuality, 41–2, 152, 317
metatheater, 6, 317
Metz, Christian, 6–8, 12–13, 15, 19, 23, 26–7, 41, 49, 52, 56, 77, 94, 108–9, 111, 120, 122, 129, 172, 180, 182, 270, 317
Michelson, Annette, 52
Mickwitz, Nina, 141
mise en abyme, 6, 22, 26, 30, 81, 317
Mister Rogers' Neighborhood (NET/PBS, 1968–2001), 50
Mittell, Jason, 37, 51, 90, 206, 209–10, 213–14
Mléčková, Kateřina, 187
Modern Family (ABC, 2009–20), 49–50
modernism, modernist, 8, 12, 35–7, 45–7, 57, 150
Modleski, Tania, 112
Mommie Dearest (Perry, 1981), 62
Moonlighting (ABC, 1985–9), 201, 205–6, 208
Moravia, Alberto, 73–5
Morning Show, The (Apple TV+, 2019–), 63

Morreale, Joanne, 48
Morricone, Ennio, 188–9
Morris, Nigel, 85, 247
mother! (Aronofsky, 2017), 28
Moullet, Luc, 74, 262
Moure, José, 112, 114, 117, 302n73
Mourgues, Nicole de, 153
Mourlet, Michel, 75
Mulvey, Laura, 94, 112, 120, 155, 188
Münsterberg, Hugo, 94
Murder, My Sweet (Dmytryk, 1944), 182
Murillo, Céline, 183–4
Murray, Michael D., 272
Muybridge, Eadweard, 52
Mwangi, Evan Maina, 39–40
My Dinner with Andre (Malle, 1981), 203
My Name Is Nobody / Il mio nome è Nessuno (Valerii 1973), 185, 187–91, 203, 284, 286

Nabokov, Vladimir, 12, 32, 181, 185
   Ada (1969), 42
   Despair (1934), 42
   King, Queen, Knave (1928), 42
   Laughter in the Dark (1932), 42, 215
   Lolita (1955), 42
   Pale Fire (1962), 42
Nama, Adilifu, 242
Napier, Susan, 39
Neupert, Richard, 43
Nichols, Bill, 286–9
Nolley, Ken, 234, 238
Nosferatu (Murnau, 1922; Herzog, 1979), 156, 176
Nöth, Winfried, 14, 123
Nouveau Roman, 43–4, 297n69
Nouvelle Vague, 16, 36, 43–4, 74–6, 262, 297n69

Ó Drisceoil, Donal, 315n82
O'Day, Marc, 223
Of Mice and Men (novel, Steinbeck, 193), 215
Office, The (BBC, 2001–3), 49
O'Healy, Aine, 129
Ohmovère, Claire, 39
Okri, Ben, 39
Olivier, Laurence, 154
   Hamlet (1948), 106, 154–5

Henry V (1944), 154
On the Trail of the Assassins (book, Garrison, 1988), 249
One Cut of the Dead / Kamera o tomeru na! (Ueda, 2017), 40, 62, 93
Orchid Thief, The (book, Orlean), 169, 171
Ortoli, Philippe, 175, 177–8, 243
Orwell, George, Orwellian, 222, 272
  1984 (1949), 146–7, 218
Otro Francisco, El (Sergio Giral, 1974), 152, 159
Our Beloved Month of August / Aquele Querido Mês de Agosto (Gomes, 2008), 293n76

Pabst, G. W. 242
  White Hell of Piz Palu, The / Die weiße Hölle vom Piz Palü (Fanck and Pabst, 1929) 241–2
Pagnoni Berns, Fernando Gabriel and Emiliano Aguilar, 244
Pain and Glory / Dolor y gloria (Almodóvar, 2019), 3
Païni, Dominique, 297n69
Palmer, R. Barton, 161–2
Parallax View, The (Pakula, 1974), 118
parody, 185–7
Past, Elena M., 129–30
Paul, R. W., 176
Pavel, Thomas G., 217
Peeping Tom (Powell, 1960), 35, 61, 64, 109
Peeters, Benoît, 141, 153
Pekar, Harvey
  American Splendor (comics, 1976–91), 44, 140–5, 305n60
  Our Cancer Year (comics, with Joyce Brabner, 1994), 140, 143
  Our Movie Year (comics, with Brabner, 2004), 144
Perfect Blue / Pāfekuto burū (Satoshi Kon, 1997), 39
Pfeifer, Barbara, 42, 296n57
Pheasant-Kelly, Fran, 197
Phillips, Gene D., 68–9
Picture of Dorian Gray, The (film, Lewin, 1945), 125
Pieldner, Judit, 306n15
Pilard, Philippe, 278
Pinter, Harold, 160

Planet of the Apes (Schaffner, 1968), 156
Plantinga, Carl, 286–7
Play It Again, Sam (Ross, 1972), 93, 95, 101–2
Player, The (Altman, 1992), 9, 62, 92, 259
Pleasantville (Ross, 1998), 100, 105
Plot Against America, The (novel, Roth, 2004; series, HBO, 2020), 44, 239–40
Poe, Edgar Allan, 39
Portrait of a Lady, The (Campion, 1996), 155–6, 160, 180, 280, 283–4
Portrait of a Lady, The (novel, James, 1880–1), 155–6
Portrait of a Lady on Fire / Portrait de la jeune fille en feu (Sciamma, 2019), 126
postmodernism, postmodernist, 6, 11–12, 17, 21–2, 36–7, 41, 44, 57, 150, 187, 198, 218, 233, 284
Prebble, John, 234, 237
Prédal, René, 112
Premier Bal (Christian-Jacques, 1941), 45
Pride and Prejudice (BBC, 1995), 154
Prisoner, The (ITV, 1967–8), 51, 100, 133, 213, 218–23, 230–1, 281–2, 285
Prom Night (Lynch, 1980), 196
Prometheus (Scott, 2012), 156
Proust, Marcel, Proustian, 129
Psycho (Van Sant, 1998), 169, 171–3
Pynchon, Thomas, 11, 44, 181
  Inherent Vice (2009), 159, 166, 168

Quart, Leonard, and Barbara Quart, 296n58
Queen Kelly (von Stroheim, 1929), 68–72, 282

Radstone, Susannah, 97, 99
Ragel, Philippe, 40–1
Ragtime (film, Forman, 1981), 42–3, 234, 296n58
Ramaeker, Paul, 118
Rancière, Jacques, 265–70, 277, 279, 288
Rapf, Joanna E., 296n58
Rated X (Esteves, 2000), 66
Raus, Tonia, 6–7, 122
Ray, Nicolas
  Bigger Than Life (1956), 74
  In a Lonely Place (1950), 61–2, 79
realist (view of cinema), 75, 85, 116–17, 120, 122, 178, 245, 284
Reality / Réalité (Dupieux, 2014), 62, 64

Reality T.V. Secrets Revealed (VH1, 2004), 49
Red Dragon (novel, Harris, 1981), 158
reflexive materialism, 265
Reisz, Karl
   French Lieutenant's Woman, The (1981), 42–3, 152, 159–65, 234
   Saturday Night and Sunday Morning (1960), 160
remediation, 124–5
Resnais, Alain
   Hiroshima mon amour (1959), 43
   I Want to Go Home (1989), 139
   Last Year at Marienbad / L'Année dernière à Marienbad (1961), 43, 46
   Night and Fog / Nuit et brouillard (1956), 247
   Smoking/No Smoking (1993), 44
Ricardou, Jean, 8, 16
Rice, Anne, 176
Richardson, Tony
   Joseph Andrews (1977), 42
   Laughter in the Dark (1986), 42
   Look Back in Anger (1959), 159
   Tom Jones (1963), 42, 159–60, 162–3
Richter, Hans, 35
Rick and Morty (Comedy Central, 2013–), 3, 48, 259
Ricœur, Paul, 285
Riffaterre, Michael, 19
Río, Elena Del, 137–9
Robbe-Grillet, Alain, 171, 296n64
   Trans-Europe-Express (1966), 43, 62
Roche, Thierry, 112, 114, 116–18, 303n79
Rocky Picture Show, The (Sharman, 1975), 96
Rodríguez, Lydia H., 181
Roger, Philippe, 172
Rolandeau, Yannick, 297n69
Rolinson, Dave, 237
Romeo + Juliet (Luhrmann, 1996), 152
Ropars-Wuilleumier, Marie-Claire, 114
Rose, Margaret, 185
Rosemary's Baby (Polanski, 1968), 46
Rosencrantz and Gildenstern Are Dead (Stoppard, play 1966; film, 1990), 44
Rosenfield, Gavriel, 312n38
Rosenstone, Robert A., 232, 249
Rossellini, Roberto
   "Miracle, The" / "Il miracolo" (1948), 63
   Rome, Open City / Roma città aperta (1945), 129
   Stromboli (Terra di Dio) (1950), 75
   Vanina Vanini (1961), 75
   Voyage in Italy / Viaggio in Italia (1954), 75
Rothwell, Kenneth Sprague, 155
Roue, La (Gance, 1923), 184
Round, Julia, 141, 143
Run of the Arrow (Fuller, 1957), 184
Rushdie, Salman
   Midnight's Children (1981), 233, 296n42
   Shame (1983), 233, 296n42
Ryan, Marie-Laure, 20–4, 27–8, 145–6

Saint'Elia, Antonio 46
Samson and Delilah (DeMille, 1949), 69
Santas, Constantine, 172
Sardar, Ziauddin, 218–19
Sarnelli, Laura, 80
Sarraute, Nathalie, 43, 296n64
Scary Movie (Wayans, 2000), 186
Schaeffer, Jean-Marie, 34, 181, 199
Schlipphacke, Heidi, 243
Schmidt, Nicolas, 22, 25–6
Scholes, Robert, 6, 38
Scorsese, Martin
   Taxi Driver (1976), 93, 251
   Hugo (2011), 264
Scott, Tony, and Nancy Welch, 264–5
Scream: The Series (MTV/Netflix, 2015–19), 51, 158
Scream Queens (Fox, 2015–16), 3–4, 51, 180
Sei chitai: Sex Zone (Adachi, 1968), 48
Seinfeld (NBC, 1989–98), 5, 16, 63, 206
Semenza, Greg M. Colón, 242
Sesame Street (NET, 1969–70; PBS, 1970–), 50–1
sex, lies and videotape (Soderbergh, 1989), 133
Shadow of the Vampire (Merhige, 2000), 62, 66, 152, 159
Shakespeare, William, 57, 137, 276, 306n15
   As You Like It, 220
   Hamlet, 106, 154–5, 306n15, 317
   Henry IV Part II, 87
   Henry V, 154–5
   King Lear, 87
   Romeo and Juliet, 87
   The Tempest, 87, 209

Shamray, Gerry, 140
Shane (Stevens, 1953), 184
Sheik, The (Melford, 1921), 156
Shepherd of the Hills, The (Hathaway, 1941), 96
Sherlock (BBC, 2010–17), 96, 205, 207–8
Shibolet, Yotam, 287–9
Shoah (Lanzmann, 1985), 247
Shooting Stars (Asquith and Bramble, 1928), 61–2, 64
Show People (Vidor, 1928), 62, 64, 67
Sibony, Daniel, 24
Silverman, Kaja, 155
Simon, Art, 249
Simpsons, The (Fox, 1989–), 36, 42, 38, 93–4, 206
Singin' in the Rain (Donen and Kelly, 1952), 16, 62, 65–7
Sirvent, Michel, 26
Siska, William C., 8, 16, 42, 122–3
Sitney, P. Adams, 10, 46–8
Sklar, Robert, 101
Skolimowski, Jerzy
   Départ, Le (1967), 122–3
   King, Queen, Knave (1972), 42
Slasher (Super Channel, 2016–), 51
Slotkin, Richard, 308n23
Smith, Imogen Sara, 55
Smith, Jack, 48
Snow White and the Seven Dwarfs (Disney, 1937), 96
Snyder, Zack
   300 (2006), 139
   Dawn of the Dead (2004), 17
   Watchmen (2009), 44, 139
Sobchack, Vivian, 123
Son of Rambow (Jennings, 2007), 66–7
Sontag, Susan, 116, 226, 244–5, 284
Sopranos, The (HBO, 1999–2007), 93, 96
Sorin, Cécile, 185
Sorlin, Pierre, 232
South Park (Comedy Central, 1997–), 48
Southern, Nile, 43, 296n60
Spark, Muriel, 181, 186
Speck, Oliver C., 8
spectatorship (theories of), 94
Sperb, Jason, 140, 145
Spielberg, Steven, 268
   Amistad (1997), 277
   Jaws (1975), 181
   Jurassic Park (1993), 84–6, 90, 108, 196
   Ready Player One (2018), 83
   Saving Private Ryan (1998), 247
   Schindler's List (1993), 247–9, 258
Spielman, Yvonne, 123
Spies, Virginie, 48
Squid Game (Netflix, 2021), 40, 83
Staiger, Janet, 94
Stam, Robert, 6–10, 12, 16, 19, 35–6, 45–7, 52, 61, 64–5, 68, 70–1, 74, 76–7, 79, 106–9, 112, 123, 132, 152, 159–60, 162, 174, 184–6, 261–3, 265, 269–70, 274, 287, 300n68
Star, The (Heisler, 1952), 62, 66, 80, 93
Star Is Born, A (Wellman, Conway and Fleming, 1937) 9, 62, 64–5, 67, 79–80, 72, 79–80
Star Is Born, A (Cukor, 1950; Pierson, 1976; Cooper, 2018), 83
Star Wars (1977–), 215–16
State of Things, The / Der Strang der Dinge (Wenders, 1982), 62
Steel, Ronald, 249, 251
Stein, Gertrude, 44, 46
Sterne, Laurence, 159
   Life and Opinions of Tristam Shandy, Gentleman, The (1759), 44, 163–5, 263
Stokes, Melvyn, and Richard Maltby, 94
Stone, Oliver
   JFK (1991), 249–51, 254, 257–9, 284
   Natural Born Killers (1994), 251
Storey, John, 223
Stranger than Fiction (Forster, 2006), 42
Strategy of the Spider, The / Strategia del ragno (Bertolucci, 1970), 42
Street Angel / Ma lu tian shi (Muzhi Yuan, 1937), 40
Stuckey, G. Andrew, 8–10, 23, 39–40, 97, 180
Sturges, John
   Magnificent Seven, The (1960), 184
   Sin of Harold Diddlebock, The (1947), 69
Suárez, Juan, 183–4
Sunset Blvd. (Wilder, 1950), 9, 28, 62, 64–5, 67–73, 79–80, 92–3, 122, 223, 227, 245, 282

Supernatural (The CW, 2005–20), 3, 51, 96, 100, 180, 206
Survivor (CBS, 2000–), 214
Swing Time (Stevens, 1936), 47
synchretic (quality of cinema), 122
Szczepanik, Petr, 123–5

Takayuki, Tatsumi, 44
Tales of Borges / Cuentos de Borges (TVE, 1992–3), 42
Tamala 2010: A Punk Cat in Space (Tol, 2010), 44
Tan, Ed S., 94
Tarantino, Quentin, 4, 9, 32, 42, 185, 191
  Django Unchained (2012), 8, 10
  Inglourious Basterds (2009), 8, 10, 69, 234, 239–44, 247, 257–9, 284
  Once Upon a Time . . . in Hollywood (2019), 9, 62, 66, 92–3, 239–40
  Pulp Fiction (1994), 200, 203, 259–60
Taurino, Giulia, and Sara Casoli, 86, 88, 70
Tel Quel, 260
Texas Chainsaw Massacre, The (Nispel, 2003), 157–8, 180
This Is Us (Fox, 2016–22), 63, 66–7, 211–13, 283
Thompson, Kristin, and David Bordwell, 36, 46, 101, 103
To Hell and Back (Hibbs, 1955), 241
Toledo, Vania Barraza, 252–3
Tom and Jerry (Hanna-Barbera, 1940–), 192
Tomasovic, Dick, 224
Tomasulo, Frank P., 112, 169–70
Top Hat (Sandrich, 1935), 103
Tore, Gian Maria, 6–7, 26, 30, 56
Toth, Josh, 38
Trinità movies (Barboni, 1970–1), 188
Tropic Thunder (Stiller, 2008), 62, 66–7
True Romance (Tony Scott, 1993), 93, 95
Truffaut, François, 178
  400 Blows, The / Les Quatre cent coups (1959), 16, 274
  Day for Night / La Nuit américaine (1973), 62, 64, 67, 80, 92–3, 306n35
Truman Show, The (Weir, 1998), 83
Trumpener, Katie, 107
Twin Peaks (ABC, 1990–1), 51, 67, 93, 199, 213, 223–31, 284

Twin Peaks: The Return (Showtime, 2017), 82, 145, 213, 226–31, 282–4
Two Tickets to Broadway (Kern, 1951), 79

Unforgiven (Eastwood, 1992), 184
Usual Suspects (Synger, 1995), 293n76

Vahdani, Alizera, 97, 99
Van Eynde, Laurent, 107
Vanelli, Marco, 129
Vertov, Dziga, 35, 45, 47, 54, 288
  Man with a Movie Camera / Chelovek s kino-apparatom (1929), 52–3, 123, 261, 286–7
Vidal, Gore, 129
Visconti, Lucino
  Bellissima (1951), 62, 65
  Terra trema, La (1948), 97
Voigts-Virchow, Eckart, 165, 306n35
Volponi, Paolo, 44–5
Vonnegut, Kurt, 181, 186

Walsh, Martin, 7
Waltz with Bashir / Vals Im Bashir (Folman, 2008), 287, 289
WandaVision (Disney+, 2021), 49, 95, 100, 106, 281
Wartenberg, Thomas E., 287
Watchmen (comics, Gibbons and Moore, 1986–7), 44, 239–40
Watchmen (HBO, 2019), 44, 239–40
Waterland (novel, Swift, 1983), 233
Watkins, Peter, 44, 234, 247, 257, 286
  Commune (Paris, 1871), La (2000), 234
  Culloden (1964), 234–9, 259, 282, 284–5
  Edvard Munch (1974), 234
  Freethinker, The / Fritänkaren (1994), 234
  Punishment Park (1971), 234
  War Game, The (1966), 234, 286
Waugh, Patricia, 8, 11, 19–22, 24, 33–4, 39, 41–4, 90, 95, 105, 108, 122, 149, 160–1, 170, 180–1, 185–6, 204, 232, 259–60, 263, 285, 296n64
Wee, Valerie, 194
Welles, Orson, 57, 77
  Citizen Kane (1941), 35, 45
  Don Quixote, 42
  Hearts of Age, The (1934), 45
Wells, Paul, 194

Wells-Lassagne, Shannon, 169, 179, 200–1
West, Mae, 56
West, Rebecca, 126, 130
Westworld (Chrichton, 1973), 83, 86–7, 90
Westworld (HBO, 2016–), 83, 86–90, 148, 158, 192, 209, 259, 281
Whalen, Tom, 174, 177
What Price Hollywood? (Cukor, 1932), 9, 62, 64–5, 67, 72
When a Stranger Calls (Walton, 1979), 194
White, Hayden 6
Wild Bunch, The (Peckinpah, 1969), 190
Wilkie, Ian, 49
Williams, Linda, 199
Winston, Brian, 288
Wire, The (HBO, 2002–8), 210–11, 282
Withalm, Gloria, 12, 23, 61
Wizard of Oz, The (Fleming, Cukor and Leroy, 1939), 103, 242
Wolf, Mark J. P., 86

Wolf, Werner 4, 6, 10–11, 13–15, 17, 19–22, 24–34, 36, 38, 40, 43, 54, 90, 123–5, 191, 208, 280, 283, 317
Wood, Robin, 194
Woolf, Virginia, 44
Worland, Rick, 194
Wright, Joe
   Atonement (2007), 154
   Pride & Prejudice (2005), 153–4

X-Files, The (Fox, 1993–2018), 51

Yacavone, Daniel, 7, 15, 25, 29, 37, 107, 123–5, 317
Yu, Chang-Min, 209–10

Zelizer, Barbie, 249
Zola, Émile, 277
Zombies on Broadway (Douglas, 1945), 186
Zucconi, Francesco, 254